CQ GUIDE TO

CURRENT AMERICAN GOVERNMENT

Spring 1997

CQ GUIDE TO

CURRENT AMERICAN GOVERNMENT

Spring 1997

Congressional Quarterly Inc.
Washington, D.C.

Congressional Quarterly Inc.

Congressional Quarterly Inc., an editorial research service and publishing company, serves clients in the fields of news, education, business, and government. It combines the specific coverage of Congress, government, and politics contained in the *Congressional Quarterly Weekly Report* with the more general subject range of an affiliated service, the *CQ Researcher*.

Congressional Quarterly also publishes a variety of books, including college political science textbooks and public affairs paperbacks on developing issues and events under the CQ Press imprint. CQ Books researches, writes, and publishes information directories and reference books on the federal government, national elections, and politics, including the *Guide to the Presidency*, the *Guide to Congress*, the *Guide to the U.S. Supreme Court*, the *Guide to U.S. Elections*, and *Politics in America*. *CQ's Encyclopedia of American Government* is a three-volume reference work providing essential information about the U.S. government. The *CQ Almanac*, a compendium of legislation for one session of Congress, is published each year. *Congress and the Nation*, a record of government for a presidential term, is published every four years.

CQ publishes the *Congressional Monitor*, a daily report on current and future activities of congressional committees, and several newsletters. The CQ FaxReport is a daily update available every afternoon when Congress is in session. An electronic online information system, Washington Alert, provides immediate access to CQ's databases of legislative action, votes, schedules, profiles, and analyses.

Contents

Introduction

Congressional Quarterly's *Guide to Current American Government* is divided into four sections—foundations of American government, political participation, government institutions, and politics and public policy—that correspond with the framework of standard introductory American government textbooks. Articles have been selected from the *Congressional Quarterly Weekly Report* to complement existing texts with up-to-date examinations of current issues and controversies.

Foundations of American Government. Fundamental aspects of the U.S. Constitution are the focus of this section. The separation of power between Congress and the president is examined in light of the legislative line-item veto, which goes into effect in 1997. And in one of its major decisions of 1996, the Supreme Court has clouded rather than clarified the issue of minority redistricting.

Political Participation. The articles in this section examine the results of the 1996 elections that returned Democratic President Bill Clinton to the White House and Republican majorities to both the Senate and the House of Representatives. One disappointing factor of the election was that only 49 percent of those eligible to vote turned out to cast ballots—the lowest turnout since the 1920s.

Government Institutions. In the wake of the 1996 congressional elections, CQ editors discuss the likely organization and agenda of the 105th Congress. Balancing the budget will remain a top priority along with campaign finance reform. CQ editors also take a look at how the president's second-term programs will likely fare in the Republican Congress. The most important cases before the Supreme Court in 1997 are also profiled.

Politics and Public Policy. This section provides in-depth coverage of two major social policy issues: welfare reform and deregulation of the electrical power industry. CQ editors also identify eleven major social policy areas that will likely challenge the leadership ability of President Clinton and the 105th Congress—ranging from balancing the budget and Medicare reform to dealing with juvenile crime and immigration reform. This report asks the questions about these issues that were rarely discussed during the campaign and provides detailed background information.

By reprinting articles largely as they appeared originally in the *Weekly Report*, the *Guide's* editors provide a handy source of information about contemporary political issues. The date of original publication is noted with each article to give the reader a time frame for the events that are described. Although new developments may have occurred subsequently, updates of the articles are provided only when they are essential to an understanding of the basic operations of American government. Page number references to related and background articles in the *Weekly Report* and the *CQ Almanac* are provided to facilitate additional research on topical events. Both are available at many school and public libraries.

Foundations of American Government

One of the pillars of the U.S. Constitution is the division of power among the executive, legislative, and judicial branches of government. The Framers set up the checks and balances among the three branches in order to keep one from becoming predominant. The first article in this section examines the passage of the legislative line-item veto, which goes into effect in January 1997. By embracing the line-item veto, Congress has decided to share its constitutional control over the federal budget — the power of the purse — with the president. Some people see the line-item veto as a useful way for the president to eliminate wasteful spending. Others see it as a dangerous gift of power to the president who can use it as a means of bullying Congress.

Opponents of the line-item veto have indicated that they will challenge its constitutionality in 1997. If the Supreme Court upholds the measure, it may mark a historic change in the division of power between the president and Congress. One political irony of the line-item veto debate is that the Republican 104th Congress passed the measure in early 1996 when Democratic President Bill Clinton's re-election was uncertain. Now with Clinton headed to a second term — a term that may be enhanced with new line-item veto power — the Republican-led 105th Congress may regret its passage.

In one of its major decisions of 1996, the Supreme Court struck down three congressional districts in Texas and one in North Carolina as unconstitutional racial gerrymandering. The Court ruled that the strangely shaped district lines were drawn up with race as the overwhelming factor. However, the Court took pains to point out that the drawing of congressional districts should still follow the 1965 Voting Rights Act, which seeks to rectify racial inequality in the political system. The question as to how states are to draw up districts that provide for the equal treatment of all races will remain clouded until the Supreme Court sets clear guidelines on redistricting.

For the 1996 elections, a panel of three federal judges in July ruled that there was not enough time to redraw the unconstitutional North Carolina district fairly. It will be redrawn in 1997. Another three-judge panel in Texas ruled differently, ordering the redrawing of the three unconstitutional districts before the November elections. In redrawing the three, ten surrounding Texas districts also had to be redrawn. This meant that the March 1996 primary results for thirteen districts had to be thrown out. In November, candidates in these districts ran in open primaries, with only those capturing a majority of the vote winning outright. It is interesting to note that all three incumbents who were from the former unconstitutional districts handily won re-election in their newly drawn districts. (They are black Democratic Reps. Sheila Jackson-Lee and Eddie Bernice Johnson and Anglo Democrat Rep. Gene Green, who represents a Hispanic-majority district.) Their re-election added weight to the argument that districts need not be drawn with race as the overriding factor for minorities to win congressional seats.

Congress Hands President The Line-Item Veto

Uncertainty remains over whether chief executive will perform radical or minor surgery

In a historic concession, the Republican-dominated Congress has given away some of its cherished power of the purse by granting the next president the equivalent of the line-item veto.

Passage of this "legislative line-item veto" bill means that congressional Republicans and their Democratic allies have potentially shifted enormous power from Congress to the president.

In clearing the bill (S 4) for President Clinton, who said he will sign it, Congress is taking a leap into a great unknown. Will future presidents limit their use of the new authority, as supporters say, to striking wasteful "pork barrel" projects from larger bills that they have little choice but to sign? Or will the president, as opponents fear, use the new authority power as a club with which to bully Congress into accepting presidential priorities?

No one knows. If the new presidential authority survives a certain constitutional challenge — and many legal scholars say it will not — it will dramatically reshape the battlefield on which Congress and the executive struggle over spending priorities. *(Story, next page)*

Jubilant supporters of the measure anticipate that the new power will wipe out the congressional practice of inserting wasteful pork barrel spending items into otherwise vital bills.

"Certainly, line-item veto is not a cure-all for budget deficits. No one is pretending it is the one big answer to all of our budget problems," said Senate Majority Leader Bob Dole, R-Kan., who would wield the power if his quest for the presidency is fulfilled. "But it is one additional tool a president can use to help keep unnecessary spending down. It's one way to fulfill our pledge to American taxpayers for less Washington spending."

CQ Weekly Report March 30, 1996

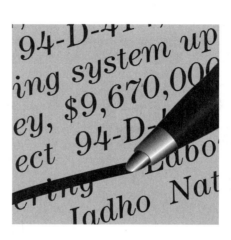

But opponents gravely warned that the new power would vest way too much power with the president. And they warned that it will backfire.

The enhanced presidential power will "upset the constitutional system of checks and balances and separation of powers, a system that was handed down to us by the constitutional framers 208 years ago, a system which has served the country well during those two centuries, a system that our children and grandchildren are entitled to have passed on to them as it was handed down to us," said Sen. Robert C. Byrd, D-W. Va.

The bill marks the biggest shift of power from one branch of government to another since 1974, when Congress passed a law (PL 93-344) to stop then-President Richard M. Nixon from "impounding" — or refusing to spend — money on projects he disliked. *(1974 Almanac, p. 145)*

Byrd, the most passionate defender of the Senate's prerogatives, led a surprisingly brief one-day debate on the bill March 27. But colleagues said the senator was resigned to defeat and feeling pressure to allow the Senate to move on to must-pass bills to raise the debt ceiling and reauthorize farm programs. Byrd allowed the measure to pass with relative dispatch — but not

before launching a withering attack on the bill. *(Excerpts, p. 4)*

The Senate adopted the conference report (H Rept 104-491) March 27 by a sweeping 69–31 vote, after voting, 58–42, to kill a motion by Byrd to recommit the measure to conference with instructions to substitute the text of a significantly milder "expedited rescissions" bill (S 14).

Nineteen Senate Democrats voted for the bill on final passage; three Republicans were opposed.

Passage of the bill gives the new GOP majority perhaps their biggest victory to date; the line-item veto likely will be the single most significant piece of the House GOP's "Contract With America" to become law.

The effort in Congress to drive the measure into law, however, involved a legislative procedure that was nothing short of extraordinary. Basically, House and Senate leaders linked the fate of the line-item measure to the essential but very unpopular bill (HR 3136) to raise the debt ceiling.

Under the maneuver, the House temporarily attached the line-item veto measure to the debt-limit bill. Had the Senate not adopted the conference report on the line-item veto by the March 29 deadline for raising the debt ceiling, the must-pass debt-limit measure would have been sent over to the Senate with the line-item measure still attached.

Technically, the House cleared the line-item bill the moment it passed the rule (H Res 391) to the debt limit bill by a vote of 232–177.

The rule contained a provision under which the House "deemed" the conference report on S 4 to have automatically been adopted and stripped the measure from the debt ceiling measure.

The maneuver also made the debt ceiling bill more palatable to conservatives — and it had the effect of putting

A Constitutional Question

Congress has sent the so-called legislative line-item veto down Pennsylvania Avenue to the White House, where President Clinton is sure to sign it. But the measure will shortly end up back on Capitol Hill — at the Supreme Court.

The "enhanced rescissions" bill (S 4) would give the president the power to automatically "cancel" items in spending bills unless he is blocked by two-thirds of Congress — and it would avoid — the enormously difficult task of amending the Constitution.

Hanging over the bill is a very simple question: Can Congress provide this authority to the president via statute instead of by amending the Constitution? Opinions vary.

"I think it is very clearly unconstitutional," said Laurence Tribe, professor of constitutional law at Harvard University. "I cannot dream up an argument for the constitutionality of this scheme."

According to Tribe and other constitutional scholars, the enhanced rescissions approach directly violates Article I of the Constitution, which vests all legislative power in Congress. The Constitution states that the president has only three options when presented with a bill: sign it into law, veto it or allow it to become law without his imprimatur.

The enhanced rescissions authority, Tribe argues, would clearly permit the president to amend a law.

In a 1983 case, *INS v. Chada*, the Supreme Court ruled: "Amendment and repeal of statutes, no less than enactment, must conform with Article I." *(1983 Almanac, p. 565)*

Defenders of the measure say it represents an entirely constitutional — and voluntary — delegation by Congress of some of its control of the budget process. This argument is made in an analysis of the enhanced rescissions concept by Johnny H. Killian, a senior specialist of American constitutional law at the nonpartisan Congressional Research Service.

"The Court has not indicated that there are any powers that may not be delegated . . . and, in fact, has pretty clearly indicated that all congressional powers may be delegated," Killian wrote in a Dec. 30, 1994, report.

The central question is the degree to which power may be delegated. According to Professor Michael J. Gerhardt of the College of William and Mary Law School, the Supreme Court has permitted Congress to delegate authority to "administrative agencies or inferior bodies." But the court has always taken a stricter approach when considering delegations of power among the titular heads of the branches of government, Gerhardt said.

"In these cases, the court has used a 'formalist' approach . . . [that] treats the text of the Constitution and the intent of its drafters as controlling and changed circumstances and broader policy outcomes as irrelevant to constitutional outcomes," Gerhardt wrote in a March 27 letter to Sen. Daniel Patrick Moynihan, D-N.Y.

Preparing for a Lawsuit

Supporters of the bill have written into the measure a provision to speed up its review by the Supreme Court. A suit is sure to be filed shortly after the bill becomes law.

Another constitutional question was raised by the Judicial Conference of the United States, the organization that represents federal judges.

In a March 15 letter to Congress, L. Ralph Mecham, secretary of the conference, wrote: "The Judiciary believes that there may be constitutional implications if the president is given independent authority to make line-item vetoes of appropriations acts. The doctrine of separation of powers recognizes the vital importance of protecting the Judiciary against interference from any president. . . . This protection needs to endure."

Supporters of the bill say, however, that they are confident the measure will survive constitutional scrutiny. Sen. Ted Stevens, R-Alaska, a reluctant supporter of the bill, said, "What we are in fact doing is giving the president the authority, in effect, to impound monies that we have given him the authority to spend."

The original Senate-passed bill contained a fundamentally different framework, devised in the mid-1980s, in which each appropriations bill would have been broken up into hundreds or thousands of individual "item" bills. That idea was created as a way to ensure its constitutionality.

Ironically, the belief by many that the bill will be struck down by the high court may have made it easier to vote for.

Sen. Kent Conrad, D-N.D., who opposed the bill, said, "I had a senator this afternoon tell me that he's going to vote for this. He doesn't believe in it. He thinks it's going to be a tragedy if it ever occurred. He said, 'I'm counting on the Supreme Court to save us from ourselves.' "

Senate opponents' backs against the wall.

Notwithstanding the procedural maneuvering, the debate on the issue for the most part was devoid of drama.

Passage in the House was a foregone conclusion, and the threat of a Byrd filibuster did not materialize. The bill had considerable Democratic support — including backing from Clinton — so cloture was not in question.

Final action capped a 12-year effort that began when President Ronald Reagan asked for the line-item veto in his 1984 State of the Union address. But prior efforts were always doomed; a 1985 attempt in the Senate was scuttled by a filibuster led by Appropriations Committee Chairman Mark O. Hatfield, R-Ore., and Democratic House leaders for years kept even mild versions of the veto power from coming to the floor. *(History, p. 5)*

To their credit, Republicans have kept their promise to pass the line-item veto despite the presence of a Democrat in the White House. But the effort has been anything but easy. The bill is being sent to Clinton only with the grudging acquiescence of GOP senators, such as Alaska's Ted Stevens and New Mexico's Pete V. Domenici, who despite voting in favor of it are reported by colleagues and aides to dislike the measure intensely.

But any attempt by reluctant Republicans to delay the bill or block it entirely would have made Republicans generally — and Dole specifically — look bad, something that Republicans are loath to do as the presidential campaign approaches. To fail to pass the

In Byrd's Words

Sen. Robert C. Byrd, D-W.Va., gave up his decadelong battle against a line-item veto on March 27 with bitter words:

"The Senate, you mark my words, is on the verge of making a colossal mistake, a mistake we will come to regret but with which we will have to live until Jan. 1 of the year 2005, at the very least. . . .

"The Senate is about to adopt a conference report, Mr. President, which Madison and the other constitutional framers and early leaders would have absolutely abhorred, and in adopting the report we will be bartering away our children's birthright for a mess of political pottage. . . .

"It is a malformed monstrosity. . . .

"This so-called line-item veto act should be more appropriately labeled 'The President Always Wins Bill.' From now on, the heavy hand of the president will be used to slap down congressional opposition wherever it may exist. . . .

"It is difficult to imagine why this body would want to deal such a painful blow, not only to itself, but to this basic structure of our constitutional form of government and to the interests of the people we represent.

"Whether the president is a Democrat or a Republican is not my concern. Whether one party or another is in power in the Congress is not my concern here. My concern is with unnecessarily upsetting the balance of powers as laid out in the Constitution, and this conference report simply gives away too much of the congressional control over the purse strings to the president."

bill would have handed Clinton an issue with which to club Republicans.

"One of the major axioms of politics is 'timing is everything.' And in this case, it means a lot," said Al Cors Jr., director of government relations for the National Taxpayers Union.

A Sorting Out Period

If the measure survives a constitutional challenge, the shift of power from Congress to the president will likely take years to sort out in the ebb and flow between the two branches.

A line-item veto in its traditional sense would permit the president to strike individual lines and items from spending or other bills. This is universally seen as requiring an amendment to the Constitution. Instead, the bill would give the president the functional equivalent of the line-item veto by granting him an enhanced rescissions authority to automatically "cancel" items in spending bills unless overturned by an act of Congress — which could then be vetoed.

The president also would be able to cancel narrowly targeted tax breaks and new entitlement programs, though most of the opportunities for its use will come on spending bills.

A principal effect of the new power in the appropriations process will be to give the administration much greater leverage during the negotiations that produce a spending bill. The president would be able to threaten a veto of a congressional item as leverage to pressure Congress to pass presidential priorities.

In fact, even some of the stoutest conservatives in Congress argue that the new power would have minimal impact on the deficit and instead would merely transfer power to the president.

"I served under three governors while in the state Legislature," said Rep. Nick Smith, R-Mich. "Every one of these governors, liberal and conservative, used the leverage of the line-item veto to get the spending they wanted."

In fact, the experience in the 43 states whose governors possess the veto has, generally speaking, produced quite limited deficit reduction.

"Evidence from the states suggests that the item veto has not been used to hold down state spending or deficits, but rather has been used by state governors to pursue their own priorities," former Congressional Budget Office director Robert D. Reischauer has said in prior congressional testimony.

"I had the line-item veto," said Sen.

Dale Bumpers, D-Ark., a former governor. "Do you know what I used it for? To get legislators in line."

On the other hand, the "veto" would also, in all likelihood, serve as a powerful disincentive for members seeking to slip items of dubious merit into larger spending bills.

In the hands of President Clinton, the measure would obviously provide leverage in his dealing with Republican appropriators.

"It would be *huge*," said an administration official deep in the ongoing talks over an omnibus end-of-year spending bill (HR 3019).

Still, an overly aggressive use of the new power might produce a backlash that could harm a future president's relationship with Congress. And Congress would always retain the power to ignore any presidential request.

In addition, the measure contains a "lockbox" mechanism that would dedicate any line-item rescission to deficit reduction. In effect, that means that any use of the veto would surrender money that could otherwise be redistributed among competing accounts. If Congress and the president see a mutual interest in spending as much of the limited pool of discretionary appropriations as possible, it would follow that they would seek to avoid the veto as much as possible.

"With the lockbox, there is little incentive for a Democratic president to use it," the administration official said.

Considering how Clinton might have used the veto if he had it is a hypothetical exercise. But it is safe to say that the $243 billion defense appropriations bill for the current fiscal year, which contains $7 billion more than Clinton asked for, would probably look a lot different. Clinton was forced to accept a host of items in exchange for allowing the measure — which contained critical financing for the Bosnia peacekeeping effort — to become law.

In a feature that may come back to haunt Congress, the bill would give the president five days to propose a rescission after he has already signed a bill into law. That is when the threat of the line-item veto may be most potent.

At that point, Congress would have lost any control over the bill, but the president would be able to threaten to cancel individual items while Congress is debating other measures.

But the majority view was that the shift of power would not be that dramatic.

"I have not known many governors

History of Line-Item Veto Effort

• **Jan. 25, 1984.** In his third State of the Union address, President Ronald Reagan calls for a constitutional amendment giving the president a line-item veto, a power he enjoyed as governor of California. In May, the Senate comes within one vote of adding a line-item veto to the fiscal 1985 deficit-reduction plan. *(1984 Almanac, p. 153)*

• **July 24, 1985.** After failing three times to stop a weeklong filibuster, Senate Majority Leader Bob Dole, R-Kan., abandons plans to consider legislation giving the president power to veto spending. Under the proposal, each item in an appropriations bill would have been packaged as a separate bill, so each could have been vetoed. *(1985 Almanac, p. 468)*

Reagan

• **Sept. 30, 1992.** Conservative Democrats, angry that Democratic House leaders have blocked a floor vote on a bill to give the president the equivalent of a weak line-item veto, team up with Republicans to hold hostage a must-pass continuing resolution for fiscal 1993. Three days later, the House overwhelmingly passes the "expedited rescissions" bill, 312–97. But Senate Appropriations Committee Chairman Robert C. Byrd, D-W. Va., keeps it from reaching the floor. Bill Clinton, who has line-item veto authority as governor of Arkansas, supports the idea during the presidential campaign. *(1992 Almanac, p. 114)*

• **March 10, 1993.** Sen. John McCain, R-Ariz., tries to attach an "enhanced rescissions" bill to legislation aimed at increasing voter registration. His amendment is rejected, 45–52.

• **July 14, 1994.** For the third time in as many years, the House again passes an expedited rescissions measure. The Senate again lets it languish. *(1994 Almanac, p. 87)*

• **Sept. 27, 1994.** More than 300 GOP House candidates sign their party's "Contract With America." The first of 10 planks calls for permanent, line-item veto authority for the president.

• **Feb. 6, 1995.** As a tribute to Reagan, the House passes on his 84th birthday a "legislative line-item veto" bill, 294–134. The president's requests to rescind spending would automatically become law unless Congress, under a complex process, blocked them by a two-thirds vote. *(1995 Weekly Report, p. 441)*

• **Feb. 14, 1995.** The Senate Budget Committee approves two competing proposals for a line-item veto. The milder version would require Congress to vote on a presidentially proposed package of spending cuts. The cuts would take effect if passed by a majority of both chambers. Under the tougher version, the proposed cuts would automatically take effect unless Congress voted by a two-thirds margin to overturn them. *(1995 Weekly Report, p. 511)*

• **March 23, 1995.** The Senate passes a line-item veto bill that takes an entirely different approach from that of the House "enhanced rescissions" bill. The Senate plan, negotiated by Dole, would require items in appropriations bills and some tax and entitlement measures to be unbundled and separately enrolled as hundreds or thousands of new bills that the president could then veto. *(1995 Weekly Report, p. 854)*

• **May 17, 1995.** In an attempt to jump-start stalled negotiations, the House takes up the Senate bill and inserts the text of its own version. But the House thumbs its nose at the Senate and does not officially request a conference. *(1995 Weekly Report, p. 1409)*

• **Aug. 1, 1995.** Senate Democrats tweak the GOP-dominated House by adopting a sense-of-the-Senate resolution urging the House to appoint conferees so that official talks could get under way. House Speaker Newt Gingrich, R-Ga., promises that House conferees will be named after Congress' August recess. *(1995 Weekly Report, p. 2346)*

• **Nov. 8, 1995.** At the second meeting of conferees, lead Senate negotiator Ted Stevens, R-Alaska, said he was willing to accept the House's "enhanced rescissions" approach. But no further talks are held in 1995. *(1995 Weekly Report, p. 3446)*

• **March 21, 1996.** Prodded by Dole, GOP negotiators agree on an enhanced rescissions bill. *(Weekly Report, p. 779)*

who have tried to forward their agenda. . . . by using the line-item veto," said Rep. Michael N. Castle, R-Del., also a

former governor.

"I think it's a very poor method of doing that. But it is very good, I think

in [eliminating] pork-type projects and the unnecessary projects. It works much better in that area," he said. ∎

Minority-District Decisions Lay No Clear Guidelines

With the Supreme Court's latest round of rulings on race-conscious House redistricting, the justices have left the topic much as they found it: a frustrating legal puzzle and certain ground for ongoing litigation.

The high court June 13 continued its assault on race-based political boundaries, striking down four congressional districts in two states as unconstitutional racial gerrymanders.

The action is likely to threaten other political districts drawn with an eye toward enhancing minority voting strength, as well as future attempts to craft such districts.

Yet the court action, which came in two separate cases, shows the justices remain sharply divided over how to balance 1965 Voting Rights Act directives, which mandated that minorities be included in the political process, with constitutional principles of equal treatment for all races.

And without a majority of justices ready to rule out race-conscious districting altogether, the court has left the practice in a murky and litigious middle ground between the permissible and the unconstitutional.

In a 5–4 split, the justices struck down three disputed congressional districts in Texas, the black-majority 18th and 30th districts in Houston and Dallas and the Hispanic-majority 29th district in Houston. They are represented by Democrats Sheila Jackson-Lee, Eddie Bernice Johnson and Gene Green, respectively. The case was *Bush v. Vera.*

And the same bloc of justices again shot down North Carolina's congressional district map. Technically, their ruling only affected the black-majority 12th district, represented by Democrat Melvin Watt. However, the 1st, the other district with a majority of black voters, was spared on a technicality and could be vulnerable to further legal attack. Democrat Eva Clayton represents it.

CQ Weekly Report June 15, 1996

Texas Districts in Trouble

Jackson-Lee   Johnson   Green

That ruling came in *Shaw v. Hunt,* the continuation of an ongoing challenge to the North Carolina districts by a group of white voters.

While the Texas and North Carolina cases involve congressional district maps, the ruling affects districting at all levels of government.

The court once more stopped short of saying there is no room for race-conscious districting.

In fact, Justice Sandra Day O'Connor, who held the controlling vote in both cases, went out of her way to specify that states can and should make special efforts to safeguard the rights of minority voters under the 1965 Voting Rights Act and its 1982 amendments. *(1982 Almanac, p. 373)*

That is of some comfort to advocates for minority-dominant districts, who have argued that they may be the only meaningful way to see that minority communities are represented.

But O'Connor's statement of principle is of limited practical use to mapdrawers because the high court shied away from clear guidelines about what states can do.

O'Connor acknowledged the conflict. "That difficulty is inevitable," she wrote in a concurrence to her own plurality opinion. "The Voting Rights Act requires the States and the courts to take action to remedy the reality of racial inequality in our political system, sometimes necessitating race-based action, while the Fourteenth Amendment requires us to look with suspicion on

the excessive use of racial considerations by the government."

O'Connor tried to lay out some guidance in her concurrence, but her efforts fell short in the eyes of many experts.

"We still have absolutely undefined standards here as to what counts as a district that passes muster — that is race-conscious but not race-driven," said Abigail Thernstrom, a prominent critic of race-conscious districting.

Pamela Karlan, a University of Virginia law professor who has defended the practice, said too much seems to depend on O'Connor's personal opinion about when race-consciousness goes too far.

"How is a district judge supposed to know what's in Justice O'Connor's mind?" Karlan asked.

That confusion is not likely to change any time soon.

Two justices who agreed with O'Connor's controlling opinion to strike down the Texas districts, Chief Justice William H. Rehnquist and Anthony M. Kennedy, are at best skeptical of race-conscious districting. Antonin Scalia and Clarence Thomas, who supported O'Connor's conclusion in the Texas case but not her reasoning, are even more hostile to reliance on race to draw district lines.

Those were the same five justices who voted to strike down the North Carolina district, joining an opinion authored by Rehnquist.

The four dissenting justices in both cases — John Paul Stevens, Ruth Bader Ginsburg, David H. Souter and Stephen G. Breyer — want to reverse course and give states greater leeway to draw race-conscious districts in the interest of ensuring minority voting strength.

Absent a change in the makeup of the court, that leaves the deciding vote to O'Connor. And O'Connor wants to continue to tread a delicate path between the competing factions.

The result, say many legal experts, is likely to be more complex districting cases before the high court.

"The court has shown they're ready to live with a lot of litigation," said Samuel Issacharoff, a voting rights expert at the University of Texas law school.

March From 'Shaw'

The case that kicked off many of the pending legal challenges to race-conscious districting was an earlier incarnation of the North Carolina dispute.

In its 1993 opinion in *Shaw v. Reno*, the Supreme Court expressed alarm at the contorted shape of the two black-majority districts in North Carolina and said they might violate the equal protection rights of the white plaintiffs. *(1993 Almanac, p. 325)*

The court went further last term, ruling in *Miller v. Johnson* that whenever race is the predominant factor in determining district lines — regular or irregular — the districts most likely are unconstitutional. *(1995 Weekly Report, p. 1944)*

Yet the *Miller* case left many unanswered questions about the proper role of race in the districting process. The ruling said that when race is the predominant factor in determining district lines, the district must be subject to "strict scrutiny" — the most demanding level of court review, and one that requires the state to prove that it took the most narrowly tailored action possible to achieve a "compelling" public policy objective.

The court did not spell out when race would be considered the "predominant" factor, rather than simply one of several influences. Nor did it specify what might serve as a "compelling" enough reason for a race-conscious district to be judged constitutional.

There were hopes, if not necessarily expectations, that the latest round of cases would resolve some of these issues. But the new opinions offer incremental clarity rather than firm guidance.

In North Carolina, the issue was how to apply strict scrutiny.

After the Supreme Court in 1993 cast doubt on the two black-majority districts, a lower court upheld them as constitutional. The district court said the state had several compelling reasons for creating the black-majority 1st and 12th districts and had taken a sufficiently targeted approach.

The Supreme Court, acting on an appeal from the white plaintiffs, dismissed the challenge to the 1st district because the plaintiffs did not live in the district. But the majority went on to strike down the 12th district, saying that its elongated and twisting boundaries did not represent a "narrowly tailored" effort to safeguard the voting strength of blacks.

North Carolina Districts at Issue

Watt   **Clayton**

The Texas case presented newer and more intriguing questions of the interplay between race and other factors in redistricting, such as incumbency and partisanship.

Texas officials acknowledged that racial considerations and their efforts to comply with the Voting Rights Act played a role in shaping the districts.

But state officials said it was not race that accounted for the odd shapes of the districts, but more traditional — and legally accepted — districting principles, such as seeking to protect incumbents.

O'Connor acknowledged that incumbency interests were a factor and also that racial grouping sometimes coincided with valid efforts to unite communities with shared political interests. But she ultimately concluded that race, and not these other considerations, was predominant.

"Despite the strong correlation between race and political affiliation, the maps reveal that political considerations were subordinated to racial classification in the drawing of many of the most extreme and bizarre district lines," she wrote.

And where race is the primary reason for abandoning compact district lines, O'Connor concluded, redistricting crosses the line into unconstitutional racial gerrymandering.

Confusion Ahead

At the heart of much of the recent litigation is the question of whether the Voting Rights Act is on a collision course with the 14th Amendment's guarantees of equal protection.

Under the terms of the Voting Rights Act, the Justice Department must "preclear" district maps in states with a history of discrimination against minority voters. The department has used that authority to pressure some states to create additional minority-dominant districts.

The Supreme Court attacked that practice in the *Miller* case, and the new rulings appear to put pressure on the department to ease up in this area.

But there is also the question of what states can or should do to comply with another portion of the Voting Rights Act — Section 2 — which allows voters or the Justice Department to challenge state actions that dilute minority voting power.

If state officials draw a minority-dominant district to avoid such a vote-dilution lawsuit, does that constitute a "compelling" state interest that would justify making significant use of race in the districting process?

While the controlling opinions in the Texas and North Carolina cases explicitly refused to answer that question, O'Connor wrote a separate opinion to specify that she believes states do have a compelling obligation to comply with this portion of law. That keeps alive a line of legal defense for race-conscious districting.

Legal experts struggled to pull other lessons from the tangle of opinions, concurrences and dissents in the two cases. Several said the Texas case may put an increased premium on neat district lines — whatever goes into drawing them.

Thernstrom was heartened by the outcome worries that states may be able to use race so long as they are less vocal about it and keep district boundaries more tidy. The message could be, "Be a little more subtle and nuanced about it and it'll be OK," she said.

Daniel Lowenstein, a voting law expert at UCLA Law School, says the rulings may affect only the most aggressive cases of race-conscious districting, leaving ample room for some minority-dominant districts. Lowenstein thinks the greatest impact will be on state autonomy, with courts stripping state legislators of their historical discretion over drawing political boundaries.

But lawyers for minority groups see a far more dramatic threat to race-conscious districting.

Penda D. Hair, director of the Washington office of the NAACP Legal Defense and Education Fund, said compactness is a significant burden that will put minorities at a disadvantage in bargaining over district lines.

"The Supreme Court has constitutionalized a double standard . . . because it is only African-Americans and Latinos that have to have compact districts in order to achieve representation of their communities of interests," Hair said. ■

Excerpts From Opinions

Below are excerpts from the opinion, concurrences and dissents in *Bush v. Vera*, the Texas redistricting case decided June 13: *(Story, p. 6)*

From Justice O'Connor's plurality opinion, joined by Justices Rehnquist and Kennedy:

The Constitution does not mandate regularity of district shape . . . and the neglect of traditional districting criteria is merely necessary, not sufficient. For strict scrutiny to apply, traditional districting criteria must be *subordinated to race.* Nor, as we have emphasized, is the decision to create a majority-minority district objectionable in and of itself.

In some circumstances, incumbency protection might explain as well as, or better than, race a State's decision to depart from other traditional districting principles, such as compactness, in the drawing of bizarre district lines. . . .

We cannot agree with the dissenters . . . that racial stereotyping that we have scrutinized closely in the context of jury service can pass without justification in the context of voting. If the promise of the Reconstruction Amendments, that our Nation is to be free of state-sponsored discrimination, is to be upheld, we cannot pick and choose between the basic forms of political participation in our efforts to eliminate unjustified racial stereotyping by government actors.

And, despite the strong correlation between race and political affiliation, the maps reveal that political considerations were subordinated to racial classification in the drawing of many of the most extreme and bizarre district lines. . . . But the fact that racial data were used in complex ways, and for multiple objectives, does not mean that race did not predominate over other considerations. The record discloses intensive and pervasive use of race as a proxy to protect the political fortunes of adjacent incumbents, and for its own sake in maximizing the minority population of District 30 regardless of traditional districting principles. . . .

Significant deviations from traditional districting principles, such as the bizarre shape and non-compactness demonstrated by the districts here, cause constitutional harm insofar as they convey the message that political identity is, or should be, predominantly racial . . . .

Legislators and district courts nationwide have modified their practices — or rather, reembraced the traditional districting practices that were almost universally followed before the 1990 census — in response to *Shaw I.* Those practices and our precedents, which acknowledge voters as more than mere racial statistics, play an important role in defining the political identity of the American voter. Our Fourteenth Amendment jurisprudence evinces a commitment to eliminate unnecessary and excessive governmental use and reinforcement of racial stereotypes. . . . We decline to retreat from that commitment today.

From Justice O'Connor's concurrence:

As the disagreement among members of this Court over District 30 shows, the application of the principles that I have outlined sometimes requires difficult exercises of judgment. That difficulty is inevitable. The Voting Rights Act requires the States and the courts to take action to remedy the reality of racial inequality in our political system, sometimes necessitating race-based action, while the Fourteenth Amendment requires us to look with suspicion on the excessive use of racial considerations by the government. But I believe that the States, playing a primary role, and the courts, in their secondary role, are capable of distinguishing the appropriate and reasonably necessary uses of race from its unjustified and excessive uses.

From Justice Stevens' dissent, joined by Ginsburg and Breyer:

I believe that the Court has misapplied its own tests for racial gerrymandering, both by applying strict scrutiny to all three of these districts, and then by concluding that none can meet that scrutiny. . . .

Even if strict scrutiny applies, I would find these districts constitutional, for each considers race only to the extent necessary to comply with the State's responsibilities under the Voting Rights Act while achieving other race-neutral political and geographical requirements. . . .

The decisions issued here today serve merely to reinforce my conviction that the Court has, with its "analytically distinct" jurisprudence of racial gerrymandering, struck out into a jurisprudential wilderness that lacks a definable constitutional core and threatens to create harms more significant than any suffered by the individual plaintiffs challenging these districts. Though we travel ever farther from it with each passing decision, I would return to the well-traveled path that we left in *Shaw I.* . . .

The great irony, of course, is that by *requiring* the State to place the majority-minority district in a particular place and with a particular shape, the district may stand out as a stark, placid island in a sea of oddly shaped majority-white neighbors. The inviolable sanctity of the [Section] 2-eligible districts will signal in a manner more blatant than the most egregious of these racial gerrymanders that "a minority community sits here: Interfere with it not." The Court-imposed barriers limiting the shape of the district will interfere more directly with the ability of minority voters to participate in the political process than did the oddly shaped districts that the Court has struck down in recent cases.

From Justice Souter's dissent, joined by Ginsburg and Breyer:

The result of this failure to provide a practical standard for distinguishing between the lawful and the unlawful use of race has not only been inevitable confusion in state houses and courthouses, but a consequent shift in responsibility for setting district boundaries from the state legislatures, which are invested with front-line authority by Article I of the Constitution, to the courts, and truly to this Court, which is left to superintend the drawing of every legislative district in the land.

Political Participation

In the 1996 elections Americans embraced the status quo, returning Democratic President Bill Clinton to the White House and Republican majorities to both the Senate and House of Representatives in Congress. Clinton carried 31 states for an Electoral College victory of 379 to 159 over Republican opponent Bob Dole. Yet Clinton fell slightly short of gaining the nod of a majority of the voters, winning 49.2 percent of the vote to Dole's 41.8 percent. Reform Party challenger Ross Perot received only 8.5 percent of the vote, less than half of what he received as an independent candidate in 1992.

Voters seem satisfied with the current split government arrangement — 1996 was the first time in U.S. history that a Democratic president and a Republican Congress had been re-elected. One possible interpretation of the mixed results might be that voters see the benefit in keeping one party from becoming too powerful — extending the system of checks and balances established in the three branches of the federal government by the Constitution to party control of two of those branches, the presidency and Congress.

The election results confirm old political trends and reveal new ones. The East has become the Democratic stronghold, along with most states in the Midwest and Pacific coast. The Republican base in the South remains secure, although Clinton became the first Democratic presidential candidate to carry Florida since 1976. Republicans also continue to maintain the political upperhand in Mountain West and Plains states. Cities and suburban areas generally went Democratic, while small towns and rural areas continued to lean Republican. The vote among men was split between the two parties, while women voters, by 17 percent, favored the Democratic ticket. The Democratic Party was also the clear choice of minorities: it received 80 percent of the black vote and 70 percent of the Hispanic vote.

One disquieting aspect of the election was widespread voter disinterest — only 49 percent of those eligible turned out to cast ballots. This was the lowest turnout percentage for a presidential elections since 1924. (Lower percentages usually turn out for congressional elections.) This was also surprising in the wake of the passage of the 1993 motor voter law, which helped contribute to record numbers of new registered voters during the past four years. The increase in voter registration did not translate into an increase in voters on election day. The drop in voter turnout continues the declining trend begun in the 1960s, when turnout reached an modern-era high of 63 percent.

The results and interpretation of the presidential race are reported in this section of the Guide. CQ editors also review the fate of state propositions on the ballot around the country, including the controversial ban on affirmative action programs in California (which passed) and a parental rights initiative in Colorado (which did not pass). House and Senate elections are covered in the Government Institutions section beginning on page 19. Unofficial vote returns are supplied in the Appendix.

ELECTION '96

Voters Choose To Keep The Players in Place

Clinton wins second term with centrist themes and pledges to work with Hill Republicans

During the elections of 1992 and 1994, voters seemed as furious as Howard Beale, the raging television anchorman in the movie "Network." Like Beale, the electorate was mad as hell and not going to take it anymore.

Anger over a sagging economy cost President George Bush his job four years ago. A very different sort of anger, over President Clinton's unsteady governance, propelled hard-charging Republicans into control of Congress in 1994.

But in 1996, Americans were no longer mad as hell. When it came time to cast their ballots, most voters coolly and dispassionately chose to ratify the existing political order. Incumbency, a dirty word in American politics just two years ago, returned to respectability Nov. 5.

A general sense of satisfaction with the status quo powered Clinton to a solid, if anticlimactic, 31-state electoral triumph over Republican Bob Dole. But the nation's contented mood was leavened with a healthy dose of skepticism, as voters reinstalled a Republican Congress to keep the president in check.

On one level, the split verdict underscored the immense advantages incumbents possess when there is peace abroad and relative prosperity at home. Hard as he tried, Dole never made the case that the economy — which has been growing steadily, if slowly, during Clinton's term — is in disastrous shape.

But the lessons drawn from the election of 1996 are likely to be more varied and complex.

From Clinton on down, most candidates found success by moving to the political middle. The president almost certainly would not have been re-elected had he not relentlessly — Republicans would say shamelessly — appropriated traditional conservative themes following the Democrats' debacle of 1994.

For Republicans, a sprint to the center also became a matter of political survival. Attacked by Democrats as heartless extremists intent on rending the social safety net, House Re-

REUTERS

publicans managed to hang on to their majority only by softening their ideological rough edges and disavowing the budgetary brinkmanship of 1995.

Still, the campaign of 1996 provided plenty of fresh evidence of the nation's long-term shift to the right. Republicans and Democrats no longer sparred over whether — but how — to balance the federal budget. In August, Clinton affixed his signature to legislation ending six decades of guaranteed federal welfare payments. *(Welfare, pp. 74–80)* While it was momentous that a Democratic president would agree to tear down one of the pillars of the New Deal, what may have been more remarkable was that he did not pay dearly for that action in his own party.

Real Conciliation?

With the president and Republicans seemingly moving in the same direction, the question now is whether this latest experiment in divided government will produce results. In the days immediately following the election, each side spoke in conciliatory terms, although it was difficult to tell whether that was just traditional post-campaign courtesy.

Clearly, the White House and Republicans will have a big stake in avoiding political warfare. On Nov. 5, voters turned thumbs down on obstructionism, rewarding both sides for the deals they forged in the final days of the 104th Congress to break stalemates over welfare, immigration and health care bills. A return to gridlock could reignite popular outrage, with unpredictable consequences for both parties.

But divided government historically has not been a prescription for legislative success. And the 105th Congress, like its predecessor, will be badly divided along partisan and ideological lines. A hangover of bitterness remains from the long, costly campaign. Once the final votes are counted, Republicans are expected to pick up two seats in the Senate, giving them a 55–45 margin, with several GOP moderates being replaced by conservatives.

CQ Weekly Report November 9, 1996

Both parties are split internally. Liberal Democrats, who swallowed their anger during the campaign when Clinton signed the welfare bill and moved to the right on other issues, will no longer be so compliant. Among Republicans, there is rivalry among social conservatives, moderates, and tax-cutting supply-siders.

Clinton will begin his second term carrying the heavy baggage of alleged ethical transgressions, including Whitewater, the White House's handling of the FBI files of prominent Republicans, and the late-breaking controversy over fundraising by the Democratic National Committee.

The ethical clouds are particularly ominous for Clinton. Exit polls indicate that, in stark contrast to former President Ronald Reagan, the nation's last two-term president, Clinton's reservoir of popular support is broad but shallow. If just one of the potential scandals swirling around the White House begins to inflict serious damage, the public could quickly turn against the president.

That may also occur if the economy stalls or an overseas crisis erupts. For a soon-to-be lame duck president who will be concerned with securing his place in history, such risks are considerable.

Republican leaders, already beginning to map their strategy for the 1998 midterm elections, have been careful not to overplay their hand on the investigations. They promised tough but fair scrutiny of a president who, while falling short of a popular majority, still managed to garner 49 percent of the vote.

Reflecting some differences over how to proceed, Senate Majority Leader Trent Lott, R-Miss., promised early hearings on the campaign funding allegations. But Banking Committee Chairman Alfonse M. D'Amato, R-N.Y., who hounded the White House for months over Whitewater, called for ending such investigations and urged that they be handled by independent counsel Kenneth Starr.

Evolution, Not Revolution

Four years ago, Clinton arrived in office with big plans. He vowed to erase the legacy of Ronald Reagan, one of the nation's most popular chief executives, remake the nation's health care system and lead a government of "bold, persistent experimentation."

But Clinton's reach exceeded his grasp. His first two years were plagued with failures and missteps, which were capped by the demise of the administration's health care plan. The electorate meted out its punishment by ending the Democrats' 40-year dominance on Capitol Hill. It is a testament to Clinton's political skills, as well as his tenacity, that he was able to recover from such a devastating blow and score a landslide electoral triumph.

Early in 1995, it was Republicans, fresh from their historic victory, who had outsized dreams. House Speaker Newt Gingrich, R-Ga., envisioned the "Contract With America" — the House GOP's legislative blueprint for a downsized government — as just a beginning. Gingrich wanted to reshape American society and elevate the office of Speaker to the point where it could rival the presidency.

But in the minds of most voters, Gingrich and the Republicans also went too far. Just as Clinton struggled to overcome his image as a classic, big-spending liberal, Republicans spent much of the campaign trying to dispel the perception that they are willing to savage Medicare to provide tax breaks to the wealthy.

At the close of this tumultuous four-year period, it has become clear that it isn't just the era of big government that ended. The time for big ideas ended as well. Americans now appear to prefer small, doable proposals to grandiose schemes, evolutionary change to revolutionary convulsions.

There has long been a consensus that expensive new government programs are no longer feasible. But voters also were wary of Republican plans to radically reduce the size of government and cut programs that benefit the middle class. And they were highly dubious that Dole could succeed in cutting taxes while balancing the budget.

The parties and their leaders have been chastened by their experiences. Clinton's second-term agenda is chock-full of minimalist initiatives that require the expenditure of little in the way of money or political capital. Thomas Mann of the Brookings Institution has referred to Clinton's agenda as "itsy-bitsy."

Instead of a national health care plan, as the president proposed in 1992, Clinton has modestly called for insuring people who are between jobs for up to six months.

Instead of a hefty, 15-percent tax cut, like the one championed by Dole, Clinton wants narrowly targeted tax breaks to defray the cost of college education and provide some relief to middle-income families.

But Clinton's most urgent task will be to fulfill his commitment to balance the budget by 2002 while simultaneously keeping the Medicare system from going broke. Unless there is a major change in policy, according to Medicare trustees, the program will be insolvent in five years.

To fulfill those goals, the president will need considerable cooperation from Republicans. In recognition of that reality, he invited GOP leaders to the White House for budget talks during the week of Nov. 11 and promised to consider Republicans for senior administration posts.

For their part, Republicans appear to be in no hurry to develop a detailed legislative agenda. In 1995, House Republicans exploded from the starting blocks in a race to enact the contract.

Sobered by their political near-death experience Nov. 5, Republicans seem content for now to let the White House take the lead — and the responsibility — for making laws. After catching flak throughout the campaign for proposing to cut Medicare, they may be particularly reluctant to give Clinton any help on that issue.

While the election did little to alter Washington's political landscape, the principal players are likely to take on new roles. Clinton played superb defense during the past two years, portraying himself as the protector of popular, middle-class programs. Now he must push his own agenda through Congress, and quickly. His status as a lame duck does not afford him the luxury of time.

After dreaming of shifting the locus of power from the White House to Capitol Hill, Republicans must be content to play a much more traditional role — disposing of the legislation proposed by the president. Their biggest challenge will be to mount a credible opposition to Clinton, without resorting to the confrontational tactics that proved so instructively unpopular. ■

> Sobered by their political near-death experience Nov. 5, Republicans seem content for now to let the White House take the lead — and the responsibility — for making laws.

ELECTION '96

Clinton's Easy Second-Term Win Riddles GOP Electoral Map

But both parties claim victory, as voters make historic choice for further split government

Although his margin was smaller than most election-eve polls suggested, President Clinton easily won a second term Nov. 5 and shredded once again the Electoral College map that Republicans had dominated for the past quarter century.

For the second straight election, Clinton swept the entire Northeast, most of the Midwest, all the Pacific Coast states (including the big prize of California), and chunks of the Mountain West and the South.

In its geographic breadth, Clinton's victory was strikingly similar to his first presidential victory four years ago. Then, he carried 32 states and the District of Columbia, worth 370 electoral votes (100 more than needed).

This time he took 31 states and the District of Columbia, good for 379 electoral votes. Of the nation's nine largest states, Clinton this year won eight (losing only Texas).

But no one was claiming the dawn of a new Democratic presidential era. Even Clinton was shy about claiming a mandate, especially given that Republicans maintained control of both chambers of Congress. Rather, both parties seemed aware that neither was to have the upper hand.

The political lineup in Washington already had been the historically unusual combination of a Democratic president and a Republican Congress, the product of Republicans' sweep of the House and Senate in the 1994 midterm elections.

But it is even more unusual to have that arrangement ratified by the voters in a presidential election. Never before had voters re-elected a Democratic president while giving Republicans both houses of Congress.

The split decision allowed both parties to claim victory. The presidential win marked a great personal comeback for Clinton, who had been widely portrayed after the 1994 Democratic debacle as a sure 1996 loser. And Republicans argued that voters had certified their conserva-

CQ Weekly Report November 9, 1996

WIN MCNAMEE

Clinton hugs Vice President Al Gore before his victory speech at the Old State House in Little Rock on Nov. 6.

tive agenda by extending their control of Congress.

But tempering the results for both parties was the clear display of voter uninterest. Turnout plummeted to below 50 percent of the voting age population for the first time in a presidential election year since women were extended the right to vote in the early 1920s. Altogether, nearly 10 million fewer votes were cast in 1996 than had been cast four years earlier.

And even though presidential candidate Ross Perot of the newly founded Reform Party fell way short of the 19 percent of the vote he received as an independent in 1992, he and an array of minor-party candidates collected a total of about 10 percent of the vote.

This second consecutive double-digit showing produced the largest third-party tally in back-to-back presidential elections since 1856 and 1860, a volatile period that gave birth to the Republican Party on the eve of the Civil War.

Good News, Bad News

For all the major candidates, the results could have been better, but they could also have been a lot worse.

Republicans lost their second straight presidential election after winning five of the previous six. But Dole's dogged effort, which climaxed with a frenetic, four-day, round-the-clock campaign blitz of diners, bowling alleys, and airport tarmacs, rallied the Republican base, helping the party reverse a decade-long downward spiral in the GOP presidential vote.

It had fallen from nearly 60 percent for President Ronald Reagan in 1984 to less than 40 percent for President Bush in 1992. Dole finished with 41 percent of the popular vote, well above his average standing in "horse race" presidential polls in the months prior to the election.

Despite a stumbling campaign that led to his being largely dismissed as too old

---

★ **THE PRESIDENT** ★

CLINTON

▪ Carried 31 states, one less than in 1992

▪ Electoral vote total of 379 was nine higher than in 1992

▪ Two-election total of 749 electoral votes surpasses the Democratic total for the previous six elections

▪ First Democrat since 1948 to win Arizona

▪ First Democrat since 1976 to win Florida

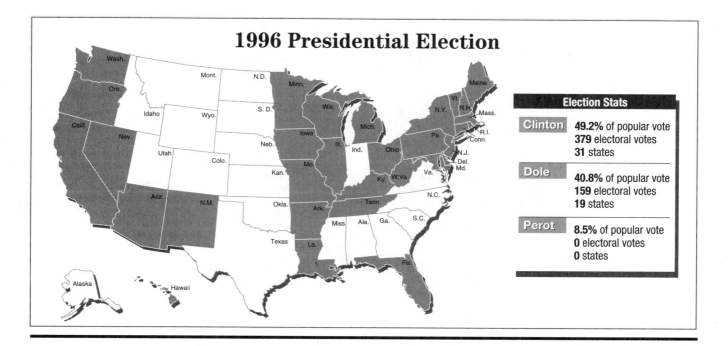

1996 Presidential Election

Election Stats

Clinton	**49.2%** of popular vote
	379 electoral votes
	31 states

Dole	**40.8%** of popular vote
	159 electoral votes
	19 states

Perot	**8.5%** of popular vote
	0 electoral votes
	0 states

For the second straight time, Clinton chewed up the Republican "L," the cornerstone of the recent GOP presidential victories.

The L-shaped bloc of states starts at the Canadian border, moves south through the Rocky Mountain and Plains states to the Mexican border, then turns east across the South to the Atlantic Ocean.

and inarticulate for the television age, Dole managed to win a disproportionate share of voters who made up their minds in the final days of the campaign, an upsurge that probably helped Republicans maintain their congressional majorities.

As for Perot, his 8 percent share of the vote was less than half his showing as a first-time candidate in 1992. But by winning more than 5 percent of the popular vote, he ensured that the nominee for his Reform Party would qualify for federal funding in 2000, albeit less than the $29 million that Perot received this year.

As for Clinton, his share of the popular vote rose from 43 percent in 1992 to 49 percent this time, according to nearly complete but unofficial returns. Yet his 8 percentage point margin of victory over Dole was less than half the lead he enjoyed in a number of public opinion surveys just a week or two before the election.

Nonetheless, Clinton is the first Democrat since Franklin D. Roosevelt in 1936 to win re-election to a second term, and his victory marked the first time since 1960 and 1964 that the Democrats had won back-to-back presidential elections.

Clinton's victory underscored the volatility of American politics in the 1990s. While his re-election looked inevitable throughout much of 1996, it seemed nearly impossible from the vantage point of late 1994, after the pummeling the Democrats took in the midterm elections.

But Clinton began to recoup in 1995, helped by missteps by congressional Republicans as they aggressively pursued their conservative "revolution" and by his own early fundraising success that scared off potential Democratic primary opposition. By early 1996, he was well ahead of Dole in the polls, and maintained a comfortable lead throughout the year.

So certain did Clinton's election appear that stories on his second term began to appear weeks before the election, and the presidential balloting Nov. 5 was widely regarded as little more than a formality.

Yet in spite of an economy that was humming and a world that was largely at peace, Clinton slumped at the end. A cascade of stories about Democratic fundraising improprieties no doubt took a toll, as did pointed attacks by Dole and Perot on the series of scandals that reflected on the character of the president, First Lady Hillary Rodham Clinton and members of the Clinton administration.

The Wilson Parallel

For much of the fall it had appeared that Clinton was poised to score a victory of significant proportions. But in the end, he followed in the more modest electoral footsteps of Democrat Woodrow Wilson, who won a first term against divided Republican opposition in 1912 with just 42 percent of the vote, then won re-election in 1916 with 49 percent.

Clinton can hope that the similarities to Wilson do not continue. Wilson's second term, dominated by U.S. engagement in World War I, unraveled in personal and political tragedy. He left office with failing health, skidding popularity, and a tattered legislative agenda, climaxing in the Republican Senate's rejection of U.S. participation in his masterwork, the League of Nations.

As it was, Wilson's presidency came in the midst of a half-century period, from 1880 through the onset of the Great Depression, in which no Democratic presidential candidate even once drew a majority of the popular vote.

Democrats are in a similar period now. They have won six presidential elections since the end of World War II, but voter approval has been grudging. Only once in the last 50 years has the Democratic nominee exceeded 50.1 percent of the popular vote (Lyndon B. Johnson in 1964).

Political Success

Measured against this modest record of electoral achievement, Clinton's re-election was a significant accomplishment. And at the least, it raised more doubts as to whether Republicans still hold an advantage on the Electoral College map.

The GOP clearly did from 1968 through 1988, when they won five of six presidential elections. But for the second straight time, Clinton chewed up the Republican "L," the cornerstone of the recent GOP presidential victories.

The L-shaped bloc of states starts at the Canadian border, moves south through the Rocky Mountain and Plains states to the Mexican border, then turns east across the South to the Atlantic Ocean. Adding Alaska, which regularly votes Republican in presidential elections, the "L" encompasses 26 states with 223 electoral votes.

When Reagan first won the White House in 1980, he carried every state in the "L" except for President Jimmy Carter's home state of Georgia. In 1984, Reagan swept all of them in his landslide win over Democrat Walter F. Mondale. So did Bush in 1988, winning every one of the 26 states, defeating Democrat Michael S. Dukakis in each by at least 5 percentage points.

Such dominance freed Republicans to campaign aggressively in California and the vote-rich states of the industrial Frost Belt, while Democrats had to frantically search for toeholds wherever they could find them.

But Clinton has made the "L" look like a piece of Swiss cheese, freeing the Democrats to go on the offensive. In 1992, Clinton took nine states in the "L." This year, he captured eight: five in the South and three in the Mountain West. Altogether, Clinton's share of electoral votes in the "L" jumped from 67 four years ago to 76 this year.

Clinton lost Colorado, Georgia, and Montana, which he had carried in 1992, but more than compensated by adding Arizona and Florida to his total. Both are states with a Republican heritage in recent presidential voting. Florida had given its electoral votes to only one Democrat since LBJ (Carter in 1976), while the last Democrat for whom Arizona had voted was Harry S. Truman 48 years ago.

But there are large numbers of retirees in both states, where Clinton's depiction of himself as the protector of Social Security, Medicare, and Medicaid against an insensitive Republican Congress resonated.

Clinton's ability to poach in this previously Republican preserve has totally changed Electoral College dynamics in the 1990s. Democrats have been able to leisurely scan the electoral map of the country, while Republicans have frenetically tried to secure their base.

Dole largely succeeded in that limited goal, holding most of the South (including Texas, North Carolina, Georgia, and Virginia) and taking most of the Mountain West and all of the Plains states, capped by an 18 percentage point victory in his home state of Kansas.

REUTERS

Presidential candidate Bob Dole delivers his concession speech to supporters Nov. 5.

But just like Bush four years ago, Dole could take only one state outside the "L" — Indiana. He failed badly in his desperate 11th-hour bid to win California, a foray that was easily rebuffed by Clinton, who carried the Golden State and its 54 electoral votes by more than 1.2 million votes.

With Dole giving up early on much of the industrial Frost Belt, Clinton also rolled to victory there. He swept New York by more than 1.6 million votes, Massachusetts by 850,000, Illinois by more than 700,000, Michigan by 500,000, Pennsylvania by more than 400,000, and Ohio by nearly 300,000 votes.

The results underscored a new political reality: The East has replaced the South as the Democrat's electoral cornerstone. Not only did Clinton sweep every eastern state for the second straight election, but with the exception of Pennsylvania, he won each one this time by at least 10 percentage points. That includes historic Republican bastions such as New Hampshire and Vermont.

And it was in the East that Clinton ran up his highest percentages of the 1996 election. He took 85 percent of the vote in the District of Columbia, 62 percent in Massachusetts, 60 percent in Rhode Island, and 59 percent in New York. By comparison, Clinton drew 54 percent of the vote in his home state of Arkansas.

Playing in Peoria

Nationwide exit polling showed the breadth of Clinton's appeal. He swept the vote of every age group, running best among young voters. He ran ahead of Dole among all education categories, except college graduates. And he won a number of key voting blocs, such as Catholics and self-described moderates.

The demographic advantage for Clinton most often mentioned during the campaign was the strong support he received from women voters. While Dole ran virtually even with Clinton among men, the incumbent ran roughly 20 percentage points ahead among women.

The outcome made it appear that the "gender gap" in presidential voting has become virtually institutionalized. It was the fifth straight election, going back to the Reagan-Carter contest of 1980, that the Democratic nominee ran better among women than men.

Clinton ran even with Dole among whites but rolled up the sort of big edge that has been typical of Democratic candidates among minority voters. Clinton took more than 80 percent of the black vote and surpassed 70 percent among Hispanics, a rebuff to GOP vice presidential nominee Jack F. Kemp's minority-outreach effort.

Dole did have his successes. He beat Clinton among upper-income voters. He won a plurality of 1992 Perot voters, a major target of his campaign. And he largely maintained the Republican base, winning the support of more than 80 percent of 1992 Bush voters who cast ballots.

Not only did Dole fend off Clinton in California's Orange County, a bastion of Sun Belt conservatism, but the unofficial returns showed him narrowly winning two populous GOP-ori-

Three-Party Vote for President

Following are the nearly complete but unofficial vote totals for the three leading candidates in the presidential race — Democrat Bill Clinton, Republican Bob Dole and Reform Party candidate Ross Perot. Percentages, though, are based on the votes cast for all candidates and do not necessarily add to 100.

State	Clinton	%	Dole	%	Perot	%	Electoral Votes
Alabama	664,503	43	782,029	51	92,010	6	9
Alaska	66,508	33	101,234	51	21,536	11	3
Arizona	612,412	47	576,126	44	104,712	8	8
Arkansas	469,164	54	322,349	37	66,997	8	6
California	4,639,935	51	3,412,563	38	667,702	7	54
Colorado	670,854	44	691,291	46	99,509	7	8
Connecticut	712,603	52	481,047	35	137,784	10	8
Delaware	140,209	52	98,906	37	28,693	11	3
District of Columbia	152,031	85	16,637	9	3,479	2	3
Florida	2,533,502	48	2,226,117	42	482,237	9	25
Georgia	1,047,214	46	1,078,972	47	146,031	6	13
Hawaii	205,012	57	113,943	32	27,358	8	4
Idaho	165,545	34	256,406	52	62,506	13	4
Illinois	2,299,476	54	1,577,930	37	344,311	8	22
Indiana	874,668	42	995,082	47	218,739	10	12
Iowa	615,732	50	490,949	40	104,462	9	7
Kansas	384,399	36	578,572	54	92,093	9	6
Kentucky	635,804	46	622,339	45	118,768	9	8
Louisiana	928,983	52	710,240	40	122,981	7	9
Maine	311,092	52	185,133	31	85,290	14	4
Maryland	924,284	54	651,682	38	113,684	7	10
Massachusetts	1,567,223	62	717,622	28	225,594	9	12
Michigan	1,941,126	52	1,440,977	38	326,751	9	18
Minnesota	1,096,355	51	751,971	35	252,986	12	10
Mississippi	385,005	44	434,547	49	51,500	6	7
Missouri	1,024,817	48	889,689	41	217,103	10	11
Montana	167,169	41	178,957	44	55,017	14	3
Nebraska	231,906	35	355,665	53	76,103	11	5
Nevada	203,388	44	198,775	43	43,855	9	4
New Hampshire	245,260	50	196,740	40	48,140	10	4
New Jersey	1,599,932	53	1,080,041	36	257,979	9	15
New Mexico	252,215	49	210,791	41	30,978	6	5
New York	3,513,191	59	1,861,198	31	485,547	8	33
North Carolina	1,099,132	44	1,214,399	49	165,301	7	14
North Dakota	106,405	40	124,597	47	32,594	12	3
Ohio	2,100,690	47	1,823,859	41	470,680	11	21
Oklahoma	488,102	40	582,310	48	130,788	11	8
Oregon	326,099	47	256,105	37	73,265	11	7
Pennsylvania	2,206,241	49	1,793,568	40	430,082	10	23
Rhode Island	220,592	60	98,325	27	39,965	11	4
South Carolina	495,878	44	564,856	50	63,324	6	8
South Dakota	139,295	43	150,508	46	31,248	10	3
Tennessee	905,599	48	860,809	46	105,577	6	11
Texas	2,455,735	44	2,731,998	49	377,530	7	32
Utah	220,197	33	359,394	54	66,100	10	5
Vermont	138,400	54	80,043	31	30.912	12	3
Virginia	1,070,990	45	1,119,974	47	158,707	7	13
Washington	899,645	51	639,743	36	161,642	9	11
West Virginia	324,394	51	231,908	37	70,853	11	5
Wisconsin	1,071,859	49	845,172	39	227,426	10	11
Wyoming	77,897	37	105,347	50	25,854	12	3
TOTALS	**45,628,667**	**49**	**37,869,435**	**41**	**7,874,283**	**8**	**538**

SOURCE: The Associated Press

A Regional Breakdown

In winning re-election Nov. 5, President Clinton ran ahead of Republican Bob Dole in both the popular and electoral vote in three of the four regions. Clinton made his strongest showing in the East, where he swept all 127 electoral votes for the second straight election. Like President George Bush four years ago, Dole had the edge only in the South.

The popular vote percentages shown below are based on the nearly complete but unofficial three-party vote for president, as tallied by the Associated Press. The winner of the popular vote in each region is indicated in **boldface**.

	Popular Vote			Electoral Vote	
	Clinton	Dole	Perot	Clinton	Dole
East	56%	35%	9%	127	0
Midwest	49	41	10	100	29
South	46	46	7	59	104
West	50	42	8	93	26

ented Southern California counties Clinton had carried in 1992, Riverside and San Diego.

But prominent bellwether counties went to Clinton. The president played well in Peoria. In 1992, he became the first Democratic nominee to carry the Illinois county since LBJ in 1964 and he won it again this year.

So too Ohio's Stark County (Canton), a bellwether county in a bellwether state that was chronicled in a series of election-year articles in The New York Times; Clinton carried it for the second straight time.

And Clinton became the first Democratic presidential nominee since Hubert H. Humphrey in 1968 to carry Michigan's Macomb County, a quintessential hotbed of socially conservative, blue-collar "Reagan Democrats."

For years, Republicans dominated presidential voting by executing a simple formula: Concede the cities to the Democrats while rolling to victory in the suburbs, small towns, and rural areas.

But Clinton stymied that formula in 1992, and he did so again in 1996. Clinton won most major urban areas, swept many of the nation's most populous suburban jurisdictions, from Suffolk County on New York's Long Island to San Bernardino County in southern California, and he made deep inroads in rural America.

Nowhere was that more evident than in Illinois' Whiteside County. It is in the heart of farm country along the Mississippi River and includes Reagan's birthplace of Tampico. Throughout its history, Whiteside has been reliably Republican in presidential voting.

Before Clinton, it had never voted for a Democratic presidential candidate. But Clinton now has carried it twice. Arguably in 1992, it took an assist by Perot for Clinton to carry the county with just 45 percent of the vote. But this time, Clinton clearly won it on his own, taking Whiteside County with an outright majority of 51 percent.

Shades of 1984, 1924

Whether Whiteside County will vote for another Democratic presidential candidate in 2000 is an open question.

In running for re-election this year, Clinton was able to exploit several unique assets. Upbeat reviews of the economy enabled him to reprise the "Morning in America" theme that Reagan used so effectively in his 1984 re-election bid.

Clinton muted differences with Republicans on volatile issues such as crime and welfare reform.

And the absence of primary opposition early this year freed Clinton to move to the political center while running ads in targeted states, tying Dole to House Speaker Newt Gingrich at a time when Dole was financially exhausted by his primary competition and unable to respond effectively. What had been a single-digit percentage point lead for Clinton over Dole at the beginning of the year quickly became a double-digit lead.

Dole tried mightily to change the odds. His campaign will be remembered for a series of dramatic thrusts: He resigned from the Senate in the spring, unveiled a 15 percent tax-cut proposal in the summer, tapped former political adversary Kemp as his running mate, and succeeded in getting Perot excluded from the October presidential debates so he could have a one-on-one shot at Clinton.

But Dole could never surmount doubts about his age (73) and communication skills. Even the nation's oldest voters (60 years and up) preferred Clinton.

Well ahead in the polls as Election Day approached, the president ran a victory lap through conservative strongholds from Orange County, Calif., to Manchester, N.H., as he stumped hard for Democratic congressional candidates.

Meanwhile, Dole was left railing against what he saw as a liberal media elite and an incumbent president he intimated was corrupt. "Where's the outrage?" Dole asked plaintively.

In pushing the ethics theme, Dole had help from Perot, who increasingly focused on Clinton's character as Election Day approached. At one point, he called Clinton the "all-time, world-record, grand-prize winner for corrupt campaign fund-

The Final Polls

Pollsters had predicted long before Election Day that President Clinton would win re-election. The margin, however, varied by several points in the closing days. Most polls prior to the election projected a wider margin of victory for Clinton than he actually received.

	Clinton	Dole	Perot
Actual popular vote	49%	41%	8%
Reuters/Zogby	49	41	8
Gallup/CNN/USA Today	52	41	7
Lou Harris	51	39	9
CBS News/New York Times	53	35	9
ABC News	51	39	7
NBC News/Wall Street Journal	49	37	9
Hotline/Battleground Poll	45	36	8

ing" and referred to the president and the first lady as "Bonnie and Clyde."

Perot, though, was not the factor that he was four years ago, when Republicans accused him of carving into their base. Unlike 1992, he was not invited to participate in the presidential debates this year, and his televised infomercials drew smaller audiences than four years ago. He did attract some media attention in late October when the Dole campaign urged him to quit the race and throw his support to Dole, an entreaty Perot refused.

The attention helped push Perot's standing from the mid-single digits to above 10 percent in a variety of polls. But the Perot uptick had abated by Nov. 5. He did not come close to winning a single state; his best showings were 14 percent in Maine and Montana. Maine had been Perot's best state in 1992, when it gave him 30 percent of the vote.

The freshness of Perot's candidacy four years ago helped produce a surge in voter turnout. A record 104.4 million ballots were cast, representing 55 percent of the voting-age population. It was the highest rate of turnout since 1972.

But this year, the downward trend in turnout resumed. Fewer than 96 million ballots were cast, according to an esti-

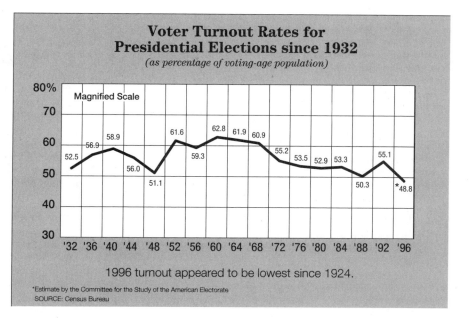

Voter Turnout Rates for Presidential Elections since 1932
(as percentage of voting-age population)

1996 turnout appeared to be lowest since 1924.

*Estimate by the Committee for the Study of the American Electorate
SOURCE: Census Bureau

mate by the Committee for the Study of the American Electorate (CSAE), which represented just 48.8 percent of the voting-age population. It was the lowest turnout rate since 1924 and the second lowest since 1824, according to the CSAE.

The rate of presidential-year turnout has been on a steady decline since the closely fought election of 1960, won by Democrat John F. Kennedy over Republican Richard M. Nixon, which drew 63 percent of the voting-age population to the polls. The turnout rate stayed above 60 percent through the 1960s, before falling to 55 percent in 1972 after the voting age was lowered from 21 to 18.

And it has continued to fall since then, with the exceptions of 1984 and 1992, when there were upticks in voter participation that proved only temporary.

Until this year, the low point for turnout in recent presidential elections came in 1988 when Bush defeated Dukakis. Then, barely 50 percent of the voting age population cast ballots.

But it was apparent throughout 1996 that the turnout rate could go lower than that this year, as viewership for the August national conventions of the Republican and Democratic parties and the October debates between Clinton and Dole fell sharply from 1992. The television networks' election night coverage had fewer watchers, too.

"This is a mandate for no one," said CSAE Director Curtis B. Gans. "The president won and the GOP's House margin was diminished."

As a result, Gans said, the new Congress will begin with neither party in a clear position to lead — and that could push the parties in either of two distinctly different directions.

"The question in the next two years," he said, "will be whether that lack of mandate for either side will foster cooperation to get things done or positioning to do battle in the next election." ∎

Presidents and Re-election

Although presidents once won second terms almost as a matter of course, the trick has proven more difficult in recent decades. Since President Nixon won re-election in 1972 with 61 percent of the vote, presidents have often had a rough ride to another term. Three have lost; two have won; and only Ronald Reagan in 1984 drew a majority of the popular vote. President Clinton's percentage this year is based on nearly complete but unofficial returns.

	Vote Share	Outcome
Harry S. Truman, D-1948	50%	Won
Dwight D. Eisenhower, R-1956	57	Won
Lyndon B. Johnson, D-1964	61	Won
Richard M. Nixon, R-1972	61	Won
Gerald R. Ford, R-1976	48	Lost
Jimmy Carter, D-1980	41	Lost
Ronald Reagan, R-1984	59	Won
George Bush, R-1992	37	Lost
Bill Clinton, D-1996	49	Won

Propositions: Pot to Parental Rights

Voters in 20 states passed judgment Nov. 5 on a wide variety of ballot initiatives, led by a California proposition that would ban affirmative action programs in public hiring, contracting and educational admissions.

The California plan (Prop. 209) won approval on a vote of 54 percent to 46 percent, a margin of victory considerably below what most polls had predicted.

The measure was controversial not only because it ended preferences based on race but because it ended preferences based on sex.

The measure, known as the California Civil Rights Initiative, was confusing to some voters in part because of its name. One of its original advocates, Ward Connerly, is a black businessman who had also worked for Gov. Pete Wilson.

The Prop. 209 campaign generated additional controversy by attempting to use footage of the "I Have A Dream" speech by the Rev. Dr. Martin Luther King Jr. in a television ad. The footage was not used after King's widow, Coretta Scott King, objected.

The measure was supported by several prominent Republicans, including Wilson, Attorney General Dan Lungren and presidential nominee Bob Dole, whose endorsement gave the initiative even more national exposure.

Opponents were led by a coalition of minorities, women and labor unions. President Clinton also expressed opposition.

Considering California's status as the most populous state and its occasional tendency to act as a political bellwether, voters in other states may seek to pass a similar initiative. Wilson acted quickly to follow through on the initiative the day after it passed, issuing an executive order directing state agencies to identify programs that provide preferences based on race or sex.

But opponents filed a lawsuit in federal district court that same day to try to block enforcement, claiming that it violated the equal protection clause of the U.S. Constitution's 14th Amendment. Proponents countered with a lawsuit of their own in state court seeking prompt enforcement.

Other ballot measures attracting attention:

• **Marijuana.** Voters in both California and Arizona approved measures designed to permit using marijuana for medical purposes when prescribed by a physician. The Arizona initiative applies only to critically ill patients. The impact of both measures was clouded by federal prohibitions against using, growing or selling marijuana.

• **Environment and wildlife.** Florida voters rejected a penny-a-pound sugar tax for cleaning up the Everglades, an initiative that was opposed by sugar companies. Maine turned down a proposal — opposed by the paper industry — to ban clear-cutting on 10 million acres of the state's northern forests.

A variety of measures to ban certain types of hunting were adopted by Alaska, Massachusetts, Colorado and Washington, while Idaho and Michigan rejected new limits on hunting.

Idaho voters also expressed disapproval of a federal contract to store nuclear waste in the state temporarily.

• **Gambling.** Gambling measures were defeated in Nebraska, Ohio, Colorado and Arkansas. Arizona approved expanding gambling in Native American casinos, and Michigan voters approved a statewide measure to allow casino gambling in Detroit.

• **Term limits.** Proponents of term limits took a new approach in many states in light of a 1995 U.S. Supreme Court ruling that prohibits states from limiting congressional terms without amending the Constitution.

Voters in nine states — Alaska, Arkansas, Colorado, Idaho, Maine, Missouri, Nebraska, Nevada and South Dakota — passed measures that will ask candidates in those states to try to pass congressional term limits. Officials in those states who decline to do so will generally have their positions noted on the ballot the next time they run.

Voters in five states — Washington, Oregon, North Dakota, Montana and Wyoming — rejected the new term limits strategy.

• **Campaign finance.** Voters in Arkansas, California and Colorado approved new contribution limits for state and local races. Maine voters approved of giving some public funding to candidates. And Montanans banned corporate spending on ballot initiatives.

• **Health care.** Oregon voters raised the state cigarette tax by 30 cents a pack, to 68 cents, to help fund health care for poor people. Californians rejected two plans to revamp the way the state's HMOs do business.

• **Parental rights.** Colorado voters rejected a state constitutional amendment that would have given parents ultimate rights in matters of educating and disciplining their children.

Proponents, led by Of the People, a conservative Christian organization, said it would protect families and act as a buffer against government interference in education and family matters. Opponents said it would make it harder to investigate charges of child abuse or devise school curriculums.

• **Taxing churches.** Colorado voters also defeated a measure that would have imposed a state tax on certain property used for religious or charitable purposes.

• **Shareholder lawsuits.** California voters rejected a plan that would have made it easier to sue companies and individuals for alleged securities fraud. The proposition attracted heavy spending from opponents in financial services and in the entrepreneurial high-tech industry.

• **Minimum wage.** Proposed increases in the minimum wage were rejected in Missouri, Montana and Colorado (for the city of Denver), but approved in California and Oregon.

> Considering California's status as the most populous state and its occasional tendency to act as a political bellwether, voters in other states may seek to pass a similar initiative on affirmative action.

Government Institutions

In 1996 the electorate turned out to reaffirm the existing party control of the federal government. Most of the articles in this section examine how the outcome of the elections will affect the organization and agenda of the 105th Congress and the executive branch. If the election results indicated one thing from the president on down to members of Congress, it was that those candidates who eschewed harsh rhetoric and fought to control the political center on the issues were the big winners.

In the Senate the Republican Party picked up two seats to increase to a 55–45 advantage over the Democrats. Conservative Senate Majority Leader Trent Lott, saw his position strengthened with the addition of new conservative members in the chamber. The GOP, however, lost ground in the House of Representatives, turning over at least seven seats to the Democratic Party. A smaller Republican majority will give Speaker of the House Newt Gingrich less room to maneuver. With ethics charge still hovering over him and many in his party less likely to follow him as adamantly as during the 104th Congress, Gingrich will likely see his power in the 105th Congress diminished.

(At press time, a few close House results reported here appear to have been reversed. In Washington state, in the 2nd District, incumbent Republican Jack Metcalf moved ahead of Democrat Kevin Quigley on the strength of absentee ballots. Similarly in 3rd District, Republican Rep. Linda Smith won a razor-thin victory over Democratic challenger Brian Baird. If these results hold, the GOP will maintain control of the state's House delegation by a 6–3 margin. In California's 46th District, absentee ballots also pushed Democrat Loretta Sanchez past nine-term Republican Rep. Robert K. Dornan. Official results for these races and a handful of other close contests have yet to be certified. There were also several recounts underway and three runoffs for Texas House seats scheduled for December. The final makeup of the 105th Congress may not be known until January 1997.)

The major area where Congress and the president collided in 1995 and 1996 was the federal budget. Balancing the budget will remain a top priority for both branches in 1997. For Republicans in Congress to regain the upper hand, they may have to abandon their revolutionary agenda and try coalition building. The moderate congressional members from both parties may emerge as the new power brokers. CQ editors also take a look at how the president's second-term programs will likely fare in the Republican Congress. President Clinton will likely attempt to advance his programs incrementally while seeking centrist positions. 1997 may also be the year that Congress and the president enact a bipartisan solution to campaign finance reform.

The final article in this section looks at important cases that the Supreme Court will likely review in 1997. These high-profile cases include the application of free speech rights to the Internet, whether the federal government overstep its powers over the states in the Brady law's waiting period for handgun purchases, the legality of assisted suicide, and presidential immunity.

Senate Steps to the Right As GOP Expands Majority

Senate now more of an ideological match for House, as new members swell conservative ranks

The Senate proved to be the Republicans' happiest hunting ground on Election Day, as the party made an apparent net gain of two seats. If certified, this gain will give the Republicans a solid 55–45 majority over the Democrats in the 105th Congress, up from 53–47 before the election.

Most of the nine new Republican members will swell the ranks of their party's conservative wing in the Senate — making the chamber more of an ideological match for the House GOP majority, whose activist agenda drove the Republican "revolution" in the 104th Congress.

Three of the new conservative Republican members — Jeff Sessions of Alabama, Tim Hutchinson of Arkansas and Chuck Hagel of Nebraska — were elected to succeed retiring Democrats. Pat Roberts of Kansas and apparent winner Gordon Smith of Oregon are conservatives who will replace more moderate retiring senators of their own party.

Hutchinson and Roberts both will be moving from the House to the Senate, as will conservatives Sam Brownback of Kansas, who won the race to fill out the remaining two years of Republican presidential nominee Bob Dole's unexpired term, and Wayne Allard of Colorado.

In both chambers, the relative strength of the two parties varies increasingly by region. Like rival street gangs, the two parties now control swaths of territory with relative ease while engaging each other primarily at the geographical margins.

Republicans are now regnant in the South, the lower Plains and the interior West, while Democrats take advantage of the different traditions and voter demographics of the East, the Upper Midwest and the Pacific Coast.

The GOP appears to be nailing down the once solidly Democratic South as the

REUTERS

Incumbent Sen. Senator Jesse Helms addresses supporters after winning a fifth term Nov. 5.

foundation of its national constituency. But the increasingly Southern and socially conservative face of the GOP may cost the party some currency in its former redoubts in suburban and rural areas of the North and Midwest, said Ronald M. Peters Jr., director of the Carl Albert Congressional Research and Studies Center at the University of Oklahoma.

Republicans won 10 of the 12 Southern seats up for contention. But even as the GOP gathers strength in the South, the traditional Republican strongholds of New England and the Great Lakes states have eroded — leaving the two parties to duel for dominance in separate parcels of the West.

"It's possible that what happens in the South only appears favorable for Republicans if they're able to hold their seats in their old base in the old Abraham Lincoln territory," Peters said.

The Republicans' two-seat gain was contingent on a three-day count of absentee ballots in Oregon, where roughly one-third of the total vote was not cast at the polling booths. Smith's narrow lead over Democrat Tom Bruggere held up, pushing the GOP's total to 55 seats — its high-water mark in the Senate following any election since 1928.

But Democrats held their own in most regions of the country. All seven Democrats seeking re-election were returned, and Democrats bagged the only incumbent trophy Nov. 5, with Democratic Rep. Tim Johnson unseating three-term Republican Larry Pressler of South Dakota.

Only one other incumbent was defeated this year: interim Sen. Sheila Frahm of Kansas, who was appointed after Dole resigned from the Senate in June but lost to Brownback in the Aug. 6 primary. Yet because a record 13 incumbent senators retired, there will be 15 freshman senators

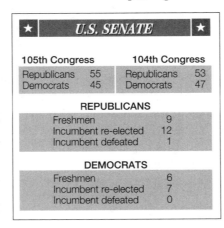

★	U.S. SENATE		★
105th Congress		**104th Congress**	
Republicans	55	Republicans	53
Democrats	45	Democrats	47

REPUBLICANS	
Freshmen	9
Incumbent re-elected	12
Incumbent defeated	1

DEMOCRATS	
Freshmen	6
Incumbent re-elected	7
Incumbent defeated	0

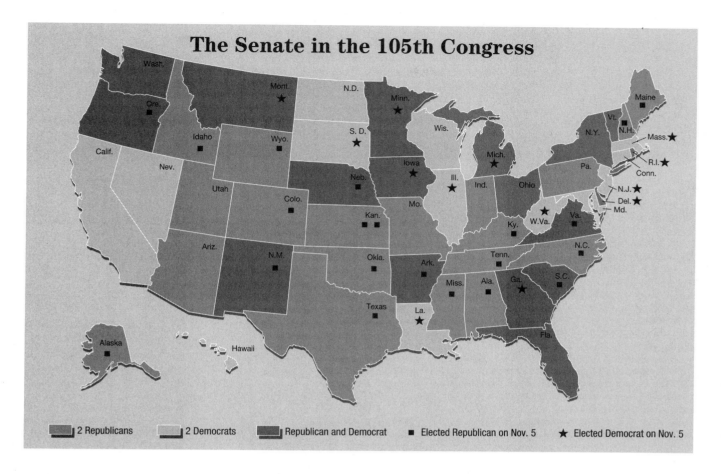

The Senate in the 105th Congress

Legend: 2 Republicans | 2 Democrats | Republican and Democrat | ■ Elected Republican on Nov. 5 | ★ Elected Democrat on Nov. 5

— in the 105th Congress, the largest incoming Senate class since the GOP landslide year of 1980.

And, in contrast to 1994, when Republicans monopolized an entire Senate class for the first time since popular election of senators was mandated by the 17th Amendment in 1913, six Democrats will be taking oaths of office in January. Democrats making the move from the House to the Senate are South Dakota's Johnson and open-seat winner Richard J. Durbin of Illinois.

Frahm and Kansas' other GOP senator, retiring moderate Nancy Landon Kassebaum, will be replaced by men — Brownback and Roberts — who defeated Democratic women candidates on Nov. 5.

Nevertheless, the number of women in the Senate remains constant at nine, with Democrat Mary Landrieu the apparent narrow winner in Louisiana and Republican Susan Collins prevailing in Maine. With Collins joining 1994 Republican winner Olympia J. Snowe, Maine replaces Kansas as the only state besides California with two women senators.

The two new women in the Senate bucked regional tides running against their respective parties to win their seats. Collins was the only Republican elected to the Senate from the East. Landrieu was one of two Democratic hopefuls in open seat races, along with Max Cleland of Georgia, able to counter the GOP's gathering dominance of the South.

Only one Southern Democrat had succeeded another to the Senate since 1978: John B. Breaux of Louisiana, who first won the Bayou State's other seat in 1986. Landrieu's victory leaves Louisiana the only state in the South with two Democratic senators.

The South

The razor-thin victories of Landrieu and Cleland — neither won more than 50 percent of the vote — masked a greater underlying Republican trend in the South. Republicans defended eight Southern seats, most with relative ease, and won seats in Alabama and Arkansas that had long been held by Democrats.

"What 1996 does is put more frosting on the cake of the Republican South," said Charles W. Dunn, who specializes in conservative politics at Clemson University.

Hutchinson now becomes the first Republican Arkansas has sent to the Senate since Reconstruction. His win was a finger in the eye of the nation's best-known Arkansan, President Clinton, whose coattails were short even as he easily carried his home state.

"The fact that Arkansas went Republican is symbolically the strongest statement that can be made about the gradual erosion of the Democratic one-party South," Dunn said.

Hutchinson overcame a head start and slight spending advantage enjoyed by the Democratic nominee, state Attorney General Winston Bryant, who proved a lackluster candidate despite a long streak of earlier statewide victories.

Under strong pressure from Republican leaders, Hutchinson abandoned his 3rd District seat to make the run for the Senate after the original GOP nominee, Mike Huckabee, withdrew to succeed Democratic Gov. Jim Guy Tucker, who resigned following a Whitewater-related conviction.

Huckabee, who had been serving as lieutenant governor, was a heavy favorite to capture the Senate prize. Hutchinson was not well-known outside his northwest Arkansas district, but was able to tar Bryant, who had won seven previous statewide races, as a career politician for once having supported a state legislative pay raise and going on state-funded trips.

He also derided Bryant for an administrative slip-up in the prosecutor's office that allowed a convicted killer to walk.

Bryant countered with TV ads laying the blame for government shutdowns in 1995 at Hutchinson's feet. But his attempts to link Hutchinson to Newt Gingrich, R-Ga., partially foundered on the shore of the Republican's vote to release the outside counsel's report on the Speaker's alleged ethics violations.

Alabama's Sessions, the other state attorney general nominated for the Senate, enjoyed greater success. As one of the brightest stars in a blossoming Alabama GOP, Sessions had been favored throughout the campaign to succeed retiring three-term Democrat Howell Heflin.

Sessions cried foul when his Democratic opponent, state Sen. Roger Bedford, stole some of his thunder on social issues: Both trumpeted their opposition to abortion and gun control and their support for prayer in public schools.

But Sessions found other torpedoes to launch at Bedford. He pilloried the Democrat for having secured state funds for a water grant that raised the value of some property Bedford co-owned. Sessions also reached into the Republican arsenal and blasted Bedford for his association with trial lawyers, labor unions and other traditional Democratic constituencies.

Some episodes from Sessions' past, centering on racially tinged remarks he made that sank his nomination for a federal judgeship in 1986, helped unify Democrats against him and keep the race close. But even Bedford conceded privately that the race was probably Sessions' to lose from the beginning.

Solid support among blacks helped propel Landrieu to her narrow victory over Republican state Sen. Louis "Woody" Jenkins. According to exit polls, she won 91 percent of the ballots cast by African-Americans in the state with the second-highest percentage of black residents.

Landrieu was aided in this cause by a late endorsement from Democratic Rep. Cleo Fields, who is black. The two had a touchy relationship: Landrieu refused to endorse Fields in the 1995 gubernatorial contest after he defeated her for a place in the runoff.

Landrieu staked out the political center, highlighting her support for federal education programs. She also lambasted Jenkins, a solid-plated conservative, with a list of "100 reasons" why he was too extreme for the Senate.

Jenkins, a leading opponent of abortion in the state Legislature, volleyed back that Landrieu was too liberal, citing her support for abortion rights and votes for tax increases she cast as a state legislator. He was aided by a former archbishop of New Orleans, who declared that it would be a "sin" to vote for Landrieu because of her abortion position.

But Jenkins' anti-tax crusade — he called for abolishing the Internal Revenue Service — backfired when it was re-

vealed his businesses had been regularly delinquent with tax payments over a six-year period.

Portraying Democratic contenders as soft on crime was a standard Republican approach across the South and the nation. Both Landrieu in Louisiana and Cleland in Georgia were lambasted by their opponents for having intervened in past parole proceedings in behalf of convicted killers. During a Nov. 3 debate, Republican nominee Guy Millner demanded of Cleland that he look into the TV camera and apologize to the family of the killer's victim.

Steady attacks by Millner, a millionaire employment agency owner, moved him surprisingly close behind Cleland in the final days of the Georgia campaign. But in the end, Cleland was able to maintain a stronger grasp of the political center than Millner, who was adamant in his opposition to abortion and drew negative publicity for holding membership, which he subsequently resigned, in a club thought restricted against blacks and Jews.

Early on, Cleland had appeared to be the ideal candidate for the state, a Vietnam War hero who previously had won statewide races by large margins. Cleland's personal story — he lost both legs and one arm in combat — helped him capture the imagination of the state, with its deep regard for military service, and may have been decisive in his narrow victory.

REUTERS

Democratic Rep. Robert Torricelli waves to supporters after defeating GOP Rep. Dick Zimmer for New Jersey Senate seat.

Republican Strom Thurmond of South Carolina looked to be potentially vulnerable because of his age (his 100th birthday will occur a month after the next time his seat comes up for election in November 2002). But Democratic businessman Elliott Close could not convince voters to turn out the political legend.

Thurmond's neighbor, Republican Jesse Helms of North Carolina, found that there were benefits to seniority, as voters rewarded the Foreign Relations Committee chairman. For the second consecutive election, Helms proved willing to play the race card against Democrat Harvey B. Gantt, a black former mayor of Charlotte.

Another veteran GOP lawmaker, John W. Warner of Virginia, found himself with a narrower victory margin than polls had indicated. His Democratic challenger, cellular phone mogul Mark Warner, drew within 6 percentage points by converting a steady stream of cash into a barrage of negative advertising. "Ten million dollars in ads has to take a toll," said Mark J. Rozell of American University, co-author of a book on Virginia politics.

"Mark Warner was effective in conveying to many voters that John Warner is not what he's advertised to be, some kind of centrist that draws support from both parties," said Rozell, adding that the ads accomplished this "by factually conveying John Warner's voting record."

Republicans Mitch McConnell of Kentucky, Thad Cochran of Mississippi, Fred Thompson of Tennessee and Phil Gramm of Texas all turned aside their Democratic challengers with relative dispatch.

| Sessions | Hutchinson | Allard | Cleland | Durbin | Brownback | Roberts | Landrieu |

New Faces in the Senate

State	104th	105th	Winner	Loser	Incumbent
Alabama	D	R	Jeff Sessions	Roger Bedford	Howell Heflin
Arkansas	D	R	Tim Hutchinson	Winston Bryant	David Pryor
Colorado	R	R	Wayne Allard	Tom Strickland	Hank Brown
Georgia	D	D	Max Cleland	Guy Millner	Sam Nunn
Illinois	D	D	Richard J. Durbin	Al Salvi	Paul Simon
Kansas	R	R	Sam Brownback	Jill Docking	Sheila Frahm
Kansas	R	R	Pat Roberts	Sally Thompson	Nancy Landon Kassebaum
Louisiana	D	D	Mary Landrieu	Louis "Woody" Jenkins	J. Bennett Johnston
Maine	R	R	Susan Collins	Joseph E. Brennan	William S. Cohen
Nebraska	D	R	Chuck Hagel	Ben Nelson	Jim Exon
New Jersey	D	D	Robert G. Torricelli	Dick Zimmer	Bill Bradley
Oregon	R	R	Gordon Smith	Tom Bruggere	Mark O. Hatfield
Rhode Island	D	D	Jack Reed	Nancy J. Mayer	Claiborne Pell
South Dakota	R	D	Tim Johnson	Larry Pressler	Larry Pressler
Wyoming	R	R	Mike Enzi	Kathy Karpan	Alan K. Simpson

| Collins | Hagel | Torricelli | Reed | Johnson | Enzi | Smith |

James M. Inhofe's 17-point re-election margin was emblematic of a dramatic Republican surge in Oklahoma. There were five Democrats in the state's eight-member congressional delegation as recently as 1994, but the entire group is Republican now.

The Midwest

Other Plains states have also shown themselves ready to embrace the GOP's socially conservative platform. Voters in Nebraska and Kansas offered work to Senate nominees who take a harder line on social issues than has been the custom of either the region or the Senate.

But voters in the Upper Midwest rejected Republican Senate hopefuls wholesale, with South Dakota turning out three-term incumbent Pressler.

Dole's home state of Kansas selected two new Republican senators, with Rep. Roberts easily winning Kassebaum's seat, which he initially had been reluctant to seek.

"Kansas is big, Kansas is back — deal with it," the often acerbic Roberts said to cheering supporters Nov. 5 after defeating Democratic state Treasurer Sally Thompson.

Brownback also found himself in the winner's circle, turning back Democratic stockbroker Jill Docking. The fast-rising Brownback, a leading agitator in the House GOP Class of 1994, has spearheaded efforts to abolish four Cabinet departments and has aligned himself with religious conservative groups since starting his career on the Hill.

His nomination over the more moderate Frahm had been portrayed as symbolic of the rift between the old and the new in the Kansas Republican Party. But he was able to bridge that gap, obtaining Frahm's support for the general election. "I think across the board Brownback sold himself as conservative but not extremist," said University of Kansas political scientist Burdett Loomis.

In Nebraska, Republican investment banker Chuck Hagel scored perhaps the year's biggest upset with his defeat of Democratic Gov. Ben Nelson for the seat of retiring three-term Democratic Sen. Jim Exon. Nelson had been re-elected to the statehouse in 1994 with 74 percent of the vote, but his statewide take shrunk to 42 percent against Hagel.

Nelson had held a polling lead from the opening gun, but found himself caught up short after Hagel reminded voters of Nelson's re-election pledge in 1994 to serve out his gubernatorial term.

Hagel, the first Republican Nebraska has sent to the Senate in 24 years, out-hustled Nelson and outspent him by about $1 million — much of that difference drawn from his own pocket. He promised a large tax break to be funded in part by the elimination of federal agencies such as the Department of Education.

Many voters apparently were concerned that Nelson's potential replacement in Lincoln, Democratic Lt. Gov. Kim Robak, would be too permissive on abortion (she supports access to the procedure, which Hagel and Nelson both oppose).

"My sense is you're getting a kind of Plains Republicanism that's both fiscally conservative and increasingly social conservative," Loomis said.

But voters in the Great Lakes state of Illinois were turned off by Republican state Rep. Al Salvi, another social conservative who had knocked off more moderate GOP Lt. Gov. Bob Kustra in the Illinois primary. Salvi lost to Democrat Durbin by a wide margin in the race to succeed popular, retiring two-term Democratic Sen. Paul Simon.

Salvi ran a smooth campaign, emphasizing budget issues and taxes. His television ads showed him frolicking with his children, helping to fend off Durbin's attempts to portray him as an extremist because of such stances as his strong opposition to abortion and many gun control measures.

But Salvi made a huge misstep in the closing days of the campaign, falsely stating that former presidential press secretary James S. Brady — a popular figure who incurred disabling injuries in the 1981 attempt to assassinate President Ronald Reagan and has since been an advocate of Democratic-led gun control efforts — had an earlier career selling machine guns.

Like Durbin, South Dakota's Johnson succeeded at portraying himself as a moderate, not the liberal his Republican opponent said he was.

The South Dakota race was acrimonious. Pressler called a TV ad in which he castigated Johnson as being too liberal for the state "the essence of my campaign." But the incumbent was hurt by revelations that campaign funds had underwritten expensive restaurant meals and travel.

The market-oriented farm law enacted this year with Pressler's support drew mixed reviews in South Dakota, where low beef prices have created anxiety about commodity price supports. Johnson was able to make the case that certain government programs, such as Medicare and education, are boons.

Other Midwestern Democrats ran even more proudly under the banner of liberalism. Incumbents Paul Wellstone of

Minnesota, Tom Harkin of Iowa and Carl Levin of Michigan, who all looked vulnerable at the beginning of the cycle, were all returned for another term.

The West

The benefits of federal programs had helped to keep some Western states in the Democratic column in the recent past. But on the scale of many westerners, the traditional appeal of highway and water projects has been outweighed by the burden of federal regulation.

So the region is now split politically, as it had been culturally for decades, between coast and interior. According to Oregon State University political scientist Bill Lunch, resentment of federal land-use policy has created a political rift between the West's rural inhabitants and those who dwell in the coastal strip from Seattle south to San Diego.

"If you think environmental protections are a good idea, that's an attractive message to voters in Portland, Seattle or San Francisco," Lunch said. "If you think it's a drag on the economy and a hindrance to personal freedom, that will sell well in Boise or Pendleton [in eastern Oregon], where Gordon Smith is from."

During an unsuccessful run against Democrat Ron Wyden in a special Senate election earlier this year, state Senate President Smith ran with the support of the socially conservative Oregon Citizens Alliance and lost. Wyden successfully pinned an extremist label on the Republican and won by a single percentage point by dominating the populous counties around Portland. In his encore bid, against Democratic high-tech entrepreneur Bruggere, Smith came down ideologically from the mountains, moderating his image to appeal to voters who reside west of the Cascade Range.

For example, he pledged to oppose a constitutional ban on abortion, despite his opposition to the procedure. Even as he made that promise, Smith, who made a fortune operating a frozen food company in eastern Oregon, spoke of how hard he had worked to make his processing plant less offensive to the environment.

In Wyoming, previously little-known Republican state Sen. Mike Enzi is going to the Senate to succeed retiring three-term GOP incumbent Alan K. Simpson. His Democratic opponent, former Secretary of State Kathy Karpan, got nowhere by trying to portray herself as a centrist on land-use policy and gun control.

Enzi, an opponent of abortion with close ties to the Christian Coalition, ridiculed Karpan as a believer in big federal bureaucracy. "Karpan ran well, but she was not able to make the inroads a Democrat needs to make to appeal to moderate Republicans and independents," commented University of Wyoming political scientist Jim King. "You have a Republican state, [it] goes Republican."

In a race with similar themes, Republicans enjoyed a similar outcome. Colorado Democrat Tom Strickland plied environmental issues and opposition to gun rights to no avail

Democrat Sen. Kerry embraces Sen. Ted Kennedy after winning re-election over Gov. William F. Weld.

Senate Membership — 105th Congress

Republicans	55
Democrats	45
Freshmen	15

This Senate roster for the 105th Congress is pending confirmation of an apparent narrow win by Democrat Mary Landrieu of Louisiana.

The Republican total of 55 seats is the GOP's highest number following an election since 1928.

Freshmen are designated with a #, seats that switched parties with a †, and 1996 winners are in *italic*.

Alabama
Richard C. Shelby (R)
Jeff Sessions (R)# †

Alaska
Ted Stevens (R)
Frank H. Murkowski (R)

Arizona
John McCain (R)
Jon Kyl (R)

Arkansas
Dale Bumpers (D)
Tim Hutchinson (R)# †

California
Dianne Feinstein (D)
Barbara Boxer (D)

Colorado
Ben Nighthorse Campbell (R)
Wayne Allard (R)#

Connecticut
Christopher J. Dodd (D)
Joseph I. Lieberman (D)

Delaware
William V. Roth Jr. (R)
Joseph R. Biden Jr. (D)

Florida
Bob Graham (D)
Connie Mack (R)

Georgia
Paul Coverdell (R)
Max Cleland (D)#

Hawaii
Daniel K. Inouye (D)
Daniel K. Akaka (D)

Idaho
Larry E. Craig (R)
Dirk Kempthorne (R)

Illinois
Carol Moseley-Braun (D)
Richard J. Durbin (D)#

Indiana
Richard G. Lugar (R)
Daniel R. Coats (R)

Iowa
Charles E. Grassley (R)
Tom Harkin (D)

Kansas
Sam Brownback (R)#
Pat Roberts (R)#

Kentucky
Wendell H. Ford (D)
Mitch McConnell (R)

Louisiana
John B. Breaux (D)
Mary Landrieu (D)#

Maine
Olympia J. Snowe (R)
Susan Collins (R)#

Maryland
Paul S. Sarbanes (D)
Barbara A. Mikulski (D)

Massachusetts
Edward M. Kennedy (D)
John Kerry (D)

Michigan
Carl Levin (D)
Spencer Abraham (R)

Minnesota
Paul Wellstone (D)
Rod Grams (R)

Mississippi
Thad Cochran (R)
Trent Lott (R)

Missouri
Christopher S. Bond (R)
John Ashcroft (R)

Montana
Max Baucus (D)
Conrad Burns (R)

Nebraska
Bob Kerrey (D)
Chuck Hagel (R)# †

Nevada
Harry Reid (D)
Richard H. Bryan (D)

New Hampshire
Robert C. Smith (R)
Judd Gregg (R)

New Jersey
Frank R. Lautenberg (D)
Robert G. Torricelli (D)#

New Mexico
Pete V. Domenici (R)
Jeff Bingaman (D)

New York
Daniel Patrick Moynihan (D)
Alfonse M. D'Amato (R)

North Carolina
Jesse Helms (R)
Lauch Faircloth (R)

North Dakota
Kent Conrad (D)
Byron L. Dorgan (D)

Ohio
John Glenn (D)
Mike DeWine (R)

Oklahoma
Don Nickles (R)
James M. Inhofe (R)

Oregon
Ron Wyden (D)
Gordon Smith (R)#

Pennsylvania
Arlen Specter (R)
Rick Santorum (R)

Rhode Island
John H. Chafee (R)
Jack Reed (D)#

South Carolina
Strom Thurmond (R)
Ernest F. Hollings (D)

South Dakota
Tom Daschle (D)
Tim Johnson (D)# †

Tennessee
Fred Thompson (R)
Bill Frist (R)

Texas
Phil Gramm (R)
Kay Bailey Hutchison (R)

Utah
Orrin G. Hatch (R)
Robert F. Bennett (R)

Vermont
Patrick J. Leahy (D)
James M. Jeffords (R)

Virginia
John W. Warner (R)
Charles S. Robb (D)

Washington
Slade Gorton (R)
Patty Murray (D)

West Virginia
Robert C. Byrd (D)
John D. Rockefeller IV (D)

Wisconsin
Herb Kohl (D)
Russell D. Feingold (D)

Wyoming
Craig Thomas (R)
Mike Enzi (R)#

against Republican Rep. Allard.

Not even a potentially damaging single issue could stall Republican Larry E. Craig's easy ride to a second Senate term in conservative Idaho. Democratic challenger Walt Minnick, a wood products millionaire, reportedly invested as much as $1 million of his own money in the race, most of which paid for television ads that accused Craig of being out of touch with residents concerned about the state's environment.

Minnick centered his efforts on opposition to a deal, sup-

REUTERS

Democrat Cleland survived an unexpectedly close race to succeed Sen. Sam Nunn in Georgia.

ported by Craig, to temporarily store nuclear waste in the state. Although voters overwhelmingly supported a ballot initiative expressing opposition to the storage, they handily re-elected Craig.

The one exception to the Republican sweep of the interior was the re-election of three-term Democrat Max Baucus in Montana. But Montana is an exceptional state, divided between a mountainous, Democratic-leaning western half with an organized labor constituency, and a rural, Republican-oriented Plains area in the east.

Though he won, Baucus had to defend himself to moderate and conservative voters angered by his support for Clinton's 1993 budget package that increased taxes and his mixed record as an environmentalist. He squeaked past Republican Lt. Gov. Dennis Rehberg with just under 50 percent of the vote.

The region's other two incumbents, Republicans Ted Stevens of Alaska and Pete V. Domenici of New Mexico, are powerful figures who sailed to easy wins. Stevens is in line to chair the Appropriations Committee in the 105th Congress; Domenici, also an Appropriations member, is the chairman of the Budget Committee.

The East

Democrats, constructing a new base along the nation's eastern corridor, won five of the region's seven Senate seats that were in play this year.

Democratic incumbents in Delaware (Joseph R. Biden Jr.) and West Virginia (John D. Rockefeller IV) walked to easy victories, as did Rep. Jack Reed, who succeeds retiring six-term Democrat Claiborne Pell in the Democratic stronghold of Rhode Island.

Massachusetts Democrat John Kerry held off a strong challenge by Republican Gov. William F. Weld, in part with help from strong Democratic candidates up and down the ballot.

In the contest between two popular officeholders, there was a good deal of voter sentiment that it would be best to keep Kerry in Washington and Weld in Boston.

Some voters also were concerned that by electing Weld they would be turning over the state to a Republican lieutenant governor with serious personal debt problems.

A strong overall Democratic voting pattern in New Jersey also propelled Rep. Robert G. Torricelli past GOP Rep. Dick Zimmer. In an expensive campaign generally considered the nation's dirtiest, both candidates tarred each other as extremists, even though both have relatively moderate voting records.

The Democrats' two losses in the East are exceptions that help prove the rule.

Republicans held the seat in Maine, with Collins, a former Senate aide, defeating Democratic former Gov. Joseph E. Brennan.

In her winning bid to succeed retiring three-term Republican moderate William S. Cohen, her former boss, Collins cast herself as the sort of independent politician Maine favors, emphasizing small-business concerns while holding liberal positions on issues such as abortion and gay rights.

But the result represented not so much her victory as Brennan's loss, as even many Democrats abandoned the veteran politician. The state party openly begged Brennan not to make the race, his 14th in 32 years. In the end, Collins narrowly edged Brennan but ran 18 points ahead of presidential nominee Dole in the state.

Republican Sen. Robert C. Smith's political near-death experience was the result of his association with social issues, particularly his graphic advocacy of a ban on so-called partial-birth abortions.

Early on election night, the major TV networks misread exit polls and declared victory for his opponent, Democratic former Rep. Dick Swett. But Smith had the last laugh by pulling out a win, although with less than 50 percent of the vote.

"New Hampshire is the quintessential state where the fiscal and social conservatives go toe-to-toe over control of the Republican Party," said Garrison Nelson, a University of Vermont political scientist.

The GOP's unsuccessful gubernatorial candidate, Ovide Lamontagne, brought social issues to the fore in New Hampshire, according to Nelson, and "that was Swett's long suit."

Although Smith had been declared the loser, he stated in his late-night victory speech that certain signs had buoyed his spirits, including a rainbow that he saw and a card given to him by a nun on which she had written, "Sen. Smith, you are the winner, praise God."

"I'm gonna put in a bill just as soon as I get back down to Washington to end exit polling," declared Smith. ∎

THE SENATE

Lott's Challenge: Finding Balance Of Challenge and Compromise

Majority leader was a big winner, but new Senate's ideological spread will test his pragmatism

SCOTT J. FERRELL

Senate Majority Leader Lott at Nov. 6 news conference on the election.

Far more conservative in membership, increasingly homogeneous in ideology and younger in demographic makeup is Trent Lott's new Senate.

Two years after hard-charging Republicans wrested control of the chamber from the Democrats, the GOP bucked the presidential tide in the Nov. 5 election, padding its lead by two Senate seats. Unofficial results give it a 55–45 edge, up from 53–47. *(Story, p. 20)*

In more ways than one, the election strengthens the hand of the Senate majority leader, a right-of-center Mississippi Republican who displayed a pragmatic streak in compromising with Democrats in the last four months of the 104th Congress.

"He is as big a winner as Clinton," Sen. Robert F. Bennett, R-Utah., said of Lott. "He was rewarded with a bigger victory than he had before."

Nearly every retiring or defeated senator has been replaced by a more conservative one, giving Lott and the Senate an ideological advantage not seen since the overwhelming Democratic membership Mike Mansfield ruled over in 1964.

For Lott, the victory of like-minded lawmakers comes at a pivotal moment as he prepares to assert his full control over the Senate for the first time since succeeding former Majority Leader Bob Dole, who resigned to focus on his presidential bid. Lott no longer presides over a Senate agenda set by Dole; the political necessities of a presidential election are past.

This gives Lott an opportunity to fill a vacuum at the top of the national Republican Party, to become the party's standard-bearer and foil to President Clinton in Congress. The defeat of Dole, the ethical woes of House Speaker Newt Gingrich, R-Ga., and the absence of a clear-cut front runner for the Republican presidential nomination in 2000 create this opportunity.

"Lott is the ideal spokesman for the party," said Steven S. Smith, a University of Minnesota political science professor who described the Republican as capable of enunciating conservative views without alienating moderate voters.

CQ Weekly Report November 9, 1996

Still, the majority leader will have to walk a fine line as he tries to keep the peace between the formidable group of GOP conservatives, who will aggressively challenge Democrats and the White House, and the diminishing group of GOP moderates straining for consensus.

On one of the first issues likely to arise in the 105th Congress, for example, a constitutional amendment requiring a balanced budget, Lott welcomes the new members who have signaled their support. In the last Congress, the balanced budget measure failed in the Senate by one vote.

But Lott will be tested as he seeks to balance the push by some conservatives for investigations of alleged Clinton administration wrongdoing and suspected fundraising irregularities by the Democratic Party against the desire by some moderate Republicans to put the probes aside to pursue bipartisan legislation.

And then there are the Democrats, a minority composed of liberal stalwarts, old and new. Lacking a 60-vote, filibuster-breaking majority, Republicans will need Democratic support to enact legislation.

After eight years in the Senate, Lott knows all too well the venerable idiosyncrasies of the chamber. "This is still the Senate, and it doesn't take a party to tie this place up, it takes a senator — one," said Lott the day after the election. "You have to find consensus and you have to be prepared to work with senators of all regions, all philosophies in both parties."

'Wait and See' Agenda

The first task for the new Senate likely will be confirmation hearings for what is shaping up as a brand new Cabinet for the Clinton administration.

Within hours of the president's re-election, the secretaries of State, Defense, Energy and Commerce as well as other top administration officials signaled their desire to leave the executive branch before Clinton's second term moves into high gear. *(Story, p. 64)*

The president also will be called upon to nominate mem-

For Gore, a 'Separation' Process

Vice President Al Gore is already a president — of the Senate. It is a part-time responsibility that entitles him to a plush office in the Capitol and gives him the singular power to break a tie vote there — a power he has used three times. Four years from now, he hopes to preside over much more than the Senate; he hopes to sport a veto pen in his pocket and move into a larger, oval-shaped office on the other end of Pennsylvania Avenue.

Gore has not declared his candidacy for president, but his moves are barely disguised. The week before Election Day, he visited New Hampshire and Iowa, each the site of a close Senate race — and each a critical, early primary season state. More importantly, he has toiled to elevate the sleepy office of vice president to a position of influence, a place from which he can boldly enter the race for president in 2000.

Gore's Role

Washington typically pokes fun at vice presidents by saying their only function is to attend the funerals of foreign dignitaries. Gore has done more than that. He has been a trusted, close and regular policy adviser to President Clinton.

In his role as Senate president, he broke tie votes three times to help push through the administration's budget and environmental agendas — all while Democrats still controlled Congress. He now faces an even more conservative Senate than the GOP-controlled 104th, and it is unclear whether any dramatic tie-breaking votes are in the offing. Regardless, it is more in his executive branch role that Gore seeks to distinguish himself.

Shortly after the January 1993 inauguration, Clinton told Gore to lead a multiagency team to "reinvent government." Six months later, Gore presented a sweeping proposal aimed at making the federal government work better and cost less. *(1993 Almanac, p. 191)*

"He is viewed as a substantial player in his own right," says Gore's former chief of staff, Roy Neel.

On a national campaign to build support for the plan, Gore also began to reinvent his public persona, which had been described as wooden. With self-deprecating humor and other devices, such as an appearance on David Letterman's "Late Show," — where he donned safety goggles and smashed a government issue ashtray, — Gore became a darling of talk show hosts.

He has been more than cute, though. Gore helped the Clinton administration — and congressional Democrats — attack the GOP-controlled Congress for its aggressive ef-

forts to scale back environmental regulations. Gore is a serious student of the environment, author of *Earth in the Balance*, and a former senator with an established record in favor of environmental protection. He was an asset when the issue became a potent weapon for Democrats. Many of Clinton's top environmental policy posts are filled by Gore associates such as Environmental Protection Agency head Carol M. Browner, a former top Senate aide.

So far, the Clinton and Gore partnership has seemed effortless. Both are moderate Southern Democrats with compatible ideologies. "It has not been difficult for him to go down the road with Bill Clinton," says Neel.

It should stay that way, at least for another two years. Gore can continue to use the office of vice president to gain attention and, he hopes, become increasingly popular. "My guess is the president will give him lots of high-profile opportunities," says Neel.

But as the second term nears the midway point, the transition from vice president to presidential candidate must begin. Gore will have to set up a national campaign operation outside the White House and make his candidacy, not the vice presidency, his top priority.

Trouble Ahead?

For his hard work as vice president, Gore rightly shares credit for some of the Clinton administration's accomplishments — particularly for being on the first Democratic ticket in 60 years to be re-elected.

But such close association with Clinton comes with perils. The GOP-controlled Congress is eager to continue probes and begin new ones into the administration. If those inquiries debilitate Clinton, Gore will be squeezed. He will have to appear loyal, but establish his independence at the same time.

"How does Gore avoid double-crossing a president . . . without fatally compromising himself?" asks Samuel T. McSeveny, professor of history at Vanderbilt University in Tennessee. "If the administration hits bad times, there's no way he can distance himself."

Policy could cause tension, too. What is good for Clinton and his legacy — such as making needed but unpopular changes in Medicare — will not necessarily be good for Gore's campaign.

"It won't be like [Vice President Hubert H.] Humphrey distancing himself from [President Lyndon B.] Johnson on his Vietnam policy," says Neel. But Gore will have to more assertively establish his own identity.

REUTERS

Gore talks to delegates Aug. 28 at the Democratic National Convention in Chicago.

bers to the Supreme Court as several of the older justices decide to retire. Even before it casts its first vote, the more conservative Senate will influence the type of nominees Clinton chooses, all but forcing the president to abandon any notion of selecting liberals or candidates lacking ties to Congress. Prominent among the names already mentioned for possible Cabinet replacements are former senators and Republicans.

On the legislative front, Senate Republicans are looking to the Democratic administration to show its hand first in solving one of the nation's more pressing problems, the near-term insolvency of the trust fund for Medicare, the nation's health insurance entitlement for the elderly. It is headed for insolvency by 2001.

Republicans paid a political price in this election as Democrats accused them of trying to solve the Medicare problem by seeking deep reductions in the program to finance a tax cut for the wealthy. Hard feelings among Republicans still linger.

The wait-and-see approach will apply to several other defining issues, including cuts in spending to achieve a balanced budget in the next century.

The scandal involving Democratic Party fundraising has provided momentum to the drive to overhaul the current system of financing political campaigns, and the chief sponsors of a bipartisan Senate bill — Republican John McCain of Arizona and Democrat Russell D. Feingold of Wisconsin — plan to introduce their legislation on the first day of the new session. *(Story, p. 66)*

But the bill still faces strong opposition — Lott has expressed his reservations — and members of the Senate may try to limit the effort to investigations of possible criminal activity by Democratic Party officials or piecemeal reform of current laws.

Several Senate Republicans believe their House counterparts did a far better job in investigating the administration during the 104th Congress and hope to match or exceed that performance. Investigations are expected on political fundraising, the White House's collection of FBI files on past Republican administration officials and the firing of employees in the White House travel office.

But the chairman of the Senate Banking Committee, Republican Alfonse M. D'Amato of New York, said he would not restart an investigation on whether the president and first lady Hillary Rodham Clinton broke any laws with their various Whitewater dealings.

D'Amato had chaired a special Senate committee that investigated the issue, but the senator, who is up for re-election in 1998, saw his ratings in New York plummet following his tenacious Whitewater inquiry. "Our job is to work in common toward the goals that the president has articulated during the campaign, many of which are goals that Republicans have been fighting for," D'Amato said Nov. 6.

A Republican agenda solely dedicated to investigating the administration could cost the GOP politically, a fact the leadership keenly recognizes.

The message of the split-decision election that sent a Democrat back to the White House and solidified the Republican hold on Congress is an endorsement of cooperation and bipartisanship.

"There really is a season for partisan politics, and it just ended today," Feingold said on Nov. 5.

Republicans will not abrogate their responsibility to investigate, according to Lott, but they will not make it their primary focus. The political season is over and the new Senate must tackle the nation's legislative problems. "We ignore them to our own peril and to the people's dissatisfaction," Lott said.

Face of the New Senate

Aside from the Senate war horses who won re-election — 93-year-old Strom Thurmond, R-S.C., and 75-year-old Jesse Helms, R-N.C. — and West Virginia's current senator, 78-year-old Democrat Robert C. Byrd, the face of the Senate is younger, less legislatively experienced and trained in the confrontational, partisan ways of the House.

Forty-nine members of the Senate have previous House experience, and 27 have served in the Senate for less than three years, which could contribute to a more polarized legislative body.

Among the newly elected senators, most of the Republicans oppose abortion rights, support overturning gun control laws, favor deep tax cuts and prefer a smaller role for the federal government — positions that put them at well-defined odds with many of their Democratic colleagues.

"My impression is more conservatives, ultraconservatives in the Republican caucus," said Sen. Joseph I. Lieberman, D-Conn.

The task for Lott, who is expected to win re-election as Majority Leader during Senate meetings Dec. 3–4, and other members of the GOP leadership will be making the new senators understand how the chamber operates.

"They will try to indoctrinate, orient freshmen to the existing culture," Bennett said. But it will be a balancing act for the leader, who worked with Democrats and the White House in ensuring the passage of welfare, immigration, clean water, minimum wage and health care legislation in the 104th Congress.

The majority leader will have the advantage of dealing with a president looking to make his historical mark in a second term and trying to draw attention toward legislative achievements and away from ethical lapses.

Lott and the Democratic leader, Tom Daschle of South Dakota, proved in the last Congress that they can work together, and expectations remain that the two will continue their cooperative relationship.

Lott will rely on a leadership team that is expected to undergo only minor changes — Don Nickles of Oklahoma as majority whip, Larry E. Craig of Idaho as chairman of the Republican Policy Committee and Connie Mack of Florida, who is expected to replace Thad Cochran of Mississippi as chairman of the Republican Conference.

Unclear is whether some of the new members will work with long-standing Republican moderates such as John H. Chafee of Rhode Island and James M. Jeffords of Vermont on bipartisan efforts.

"A lot depends on new members and their inclination to join some of the others," said Sen. Byron L. Dorgan, D-N.D.

Lott showed that he still holds to some Senate tradition when he indicated that McCain would likely assume the chairmanship of the Commerce, Science and Transportation Committee based on his seniority. The lone incumbent defeated Nov. 5 was Sen. Larry Pressler, R-S.D., who served as chairman of the panel.

Following is a wrap-up of the major changes to Senate committees:

Agriculture, Nutrition and Forestry

Changes in the top positions on this committee are unlikely, with Richard G. Lugar, R-Ind., remaining as chairman, and Patrick J. Leahy of Vermont continuing as the ranking Democrat. The two lawmakers have long had a close working relationship on this generally bipartisan panel, and that is expected to continue.

There may be other movement, however. Republicans will probably try to find a spot for Kansas freshman Pat Roberts, who chaired the House Agriculture Committee in the 104th Congress. Democrats need to replace retiring Sens. Howell Heflin of Alabama and David Pryor of Arkansas — both steadfast supporters of Southern crops such as peanuts and cotton.

Lugar

The committee's agenda is expected to be light in the next two years, since the 104th cleared two major agriculture bills: an omnibus farm bill (PL 104-127) known as "Freedom to Farm," and a rewrite of pesticides law (PL 104-170). With Congress remaining under GOP control, the Republican-crafted farm law will probably remain unchanged.

Lugar, who says he wants to reduce the nation's dependence on foreign oil, may use the scheduled reauthorization of research programs to funnel more money into the development of home-grown "biofuels." These fuels, such as corn-derived ethanol, are produced from plant and animal byproducts.

Appropriations

Ted Stevens, R-Alaska, is set to take over the chairmanship from the departing Mark O. Hatfield, R-Ore., a change that will probably be more evident in style than substance. Where Hatfield was soft-spoken and gracious, Stevens has a fiery temper, an intimidating manner and a combative way of getting what he wants.

At the same time, the longtime appropriator is viewed as solidly in the mainstream of the traditionally bipartisan committee, which has clashed with its House counterpart the past two years over efforts to raise domestic spending levels that many Republican senators thought were too low.

Though Stevens has been chairman of the Defense subcommittee and can be expected to guard the Pentagon's share of the appropriations pie, he is widely viewed as a protector of domestic programs as well, many of which have found their way to Alaska over the years. Stevens also gets along well with ranking Democrat Robert C. Byrd of West Virginia, which is essential to keep the committee running smoothly.

There are two vacancies on the panel — Hatfield's and the seat being vacated by the retiring J. Bennett Johnston, D-La. This is still viewed as a premium committee, but diminishing budget resources and the shift of political emphasis to tax policy has already caused one defection to the Finance Committee, Phil Gramm, R-Texas. Insiders wonder if there will be more.

The panel's chief worry next year will be figuring out a way to avoid the bruising fights of the past two years, when what even some Republicans considered an unrealistically low appropriations cap sparked lengthy battles between House and Senate appropriators and between appropriators and President Clinton, who managed to force the number up in both years. The fiscal 1998 discretionary spending cap set by the fiscal 1997 budget resolution (H Con Res 178) adopted in June — about $494 billion — is lower than the fiscal 1997 discretionary appropriations agreed to by negotiators in September: $503 billion.

Armed Services

No challenge is anticipated to the chairmanship of Strom Thurmond of South Carolina, who was re-elected for a seventh full term at age 93. When Thurmond took over Armed Services in 1995, some Republicans groused that he would not be up to the job. Indeed, during his first year as chairman, the annual defense authorization bill nearly fell apart.

But in 1996, the committee worked relatively well, and the Republican staff ran far more smoothly with a new director, Romie L. "Les" Brownlee, a retired Army officer who had worked since 1983 as an aide to John W. Warner of Virginia, the committee's second-ranking Republican.

Of the three Republicans with considerable experience who ranked immediately behind Thurmond in seniority in the 104th, Warner remains, but centrist William S. Cohen of Maine is retiring, and John McCain of Arizona will not be able to devote as much time to defense matters. McCain will succeed the defeated Larry Pressler of South Dakota as chairman of the Commerce Committee.

Potentially the most dramatic change in the committee's lineup is at the top of the Democratic ranks, where liberal Carl Levin of Michigan succeeds retiring conservative Sam Nunn of Georgia. Both have reputations as highly effective inquisitors who master the substance of any issue they take up. But Nunn was one of the many centrist Democrats who backed GOP-sponsored additions to Clinton's defense budgets, while Levin opposed them.

On the other hand, Levin is a proven legislative operator who for years effectively led a major Armed Services subcommittee on which he was the only liberal.

To head the Democratic staff, Levin has hired David S. Lyles, a veteran of more than a decade's service on the committee staff. Lyles also was staff director of the 1995 base-closing commission.

Banking, Housing and Urban Affairs

The lineup of the Banking Committee remains almost unchanged, but its agenda for the 105th Congress is likely to look much different than that of the past two years.

Chairman Alfonse M. D'Amato, R-N.Y., is up for re-election in 1998, and he is expected to spend less time on Whitewater and more time on legislation.

D'Amato's lengthy and partisan hearings into the Whitewater controversy did not help his political standing in New York. But he has earned favorable press for an investigation into assets that were taken from Jewish Holocaust victims and placed in Swiss bank accounts, and he may seek to move a bill to help the victims. D'Amato also may resurrect a pro-consumer plan to ban certain automated teller machine surcharges.

Over the past two years, D'Amato did not seek to advance legislation to overhaul banking law, but lobbyists following the issue believe that he will wade in during the 105th Congress. He also has said a priority will be to create a common charter for banks and thrifts to build on this year's successful effort to shore up the Savings Association Insurance Fund.

The current ranking Democrat is Paul S. Sarbanes of Maryland, but he may opt to succeed Claiborne Pell of Rhode Island as the top Democrat on Foreign Relations if Joseph R. Biden Jr. of Delaware does not do so. If Sarbanes moves, Christopher

J. Dodd of Connecticut would assume the top Democratic spot. Dodd and D'Amato, despite their reputations as political partisans, have a good relationship on legislative issues.

Budget

Pete V. Domenici of New Mexico will continue as chairman of this committee, but New Jersey's Frank R. Lautenberg is expected to become ranking Democrat. The left-of-center Lautenberg, a harsh critic of GOP budget proposals, would succeed the more moderate Jim Exon of Nebraska, who is retiring.

Democratic retirements leave three panel vacancies, the seats of Exon, J. Bennett Johnston of Louisiana, and Paul Simon of Illinois. Republicans have just one empty seat, that of

Domenici   **Lautenberg**

Hank Brown of Colorado, who also is retiring. There have been calls to shrink the size of the committee, but that is not deemed likely.

While Domenici and Lautenberg will almost surely be at odds over most key budget issues, both are appropriators, and

both may want to increase the amount of money set to go to appropriations this year — a figure set by the annual budget resolution.

Pressure from President Clinton and unhappiness among Senate Republicans (and some in the House) have forced the GOP Congress to exceed its initial appropriations limits in each of the past two years. The fiscal 1997 budget resolution (H Con Res 178) set what some GOP appropriators privately say is an unrealistically low limit for fiscal 1998.

The committee's top priority will be to craft a plan to balance the budget by 2002. Although steadily shrinking deficit projections will make it easier to balance the budget, any faint hope of quick bipartisan agreement seems to have been destroyed by campaign rancor: Republicans are furious at what they contend was Democratic demagoguery on Medicare and have already rejected feelers from the White House about working on a common budget.

Commerce, Science and Transportation

The defeat of Larry Pressler, R-S.D., the only Senate incumbent to lose this year, will likely mean big changes for the Commerce Committee. His successor as chairman will be John McCain, R-Ariz., one of the most staunchly pro-deregulation senators.

McCain was one of just five members who voted against this year's telecommunications bill (PL 104-104), and the only one to do so because he felt it did not go far enough in reducing regulations.

McCain may get a chance to put his stamp on telecommunications issues in the 105th. A federal appeals court judge in St. Louis has halted a Federal Communications Commission rule enforcing the bill's requirements on local Bell companies.

These requirements and other FCC rules stemming from the law could be re-examined in new legislation next year.

SCOTT J. FERRELL

McCain, shown at an Indian Affairs Committee meeting in August 1995, will chair the Commerce Committee.

The committee may have considerable leverage over the administration on telecommunications issues; President Clinton will be seeking to fill as many as four vacancies on the five-member commission during the 105th Congress.

Other than at the top, the committee's makeup will not change much. In addition to Pressler, only retiring Sen. Jim Exon, D-Neb., will not be back. The two seats may not be filled. Ernest F. Hollings of South Carolina will remain the ranking Democrat.

Energy and Natural Resources

For the past two years, Frank H. Murkowski has chaired the committee with an eye on natural resource issues but far less concern for the energy questions under his jurisdiction. That should change in the 105th Congress, as pressure mounts from House members and lobbyists to deregulate the nation's last major monopoly: the $208 billion electric power industry.

The Alaska Republican, skeptical that the federal government should step into a complex issue now being handled by the states, has counseled a go-slow approach. But he is likely to face pressure to move ahead from the panel's new ranking Democrat, Dale Bumpers of Arkansas, as well as from the House and the Clinton administration.

Bumpers, an outspoken liberal, succeeds retiring Sen. J. Bennett Johnston of Louisiana as top Democrat. Johnston is a consummate deal-maker, who often sided with the GOP on energy issues.

Also retiring are Republican Mark O. Hatfield of Oregon and Bill Bradley of New Jersey. Bradley was the Democrat most likely to stand in the way of efforts to loosen federal controls over natural resources.

Murkowski also probably will move quickly to revive a nuclear waste bill (S 1936) that died in House in the 104th Congress. Election year politics helped defeat the measure, which would have mandated the construction of a temporary nuclear waste storage site in Nevada.

Environment and Public Works

Most members are expected to return to this committee, where Chairman John H. Chafee, R-R.I., is the moderating force on a panel dominated by conservative Republicans. No major shuffles are expected on the subcommittees.

The two or three major environmental issues expected to dominate — endangered species protection, the superfund hazardous waste program, and possibly the clean water act — will pose big challenges.

Republican Dirk Kempthorne of Idaho is expected to take the lead on revamping endangered species; he and Chafee face a difficult task in bridging differences between Western conservatives, who contend that the law imposes excessive restrictions on property owners, and liberals from the Northeast.

Other priorities will include revamping the superfund hazardous waste law and reauthorizing omnibus highway legislation known as the Intermodal Surface Transportation Efficiency Act. The law determines the amount of highway and public transit funds that is allotted to the states.

Finance

GOP leaders are likely to continue to exert considerable influence over this committee, whose chairman, William V. Roth Jr. of Delaware, is well-liked but widely viewed as a weak leader. In the 104th Congress, the committee's GOP majority did little to drive policy, and individual senators easily pushed special-interest measures into legislation.

That led to a swirl of rumors that other senators — most notably Orrin G. Hatch of Utah — were angling for Roth's job.

In response, Roth recently released a letter from Hatch pledging that he would not challenge Roth.

The atmosphere of shifting alliances and power plays is likely to continue in the 105th Congress, and party-line votes will be the norm. Leading the conservatives is the increasingly visible Don Nickles of Oklahoma, who is also majority whip.

The committee is expected to revisit budget-related issues such as spending reductions in Medicare and Medicaid and cuts in taxes.

There could be more action than last year on trade issues, where Roth has maintained the committee's tradition of bipartisanship. The other chance for bipartisan cooperation is through the close friendship and political partnership of John H. Chafee, R-R.I., and John B. Breaux, D-La., who together drafted balanced-budget and welfare proposals in the 104th Congress and a health care overhaul plan in the 103rd.

Democrats will continue to be led by Daniel Patrick Moynihan, D-N.Y., who cares deeply about welfare policy and is expected to work to moderate some of the policies in the overhaul bill (PL 104-193) that became law last summer.

Republicans and Democrats each will have two vacancies to fill.

Foreign Relations

Jesse Helms, who survived another tough challenge to win a fifth term, is likely to keep his chairmanship.

Helms will try to revive his prized foreign policy reorganization plan, which failed in the face of concerted opposition from Democrats and the Clinton administration.

Staff Director James W. "Bud" Nance, Helms' boyhood friend, indicated that the chairman wants to work with the White House to reach agreement on a modified version of the reorganization plan, which originally would have required the consolidation of three independent foreign policy agencies — the Agency for International Development, United States Information Agency and Arms Control and Disarmament Agency — with the State Department.

The panel's first task will probably be to confirm a successor to Secretary of State Warren Christopher, who announced Nov. 7 that he is resigning.

Aside from Helms, the committee will have a different look next year. Ranking Democrat Claiborne Pell of Rhode Island is retiring, and Joseph R. Biden Jr. of Delaware is in line to replace him. But Biden, who is ranking Democrat on the Judiciary Committee, may opt to stay in that post.

Paul S. Sarbanes of Maryland is next in line, but he is ranking Democrat on the Banking Committee. If Biden and Sarbanes decline to take the ranking Democrat slot on Foreign Relations, it would fall to Christopher J. Dodd of Connecticut.

There will be changes ahead on the Republican side as well. Republican Nancy Landon Kassebaum of Kansas, the chairman of the African Affairs Subcommittee and a moderate voice on the committee, is retiring. So is Colorado Republican Hank Brown, who has chaired the subcommittee on Near Eastern and South Asian Affairs.

Governmental Affairs

Just three years into his first term, Fred Thompson of Tennessee is likely to take over as chairman, filling the vacancy left by Alaskan Ted Stevens, who appears headed for the Appropriations Committee. Thompson has wholeheartedly embraced GOP efforts to move power from Washington to the states and loosen federal regulations. He also supported congressional term limits and proposals to overhaul campaign finance rules. He backed legislation during the 104th Congress that would have required agencies to perform a detailed cost-benefit analysis before enacting new regulations.

A Thompson-led panel is almost certain to revisit legislation from the 104th Congress dubbed the "10th Amendment Enforcement Act." The measure, a favorite among GOP governors, seeks to protect state powers by requiring all branches of the federal government to take steps to ensure they do not enact laws or promulgate rules that interfere with powers intended for the states.

John Glenn of Ohio will likely remain the panel's ranking Democrat.

Indian Affairs

Arizona Republican John McCain plans to chair both the Indian Affairs Committee and the Commerce, Science and Transportation Committee. GOP Conference rules prohibit a member from serving as chairman of more than one standing committee, but Indian Affairs is among five panels not considered to be such a committee, according to party rules changes scheduled to take effect in January. A standing committee is defined by Republicans as a permanently authorized committee with broad legislative mandates; Indian Affairs has a narrow focus.

As chairman, McCain is likely to proceed with plans to expand federal regulation of the booming Indian gaming industry, to overhaul the troubled Bureau of Indian Affairs, and to revive a bill to expedite the legal process for adopting American Indian children. He also may tackle the difficult issue of settling claims of Indian tribes that contend their trust accounts have not been properly handled by the federal government.

McCain is expected to continue to work closely with Daniel K. Inouye of Hawaii, an active defender of Indian rights, who is likely to be the panel's ranking Democrat.

Judiciary

Orrin G. Hatch of Utah will continue as chairman of the Judiciary Committee, which is likely to keep up a focus on anti-crime and anti-drug legislation. With Republicans retaining the majority, another proposal to amend the Constitution to require a balanced budget is in the offing, as are more hearings on the White House's handling of FBI files. And a second stab at restrictions on legal immigration is fairly likely, depending on who chairs the immigration subcommittee after Alan K. Simpson of Wyoming retires.

Kyl

The most likely replacement is Jon Kyl, R-Ariz. If he declines, the post will go to one of two senators with a much more pro-immigration posture than either Simpson or Kyl — Mike DeWine of Ohio or Spencer Abraham of Michigan.

Supreme Court Justices William H. Rehnquist and John Paul Stevens are reportedly considering retirement, leaving the possibility that Hatch will chair his first confirmation hearings on a nominee to the high court.

Four of the committee's 18 members — Simpson, Hank Brown, R-Colo., Paul Simon, D-Ill., and Howell Heflin, D-Ala. — are stepping down. All were conciliators who did not hesitate to work with members of the opposite party. It is not clear who will succeed them.

Ranking Democrat Joseph R. Biden Jr. of Delaware has considered moving to the top Democratic spot on the Foreign Relations Committee if it became less contentious than it has been under Chairman Jesse Helms, R-N.C. But with Helms showing no inclination to shift to the Agriculture chairmanship, Biden will probably keep the top slot at Judiciary.

Labor and Human Resources

A few key retirements are remaking the Labor and Human Resources Committee into a peculiarly polarized body. Some of the most liberal senators will clash with some of the most conservative, and presiding over it all will be the most moderate of Republicans.

The retirement of Chairwoman Nancy Landon Kassebaum of Kansas has cleared the way for GOP maverick James M. Jeffords of Vermont to take the gavel. He will have to control an unruly bunch. The retirements of conciliatory Democrats Claiborne Pell of Rhode Island and Paul Simon of Illinois leave behind the nexus of Democratic liberalism in the Senate: Edward M. Kennedy of Massachusetts, Christopher J. Dodd of Connecticut, Tom Harkin of Iowa, Barbara A. Mikulski of Maryland and Paul Wellstone of Minnesota.

They will inevitably clash with conservative Republicans such as Lauch Faircloth of North Carolina, Mike DeWine of Ohio and John Ashcroft of Missouri, all of whom are anxious to enact legislation to free up businesses from what they see

as onerous restrictions imposed by federal labor law and the Food and Drug Administration (FDA).

Jeffords will likely move quickly on a bill to allow employers to offer their workers compensatory time off in lieu of overtime pay and another to clarify that employers can set up workplace employee-management teams. But he is likely to avoid some of the hot-button issues, such as legislation to allow employers to permanently replace striking workers, that enraged the unions in the 104th Congress.

Legislation that created the federal higher-education student loan program will be up for reauthorization, and members will tackle a bill to revise federal support for the education of children with disabilities. The panel may continue working on incremental health care legislation; Kennedy wants to expand coverage to children and the unemployed.

Rules and Administration

This panel is usually out of the spotlight because it generally handles low-profile issues and rarely produces legislation. Overseeing Senate administration, the *Congressional Record* and the Botanical Garden does not make headlines. But another issue under the panel's jurisdiction — campaign finance — was a major story during the past election cycle, and both parties vow to make it a priority in the 105th Congress.

Virginia's John W. Warner will likely return as chairman, and Wendell H. Ford of Kentucky will remain the ranking Democrat. Retirements are opening up two slots that are now held by Mark O. Hatfield, R-Ore., and Claiborne Pell, D-R.I.

Warner

Panel member Mitch McConnell, R-Ky., has been an effective opponent of many initiatives to overhaul campaign finance laws, contending that limiting contributions to political candidates would infringe on constitutional freedom of speech. He may also stay on as chairman of the Senate Ethics committee and become chairman of the GOP Senate campaign committee, positions that would make him a player in the debate.

Ethics

In the year following an election, the Select Committee on Ethics typically deals with complaints filed by political opponents, and 1997 should be no exception.

At least one allegation has been leveled by the North Carolina Democratic Party, which has filed an ethics complaint against Republican Jesse Helms for failing to file reports on rental properties he owns with his wife.

Helms edged Democrat Harvey B. Gantt to win a fifth term.

Mitch McConnell of Kentucky is expected to remain as chairman of the committee, but he also is likely to be elected chairman of the National Republican Senatorial Committee, which could present several conflicts of interest.

Democrat Byron L. Dorgan of North Dakota will step down as vice chairman, elevating Harry Reid of Nevada to the post. Senate Minority Leader Tom Daschle, D-S.D., will decide which Democrat, likely a freshman, will fill the vacancy on the committee.

The panel dealt with few complaints in 1996 after disposing of its major case, the investigation of former Sen. Bob Packwood, R-Ore., on charges of sexual misconduct and abuse of office, in 1995.

Intelligence

Chairman Arlen Specter, R-Pa., is required to leave the committee because he has served on the panel for eight years, the maximum allowed. That will open the chairmanship to Richard G. Lugar of Indiana or Richard C. Shelby of Alabama.

To take the top spot at Intelligence, Lugar would have to give up the chair at Agriculture.

Either Lugar or Shelby would likely pursue a less ambitious agenda than Specter, who sponsored a structural overhaul of the intelligence community. That plan, which would have strengthened the director of Central Intelligence at the expense of the secretary of Defense, was scuttled by stiff opposition from the Pentagon and its congressional allies.

Among other tasks, the committee will probably have to confirm a new director of Central Intelligence. John M. Deutch is expected to step down from that post to succeed William J. Perry, who has told President Clinton he will resign as secretary of Defense.

Shelby

Kerrey

Vice Chairman Bob Kerrey of Nebraska, who worked closely with Specter on his reorganization plan, will remain the committee's senior Democrat.

Small Business

The committee does not appear to be in store for any dramatic changes next year. Republican Christopher S. Bond of Missouri is expected to resume his role as chairman and will likely continue with his agenda of streamlining functions within the Small Business Administration and reducing regulations on small businesses.

One priority will be an effort to increase tax deductions for the health care expenses of self-employed people.

The panel's ranking Democrat, Dale Bumpers of Arkansas, is likely moving to the top spot at Energy and Natural Resources.

Carl Levin of Michigan is in line for the ranking minority position at Armed Services. As a result of these moves, Tom Harkin of Iowa could move up to the ranking spot on Small Business.

Special Aging

Charles E. Grassley, R-Iowa, is in line to chair the committee, following the retirement of Chairman William S. Cohen, R-Maine, and the defeat of the panel's second-ranking Republican, Larry Pressler of South Dakota.

The committee has no authority to report legislation, but gains influence from its ability to draw attention to the needs of older Americans. Its investigative staff compiles information on the health, income, employment and housing of, as well as assistance to, older Americans.

Grassley is likely to emphasize protection of entitlement programs such as Medicare.

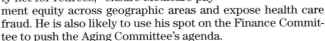
Grassley

A Grassley aide said the chairman-to-be would work to "preserve a viable safety net for retirees," ensure Medicare payment equity across geographic areas and expose health care fraud. He is also likely to use his spot on the Finance Committee to push the Aging Committee's agenda.

John B. Breaux of Louisiana is in line to become the ranking Democrat, following the retirement of David Pryor of Arkansas.

An aide said Breaux would focus on ensuring that Medicare and Social Security remain solvent. Like Grassley, Breaux is a member of the Finance Committee.

Veterans' Affairs

With the retirement of Alan K. Simpson, R-Wyo., the veterans committee will likely regain its image as a bipartisan, veteran-friendly panel.

Simpson often clashed during the 104th Congress with ranking Democrat John D. Rockefeller IV of West Virginia over decisions to extend benefits to more veterans, including those exposed to Agent Orange. Simpson maintained that Democratic efforts were based more on emotion and politics than on sound science.

Arlen Specter, R-Pa., will likely take over as chairman, and few observers believe he will be as eager as Simpson to challenge the priorities of influential veterans groups. Rockefeller will remain the panel's ranking Democrat.

The committee is likely to look into Persian Gulf Syndrome, an illness affecting U.S. soldiers who fought in the 1990–91 war against Iraq.

The 104th Congress extended priority medical treatment to Persian Gulf veterans through fiscal 1998. But with new Pentagon disclosure that thousands more veterans may have been exposed to chemical weapons in the Gulf than previously thought, the issue undoubtedly will command a series of investigative hearings.

The panel is also expected to look into changing the process by which veterans are awarded compensation benefits.

HOUSE VOTE

Despite Push, Democrats Fail To Topple GOP

But strong showing helps slow momentum left from Republican gains in '94

Despite strong financial backing from organized labor and a brisk tailwind from President Clinton's re-election victory, Democrats fell short of recapturing control of the House, as Republicans won their first back-to-back majorities in the chamber since the 1920s.

To regain control, Democrats needed a net gain of 19 seats from their last headcount in the 104th Congress (including the vote of a usual ally, liberal independent Rep. Bernard Sanders of Vermont).

Pending final certification, Democrats this year apparently won more than 20 seats that were held by Republicans in the 104th Congress. But Republicans captured a baker's dozen of Democratic-held seats, leaving the Democrats a painful few seats shy of their magic number.

Still, the Democrats did manage to cut into the GOP majority and disrupt the momentum that had seemed so strong for the Republicans in the elections of 1994, when they gained a net of 52 seats, and the ensuing rash of party-switching that brought them five more in 1995.

There is some doubt about the outcomes in a handful of close races, and party control of two House seats in Texas will be decided in Dec. 10 runoffs. *(Texas, p. 43)*

But if all the candidates who led in unofficial but nearly complete returns as of Nov. 8 become members of the 105th Congress, the Democrats will have gained a net of nine seats, leaving a party breakdown in the House of 227 Republicans and 207 Democrats, with Sanders the lone independent. *(Election results, p. 110)*

"We would prefer to have won control, but we made a very strong showing," said Rep. Martin Frost, D-Texas, chairman of the Democratic Congressional Campaign Committee.

National Democratic officials and their House candidates across the country attempted to nationalize the individ-

CQ Weekly Report November 9, 1996

DEBORAH KALB

Ohio Democrat Ted Strickland talks to supporter Em Lowe.

ual House elections — just as the Republicans had in 1994, when they produced the "Contract With America" and painted President Clinton as a villain.

This time around, Democrats attempted to tie their GOP opponents to House Speaker Newt Gingrich, R-Ga., whose brash leadership of the congressional Republican "revolution" made him the most unpopular national political leader, according to public opinion polls.

Democrats attempted to tar their GOP opponents for backing the Republican leadership's proposals to reduce the growth in spending on Medicare, Medicaid and education — portrayed in Democratic rhetoric as spending "cuts" — and supporting efforts to rein in government regulations, which Democrats cast as "anti-environment" and "anti-safety."

Democrats were aided in their efforts by the AFL-CIO's $35 million "educational" campaign that largely attacked Republican incumbents.

Throughout the campaign, and even after it ended, GOP leaders said that the "Washington union bosses" were trying to buy back the House for the Democrats.

Given that these attacks fell short of their goal of overturning Republican control, GOP leaders declared victory despite their net loss of seats. But their bold pre-election predictions of a 15-to-25 seat net gain were far off the mark.

Rep. Bill Paxon, R-N.Y., head of the National Republican Congressional Committee, said while he failed to "predict the score," the Republicans did win the game by holding on to their majority for a second cycle. The last time the GOP returned a majority to the House was following the 1928 election. (They won a narrow majority of House seats again in 1930, but deaths of several Republican members created vacancies that allowed the Democrats to organize the House.)

"We cemented our historic gains in the House and laid a solid foundation for a long-term Republican majority," Paxon said.

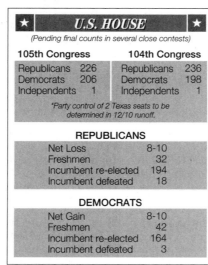

★	U.S. HOUSE	★
(Pending final counts in several close contests)		

105th Congress		104th Congress	
Republicans	226	Republicans	236
Democrats	206	Democrats	198
Independents	1	Independents	1

Party control of 2 Texas seats to be determined in 12/10 runoff.

REPUBLICANS	
Net Loss	8-10
Freshmen	32
Incumbent re-elected	194
Incumbent defeated	18

DEMOCRATS	
Net Gain	8-10
Freshmen	42
Incumbent re-elected	164
Incumbent defeated	3

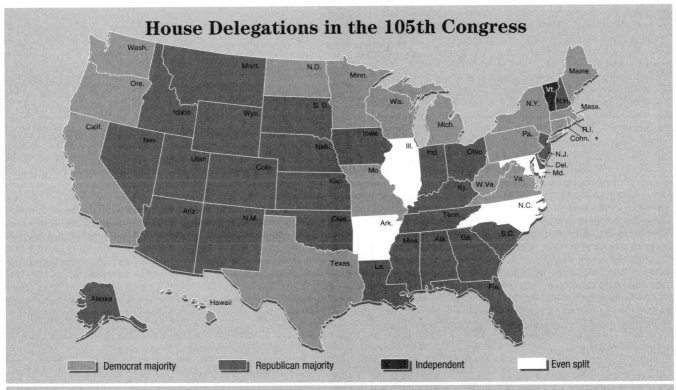

House Delegations in the 105th Congress

Democrat majority   Republican majority   Independent   Even split

	Current Lineup	New Lineup	Net Dem. Change		Current Lineup	New Lineup	Net Dem. Change		Current Lineup	New Lineup	Net Dem. Change		Current Lineup	New Lineup	Net Dem. Change		Current Lineup	New Lineup	Net Dem. Change
Ala.	4D 3R	2D 5R	-2	Hawaii	2D 0R	2D 0R	0	*Mass.	8D 2R	10D 0R	+2	N.M.	1D 2R	1D 2R	0	S.D.	1D 0R	0D 1R	-1
Alaska	0D 1R	0D 1R	0	Idaho	0D 2R	0D 2R	0	Mich.	9D 7R	10D 6R	+1	N.Y.	17D 14R	18D 13R	+1	Tenn.	4D 5R	4D 5R	0
*Ariz.	1D 5R	1D 5R	0	Ill.	10D 10R	10D 10R	0	Minn.	6D 2R	6D 2R	0	N.C.	4D 8R	6D 6R	+2	*Texas	18D 12R	16D 14R	-2
Ark.	2D 2R	2D 2R	0	Ind.	4D 6R	4D 6R	0	Miss.	3D 2R	2D 3R	-1	N.D.	1D 0R	1D 0R	0	Utah	1D 2R	0D 3R	-1
*Calif.	26D 26R	28D 24R	+2	Iowa	0D 5R	1D 4R	+1	*Mo.	6D 3R	5D 4R	-1	Ohio	6D 13R	8D 11R	+2	Vt.	0D 0R 1I	0D 0R 1I	0
Colo.	2D 4R	2D 4R	0	Kan.	0D 4R	0D 4R	0	Mont.	1D 0R	0D 1R	-1	Okla.	1D 5R	0D 6R	-1	Va.	6D 5R	6D 5R	0
Conn.	3D 3R	4D 2R	+1	Ky.	2D 4R	1D 5R	-1	Neb.	0D 3R	0D 3R	0	*Ore.	3D 2R	4D 1R	+1	*Wash.	2D 7R	5D 4R	+3
Del.	0D 1R	0D 1R	0	La.	2D 5R	2D 5R	0	Nev.	0D 2R	0D 2R	0	*Pa.	11D 10R	11D 10R	0	W.Va.	3D 0R	3D 0R	0
Fla.	8D 15R	8D 15R	0	Maine	1D 1R	2D 0R	+1	N.H.	0D 2R	0D 2R	0	R.I.	2D 0R	2D 0R	0	Wis.	3D 6R	5D 4R	+2
Ga.	3D 8R	3D 8R	0	Md.	4D 4R	4D 4R	0	N.J.	5D 8R	6D 7R	+1	S.C.	2D 4R	2D 4R	0	Wyo.	0D 1R	0D 1R	0

*Races where the outcome could change pending final counting of ballots: Ariz.-6, Calif.-42, Calif.-46, Ore.-5, Wash.-2. Final results subject to recount in Mass.-6 and Pa.-13. Final results to be determined in Dec. 10 runoffs in Texas-8, Texas-9 and Texas-25. Vacancies in Mo.-8 and Texas-2 counted in "current lineup" as if in party of last person holding seat.

The GOP was bolstered by its strength in the South — the only region in the country where the party had a net gain of House seats. Republicans will occupy 83 Southern seats in the 105th Congress to 54 for the Democrats (barring any changes resulting from the Dec. 10 Texas runoffs).

Even as they were picking up seats in the South, Republicans saw their strength in the East continue to erode. Barring any changes that could result from recounts, Democrats will have 60 of the seats in the East in the 105th Congress, compared with 39 for Republicans.

The Nov. 5 results show that 73 new members (31 Republicans and 42 Democrats) were elected to the House. A 74th new member certainly will be elected from Texas on Dec. 10, when two Republicans compete in a runoff to succeed retiring 8th District GOP Rep. Jack Fields.

The book is not quite yet closed on the freshman Class of 1996. Two other Texas races, these involving incumbents fighting for re-election against serious challengers, also will be decided in Dec. 10 runoffs. These unusual runoffs were necessitated by a court-enforced redistricting plan.

And as of Nov. 8, a handful of the Nov. 5 races were still too close to call, pending final canvassing, or were subject to challenge by the trailing candidate.

In California's 46th District, the race between GOP Rep. Robert K. Dornan and Democratic financial adviser Loretta Sanchez was neck and neck, with Dornan holding a narrow lead and many absentee ballots outstanding.

Several other races in California, Oregon and Washington have apparent winners, but a heavy reliance on absentee or mail-in voting in those states left thousands of ballots still to be counted.

In other contests, GOP Reps. J. D. Hayworth of Arizona and Jon D. Fox of Pennsylvania were leading their Democratic opponents but challenges or certification of the results in those races could change the outcome. Peter G. Torkildsen, R-Mass., who apparently lost by a narrow margin, is requesting a recount; Bill Orton, D-Utah, has asked for an investigation into the election that he apparently lost.

As of Nov. 8, 18 Republican incumbents and three Democratic incumbents were defeated. The total of 21 defeated incumbents is considerably smaller than the 34, all Democrats, who were unseated in the 1994 GOP sweep.

The biggest toll was among the mainly conservative and contentious GOP freshman class. But even within this group

New House Members

Following is a list of House freshmen as of Nov. 8. The outcome of three Texas races will be decided in Dec. 10 runoffs.

State, District	Winner	State, District	Winner
Ala. (3)	Bob Riley, R	Mont. (AL)	Rick Hill, R
Ala. (4)	Robert Aderholt, R	Nev. (2)	Jim Gibbons, R
Ark. (1)	Marion Berry, D	N.H. (1)	John E. Sununu, R
Ark. (2)	Victor F. Snyder, D	N.J. (8)	William J. Pascrell Jr., D
Ark. (3)	Asa Hutchinson, R	N.J. (9)	Steven R. Rothman, D
Calif. (10)	Ellen Tauscher, D	N.J. (12)	Mike Pappas, R
Calif. (22)	Walter Holden Capps, D	N.Y. (4)	Carolyn McCarthy, D
Calif. (24)	Brad Sherman, D	N.C. (2)	Bobby R. Etheridge, D
Calif. (27)	James E. Rogan, R	N.C. (4)	David E. Price, D
Colo. (1)	Diana DeGette, D	N.C. (7)	Mike McIntyre, D

Rogan   McGovern   Sununu   McCarthy   McCarthy   Granger

State, District	Winner	State, District	Winner
Colo. (4)	Robert W. Schaffer, R	Ohio (6)	Ted Strickland, D
Conn. (5)	James H. Maloney, D	Ohio (10)	Dennis Kucinich, D
Fla. (2)	Allen Boyd Jr., D	Okla. (3)	Wes Watkins, R
Fla. (11)	Jim Davis, D	Ore. (2)	Bob Smith, R
Fla. (19)	Robert Wexler, D	Ore. (5)	Darlene Hooley, D
Ill. (5)	Rod R. Blagojevich, D	Pa. (5)	John E. Peterson, R
Ill. (7)	Danny K. Davis, D	Pa. (16)	Joseph R. Pitts, R
Ill. (20)	John M. Shimkus, R	R.I. (2)	Robert A. Weygand, D
Ind. (7)	Ed Pease, R	S.D. (AL)	John Thune, R
Ind. (10)	Julia Carson, D	Tenn. (1)	Bill Jenkins, R
Iowa (3)	Leonard L. Boswell, D	Tenn. (9)	Harold E. Ford Jr., D
Kan. (1)	Jerry Moran, R	Texas (1)	Max Sandlin, D
Kan. (2)	Jim Ryun, R	Texas (2)	Jim Turner, D
Kan. (3)	Vince Snowbarger, R	Texas (5)	Pete Sessions, R
Ky. (3)	Anne Northup, R	Texas (12)	Kay Granger, R
La. (5)	John Cooksey, R	Texas (14)	Ron Paul, R
La. (7)	Chris John, D	Texas (15)	Ruben Hinojosa, D
Maine (1)	Tom Allen, D	Texas (16)	Silvestre Reyes, D
Mass. (3)	Jim McGovern, D	Utah (2)	Merrill Cook, R
Mass. (6)	John F. Tierney, D	Utah (3)	Chris Cannon, R
Mass. (10)	William D. Delahunt, D	Va. (5)	Virgil H. Goode Jr., D
Mich. (8)	Deborah Ann Stabenow, D	Wash. (2)	Kevin Quigley, D
Mich. (15)	Carolyn Cheeks Kilpatrick, D	Wash. (3)	Brian Baird, D
Miss. (3)	Chip Pickering Jr., R	Wash. (9)	Adam Smith, D
Mo. (7)	Roy Blunt, R	Wis. (3)	Ron Kind, D
Mo. (8)	Jo Ann Emerson, R	Wis. (8)	Jay Johnson, D
Mo. (9)	Kenny Hulshof, R		

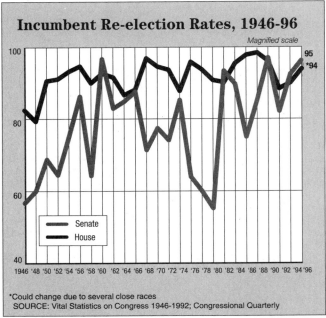

Incumbent Re-election Rates, 1946-96

Magnified scale

100
95
*94
80
60
40

1946 '48 '50 '52 '54 '56 '58 '60 '62 '64 '66 '68 '70 '72 '74 '76 '78 '80 '82 '84 '86 '88 '90 '92 '94 '96

— Senate
— House

*Could change due to several close races
SOURCE: Vital Statistics on Congress 1946-1992; Congressional Quarterly

MARILYN GATES-DAVIS

that was heavily targeted for challenges by Democrats, only 13 of the 71 members seeking re-election were sent packing.

The GOP salvaged its continued hold on the House with its performance in open seats, those districts vacated by incumbents who retired, ran for other office or were defeated in their House primaries earlier this year. Of the 53 such seats, Republicans won 29, 10 of which had been given up by Democratic incumbents. Democrats won 24, only four of which had been held by Republicans.

There will be homecomings for five new members, who had served in the House: Republicans Bob Smith of Oregon, Ron Paul of Texas, and Wes Watkins of Oklahoma (who served as a Democrat during his earlier House tenure) and Democrats David Price of North Carolina and Ted Strickland of Ohio.

In Missouri's 8th District, Republican Jo Ann Emerson is succeeding her husband, Bill Emerson, who died in June.

The following is a state-by-state look at seats that changed hands Nov. 5:

The East

The East proved to be prime Democratic territory, and Massachusetts was the Democrats' crown jewel. Pending the outcome of Torkildsen's race, Democrats apparently swept the entire 10-member House delegation. Not only did Democrats hold all their House seats in the region, but they appeared to have picked up six seats previously held by Republicans.

• **Massachusetts:** Clinton dominated the contest with 62 percent of the vote, and it was one place that he appeared to have real "coattails." In the 3rd District, Democrat Jim McGovern, a former congressional aide, defeated two-term Republican Rep. Peter I. Blute. In an effort to link the relatively moderate Blute to Gingrich, McGovern ran an ad that said, "If you wouldn't vote for Newt, why would you ever vote for Blute?"

Torkildsen apparently lost the rematch of his close 1994 race against lawyer John F. Tierney in the 6th District.

• **Connecticut:** Democrats scored an upset in the 5th, with Democrat James H. Maloney's defeat of three-term Rep. Gary A. Franks, one of two black Republicans in the 104th

Congress. Maloney, a former state senator, focused his campaign on tying Franks, an iconoclastic conservative within the Congressional Black Caucus, to Gingrich and the GOP agenda.

• **Maine:** One of the most vulnerable Republican freshmen, James B. Longley Jr., lost his re-election bid to Democrat Tom Allen, a former Portland mayor, in Maine's 1st District Longley was hammered by Allen on such issues as education and the environment, and also was a major labor union target.

• **New Jersey:** Freshman Republican Rep. Bill Martini failed to win a second term in the 8th District, losing to Democrat William J. Pascrell Jr., the mayor of Paterson. Although Martini is relatively moderate, Pascrell succeeded in burdening him with his steady support in early 1995 for Gingrich and the Contract with America.

• **New York:** The only change in New York's 31-member House delegation was in the Democrats' favor. Gun-control activist Carolyn McCarthy, the Democratic nominee, defeated freshman Republican Rep. Daniel Frisa in the normally Republican 4th District. The contest mixed national politics with an intensely personal cause: McCarthy, whose husband was killed and son wounded in the 1993 Long Island Railroad massacre, entered politics after her congressman, Frisa, voted to repeal the assault weapons ban.

The South

Republicans offset their Eastern setback by expanding their base in the South. They captured seven of the 19 seats vacated by retiring Democrats in the South, while losing only one of their own open seats in the region.

Some Races Still Unresolved

The final outcomes in some close races have yet to be decided. In California's 46th District, Republican Rep. Robert K. Dornan held a slim lead over his Democratic challenger, Loretta Sanchez. In the 42nd District, Democrat George E. Brown Jr. appeared to have won a narrow victory over Republican Linda M. Wilde. Also on the West Coast, Democrat Darlene Hooley appeared to have defeated Republican Rep. Jim Bunn in Oregon's 5th District, and Democrat Kevin Quigley seemed to have overtaken Republican Rep. Jack Metcalf in Washington's 2nd District. In Arizona's 6th District, Republican Rep. J. D. Hayworth scored a narrow victory over Democrat Steve Owens, but some absentee ballots were still being counted.

A recount is under way in at least one close contest. In Massachusetts' 6th District, where Democrat John Tierney narrowly defeated Republican Rep. Peter G. Torkildsen, Torkildsen has asked for a recount. A recount is also possible in Pennsylvania's 13th District, where Republican Rep. Jon D. Fox scored a 10-vote victory over Democrat Joseph M. Hoeffel.

In three Texas districts, final outcomes will not be decided until runoffs slated for Dec. 10. In the 8th District, two Republicans, Gene Fontenot and Kevin Brady, are fighting it out. In the 9th, Republican Rep. Steve Stockman faces Democrat Nick Lampson. And in the 25th, Democratic Rep. Ken Bentsen is likely to face Republican Dolly Madison McKenna, who finished second in last week's election. But the third-place finisher, Democrat Beverley Clark, who nearly overtook McKenna, could ask for a recount by Nov. 12.

Incumbents Survive Redistricting

When Supreme Court decisions forced the redrawing of black and Hispanic House districts in several states, some observers expected the affected incumbents to suffer on Election Day.

But in the four affected states that held their House races using the new maps Nov. 5, no minority incumbent member was turned out of office.

McKinney

Bishop

Ironically, the first victims of the remapping might be two Anglo incumbents in Texas who have been forced into runoffs Dec. 10 because of the new district lines.

Congressional maps in Texas, Florida, Georgia and Louisiana were redrawn this year in the wake of Supreme Court decisions in 1995 and 1996 that cast heavy doubt on the constitutionality of using race as the main factor in redistricting decisions.

Civil rights activists had predicted that reducing the black or Hispanic population in the affected districts from a majority to a minority would spell defeat for black or Hispanic members elected under the old lines (such as Democrats Cynthia A. McKinney and Sanford D. Bishop Jr. of Georgia).

"It becomes harder to make the argument that these districts make it impossible for black (and other minority) candidates to win," said Merle Black, a political scientist at Emory University.

However, the new round of redistricting did produce one casualty even before the election was held.

Black Democratic Rep. Cleo Fields of Louisiana decided not to seek a third term after the new map adopted by a federal three-judge panel, which struck down the black-majority 4th District he represented, left him with no obvious district to run in for re-election. The judges' map significantly reduced the black population in the new 4th.

In Florida, the black-majority 3rd District, represented by two-term black Democratic Rep. Corrine Brown, was found unconstitutional in April. The state Legislature created a new map that reduced the number of blacks from a majority to a minority of the 3rd's population. Despite this, Brown had little trouble securing a third term.

Georgia's congressional map was redrawn after two of the state's three black-majority districts were found unconstitutional. In redrawing the state's lines, a federal three-judge panel left only one of those black-majority districts intact, the 5th held by black Democratic Rep. John Lewis.

As a result, McKinney and Bishop were forced to run in districts with black populations significantly reduced from those they had been elected to in 1992 and 1994.

McKinney was seen as the state's most vulnerable incumbent but emerged victorious with 58 percent of the vote Nov. 5. Bishop also won re-election to his newly drawn district but had a smaller margin of victory. At the same time, Democratic hopes of knocking off a handful of Republican incumbents, who were expected to have more trouble running in districts with higher black populations, did not materialize.

As in Georgia, a federal panel of three judges redrew Texas' map earlier this year after three minority-majority districts in the Lone Star state were found to be unconstitutional. All three of the incumbents whose districts were struck down were re-elected in their new districts.

They are black Democratic Reps. Sheila Jackson-Lee and Eddie Bernice Johnson and Anglo Democrat Gene Green, who had represented a Hispanic-majority district. *(Texas, p. 43)*

• **Alabama:** Two Democratic open seats in Alabama fell to Republicans by narrow margins, giving a 5–2 advantage in the state's House delegation to the advancing GOP.

In the 3rd District, GOP car dealer Bob Riley captured the seat of Democratic Rep. Glen Browder, who made an unsuccessful bid for the Democratic Senate nomination. Riley dismissed Democratic state Sen. Ted Little's claim of being a fiscal conservative and attacked him as "too liberal for Alabama."

The GOP also gained a seat in the 4th District race to succeed Democrat Tom Bevill. Republican Robert Aderholt, a municipal court judge, overcame Democratic former state Sen. Bob Wilson Jr.'s early lead in the polls.

• **Kentucky:** Rep. Mike Ward — the only freshman Democratic incumbent to lose re-election this fall — was unable to repel a well-funded attack from GOP state Rep. Anne Northup. She accused Ward, who in 1994 had barely won the open, Louisville-based 3rd District seat, of taking positions that were too far to the left for the district.

• **Louisiana:** The redrawing of the state's congressional map prior to this year's elections resulted in no net changes in its House delegation, leaving a 5–2 Republican edge.

The court-ordered remap prompted Democratic Rep. Cleo Fields not to seek re-election and left the newly drawn, heavily conservative 5th District without an incumbent. Republican physician John Cooksey won the 5th by easily defeating Democratic state Rep. Francis Thompson.

But Democrats balanced that loss, as Democratic former state Rep. Chris John picked up the 7th District seat vacated by GOP Rep. Jimmy Hayes, who made an unsuccessful bid for the Senate.

• **Mississippi:** The retirement of 15-term conservative Democratic Rep. G. V. "Sonny" Montgomery opened up his Republican-leaning 3rd District seat to a GOP takeover. Republican Charles W. "Chip" Pickering Jr., a former aide to Sen. Trent Lott, R-Miss., easily captured the seat, defeating Democratic lawyer John Arthur Eaves Jr. Republicans now hold a 3–2 edge in the state's House delegation.

• **Oklahoma:** Oklahoma is now the southern Republican mirror image to the Democrats' Massachusetts redoubt. The Sooner State has an all-GOP delegation, with Watkins' Republican pickup of the 3rd District, which had been the state's lone Democratic House seat. Watkins, who had represented the district as a Democrat from 1977 to 1991, defeated Democ-

House Membership in 105th Congress

Alabama

1 Sonny Callahan (R)
2 Terry Everett (R)
3 Bob Riley (R)#
4 Robert Aderholt (R)#
5 Robert E. "Bud" Cramer (D)
6 Spencer Bachus (R)
7 Earl F. Hilliard (D)

Alaska

AL Don Young (R)

Arizona

1 Matt Salmon (R)
2 Ed Pastor (D)
3 Bob Stump (R)
4 John Shadegg (R)
5 Jim Kolbe (R)
6 J.D. Hayworth (R)

Arkansas

1 Marion Berry (D)#
2 Victor F. Snyder (D)#
3 Asa Hutchinson (R)#
4 Jay Dickey (R)

California

1 Frank Riggs (R)
2 Wally Herger (R)
3 Vic Fazio (D)
4 John T. Doolittle (R)
5 Robert T. Matsui (D)
6 Lynn Woolsey (D)
7 George Miller (D)
8 Nancy Pelosi (D)
9 Ronald V. Dellums (D)
10 Ellen Tauscher (D)#
11 Richard W. Pombo (R)
12 Tom Lantos (D)
13 Pete Stark (D)
14 Anna G. Eshoo (D)
15 Tom Campbell (R)
16 Zoe Lofgren (D)
17 Sam Farr (D)
18 Gary A. Condit (D)
19 George P. Radanovich (R)
20 Cal Dooley (D)
21 Bill Thomas (R)
22 Walter Holden Capps (D)#
23 Elton Gallegly (R)
24 Brad Sherman (D)#
25 Howard P. "Buck" McKeon (R)
26 Howard L. Berman (D)
27 James E. Rogan (R)#
28 David Dreier (R)
29 Henry A. Waxman (D)
30 Xavier Becerra (D)
31 Matthew G. Martinez (D)
32 Julian C. Dixon (D)
33 Lucille Roybal-Allard (D)
34 Esteban E. Torres (D)
35 Maxine Waters (D)
36 Jane Harman (D)
37 Juanita Millender-McDonald (D)
38 Steve Horn (R)
39 Ed Royce (R)
40 Jerry Lewis (R)
41 Jay C. Kim (R)
42 George E. Brown Jr. (D)
43 Ken Calvert (R)
44 Sonny Bono (R)
45 Dana Rohrabacher (R)
46 Robert K. Dornan (R)
47 Christopher Cox (R)
48 Ron Packard (R)
49 Brian P. Bilbray (R)
50 Bob Filner (D)
51 Randy "Duke" Cunningham (R)
52 Duncan Hunter (R)

Colorado

1 Diana DeGette (D)#
2 David E. Skaggs (D)
3 Scott McInnis (R)
4 Robert W. Schaffer (R)#
5 Joel Hefley (R)
6 Dan Schaefer (R)

Connecticut

1 Barbara B. Kennelly (D)
2 Sam Gejdenson (D)
3 Rosa DeLauro (D)
4 Christopher Shays (R)
5 James H. Maloney (D)#
6 Nancy L. Johnson (R)

Delaware

AL Michael N. Castle (R)

Florida

1 Joe Scarborough (R)
2 Allen Boyd Jr. (D)#
3 Corrine Brown (D)
4 Tillie Fowler (R)
5 Karen L. Thurman (D)
6 Cliff Stearns (R)
7 John L. Mica (R)
8 Bill McCollum (R)
9 Michael Bilirakis (R)
10 C.W. Bill Young (R)
11 Jim Davis (D)#
12 Charles T. Canady (R)
13 Dan Miller (R)
14 Porter J. Goss (R)
15 Dave Weldon (R)
16 Mark Foley (R)
17 Carrie P. Meek (D)
18 Ileana Ros-Lehtinen (R)
19 Robert Wexler (D)#
20 Peter Deutsch (D)
21 Lincoln Diaz-Balart (R)
22 E. Clay Shaw Jr. (R)
23 Alcee L. Hastings (D)

Georgia

1 Jack Kingston (R)
2 Sanford D. Bishop Jr. (D)
3 Mac Collins (R)
4 Cynthia A. McKinney (D)
5 John Lewis (D)
6 Newt Gingrich (R)
7 Bob Barr (R)
8 Saxby Chambliss (R)
9 Nathan Deal (R)
10 Charlie Norwood (R)
11 John Linder (R)

Hawaii

1 Neil Abercrombie (D)
2 Patsy T. Mink (D)

Idaho

1 Helen Chenoweth (R)
2 Michael D. Crapo (R)

Illinois

1 Bobby L. Rush (D)
2 Jesse L. Jackson Jr. (D)
3 William O. Lipinski (D)
4 Luis V. Gutierrez (D)
5 Rod R. Blagojevich (D)#
6 Henry J. Hyde (R)
7 Danny K. Davis (D)#
8 Philip M. Crane (R)
9 Sidney R. Yates (D)
10 John Edward Porter (R)
11 Jerry Weller (R)
12 Jerry F. Costello (D)
13 Harris W. Fawell (R)
14 Dennis Hastert (R)
15 Thomas W. Ewing (R)
16 Donald Manzullo (R)
17 Lane Evans (D)
18 Ray LaHood (R)
19 Glenn Poshard (D)
20 John M. Shimkus (R)#

Indiana

1 Peter J. Visclosky (D)
2 David M. McIntosh (R)
3 Tim Roemer (D)
4 Mark E. Souder (R)
5 Steve Buyer (R)
6 Dan Burton (R)
7 Ed Pease (R)#
8 John Hostettler (R)
9 Lee H. Hamilton (D)
10 Julia Carson (D)#

Iowa

1 Jim Leach (R)
2 Jim Nussle (R)
3 Leonard L. Boswell (D)#
4 Greg Ganske (R)
5 Tom Latham (R)

Kansas

1 Jerry Moran (R)#
2 Jim Ryun (R)#
3 Vince Snowbarger (R)#
4 Todd Tiahrt (R)

Kentucky

1 Edward Whitfield (R)
2 Ron Lewis (R)
3 Anne Northup (R)#
4 Jim Bunning (R)
5 Harold Rogers (R)
6 Scotty Baesler (D)

Louisiana

1 Robert L. Livingston (R)
2 William J. Jefferson (D)
3 W.J. "Billy" Tauzin (R)
4 Jim McCrery (R)
5 John Cooksey (R)#
6 Richard H. Baker (R)
7 Chris John (D)#

Maine

1 Tom Allen (D)#
2 John Baldacci (D)

Maryland

1 Wayne T. Gilchrest (R)
2 Robert Ehrlich Jr. (R)
3 Benjamin L. Cardin (D)
4 Albert R. Wynn (D)
5 Steny H. Hoyer (D)
6 Roscoe G. Bartlett (R)
7 Elijah E. Cummings (D)
8 Constance A. Morella (R)

Massachusetts

1 John W. Olver (D)
2 Richard E. Neal (D)
3 Jim McGovern (D)#
4 Barney Frank (D)
5 Martin T. Meehan (D)
6 John F. Tierney (D)#
7 Edward J. Markey (D)
8 Joseph P. Kennedy II (D)
9 Joe Moakley (D)
10 William D. Delahunt (D)#

Michigan

1 Bart Stupak (D)
2 Peter Hoekstra (R)
3 Vernon J. Ehlers (R)
4 Dave Camp (R)
5 James A. Barcia (D)
6 Fred Upton (R)
7 Nick Smith (R)
8 Deborah Ann Stabenow (D)#
9 Dale E. Kildee (D)
10 David E. Bonior (D)

Lineup

Republicans	226	**Freshmen**	32
Democrats	206	**Freshmen**	42
Independents	1		0

NOTE: Party control of two Texas seats to be determined in a Dec. 10 runoff.

 # Freshman representative.

---

11 Joe Knollenberg (R)
12 Sander M. Levin (D)
13 Lynn Rivers (D)
14 John Conyers Jr. (D)
15 Carolyn Cheeks Kilpatrick (D)#
16 John D. Dingell (D)

Minnesota

1 Gil Gutknecht (R)
2 David Minge (D)
3 Jim Ramstad (R)
4 Bruce F. Vento (D)
5 Martin Olav Sabo (D)
6 William P. "Bill" Luther (D)
7 Collin C. Peterson (D)
8 James L. Oberstar (D)

Mississippi

1 Roger Wicker (R)
2 Bennie Thompson (D)
3 Charles W. "Chip" Pickering Jr. (R)#
4 Mike Parker (R)
5 Gene Taylor (D)

Missouri

1 William L. Clay (D)
2 James M. Talent (R)
3 Richard A. Gephardt (D)
4 Ike Skelton (D)
5 Karen McCarthy (D)
6 Pat Danner (D)
7 Roy Blunt (R)#
8 Jo Ann Emerson (R)#
9 Kenny Hulshof (R)#

Montana

AL Rick Hill (R)#

Nebraska

1 Doug Bereuter (R)
2 Jon Christensen (R)
3 Bill Barrett (R)

Nevada

1 John Ensign (R)
2 Jim Gibbons (R)#

New Hampshire

1 John E. Sununu (R)#
2 Charles Bass (R)

New Jersey

1 Robert E. Andrews (D)
2 Frank A. LoBiondo (R)
3 H. James Saxton (R)
4 Christopher H. Smith (R)
5 Marge Roukema (R)
6 Frank Pallone Jr. (D)
7 Bob Franks (R)
8 William J. Pascrell Jr. (D)#
9 Steve R. Rothman (D)#
10 Donald M. Payne (D)
11 Rodney Frelinghuysen (R)
12 Mike Pappas (R)#
13 Robert Menendez (D)

New Mexico

1 Steven H. Schiff (R)
2 Joe Skeen (R)
3 Bill Richardson (D)

New York

1 Michael P. Forbes (R)
2 Rick A. Lazio (R)
3 Peter T. King (R)
4 Carolyn McCarthy (D)#
5 Gary L. Ackerman (D)
6 Floyd H. Flake (D)
7 Thomas J. Manton (D)
8 Jerrold Nadler (D)
9 Charles E. Schumer (D)
10 Edolphus Towns (D)
11 Major R. Owens (D)
12 Nydia M. Velazquez (D)
13 Susan Molinari (R)
14 Carolyn B. Maloney (D)
15 Charles B. Rangel (D)
16 Jose E. Serrano (D)
17 Eliot L. Engel (D)
18 Nita M. Lowey (D)
19 Sue W. Kelly (R)
20 Benjamin A. Gilman (R)
21 Michael R. McNulty (D)
22 Gerald B.H. Solomon (R)
23 Sherwood Boehlert (R)
24 John M. McHugh (R)
25 James T. Walsh (R)
26 Maurice D. Hinchey (D)
27 Bill Paxon (R)
28 Louise M. Slaughter (D)
29 John J. LaFalce (D)
30 Jack Quinn (R)
31 Amo Houghton (R)

North Carolina

1 Eva Clayton (D)
2 Bobby R. Etheridge (D)#
3 Walter B. Jones Jr. (R)
4 David E. Price (D)#
5 Richard M. Burr (R)
6 Howard Coble (R)
7 Mike McIntyre (D)#
8 W.G. "Bill" Hefner (D)
9 Sue Myrick (R)
10 Cass Ballenger (R)
11 Charles H. Taylor (R)
12 Melvin Watt (D)

North Dakota

AL Earl Pomeroy (D)

Ohio

1 Steve Chabot (R)
2 Rob Portman (R)
3 Tony P. Hall (D)
4 Michael G. Oxley (R)
5 Paul E. Gillmor (R)
6 Ted Strickland (D)#
7 David L. Hobson (R)
8 John A. Boehner (R)
9 Marcy Kaptur (D)
10 Dennis J. Kucinich (D)#
11 Louis Stokes (D)
12 John R. Kasich (R)
13 Sherrod Brown (D)
14 Tom Sawyer (D)
15 Deborah Pryce (R)
16 Ralph Regula (R)
17 James A. Traficant Jr. (D)
18 Bob Ney (R)
19 Steven C. LaTourette (R)

Oklahoma

1 Steve Largent (R)
2 Tom Coburn (R)
3 Wes Watkins (R)#
4 J.C. Watts (R)
5 Ernest Istook (R)
6 Frank D. Lucas (R)

Oregon

1 Elizabeth Furse (D)
2 Bob Smith (R)#
3 Earl Blumenauer (D)
4 Peter A. DeFazio (D)
5 Darlene Hooley (D)#

Pennsylvania

1 Thomas M. Foglietta (D)
2 Chaka Fattah (D)
3 Robert A. Borski (D)
4 Ron Klink (D)
5 John E. Peterson (R)#
6 Tim Holden (D)
7 Curt Weldon (R)
8 James C. Greenwood (R)
9 Bud Shuster (R)
10 Joseph M. McDade (R)
11 Paul E. Kanjorski (D)
12 John P. Murtha (D)
13 Jon D. Fox (R)
14 William J. Coyne (D)
15 Paul McHale (D)
16 Joseph R. Pitts (R)#
17 George W. Gekas (R)
18 Mike Doyle (D)
19 Bill Goodling (R)
20 Frank R. Mascara (D)
21 Phil English (R)

Rhode Island

1 Patrick J. Kennedy (D)
2 Robert A. Weygand (D)#

South Carolina

1 Mark Sanford (R)
2 Floyd D. Spence (R)
3 Lindsey Graham (R)
4 Bob Inglis (R)
5 John M. Spratt Jr. (D)
6 James E. Clyburn (D)

South Dakota

AL John Thune (R)#

Tennessee

1 Bill Jenkins (R)#
2 John J. "Jimmy" Duncan Jr. (R)
3 Zach Wamp (R)
4 Van Hilleary (R)
5 Bob Clement (D)
6 Bart Gordon (D)
7 Ed Bryant (R)
8 John Tanner (D)
9 Harold E. Ford Jr. (D)#

Texas

1 Max Sandlin (D)#
2 Jim Turner (D)#
3 Sam Johnson (R)
4 Ralph M. Hall (D)
5 Pete Sessions (R)#
6 Joe L. Barton (R)
7 Bill Archer (R)
8 Runoff Dec. 10
9 Runoff Dec. 10
10 Lloyd Doggett (D)
11 Chet Edwards (D)
12 Kay Granger (R)#
13 William M. "Mac" Thornberry (R)
14 Ron Paul (R)#
15 Ruben Hinojosa (D)#
16 Silvestre Reyes (D)#
17 Charles W. Stenholm (D)
18 Sheila Jackson-Lee (D)
19 Larry Combest (R)
20 Henry B. Gonzalez (D)
21 Lamar Smith (R)
22 Tom DeLay (R)
23 Henry Bonilla (R)
24 Martin Frost (D)
25 Runoff Dec. 10
26 Dick Armey (R)
27 Solomon P. Ortiz (D)
28 Frank Tejeda (D)
29 Gene Green (D)
30 Eddie Bernice Johnson (D)

Utah

1 James V. Hansen (R)
2 Merrill Cook (R)#
3 Chris Cannon (R)#

Vermont

AL Bernard Sanders (I)

Virginia

1 Herbert H. Bateman (R)
2 Owen B. Pickett (D)
3 Robert C. Scott (D)
4 Norman Sisisky (D)
5 Virgil H. Goode Jr. (D)#
6 Robert W. Goodlatte (R)
7 Thomas J. Bliley Jr. (R)
8 James P. Moran (D)
9 Rick Boucher (D)
10 Frank R. Wolf (R)
11 Thomas M. Davis III (R)

Washington

1 Rick White (R)
2 Kevin Quigley (D)#
3 Brian Baird (D)#
4 Richard "Doc" Hastings (R)
5 George Nethercutt (R)
6 Norm Dicks (D)
7 Jim McDermott (D)
8 Jennifer Dunn (R)
9 Adam Smith (D)#

West Virginia

1 Alan B. Mollohan (D)
2 Bob Wise (D)
3 Nick J. Rahall II (D)

Wisconsin

1 Mark W. Neumann (R)
2 Scott L. Klug (R)
3 Ron Kind (D)#
4 Gerald D. Kleczka (D)
5 Thomas M. Barrett (D)
6 Tom Petri (R)
7 David R. Obey (D)
8 Jay Johnson (D)
9 F. James Sensenbrenner Jr. (R)

Wyoming

AL Barbara Cubin (R)

BY JULIANA GRUENWALD

GOP hopeful Dolly Madison McKenna, shown campaigning Oct. 21, made the Dec. 10 runoff for a Texas seat.

ratic state Sen. Darryl Roberts.

• **North Carolina:** Rebounding from a terrible 1994 campaign, North Carolina Democrats regained some of the ground they lost by ousting GOP freshman Reps. Fred Heineman and David Funderburk.

In the 2nd District, Democrat Bobby R. Etheridge used a late-media blitz to question Funderburk's veracity, by reminding voters of a 1995 auto accident in which Funderburk initially claimed his wife was driving but later pleaded no contest to driving on the wrong side of the road.

Heineman was ousted in the 4th District by comeback winner Price, the Democrat he unseated in 1994. Heineman, who in 1995 argued that individuals with large six-figure incomes were "middle class," was criticized as being insensitive to the average voters' concerns.

• **Texas:** Republicans had hopes of picking up as many as four of the state's six seats vacated by retiring Democrats, but had to settle for a two-seat gain.

In the 5th, GOP businessman Pete Sessions won on his second try by prevailing over Democratic lawyer John Pouland. Sessions succeeds Democratic Rep. John Bryant, who gave up the seat for what would be a failed try for the Democratic Senate nomination.

In the 12th District race to succeed retiring Democrat Pete Geren, Republican Kay Granger, the former mayor of Fort Worth, easily defeated Democrat Hugh Parmer, another former Fort Worth mayor.

The Midwest

Democrats managed to reverse some of the losses they suffered here in 1994 by capturing a net gain of four seats, two in Wisconsin alone. Nonetheless, Republicans scored an upset in Missouri, where 10-term Democratic Rep. Harold L. Volkmer was defeated.

• **Illinois:** As widely expected, Republican freshman Michael Patrick Flanagan was trounced in the 5th District contest by Democratic state Rep. Rod Blagojevich. The 1994 victory by the little-known Flanagan in the normally Democra-

tic Chicago-based district was seen as a direct response to voter anger with Democratic Rep. Dan Rostenkowski, the veteran incumbent who was facing a multicount federal indictment on corruption charges.

Republicans evened the score, however, in the downstate 20th, where John M. Shimkus narrowly defeated Democratic state Rep. Jay C. Hoffman in the race to succeed Democratic Rep. Richard J. Durbin, who was elected to the Senate. The margin was quite narrow — about 1,200 votes — and as of Nov. 8 Hoffman was mulling a request for a recount.

• **Iowa:** Democrats, who had been shut out of the five-member Iowa House delegation in the 104th Congress, now have one member — though just barely. Democrat Leonard L. Boswell, who had served as state Senate president, defeated Republican Mike Mahaffey, a lawyer and former state GOP chairman, by just 1 percentage point for the 3rd District seat vacated by Republican incumbent Jim Ross Lightfoot, who lost his bid for the Senate.

• **Michigan:** Freshman Republican Rep. Dick Chrysler lived up to his billing as one of the most vulnerable in his class, losing to Democratic former state Sen. Deborah Ann Stabenow in the Lansing-based 8th District. Chrysler was one of labor's top targets, and Stabenow successfully tied him to Gingrich and the Republican agenda.

• **Missouri:** The second time was a curse for Volkmer in the 9th. He lost to his 1994 GOP opponent Kenny Hulshof, who had narrowly missed an upset in their first meeting.

Meanwhile, in a complicated scenario in the 8th District, Jo Ann Emerson claimed her late husband's seat in a three-way battle. Although ballot technicalities forced her to run as an independent against a Republican and a Democrat, Emerson will serve as a Republican in the 105th. Running as a Republican, Emerson also won a special election the same day to fill the last two months of Bill Emerson's unexpired term.

• **Ohio:** Hoping for big gains in a state where they lost four House seats in 1994, Ohio Democrats split the difference. They picked up two this time around as they defeated sophomore Rep. Martin R. Hoke and freshman Rep. Frank A. Cremeans.

In the 10th District, Hoke lost to Democratic state Sen. Dennis Kucinich, who has staged a political comeback since his controversial tenure as Cleveland mayor in the late 1970s, when the city fell into financial default.

It was a turnabout in the 6th District, where former one-term Democratic Rep. Strickland dumped Cremeans by 51 to 49 percent. The candidates' percentages were exactly reversed from the 1994 outcome.

BY ALAN GREENBLATT

Aderholt campaigns Oct. 18 in a store in Walnut Grove, Ala.

Runoffs Set in Three Texas Districts

Candidates in three House districts in the Houston area must face off for one more round of electioneering before a winner is determined.

Runoff elections will be held Dec. 10 in the 8th, 9th and 25th Districts, where no candidate received a majority of the vote Nov. 5.

The potential for runoffs was created this summer after a federal three-judge panel re-drew 13 districts in Texas. The judges were responding to a June Supreme Court ruling striking down three districts as examples of unconstitutional racial gerrymandering.

In redrawing the three unconstitutional districts, the judges found it necessary to alter 10 surrounding districts as well.

To effectuate the new map immediately, the judges threw out the results of the state's primary in all 13 altered districts, re-opened candidate filing and ordered that all the candidates run on the same ballot Nov. 5. Where no one candidate won a majority, a runoff was directed between the top two finishers regardless of party. There is no partisan suspense in the 8th District, vacated by retiring Republican Rep. Jack Fields, because the top finishers were both Republicans: state Rep. Kevin Brady and physician Gene Fontenot.

Brady had defeated Fontenot in an April 9 primary runoff, and he has the backing of most of the state's GOP congressional delegation and Gov. George W. Bush. But he will once again have to overcome Fontenot's sizable checkbook.

The outcome in the two other runoff races is less certain. Two freshman members, Democrat Ken Bentsen and

Ken Bentsen

Steve Stockman

Republican Steve Stockman, are both in danger of losing their seats. But the greater pressure is likely to be on Bentsen.

"Runoff races [in Texas] almost always benefit Republicans," according to Robert Stein, a political scientist at Rice University in Houston. "They do a better job of getting [their] vote out."

With 11 candidates in the race for the 25th District, Bentsen finished first, but had little chance of topping 50 percent. Barring any changes from a recount, Bentsen's runoff opponent will be GOP businesswoman Dolly Madison McKenna, the 1992 GOP nominee who lost a bid for the 1994 Republican nomination in this district to Fontenot.

McKenna, who got past seven other GOP contenders, squeaked by Democrat Beverley Clark, who was considering asking for a recount, by about 200 votes to clinch a spot in the runoff. McKenna is a moderate who supports abortion rights.

But McKenna may have trouble uniting Republicans, particularly GOP Christian activists, around her bid.

In the 9th, Stockman was forced into a runoff with Nick Lampson, the former Jefferson County tax assessor, after the Republican narrowly fell short of capturing a majority of the vote on Election Day. Despite being viewed as one of the most endangered incumbents, Stockman may have gotten a break because of the redistricting changes.

Lampson might well have unseated Stockman on Nov. 5 had a second Democrat, teacher Geraldine Sam, not jumped into the race after the district was redrawn. Sam captured 9 percent of the vote, while Lampson took 44 percent, making the combined Democratic vote 53 percent.

• **South Dakota:** Republicans grabbed an open-seat pickup of South Dakota's lone House seat, vacated when Democratic Rep. Tim Johnson left for his successful bid against Republican Sen. Larry Pressler. In the contest between two former Senate aides, Republican John Thune easily outran Democrat Rick Weiland.

• **Wisconsin:** The GOP's loss of two open seats here has given Democrats a 5–4 lead in Wisconsin's House delegation. Democratic prosecutor Ron Kind will succeed moderate GOP Rep. Steve Gunderson in the 3rd. Benefiting from the district's overall Democratic lean, Kind defeated Republican Jim Harsdorf, a dairy farmer and former state legislator who was hampered by Gunderson's refusal to endorse him.

A bigger surprise occurred in the 8th, where Democratic newscaster Jay Johnson defeated GOP state Assembly Speaker David Prosser Jr. to succeed retiring conservative GOP Rep. Toby Roth. The 8th generally has leaned Republican, but Prosser had a difficult time overcoming Green Bay media personality Johnson's strong advantage in name identification.

The West

Democrats had predicted they would do well along the Pacific Coast, and they did, picking up what appeared to be at least five seats in the three-state region of Washington, Oregon and California (several races were still too close to call). But those gains were mitigated by a GOP pickup of one seat each in Montana and Utah.

• **California:** California's House delegation, which had been balanced at 26 Democrats and 26 Republicans before Election Day, will show a slight Democratic tilt in the 105th Congress, as Democrats defeated at least two GOP incumbents.

In the 22nd District, freshman Republican Rep. Andrea Seastrand lost her re-election bid to Democrat Walter Holden Capps, a college professor whom she had narrowly defeated in 1994. She was targeted for defeat by organized labor, abortion rights groups and environmental organizations.

The San Francisco Bay area apparently lost its only Republican member, as Democratic businesswoman Ellen Tauscher held a 2 percentage point edge over 10th District GOP Rep.

Congressional Departures

House Vacancies

Missouri 8th (Bill Emerson, R, died June 22)
Texas 2nd (Charles Wilson, D, resigned)

Defeated for Re-election

Senate

Larry Pressler, R-S.D.

House

Bill Baker, R-Calif. (10)
Peter Blute, R-Mass. (3)
Jim Bunn, R-Ore. (5)
Dick Chrysler, R-Mich. (8)
Frank A. Cremeans, R-Ohio (6)
Michael Patrick Flanagan, R-Ill. (5)
Gary Franks, R-Conn. (5)
Dan Frisa, R-N.Y. (4)
David Funderburk, R-N.C. (2)
Fred Heineman, R-N.C. (4)
Martin R. Hoke, R-Ohio (10)
James B. Longley Jr., R-Maine (1)
Bill Martini, R-N.J. (8)
Jack Metcalf, R-Wash. (2)
Bill Orton, D-Utah (3)
Andrea Seastrand, R-Calif. (22)
Linda Smith, R-Wash. (3)
Randy Tate, R-Wash. (9)
Peter G. Torkildsen, R-Mass. (6)
Harold L. Volkmer, D-Mo. (9)
Mike Ward, D-Ky (3)

Defeated for Renomination

Senate

Sheila Frahm, R-Kan.

House

Barbara-Rose Collins, D-Mich. (15)
Greg Laughlin, R-Texas (14)

Defeated for Senate Nomination

Glen Browder, D-Ala. (3)
John Bryant, D-Texas (5)
Jim Chapman, D-Texas (1)
Jimmy Hayes, R-La. (7)

Defeated for Gubernatorial Nomination

Bill Zeliff, R-N.H. (1)

Retiring

Senate

Bill Bradley, D-N.J.
Hank Brown, R-Colo.
William S. Cohen, R-Maine
Jim Exon, D-Neb.
Mark O. Hatfield, R-Ore.
Howell Heflin, D-Ala.
J. Bennett Johnston, D-La.
Nancy Landon Kassebaum, R-Kan.
Sam Nunn, D-Ga.
Claiborne Pell, D-R.I.
David Pryor, D-Ark.
Paul Simon, D-Ill.
Alan K. Simpson, R-Wyo.

House

Anthony C. Beilenson, D-Calif. (24)
Tom Bevill, D-Ala. (4)
Bill Brewster, D-Okla. (3)
William F. Clinger, R-Pa. (5)
Ronald D. Coleman, D-Texas (16)
Cardiss Collins, D-Ill. (7)
Wes Cooley, R-Ore. (2)
E. "Kika" de la Garza, D-Texas (15)
Cleo Fields, D-La. (4)
Jack Fields, R-Texas (8)

Harold E. Ford, D-Tenn. (9)
Pete Geren, D-Texas (12)
Sam M. Gibbons, D-Fla. (11)
Enid Greene, R-Utah (2)
Steve Gunderson, R-Wis. (3)
Mel Hancock, R-Mo. (7)
Andrew Jacobs Jr., D-Ind. (10)
Harry A. Johnston, D-Fla. (19)
Blanche Lambert Lincoln, D-Ark. (1)
Jan Meyers, R-Kan. (3)
G. V. "Sonny" Montgomery, D-Miss. (3)
Carlos J. Moorhead, R-Calif. (27)
John T. Myers, R-Ind. (7)
L. F. Payne Jr., D-Va. (5)
Pete Peterson, D-Fla. (2)
James H. Quillen, R-Tenn. (1)
Charlie Rose, D-N.C. (7)
Toby Roth, R-Wis. (8)
Patricia Schroeder, D-Colo. (1)
Gerry E. Studds, D-Mass. (10)
Ray Thornton, D-Ark. (2)
Barbara F. Vucanovich, R-Nev. (2)
Robert S. Walker, R-Pa. (16)
Pat Williams, D-Mont. (AL)
Charles Wilson, D-Texas (2)

Ran for Senate

Wayne Allard, R-Colo. (4)
Sam Brownback, R-Kan. (2)
Richard J. Durbin, D-Ill. (20)
Tim Hutchinson, R-Ark. (3)
Tim Johnson, D-S.D. (AL)
Jim Ross Lightfoot, R-Iowa (3)
Jack Reed, D-R.I. (2)
Pat Roberts, R-Kan. (1)
Robert G. Torricelli, D-N.J. (9)
Dick Zimmer, R-N.J. (12)

Bill Baker. Tauscher linked Baker to Gingrich, and criticized Baker's opposition to the ban on certain assault weapons.

• **Montana:** Veteran Democratic Rep. Pat Williams had thwarted GOP ambitions in Montana, which has a relatively even partisan split. But Williams did not seek re-election, and GOP businessman Rick Hill dashed through the opening. A former state Republican Party chairman, Hill defeated Democrat Bill Yellowtail, a former state senator and ex-regional director of the Environmental Protection Agency, to pick up the state's lone House seat. The race was marked by revelations about both candidates' pasts and was close through most of the campaign, but Hill had more money for television ads.

• **Oregon:** In the 5th District, GOP freshman Rep. Jim Bunn apparently was unseated by Democrat Darlene Hooley, a Clackamas County commissioner, in a close contest.

• **Washington:** One of the most volatile states in the country in recent House elections, Washington continued its pendulum-like behavior. Republicans, who had picked up six seats in a momentous 1994 surge, apparently lost three seats this year, giving Democrats a 5–4 seat edge in Washington's House delegation. This rebound is tentative, though, pending the counting of a mountain of absentee ballots in each of the close contests.

Heavily targeted by Democrats and their support groups, GOP Rep. Randy Tate lost the politically competitive suburban Seattle 9th District to a Democratic "rising star," state Sen. Adam Smith. Smith criticized Tate for supporting Republican initiatives on Medicare and the environment.

In the 3rd District, GOP Rep. Linda Smith, known as an outspoken advocate of campaign finance reform, apparently lost a close race to Democrat Brian Baird, a psychology professor. Baird accused Smith of not living up to her rhetoric on campaign finance issues, and said her reformist image masked a policy agenda that was too far right for the district.

In the 2nd District, Democratic state Sen. Kevin Quigley held a 1 percentage point edge over GOP freshman Rep. Jack Metcalf. A political veteran and conservative stalwart, Metcalf was something of a surprise winner in 1994 when he took the 2nd, which has a modest Democratic tilt.

• **Utah:** Orton's unprecedented Democratic reign in the traditionally Republican 3rd District apparently came to an end. The Republican nominee, venture capitalist Chris Cannon, poured about $1.6 million of his own money into the race, enabling him to score with charges that Orton was more liberal than he claimed and was ineffective. ∎

THE HOUSE

Members Move To Claim Center As Voters Demand Moderation

Ambitious agenda will yield to more cautious program when Republicans take second crack at Hill control

House Republicans may have read too much into the election that brought them to power two years ago, but they have a good grasp of the meaning of Nov. 5. It was not a revolution, it was a second chance. To ensure that the message was clear, voters narrowed the GOP majority sufficiently to discourage any residual bravado.

Now, the people who stormed the Capitol in the aftermath of the 1994 elections are searching for ways to function in the new, post-revolutionary order.

Voters have signaled that centrism and moderation will be rewarded, and neither was a defining strength of the first Republican-controlled House in four decades. Rather, returning lawmakers are looking for guidance to the final weeks of the 104th Congress, when they put their strong differences with President Clinton aside to push through initiatives that turned out to be popular with voters.

Republicans are also blowing the dust off the old House operating manual. Bipartisanship is making a comeback, at least in the early rhetoric of House leaders and the White House. And committees likely will be the centers of legislative activity, superseding all-Republican task forces created and controlled by the Speaker.

In 1994, when the GOP took control of the House, Speaker Newt Gingrich, R-Ga., and his top lieutenants rushed to Washington and claimed a broad mandate for their "Contract With America." Today, the post-election mood could not be more different.

Gingrich, whose politics and persona became a liability in many re-election campaigns, is being edged from center stage by an ascendant Trent Lott, the Republican Senate majority leader from Mississippi. *(Box, p. 46; story, p. 27)*

Although Gingrich called the election results "pretty amazing, a truly historic moment," that was not the overriding sentiment.

The mood was relief, not euphoria. Most Republican

REUTERS

Newt Gingrich, peeking over a booth as he votes Nov. 5 in Marietta, Ga., returns as House Speaker, though likely in a less stellar role.

House members know how close they came to the abyss in the closing weeks of the campaign, how near they were to *not* becoming the first Republican majority since Herbert C. Hoover's day to win back-to-back House elections.

They can take heart that the election affirmed their basic philosophy of government: A national survey of voters showed that more Americans fear a Congress that is too liberal than one that is too conservative, a sign of the center-right tilt of the electorate. And Clinton was re-elected in large part because he moved away from the left in the direction of the House's conservative ideas.

"We've all learned a great deal," said Majority Leader Dick Armey of Texas. "The president pretty well ran on our themes. And I think that gives us a great deal of opportunity to work together and to move forward on the commonly shared legislative agenda."

But House Republicans are chastened by the backlash to the more extreme elements of their agenda and to bare-knuckled tactics like government shutdowns.

Chief Deputy Whip Dennis Hastert, R-Ill., described the new mood of the House this way: "We have to work together to get bipartisan support. That's how we will put our mark on history."

Ronald M. Peters Jr., director of the Carl Albert Congressional Research and Studies Center at the University of Oklahoma, said, "What Republicans ought to be aiming for is a long-term majority where the center of gravity lies with them. If they can do that, policy will flow in their direction."

Less GOP Maneuvering Room

As a result of the election, the House GOP conference, the group of all House Republicans, is slightly more conservative than it was before. Although some of the more ardent members of the caucus' hard right were defeated, including 13 of the 74 freshmen, several moderates also lost. The new Republican freshmen are about as conservative as they were in 1994.

CQ Weekly Report November 9, 1996

Now That Voters Have Spoken . . .

"Be bloody, bold, and resolute; laugh to scorn the power of man, for none of woman born shall harm Macbeth."
—Macbeth, Act 4, Scene 1.

He has become the political version of a Shakespearean tragic hero, a figure of once-historic proportions reduced by his equally outsized frailties and a legion of enemies committed to his destruction.

House Speaker Newt Gingrich, R-Ga., who rose to power two years ago to seize the stage like few congressional leaders before him, returns to a vastly diminished kingdom to undertake a period of rebuilding.

REUTERS

At the Christian Coalition gathering in Washington on Sept. 13, Gingrich, holding an ice bucket, says that he has saved more than $400,000 a year by not having ice delivered to members.

knew, that the magic of two years ago has been spent.

Having hooked their fortunes to Gingrich's, GOP incumbents everywhere were taken to task for their allegiance to the Speaker. To further exacerbate the guilt by association, issues unrelated to their political relationship with Gingrich hurt Republican incumbents as well, including Gingrich's extreme personal unpopularity with the public and an ongoing formal ethics case that raises the possibility that the Speaker misled investigators.

Notable among the wounded was Rep. Nancy L. Johnson, R-Conn., chairman of the House ethics committee. She was repeatedly attacked by her opponent for stonewalling the over two-year probe. After enjoying re-election margins in the past two cycles of 64 percent and 70 percent respectively, she eked out just a 1 percentage point lead over Democrat Charlotte Koskoff, according to unofficial results.

His circumstances are in marked contrast to those of 1994, when, after leading the Republican takeover of Congress, he was rewarded with a rare level of loyalty from his subjects. His strategic decisions were unchallenged, his every utterance studied for its potential prophecy and his ability to consolidate power seemed limitless.

The Nov. 5 election returned Republicans to the majority and Gingrich to the top House leadership spot. But the speakership now seems more like a job than the locus of a political movement. His challenge in the 105th Congress is to redefine his role and reinvent himself.

"Newt will stay as Speaker but he won't go back to being the sort of deity that he was once revered as," said Barbara Sinclair, a congressional expert at the University of California at Riverside. "They won't be thinking that he's always right and so tactically brilliant."

Gingrich will have to be more selective about his political fights with the White House and work harder to keep fractious conservative and moderate wings of the party united. Perhaps most difficult for Gingrich, he will also have to be more circumspect in style, avoiding the kind of inflammatory public remarks that have made him a poor spokesman for the party.

During the campaign, Gingrich acknowledged in an interview with Congressional Quarterly that salvaging his image could take as long as 20 years. But some of the GOP rank and file are demanding immediate changes in the way he handles himself as one of the country's most widely recognized Republicans.

"He has to appear less strident," said Rep. Christopher Shays, R-Conn., a leading moderate who has remained loyal to Gingrich. "I don't think it will take 20 years, but it will take 20 years if he slips. He has no margin of error."

The election bore out what many Republicans already

GOP challengers were slightly more immune to the Gingrich effect than incumbents, but nonetheless were tied to him in television advertising even though they never had cast a single vote with him.

Gingrich himself stayed out of sight, usually appearing at fundraisers attended by the faithful. Splashy public appearances were rare. A leader who began his reign talking about a transformation of American politics and predicting that democratic legislatures worldwide would mimic his success seemed drained of the grand elements of his vision. In his appearances, the Speaker would schlep to the podium a plastic ice bucket to emphasize GOP frugality in cutting free ice delivery to House offices.

"Newt is poison," said Martin Frost of Texas, who as chairman of the Democratic House campaign effort led the anti-Gingrich crusade.

GOP's Dwindling Allegiance

Two years ago, Gingrich occupied a position that played to his strengths. He had the stature to dictate the agenda and a command over a unified army prepared to move that agenda without a lot of help from Democrats, who dislike the Speaker with an intensity beyond their political differences with him. They remember the days then-minority leader Gingrich portrayed their congressional majority as evil and corrupt.

The election officially closed that phase of his speakership. Although he still commands a remarkable level of loyalty from Republicans who credit him with their initial success, so many of them disavowed him in the campaign that

. . . Speaker Faces Climb Back to Grace

SCOTT J. FERRELL

REUTERS

In photo at left, Gingrich and Lott answer questions on welfare overhaul at news conference July 24. Above, Gingrich and Clinton make joint appearance June 11, 1995, at senior citizens center in Clairemont, N.H.

Republicans' allegiance is collectively weaker than it was before.

Also, Clinton's re-election victory and the narrower GOP majority in the House mean the Republicans will have to deal with Democrats and participate in coalition-building more than they did their first two years.

Paul M. Weyrich, president of the conservative Free Congress Foundation, said: "He prevailed in the 104th mainly because he could keep his troops in line with the leadership position. When you see such a slim margin, it starts to get really difficult to do that."

More suited than Gingrich to the diplomatic demands of the next two years is Senate Majority Leader Trent Lott of Mississippi, who worked with Democrats to forge some of the major legislative successes of the last Congress. *(Story, p. 27)*

Like Gingrich, Lott is telegenic, an important quality to a party hoping to improve its message delivery. And Lott is not prone to the kind of spontaneous gaffes that have marred Gingrich's ability to carry the GOP message, from his impolitic prediction that Medicare would someday "wither on the vine" to his excessively personalized lament about being snubbed by Clinton aboard Air Force One.

"Newt Gingrich will be more of a stage manager in this Congress than a leading actor," said John J. Pitney, associate government professor at Claremont McKenna College in California.

Yet his certain return to the Speaker's job gives Gingrich a place to begin his reconstruction. He is unlikely to be challenged when House Republicans meet to select leaders Nov. 20. No one has the stature to take his place, and there is insufficient time for anyone to mount a kill-the-king coup.

Although Lott may well become Congress' main liaison to the White House, Gingrich maintains the ability to help coax balky Republicans into centrist deal-making.

"Newt can set the stage in terms of being compromising rather than obstructionist," said Burdett A. Loomis, a University of Kansas political scientist.

Some analysts discount Gingrich's terrible relationship with Democrats as a handicap in forging the centrist legislative coalitions that many see as vital to the success of both Clinton and the 105th Congress.

"Politicians know how to get along with one another when it's in their interest to do so," said Brookings Institution analyst Thomas E. Mann.

"We were already seeing the emergence of a more pragmatic Newt Gingrich" in the 104th Congress, said David E. Skaggs, D-Colo. "If anything, he is a very shrewd reader of reality. He is not going to get bitten again."

The wild card for Gingrich is the ongoing investigation by the ethics panel and special counsel James M. Cole, which delves into a GOP political action committee and several foundations Gingrich used to raise money.

Unlike other elements of the Speaker's rehabilitation, the ethics case is outside his control and could prove politically fatal if the committee decides to formally charge him with violations.

Already, there are faint whispers in the palace. In the Nov. 25 issue, the conservative National Review calls on Gingrich to abdicate the speakership temporarily so he can concentrate on clearing himself.

Washington editor Kate O'Beirne argues that if the Speaker does not step aside, he will be "bled to death by Democrats using ethics charges as leeches."

But there are fewer Republicans and more Democrats overall. The GOP leadership, which had little room to maneuver when the party ratio favored them 235–197 in the 104th Congress, is now in an even tighter squeeze with a likely ratio of 227–207 and one independent, according to unofficial results.

The new political dynamic could give Republican moderates power beyond their small number. "Any 10 people, if they band together, can prevent something from happening," said Rep. Michael N. Castle, R-Del.

That is the kind of role moderates played during political fights like raising the minimum wage last year. House Majority Leader Armey had been determined to stop the Democrat-led proposal until moderates threatened to cross party lines. The leadership was forced to bring a bill to the floor, where it passed.

The role of conservative Democrats, the self-described "Blue Dogs," could also grow as both parties court the center to avoid appearing extreme. The collective lesson of the last two elections seems to be that voters do not like extremes: Clinton was punished in the 1994 midterm election for policies that were too liberal, just as Republican lawmakers suffered a voter backlash in this election.

"We can spend the next two years jockeying for tactical position between the two parties, or we can solve some problems," said Rep. David E. Skaggs, D-Colo. "I would prefer to solve some problems."

"In order to resolve conflicts, the Republicans and Democrats are going to have to broaden their base," said William F. Connelly Jr., a politics professor at Washington and Lee University.

Tactically, the House Republicans learned last year that they cannot force Clinton to sign their legislation, and that the quickest way to get something done is to find middle ground with the president, as distasteful as that is for the conservative true believers. Clinton's overwhelming re-election victory assures that they will have to continue to do so.

Gingrich and Armey have already begun discussions about a new way of governing. Their staffs say there will be more bipartisan work at the committee level, with leaders holding more extensive briefings with committee chairmen, who were shoved aside during the contract stampede. Also, the approach will be more incremental, they say. The House is unlikely to crusade for the abolition of three Cabinet departments as it did in its first term.

"This will be a small-step Congress," said John J. Pitney, associate government professor at Claremont McKenna College in California. "It will not produce landmark legislation or remake America with policy changes."

The leadership also plans to air its proposals before a wider House audience and to attempt to sell its ideas to the public before bills hit the floor. That means including a wide spectrum of Republicans and also Democrats in the process.

Increased bipartisanship is not one of Gingrich's strengths. Democrats villainized him in an avalanche of campaign televi-

MARY IUVONE

Speaker Gingrich and Majority Leader Armey confer at a Republican economic strategy meeting July 23.

sion advertising. And they pressed for the ethics probe being conducted by special counsel James M. Cole.

Lott, who works well with Democrats, is more likely to become Congress' liaison to the White House. Lott's political star is ascending. His Senate majority grew larger, not smaller, in the election. And he does not have the baggage of widespread unpopularity with the public that Gingrich does.

Changing Fortunes

Posing the greatest threat to the newly launched quest for bipartisanship is the ethics issue.

House Republicans have showed no sign of abating their multifront attack on Clinton's ethics. The controversy over large donations to the Democratic Party from foreigners, which erupted during the campaign, will be added to a long roster of issues pressed by Republicans. They include the Whitewater land deal, alleged White House abuses of FBI files and alleged cronyism in the Travel Office.

For their part, House Democrats have announced no cease-fire in their pursuit of ethics charges against Gingrich. Democrats have lodged numerous complaints, some of which were dismissed and some of which were deemed serious enough for further investigation by Cole. *(1996 Weekly Report, p. 2521)*

"It's like two cars driving down the highway. There is the ethics investigation car and the policy car," said Burdett A. Loomis, a University of Kansas political scientist. "If the ethics investigation car veers into the policy car and smashes it, then little will happen. If you keep the cars separated, things can actually get done."

Initially, the two parties will also struggle for control of the agenda. House Republicans, who feel burned by Clinton for their bold attempts to balance the federal budget, are already determined to have the president move first and propose solutions to tough problems.

Foremost among those is the question of checking the rapid growth of the financially troubled Medicare program for the elderly — an issue that helped the Democrats tar the Republicans as heartless extremists in the campaign.

Armey said that once Clinton gets the annual report on the financial health of Medicare, the House will wait to see what he does. "His trustees will give a report," he said. "We would expect the president to examine that report and to make his recommendations to Congress."

Thomas E. Mann, a Brookings Institution political scientist, said, "We have neither the situation of the president in early 1993 or of Gingrich in early 1995, where it was absolutely clear where the initial program would come from. It will be a combination of initiatives from the White House and Congress."

General policy areas are being discussed by House leaders, including some holdovers from the previous, tumultuous Congress. They include: deficit reduction and balancing the budget, drug abuse and crime, health care, and banking and utility overhauls.

"The power is going to come from the center, but this is ultimately a Republican majority, and we are going to continue to pursue the same issues we pursued over the last two years," said Republican Christopher Shays of Connecticut.

Harold Rogers, R-Ky., said both Democrats and Republicans have been bloodied in the last two elections, making a course other than the strident partisanship that marked that period desirable for both sides.

"I think we learned our lessons, and they learned theirs. Both sides will be more measured," he said. "I think we will see a more moderated Congress."

Following is a look at changes in House committees for the 105th Congress:

Agriculture

This committee faces a large turnover at the top. Chairman Pat Roberts of Kansas has won election to the Senate; ranking Democrat E. "Kika" de la Garza of Texas is retiring. Two subcommittee chairmen also are leaving: Wayne Allard of Colorado, who heads to the Senate with Roberts, and Steve Gunderson of Wisconsin, who is retiring.

Smith

GOP leaders already have promised the chairmanship to Bob Smith of Oregon, who served in the House from 1983 to 1995. The offer drew Smith out of retirement to run successfully for an open seat.

Because of Oregon's strong timber industry, Smith is likely to encourage more harvesting on public lands. The Agriculture Committee has joint jurisdiction over such issues with the Resources Committee.

Smith, a livestock producer, will probably side with cattlemen over issues such as opening up environmentally sensitive land to grazing. He also is expected to be an advocate for wheat exports, an important source of revenue in Oregon.

The subcommittee chairmanships may go to Republicans John T. Doolittle of California, Robert W. Goodlatte of Virginia or Richard W. Pombo of California. The key Democratic power broker is likely to be Charles W. Stenholm of Texas, a moderate with close ties to the cotton industry.

The 49-member panel may shrink next year. There has been talk among some Republican leaders of eliminating it, although that appears unlikely because such a move could hurt the GOP politically in rural districts.

Overall, the committee is likely to assume a lowered profile in the next two years, because Congress finished work last year on two major pieces of agriculture legislation — an omnibus farm bill (PL 104-127) known as "Freedom to Farm," and a rewrite of pesticides law (PL 104-170).

The committee will have to reauthorize about $1.7 billion in agriculture research programs that expire next year.

Appropriations

Robert L. Livingston, R-La., is expected to continue as chairman, despite the desire of the more-senior Joseph M. McDade — acquitted of federal bribery and racketeering charges in August — to take over the job he argues his seniority entitles him to. The same dynamic that prompted Speaker Newt Gingrich, R-Ga., to elevate Livingston above three more-se-

nior colleagues in early 1995 also applies to McDade: Livingston is viewed as more sympathetic to the GOP revolution and less of an old-school appropriator.

McDade, R-Pa., could wind up as chairman of the Military Construction subcommittee, one of three subcommittees where departing "cardinals" have left openings. Ernest Istook, R-Okla., is in line to take over Treasury-Postal Service, and Joe Knollenberg, R-Mich., could become chairman of the Energy and Water Development panel.

There are six vacancies on the Democratic side. First shot at filling those seats presumably goes to Democrats who had to get off the committee when the GOP took over in 1995: Rosa DeLauro of Connecticut; Carrie P. Meek of Florida; James P. Moran of Virginia; John W. Olver of Massachusetts and Ed Pastor of Arizona. Former committee member David E. Price of North Carolina, defeated for re-election in 1994, is returning to Congress in 1997. David R. Obey of Wisconsin is expected to retain his spot as ranking Democrat.

The crucial issue for the committee this year — as it has been for the past two — is that its huge workload not get bogged down in fights between deficit-conscious House GOP leaders, more spending-prone Senate appropriators and President Clinton, who has consistently pushed to raise the appropriations limit set by the annual budget resolution.

Some insiders say the limit set for fiscal 1998 discretionary appropriations — about $494 billion — is unrealistically low, about $9 billion less than the $503 billion Congress and Clinton compromised on for fiscal 1997. A failure to raise it in the new budget resolution next spring would guarantee another protracted fight.

A push to reorganize the jurisdictions of the 13 Appropriations subcommittees is unlikely to go anywhere, in part because the Senate is said to be uninterested.

Banking and Financial Services

Jim Leach of Iowa is expected to retain the chairmanship of the committee even though he had an uneven first two years at the helm. Over the span of a failed 18-month effort to overhaul banking law, Leach earned a reputation for not always consulting with his colleagues and sometimes pushing quixotic initiatives.

Texan Henry B. Gonzalez, who has been absent or inactive during much of the panel's deliberations since losing the chairman's gavel that he wielded for six years, may be challenged for the panel's top Democratic spot. An intensely proud man, Gonzalez has displayed little interest in waging losing battles or deferring to Leach, with whom he has a rocky relationship.

Two senior Democrats — John J. LaFalce of New York and Bruce F. Vento of Minnesota — may take on Gonzalez.

LaFalce is clearly tilting toward a bid; he is among the most bank-friendly members on the Democratic side of the panel, which is generally dominated by pro-consumer urban liberals. That trend is likely to continue; bank-friendly Democrat Bill Orton of Utah was defeated, and moderate Texas Democrat Ken Bentsen faces a difficult runoff.

The lineup of major subcommittee chairmen appears likely to remain stable, with Marge Roukema of New Jersey retaining financial institutions and Rick A. Lazio of New York heading the housing subcommittee.

More than half the GOP majority on the committee in the 104th Congress were freshmen, but several — including Dick Chrysler of Michigan, Frank A. Cremeans of Ohio and Fred Heineman of North Carolina — lost re-election bids.

Items on the panel's agenda include a possible revisit of efforts to repeal the Depression-era Glass-Steagall Act and an attempt to create a common charter for banks and thrifts.

Budget

John R. Kasich, R-Ohio, who earned high marks as chairman in the 104th Congress, will return to the post in the 105th. It will take a Democratic Caucus rules change to allow Martin Olav Sabo of Minnesota to return as top committee Democrat, but that is expected.

The change of rules also could permit key conservative Texas Democrat Charles W. Stenholm to remain on the committee for a fifth term. But whatever chance there was to find bipartisan common ground on the budget in the new Congress has sharply diminished with the departure of several other "Blue Dogs": Moderate Democrat Bill Orton of Utah lost his race, Glen Browder of Alabama lost a Senate primary, and Harry A. Johnston of Florida is retiring.

Kasich   **Sabo**

On the GOP side, Robert S. Walker of Pennsylvania, a close ally of Speaker Newt Gingrich, R-Ga., is retiring. But David L. Hobson of Ohio, who also sits on the Appropriations Committee, will continue to play a liaison role between the two panels.

Kasich and his GOP colleagues are likely to come under pressure to loosen the restrictions on appropriations for fiscal 1998 set by the fiscal 1997 budget resolution (H Con Res 178). Pressure from President Clinton and bipartisan agitation from members of Congress has already combined to raise the appropriations limits set by GOP budgets the past two years.

The committee's top priority will be to draft a plan to balance the budget by 2002. A key question will be what to do about Medicare; Republican anger over what they thought was demagoguery on this issue by Democrats has further reduced chances of quick bipartisan action on a balanced-budget plan this year. Republicans are determined to wait for Clinton to go first.

Commerce

With Chairman Thomas J. Bliley Jr. of Virginia and his Republican lieutenants still in charge, the Commerce Committee is on track to launch the next great deregulatory battle: electric power.

But a narrower margin between Republicans and Democrats will bolster the influence of the powerful ranking Democrat, John D. Dingell of Michigan. And Dingell has made clear he will try to slow down or kill any quick efforts to enact broad legislation that mandates retail competition in the electricity industry.

Besides electricity restructuring, committee members hope to address one of the largest environmental issues left hanging by the 104th, a revision of the superfund law governing toxic waste cleanups. The committee also will try to re-

vive stalled efforts to overhaul the Food and Drug Administration, introduce more competition in the satellite industry, resurrect nuclear waste storage legislation and monitor the implementation of the mammoth telecommunications law of 1996 (PL 104-104).

Economic and Educational Opportunities

The battle over the control of Congress is over, but partisan feuding on the Economic and Educational Opportunities Committee is just getting going. The big question: Will Republicans seek revenge for the way labor groups aggressively attacked them during their campaigns or will they put aside differences in the name of passing legislation?

The departure of Steve Gunderson, a moderate Republican from Wisconsin, likely will widen the gap between the parties on this committee. Gunderson was widely respected as the voice of reason, striking deals between the committee's predominantly pro-labor Democrats and pro-business Republicans.

At times under Democratic control, the committee was considered one of the most liberal in Congress. But under the rule of Chairman Bill Goodling, R-Pa., it has taken a much more conservative tone, with an agenda that includes shrinking government, streamlining programs and eliminating duplication of services.

Goodling   **Clay**

More of the same is anticipated in the 105th Congress. The committee is expected to revisit several bills that did not make it in the 104th, including a measure to allow workers to get compensatory time off instead of overtime pay, a job training bill that would consolidate the federal government's widely disparate programs and a proposed overhaul of the Individuals with Disabilities Education Act, a program that guarantees a disabled child's right to a free education. The panel also may address the Higher Education Act, which expires in 1998.

Liberal Rep. William L. Clay of Missouri will remain the ranking Democrat, enabling him to keep up his uniquely poetic needling of Goodling.

All told, the committee will lose four Republicans and two Democrats through retirement, electoral defeat or moves to the other chamber. Pat Williams of Montana, who is retiring, was the ranking Democrat on the Subcommittee on Postsecondary Education, Training and Life-Long Learning. All subcommittee chairmen are expected to keep their jobs.

But there is not likely to be much jockeying to fill spots on this committee. After a costly and bitter election season, Republicans are leery of battling with labor, and education has never been a big draw for either side.

Government Reform and Oversight

Indiana Republican Dan Burton is expected to assume the chairmanship, where he is likely to make Clinton administration officials squirm.

Burton would replace William F. Clinger of Pennsylvania, who is retiring. Clinger was a dogged investigator, but Burton is a fierce partisan who routinely accuses administration officials of lying.

In a statement released Nov. 6, Burton promised not to conduct witch hunts. But he vowed to continue the probe launched by Clinger into the administration's handling of hundreds of FBI files on prominent Republicans. The panel also may delve into the administration's campaign fundraising practices.

Two years ago, Burton shocked members of both parties by delivering a floor speech in which he cast doubt on a special prosecutor's investigation into the apparent suicide of former White House counsel Vincent W. Foster Jr. Burton broadly hinted that Foster had been murdered and his body secretly moved to the spot where U.S. Park Police discovered it.

While the committee is expected to spend the bulk of its time delving into the administration's alleged ethical transgressions, Burton also wants to pursue postal reform legislation and oversee governmental procurement issues.

With the retirement of Illinois Democrat Cardiss Collins, Californian Henry A. Waxman is expected to become the committee's senior Democrat. Waxman is likely to challenge Burton aggressively, particularly if the chairman pursues a full slate of investigations. Tom Lantos of California, another Democrat with a zeal for partisan combat, ranks behind Waxman.

The panel's list of junior Republicans has been depleted. Bill Zeliff of New Hampshire, chairman of the National Security, International Affairs and Criminal Justice Subcommittee, gave up his seat for an unsuccessful gubernatorial bid. Freshmen Randy Tate of Washington and Dick Chrysler of Michigan were defeated for re-election.

House Oversight

Bill Thomas of California will continue to lead this committee, which controls the internal workings of the House. Thomas, who has conducted the panel with more openness and held more frequent meetings than his Democratic predecessors on the old House Administration Committee, is expected to continue efforts to overhaul the campaign finance system.

A staunch partisan who nonetheless has forged a working relationship with Democrats on institutional matters, Thomas has guided an independent audit of House operations, cut committee spending by nearly one-third and privatized certain internal operations.

Vic Fazio of California should return as ranking Democrat.

International Relations

New York Republican Rep. Benjamin A. Gilman once was known as "gentle Ben" for his mild-mannered demeanor. But after his harsh attacks on the Clinton administration's foreign policy, that moniker no longer fits.

Gilman, 73, is expected to retain his post as chairman of the International Relations Committee, which has conducted hard-hitting investigations into administration policies toward Bosnia, Haiti and Cuba.

Gilman has sometimes rankled GOP conservatives with his moderate views on social policy. But his transformation into a fierce partisan — at least on international issues — has probably secured his hold on the chairmanship. In addition, he enjoys strong support from the American Israel Public Affairs Committee, the pre-eminent pro-Israel lobbying group.

Aside from pursuing various investigations, including a probe into the administration's campaign fundraising in foreign countries, the committee will make another try at enacting a foreign aid authorization bill. No such legislation has become law since 1985.

The panel will lose a host of members, including Toby Roth of Wisconsin, chairman of the International Economic Policy and Trade Subcommittee, who is retiring. Among the other Republicans departing are Jan Meyers of Kansas, who also is retiring, and Sam Brownback, also of Kansas, who won election to the Senate.

The anticipated departure of Indiana Republican Dan Burton, who is expected to assume the chairmanship of the Government Reform and Oversight Committee, will open up the chairmanship of the Western Hemisphere Subcommittee. Ileana Ros-Lehtinen, currently chairman of the Africa subcommittee and a harsh critic of Cuba, is in line to take that spot.

Democrats will once again be led by Lee H. Hamilton of Indiana, one of his party's leading voices on foreign policy. Robert G. Torricelli of New Jersey, a key player on U.S. policy toward Cuba and Central America, was elected to the Senate.

FILE PHOTO

Judiciary Chairman Hyde and Rep. Thomas J. Bliley Jr., R-Va., after passage of product liability legislation in March 1995.

Judiciary

Henry J. Hyde of Illinois returns as chairman for a term that promises more of the social conservative legislation that marked the 104th Congress: constitutional amendments to protect religious liberties and force a balanced budget and anti-crime and anti-drug legislation. Lamar Smith, R-Texas, will continue his quest for legal immigration restrictions while trying to get back what he lost in this year's measure to restrict illegal immigration (PL 104-208).

Two highly coveted openings are the chairmanship and top Democratic spot on the Courts and Intellectual Property Subcommittee, led this year by retiring Reps. Carlos J. Moorhead, R-Calif., and Patricia Schroeder, D-Colo. With a major effort in the offing to rewrite copyright laws for cyberspace, senior Republicans are considering giving up other prestigious assignments to lead this panel.

Bill McCollum of Florida might give up the chairmanship of the Crime Subcommittee, for example. Another possibility is F. James Sensenbrenner Jr. of Wisconsin, but only if the Science

Committee — which he is in line to chair — is eliminated.

Howard Coble, R-N.C., is the most senior member of the subcommittee who does not have an attractive alternative. But Hyde has been known to ignore seniority in filling chairmanships and may turn to Robert W. Goodlatte, R-Va., or Elton Gallegly, R-Calif. Sonny Bono, also of California, wants the post but is a long shot.

On the Democratic side, Barney Frank of Massachusetts, whose district is home to many software companies, is leaning toward giving up the Constitution Subcommittee and passing on Immigration in favor of Intellectual Property.

In fact, no one is rushing to become ranking Democrat on the Immigration subcommittee, even though the 105th Congress is likely to take up major immigration legislation. The subcommittee is extremely polarized, and Democrats do not expect to have much say in the debate. The ranking spot on Immigration may fall to Xavier Becerra of California, currently the subcommittee's most junior member.

National Security

The key question facing the committee will be settled outside its ranks: Will deficit hawks in the House Republican Conference succeed in scaling back the money the GOP tries to add to President Clinton's defense budgets?

Among committee Republicans, Chairman Floyd D. Spence of South Carolina was easily re-elected, as were all the subcommittee chairmen except conservative firebrand Robert K. Dornan of California, whose margin was razor-thin. Dornan's survival makes it likely that the committee will, once again, clash with the Senate and the Pentagon over the policy on personnel missing in combat.

Spurred by two other subcommittee chairmen, Duncan Hunter, R-Calif., and Curt Weldon, R-Pa., the panel likely will try again to accelerate deployment of anti-missile defenses, though Clinton has had little trouble blunting past efforts.

Led by Saxby Chambliss, R-Ga., and others, the committee will anchor congressional opposition to Pentagon plans to cut operating costs by privatizing some base operations and maintenance activities.

Senior Democrat Ronald V. Dellums of California has balanced his desire to slash the Pentagon budget with the desires of Democratic defense hawks who support the GOP's spending increases.

With the retirement of liberal Patricia Schroeder of Colorado, most of the committee's other prominent Democrats are lawmakers such as Ike Skelton of Missouri, Norman Sisisky of Virginia and John M. Spratt Jr. of South Carolina, all strong Pentagon supporters.

Resources

Under the leadership of Chairman Don Young of Alaska, the Resources Committee proved among the most contentious House panels, populated by Western conservatives who often faced off against more moderate Republicans and liberal Democrats. The atmosphere is not likely to change, despite the departure of some members.

Members who are leaving include Republicans Wayne Allard of Colorado, who won election to the Senate, and Wes Cooley of Oregon, who is retiring. Both have helped solidify the panel's rightward direction.

FILE PHOTO

Both Moakley, left, and Solomon, shown at a Rules Committee hearing in 1995, will remain at the helm of the panel.

George Miller of California, the ranking Democrat and Young's ideological opposite, remains on the panel, which includes just a handful of GOP moderates, including H. James Saxton, R-N.J., and Wayne T. Gilchrest, R-Md.

Moreover, the ideological divisions will be played out during debates on a series of land management issues — difficult to resolve in even the most bipartisan Congress. On the committee's plate are efforts to rewrite the endangered species law, overhaul mining regulations, address the health of the nation's forests and revamp the national parks. In recent years, the committee has deadlocked on those issues.

Rules

Both parties have vacancies to fill on the crucial Rules Committee, though the top slots likely will remain unchanged, with Gerald B. H. Solomon, R-N.Y., staying on as chairman and Joe Moakley, D-Mass., as ranking Democrat.

Appointments to the committee will be made directly by each party's leader because of the panel's critical function: It determines how and whether a bill is considered on the floor and which amendments and motions are allowed. This important gatekeeper's role also means that the lopsided ratio of nine Republicans to four Democrats — stacked to give the majority party control over legislation — will probably go unchanged even though the GOP will have a narrower majority in the 105th Congress.

The two GOP vacancies stem from the retirements of James H. Quillen of Tennessee and Enid Greene of Utah. It is unclear who will succeed them. Greene's departure leaves Republicans, who say they strive for diversity on the panel, with only one woman on the committee and with no members from the large class elected in 1994.

A Democratic vacancy opened with the retirement of Anthony C. Beilenson of California. Democrats will give first consideration to those who had to give up their seats when Democrats lost control of the House in 1994. The leading candidate to regain a seat is Louise M. Slaughter of New York.

The committee may consider procedural changes suggested by a task force headed by David Dreier, R-Calif., the committee's vice chairman. Among the recommendations: creating ad hoc committees to consider specific legislative proposals, encouraging each authorizing committee to create an oversight panel or have an investigative team, and allowing members to be considered in attendance at panel hearings if they monitor a live television broadcast.

Science

Under Chairman Robert S. Walker, R-Pa., in the 104th Congress, the Science Committee was transformed from a sleepy, nonpartisan panel into a battleground for partisan warfare.

Now that Walker is retiring and F. James Sensenbrenner Jr., R-Wis., is succeeding him, the hostilities may decline. While Sensenbrenner shares Walker's partisan edge, he does not have the power base off the committee that Walker had. Walker, a close friend of Speaker Newt Gingrich, R-Ga., ran the committee from a position of strength. Democrats accused him of running it as his personal fiefdom.

Sensenbrenner, by contrast, may have to spend more time consulting with his committee members to build support for bills. The result could be a softening of the partisanship in the 105th.

George E. Brown Jr. of California returns as ranking Democrat after surviving another tough re-election bid.

As far as legislation is concerned, there is little reason to believe the committee will be anything but the also-ran panel it has been in recent years.

It routinely approves authorization bills that are ignored by the Senate, which prefers to deal with science policy on appropriations bills. During the 104th Congress there was talk of eliminating the committee. There is an outside chance that it could actually happen in the 105th.

Sensenbrenner

Intelligence

Under the chairmanship of Larry Combest, R-Texas, the committee will resume its ambitious effort to overhaul the structure of the nation's spy system and expand the powers of the director of Central Intelligence.

Opposition from the Pentagon, which resisted any reduction in its authority, and the Defense Department's congressional allies forced the intelligence panel to accept only modest changes in 1996.

Members serve on the committee at the request of the Speaker and the Minority Leader, and the two will have several vacancies to fill. The departures include Robert G. Torricelli, D-N.J., who was elected to the Senate; Ronald D. Coleman, D-Texas, who is retiring, and Robert K. Dornan, R-Calif., the chairman of the Technical and Tactical Intelligence Subcommittee, who has completed his eight-year term on the panel.

Jane Harman, D-Calif., joined the panel late in the 104th Congress, succeeding Bill Richardson, D-N.M., whose term had expired. But Richardson said he plans to return when Coleman retires. One of the first items on the agenda for the committee will be determining whether Richardson, whose term had expired, can serve a new term on the panel.

Small Business

This committee, spared elimination two years ago in part because it was the only one led by a woman, faces an uncertain future now that Chairwoman Jan Meyers of Kansas is retiring.

If the panel survives, Larry Combest, who maintained his seniority while taking a leave of absence, is in line to become chairman. However, the Texas Republican has not yet decided whether he would rather chair Small Business or head an Agriculture subcommittee.

Joel Hefley, Colo., ranks just below Combest, but he has a subcommittee chairmanship on the National Security Committee that he may not want to relinquish.

That could put Small Business in the hands of James M. Talent of Missouri, who has chaired the Regulation and Paperwork Subcommittee in the 104th. But Republican leaders could tap another woman from the committee. Republican Linda Smith of Washington, who chairs the Tax and Finance Subcommittee, lost her bid for re-election. Sue W. Kelly, N.Y., and Sue Myrick, N.C., are possible candidates.

The lineup of subcommittee chairmen will probably not change much. Smith's defeat opens up her subcommittee; if Talent is named chairman, his subcommittee also would open up.

Standards of Official Conduct

The makeup of this controversial committee in the 105th Congress is up in the air. Several members want to get off the unpopular panel, but may be stuck there while the panel struggles to finish its biggest case, the investigation of House Speaker Newt Gingrich, R-Ga.

Service on the Committee on Standards of Official Conduct, as the committee is officially known, requires members to investigate and judge the alleged wrongdoings of their colleagues — among the least desirable assignments in the House. And seven of the current 10 members of the panel have hit their six-year service limits.

But the committee has yet to resolve the ongoing ethics case against Gingrich, who is under investigation by special counsel James M. Cole. If the panel finishes by the start of the new Congress in January, the Speaker and House minority leader would simply appoint replacements for departing members.

If it does not finish by then, the four members who have served on the investigatory subcommittee in the Gingrich case may be asked to stay on until they decide whether or not to formally charge the Speaker. If formal charges are brought, then the subcommittee would disband and the newly appointed committee would take over the next phase of the case, a trial-like phase to pass judgment on the charges.

One question that may arise is who appoints the new committee if formal charges are lodged. It would be inappropriate for Gingrich to name them, so the responsibility would fall to someone else in leadership or to the Republican conference, the group of all House Republicans.

Among the members who have served out their terms are Chairwoman Nancy L. Johnson, R-Conn., and the ranking Democrat, Jim McDermott of Washington. The three who have not are Republican Steven H. Schiff of New Mexico and Democrats Robert A. Borski of Pennsylvania and Tom Sawyer of Ohio.

FILE PHOTO

Johnson, shown with Jim McDermott, D-Wash., in December 1995, nearly lost her re-election bid Nov. 5.

Further muddying the picture is Johnson's close call. She nearly lost her House seat Nov. 5 to Democrat Charlotte Koskoff, who accused Johnson of stonewalling the investigation to protect Gingrich.

Until becoming caught up in the ethics controversy surrounding Gingrich, Johnson had no trouble defending her seat. She was re-elected with 64 percent of the vote two years ago and with 70 percent in 1992.

The touchy problem of how to reconstitute the committee will have to be hashed out by House leaders during organizational meetings for the new Congress, which begin Nov. 18.

Transportation and Infrastructure

This committee will assume a higher profile in 1997, because of the scheduled reauthorization of omnibus highway legislation, known as the Intermodal Surface Transportation Efficiency Act, or ISTEA.

Because of the scope of that bill, which determines the amount of highway and public transit funds that is allotted to the states, House leaders may add lawmakers to the 64-member committee.

Most of the veteran members are returning.

Chairman Bud Shuster, R-Pa., an accomplished dealmaker, will likely use the highway bill as leverage to advance other transportation initiatives, including legislation to take the four transportation trust funds off-budget. Such an accounting change could free federal dollars for infrastructure but is strongly opposed by deficit hawks.

The committee is expected to take up legislation making changes to the troubled national passenger railroad, Amtrak, and weaning it from federal aid.

It also may consider legislation to turn the Federal Aviation Administration into an independent agency.

Key committee Democrats will continue to be ranking member James L. Oberstar of Minnesota, who has a close working relationship with Shuster, and Nick J. Rahall II of West Virginia, the senior Democrat on the Surface Transportation subcommittee and a staunch labor ally.

Veterans' Affairs

Chairman Bob Stump, R-Ariz., is likely to continue leading this committee in a bipartisan, collegial fashion. The big change will come on the minority side, where liberal Lane Evans of Illinois is expected to succeed G. V. "Sonny" Montgomery of Mississippi as ranking Democrat. Montgomery is retiring after a 30-year career devoted mainly to unflagging support of the nation's veterans. Evans, an ardent advocate for Vietnam War veterans, clashed with Montgomery on several issues and sought unsuccessfully to oust him from the committee chairmanship in 1992.

Persian Gulf Syndrome, an illness among Persian Gulf War veterans thought to be connected to exposure to Iraqi chemical weapons, is likely to dominate the early agenda. Steve Buyer, R-Ind., a Persian Gulf veteran who said he suffered from the illness, will be a leader on the issue. Evans and Joseph P. Kennedy II, D-Mass., are likely to press for increased treatment and compensation for veterans with the syndrome.

The committee also will oversee the implementation of a new law (HR 3118 — PL 104-262) overhauling the way the Department of Veterans Affairs (VA) provides medical treatment, and review the complex disability benefits system. A VA-sponsored commission is scheduled to release a review of the existing system by January.

The departure of Tim Hutchinson, R-Ark., who won a Senate seat, leaves open the chairmanship of the Hospitals and Health Care Subcommittee. Aides speculate that Buyer might prefer that post to his current chairmanship of the Education, Training, Employment and Housing Subcommittee. If Buyer shifts, Jack Quinn, R-N.Y., may fill the education chairmanship. Terry Everett, R-Ala., will likely remain chairman of the Compensation, Pension, Insurance and Memorial Affairs Subcommittee.

Ways and Means

With few changes in the lineup among senior members, the temperament of the panel will remain largely the same. The only potential wild card is the relationship between the returning chairman, Bill Archer of Texas, a strong conservative, and the new senior Democrat, Charles B. Rangel of New York, a liberal known for his brash and sometimes provocative style.

In the 104th, the two lawmakers exhibited the compatibility of oil and water. However, now that Rangel has moved up to ranking Democrat (Sam M. Gibbons of Florida is retiring), some committee watchers say he will be more restrained. Archer says he wants the panel to work in a more bipartisan manner.

Archer also would like to shrink the committee to the size it was at the beginning of the 104th Congress: 36. By the end of last session, Archer had been forced to expand to accommodate two former Democrats who, in switching to the GOP, asked for seats on the committee.

The agenda will focus on many of the same budget-related policy issues — Medicare and taxes — as last year, assuming that Congress decides to pursue a balanced-budget plan. Bipartisan commissions are expected to be named to examine Medicare and Social Security, but the committee is likely to take actions to keep Medicare solvent for 10 years before any commission issues a report.

Any budget package will likely include a $500-per-child tax credit and cuts in capital gains and estate taxes. Archer also has pledged to look at transportation excise taxes, including the airline ticket tax and highway-related taxes.

The Class of 1996 Reflects Mixed Verdict of Voters

Portrait of freshmen highlights a potential conflict over approach to governing in 105th Congress

The 105th Congress already has a place in the history books, thanks to the voters' split decision on Nov. 5. For the first time, Americans re-elected Republican majorities in the House and Senate and also granted a second term to a Democratic president.

The class of 1996 reflects the mixed verdict of the November election. In the Senate, three-fifths of the newcomers are Republican, while in the House, almost three-fifths of the freshmen are Democrats.

This is a break in the pattern from recent elections. In 1992, both the House and Senate freshman groups were predominantly Democratic. In 1994, all the Senate freshmen and the overwhelming majority of House freshmen were Republicans.

This year's nine freshman GOP senators — including three who captured open Democratic seats — will help boost their party from 53 Senate seats in the 104th Congress to 55 seats in the 105th — a level of strength the party has not enjoyed since Ronald Reagan's first term as president. And in 1998, Democrats must defend a majority of the Senate seats at stake.

In the House, by contrast, Republicans saw their edge in the 104th Congress sliced almost in half on Election Day, as 22 Democrats ousted GOP incumbents or captured Republican open seats. With three Texas races to be decided on Dec. 10 and some results still open to challenge, it looks like Democrats will head into the 1998 election needing only a 10-seat gain to win a House majority.

The other obvious conclusion to draw from the class of 1996 is that its ideological coloration gives little reason to expect an end to the pitched battles over governing philosophy that dominated the last Congress and the recent campaign.

Among the House freshmen, for example, are Republicans with strongly held views on issues such as abortion and gun owners' rights, who drew grass-roots backing from conservative Christian activists. Other freshman Republicans are more

THE ASSOCIATED PRESS

Democrat Mary Landrieu, husband Frank Snellings and son, Connor, celebrate in New Orleans her victory Nov. 5 in a tight Senate race.

business-oriented, focusing less on social issues than on cutting federal taxes, spending and regulations.

And in Democratic ranks, there are a dozen left-of-center freshmen whose campaigns benefited handsomely from AFL-CIO advertising targeted at GOP incumbents whom organized labor regarded as anti-union.

In the Senate, virtually all the freshman GOP senators rate as more conservative than the people whose seats they are taking. But the chamber's six Democratic first-termers should counter the rightward tug.

Senate: Rightward Swing

Two Southern states and one in the Midwest gave conservative Republicans their clearest-cut ideological gains: Democrats Jim Exon in Nebraska, Howell Heflin in Alabama and David Pryor in Arkansas were generally regarded as politically moderate senators, but with their retirements in 1996, voters in each of those states elected conservative Republicans — businessman Chuck Hagel in Nebraska, two-term Rep. Tim Hutchinson in Arkansas and Jeff Sessions, the Alabama attorney general.

Also, there is a noticeable shift to the right even in some of the states where one Republican is simply replacing another. In Kansas, the Senate delegation for years consisted of conservative pragmatist Bob Dole and moderate-minded Nancy Landon Kassebaum, who backed abortion rights and some gun-control efforts. In the 105th, Kansas' senators will be Sam Brownback, a resolutely conservative activist in the GOP House class of 1994, and Pat Roberts, who, like his House colleague Brownback, has a more conservative posture on social issues than did Kassebaum.

In Wyoming, Republican state Sen. Mike Enzi got campaign help from abortion foes in winning the seat vacated by GOP veteran Alan K. Simpson, who supported abortion rights. There is a similar distinction on social issues between Colorado Rep. Wayne Allard and the Republican he is replacing in the Senate, Hank Brown.

CQ Weekly Report November 9, 1996

Among the Senate's new Democrats, Rep. Tim Johnson of South Dakota has the distinction of being the only 1996 conqueror of a Senate incumbent — Republican Larry Pressler. Though Johnson is mostly known as a solid specialist in agricultural issues and other rural concerns, he also is plainly less conservative than Pressler.

Democratic Reps. Richard G. Durbin in Illinois, Jack Reed in Rhode Island and Robert J. Torricelli in New Jersey have voted a progressive line in the House, and former Georgia Secretary of State Max Cleland nudged past a staunchly conservative GOP foe by promising to vote in the fashion of outgoing Democrat Sam Nunn.

In Louisiana, former state Treasurer Mary L. Landrieu is a couple of notches to the left of retiring Democrat J. Bennett Johnston. Landrieu should find some common ground with the other woman new to the Senate, Susan Collins of Maine, a rare moderate Republican in the mold of her predecessor, William S. Cohen.

There will be nine women in the new Senate, the same as in the 104th Congress. Newcomers Collins and Landrieu balance the departures of Kassebaum, who retired, and her Kansas colleague Sheila Frahm, who lost in the primary to Brownback. (She had been appointed to replace Dole when he left the Senate). Two states, Maine and California, will have all-women Senate delegations in the 105th.

House: Republican Losses

When it convenes in January, the House will be missing some of the most conservative Republicans who helped make the chamber a theater for partisan combat in 1995. Fourteen of the 18 Republican incumbents who lost were class of 1994 freshmen, and the party's other four losers were all first elected in either 1990 or 1992.

The freshman GOP casualties included Michigan's Dick Chrysler, an ardent supporter of the House GOP's "Contract With America." He lost to former Democratic state Sen. Deborah Ann Stabenow in one of the AFL-CIO's premier target races. Two former Democratic House members avenged their 1994 losses to staunch GOP conservatives: Ohio's Ted Strickland bested Frank A. Cremeans and North Carolina's David Price defeated Republican freshman Fred Heinemann.

Connecticut state Sen. James H. Maloney scored a big coup for the Democratic Party by upsetting three-term Republican Gary A. Franks, one of only two blacks in the House GOP. The national Republican Party liked to showcase the conservative Franks, who touted an autobiographical book on a national publicity tour.

There will be 37 black House members in the 105th Congress (not counting non-voting members), compared with 38 in the 104th. With Franks' defeat and the redistricting-forced retirement of Louisiana's Cleo Fields (who was replaced by a white), the net loss for blacks would have been two without the Indiana victory of black Democrat Julia Carson, who succeeds retiring white Democratic Rep. Andrew Jacobs Jr.

The Hispanic Caucus grows by one in the 105th, to 18. Texas Democrat Silvestre Reyes replaces Ronald D. Coleman, who retired. The only Hispanic member who retired, Democrat E. "Kika" de la Garza, will be succeeded by Democrat Ruben Hinojosa.

Although most of the GOP incumbents who fell were conservatives, Democrats in Massachusetts toppled two class of 1992 Republicans of a more moderate stripe. Rep. Peter I. Blute lost to Jim McGovern, a longtime aide to Democratic Rep. Joe Moakley, and Rep. Peter G. Torkildsen lost in a rematch against lawyer John F. Tierney. And in New Jersey, Democratic state Sen. and Paterson Mayor William J. Pascrell defeated one of the leading freshman GOP moderates, Bill Martini.

Only three GOP challengers succeeded in ousting House Democratic incumbents: Kentucky state Rep. Anne Northup defeated freshman Democrat Mike Ward; businessman Chris Cannon turned out three-term Utah Democrat Bill Orton; and former prosecutor Kenny Hulshof won his rematch against 10-term Missouri Democrat Harold L. Volkmer.

The key factor enabling the Republican Party to retain its House majority was its success in open-seat races. Republicans held on to 19 of their own open districts, including three in Kansas and two apiece in Pennsylvania, Texas and Missouri.

Republicans also retained two open seats where scandal had forced the retirement of freshman GOP incumbents. In Utah, businessman Merrill Cook succeeds Enid Greene, and in Oregon, former Rep. Bob Smith returns to the seat that was held for a term by Wes Cooley. Smith, who served from 1983 to 1995, has been promised the chairmanship of the Agriculture Committee.

And Republicans were able to capture 10 open districts that had been in Democratic hands in the 104th — seven of them in the South, two in the rural West and one in rural southern Illinois.

These GOP successes helped offset the party's House incumbent defeats, and they lend credibility to Republican claims that in some parts of the country at least, traditionally Democratic voters are moving away from past electoral behavior and aligning with the GOP. ■

Budget Will Still Be the Issue To Test Moderates' Muscle

Conventional post-election wisdom has it that, after years as second-class citizens, moderates from both parties will finally come into their own as power brokers and swing votes in the new Congress. But wait a minute.

While moderates have already shown they can pull their more radical colleagues toward them on some legislation, the issue that brought many moderates to the center in the first place — the budget — remains their most galling failure. It could very well remain that in the next Congress.

Not since "Boll Weevil" Democrats defected to join a solid bloc of House Republicans to back President Ronald Reagan's budget in 1981 have centrists of either party been able to forge a significant cross-aisle budget victory. Despite persistent attempts by House and Senate centrists in 1995 and 1996, they could not form a majority in the middle behind their compromise budget proposals.

The fact is that while moderates have already had some success in luring their party wings away from extreme positions in some areas, they have failed to pry most of their colleagues away from hard-line positions on core, party-defining issues such as tax cuts and the government's proper role in running programs such as Medicaid and Medicare. Without some compromise on issues like these, there can be no fundamental agreement on the budget.

This could be the real test, not just of moderates' political potency, but of all the centrist rhetoric dished up by party leaders in the days after the elections.

Budget experts say falling deficit numbers and broad acceptance of the goal of a balanced budget by 2002 make next year the perfect time for the parties to come together on a bipartisan package that could finally put the deficit behind them. But Republican anger over what they call the Democrats' "Medi-scare" campaign rhetoric has poisoned chances for quick action and could drive the budget debate back into the same polarized, revenge-seeking mode that blocked action in the last Congress.

"There will either be a centrist budget or there will be no budget," said key House conservative Democrat Charles W. Stenholm of Texas. "On almost any area you want to talk about, there will either be a centrist position that can pass and get through the Senate or there will be political posturing."

Centrists like Stenholm have been urging their House col-

Stenholm

Boehlert

Breaux

Lieberman

leagues toward the so-called sensible center for years, with only occasional success. But the back-to-back failures of radical proposals from both parties — President Clinton's sweeping health care reform plan in 1994, and House Speaker Newt Gingrich's budget package and government shutdown in 1995 — have left chastened leaders looking for a new way to do business.

Gingrich, R-Ga., now talks of finding "common ground" with Clinton, and Democratic congressional leaders are preaching accommodation. "People want moderate, modest, practical, sensible solutions," House Minority Leader Richard A. Gephardt, D-Mo., told *The Washington Post.*

After years of ignoring or just barely tolerating the sort of Democrats who defected to Reagan in 1981, liberal Democratic leaders are wooing them. "That's the only way that we're going to be able to operate," said a senior House Democratic aide.

Hot Times in the Senate

Surprisingly, prospects for moderation seem better in the House than they do in the Senate. While the once-radically polarized House seems to be moving toward the center, the traditionally centrist Senate seems headed the other way, as moderates exit and are replaced by hard-liners.

"Rather than the Senate being the saucer in which to pour the tea to cool, in fact it's likely to turn up the heat," said Brookings Institution congressional scholar Thomas E. Mann, reversing the old George Washington dictum about the deliberative Senate being the place where hotheaded House legislation gets a chance to cool.

"There's an irony here," said centrist Senate Democrat Jospeh I. Lieberman of Connecticut. "Both parties have moved right, but that rightward movement has brought more Democrats to the center and more Republicans to the edge."

Senate-watchers point to the exodus of moderate senators such as Nancy Landon Kassebaum, R-Kan., Jim Exon, D-Neb., and Hank Brown, R-Colo., and the corresponding arrival of harder-edged replacements such as Wayne Allard, R-Colo., Sam Brownback, R-Kan., and Chuck Hagel, R-Neb.

"If you read their backgrounds, [they are] pretty much the profile of an ideologue," said centrist Democratic Sen. John B. Breaux of Louisiana. "But sometimes when you get to the Senate, ideologues become more pragmatic," he added hopefully.

Not likely, said Mann. "Most of the moderates have left. . . . Now they think [Senate Majority Leader] Trent [Lott] is too soft."

The success of any moderate agenda in the Senate de-

Thin Margins Did Not Equal Gridlock

It's two weeks after the election. The House membership meets to organize but is immediately thrown into confusion. One party has a two-vote majority — but five seats from one state have yet to be decided. Chaos ensues.

This scenario could have easily flowed from this year's elections. But the time was 1838, when it took two weeks and 11 ballots to decide the race for Speaker.

Since 1789, the House majority has had a controlling margin of 10 or fewer seats on 14 occasions. Unofficial results of this year's election show that the House Republicans' margin of control may have narrowed to about twice that. Still, even thin margins of 10 or fewer do not necessarily result in a House consumed by partisanship and unable to function.

Historic legislation, such as the Glass-Steagall Act, the Sherman Antitrust Act, and both the enactment and the repeal of Prohibition, were passed by Congresses in which House control was tenuous. Still, those sessions were marked by frequent outbursts that would make the partisan jabs of the 104th Congress look genial.

Virtually all these Houses were elected during times of great national turbulence. War, depression, the slavery debate and the growing pains of the new nation all occurred when the leaders of the House had to run the chamber with virtually no votes to spare.

The Ways and Means

For three of the first four Congresses (2nd, 3rd and 4th), the House was run by a narrow majority. Two of the three sessions were controlled by the Federalists, the party of President George Washington.

During those Congresses, forces led by Federalist Alexander Hamilton (who was Treasury secretary for most of this period), battled with Secretary of State Thomas Jefferson (and his forces led by James Madison) over the direction of the new country. Hamilton argued for a strong central government; Jefferson for power to the states.

By the 4th Congress, suspicion of Hamilton and his economic plans led to the creation of one of the first permanent standing committees — Ways and Means.

The years between 1825 and the start of the Civil War in 1861 saw some of the nastiest and most violent debates in the history of the House. Five Houses during this period (the 19th, 25th, 26th, 30th and 31st) were controlled by thin margins. In 1838, a pro-slavery freshman, William J. Graves, Whig-Ky., was so incensed by comments made by another freshman, Jonathan Cilley, D-Maine, that he challenged Cilley to a duel and killed him. The House investigated but decided to take no action because there had been no breach of Cilley's privileges in the House. (By the 31st Congress (1849–51), members routinely brought guns and knives to the floor.)

The 26th Congress (1839–41) began with 120 Democrats and 118 Whigs, with five New Jersey seats being contested. After nearly two weeks of bitter debate, the House finally agreed to begin voting for Speaker on Dec. 14. After 11 ballots, Whig Robert M. T. Hunter of Virginia beat 13 candidates for the job on Dec. 16. Similarly, the contest over Speaker in the 31st Congress (1849–51) lasted three weeks.

These closely divided Houses passed laws admitting various states into the union and creating the first sub-treasuries to hold federal monies. Members also thought, briefly, that they had settled the slavery question with passage of the Compromise of 1850, which governed the admittance of California, New Mexico and Utah under terms acceptable to both sides.

Times of War

The House also has found itself closely divided during times of war. Five of the 13 narrowly controlled Houses (the 4th, 5th, 65th, 78th and 83rd) were elected shortly before or during a war.

At the end of the 4th Congress, vicious debate broke out over the terms of Jay's Treaty, which sought to end British retaliation for the neutrality the United States had adopted during the French Revolution.

Former Speaker Frederick Muhlenberg of Pennsylvania was stabbed in the back by his brother-in-law in a fight over the treaty. Matthew Lyon, R-Vt., spat tobacco juice into the face of Connecticut Federalist Roger Griswold during a heated exchange.

Voters cut the Democrats' House margin from 106 seats to 10 during the midterm 1942 elections (the 78th Congress). And the Korean War and the election of President Dwight D. Eisenhower in 1952 ousted Democrats from House control, giving the GOP a narrow, 10-seat margin.

Legislation virtually spewed from these closely divided Congresses. The 5th Congress passed the original Alien and Sedition Act, which made it a crime to speak against the government about the war effort. The 65th Congress added the Espionage Act, which allowed a great deal of postal censorship, and the Trading with the Enemies Act.

The 65th Congress also passed Prohibition, the 18th amendment to the Constitution. The House passed a resolution to send the women's suffrage amendment to the states. During World War II, Congress enacted the GI Bill of Rights, which guaranteed aid to returning veterans.

The Houses of the 25th and 72nd Congresses had narrow margins as the country struggled through deep economic problems. The 1836 elections saw Democratic control of the House narrowed to a one-vote margin over the Whigs. The Panic of 1837 followed the election, leading to bank failures and high unemployment. In 1931, the House went from Republican to Democratic control following the midterm election of Herbert Hoover. The dogged fights between Hoover and the House led to the elevation of Democratic House Speaker John Nance Garner as vice presidential candidate on the 1934 Democratic ticket, the only Speaker to be elected on a national ticket.

> War, depression, the slavery debate and the growing pains of the new nation all occurred when House leaders had to run the chamber with virtually no votes to spare.

pends heavily on Lott, R-Miss., who got where he is with the support of the Senate's increasingly conservative Republican conference. Lieberman argued that middle-of-the-roadism and a strategic alliance with Democrats is the only way Lott can succeed.

"Neither the liberals nor the conservatives have enough votes to achieve a majority with a hard ideological program," Lieberman said. "Trent Lott can be a very productive majority leader working with the president and centrist Democrats." Perhaps, but is not that a recipe for political suicide? "It's not going to be easy for him to do that in a caucus that has moved somewhat to the right," Lieberman conceded.

Making the Difference

House moderates seem to have more reason to be sanguine about their prospects, and indeed they already claim substantial success.

Centrist House Republican Sherwood Boehlert of New York said it was moderates who shaped most of the major legislative achievements that turned things around for the GOP House in the months leading up to the elections. Boehlert pointed to the toned-down welfare reform bill, the minimum wage increase, a rush of environmental legislation and higher spending for education. All of it bore the moderates' fingerprints, he insisted. "Moderates came into their own in 1996," he said. "In 1997, moderates will make the difference."

Moderates claim success on these issues and more, but this raises a chicken-and-egg question: Are those achievements the work of the centrists, or were the centrists just bystanders in a process in which leaders were headed for the center anyway?

Congressional scholar James A. Thurber said the most powerful force behind most of the centrist legislation at the end of the last Congress was a realization by leaders that they had to run to the middle, and by House committee chairs — House Appropriations Chairman Robert L. Livingston, R-La., is the chief example — that they had to shrug off a hard-line agenda if they wanted to get something done.

"The moderates are going to say they did it," said Thurber, who is director of American University's Center for Congressional and Presidential Studies. But "I don't think the moderates did it by themselves. The electorate helped."

When polls showed voters blaming Republicans 2-to-1 for the government shutdown last year, leaders like Gingrich and former Senate Majority Leader Bob Dole, R-Kan., concluded they were too far out of the mainstream and tried to steer their party back. Gingrich suffered public humiliation when he first tried to persuade the GOP rank and file to relent and reopen the government, only to have the idea swatted down by angry conservatives who wanted to continue to play hardball with the White House.

One key to deciding how much credit to give moderates for legislative changes of direction is to determine whether their votes really made a difference in passing legislation that would otherwise have failed. Centrists are rarely more powerful than when they follow through on threats to abandon their own party and vote with the enemy to make their point.

That is what Boll Weevil Democrats did in 1981, when they turned their backs on party leaders to embrace the Reagan budget and tax plans. It is a high-risk strategy that tends to infuriate party leaders. When Rep. Breaux traded his vote on a tax bill to the Reagan White House in 1981 for promises to help Louisiana agriculture, House

Rules Committee Chairman Richard Bolling, D-Mo., confronted his junior colleague and called him a "cheap whore." As the irreverent and unrepentant Breaux told the story at the time, he shot back, "That's not true! I'm not cheap!"

GOP Moderates Revolt

In at least one instance in 1995, House Republican moderates put relations with their party leaders at similar risk by walking away on a key vote on a controversial environmental issue. As part of their drive to scale back government regulation, GOP leaders had approved the attachment of 17 legislative riders to the VA-HUD appropriations bill, all of them designed to bar or restrict various regulatory activities by the Environmental Protection Agency (EPA). That struck Boehlert and other GOP moderates as grossly excessive, and on July 28, they backed a Democratic amendment to strip the language.

In a stunning blow to the GOP House leadership, the amendment prevailed on a narrow 212–206 vote. Fully 51 Republicans joined with a strong majority of Democrats. Embarrassed GOP leaders pulled the bill, and when they brought it back up again three days later, they managed to eke out a 210–210 tie that killed the amendment. Pro-environment Republicans had made their point, however, and the riders were later dropped. (*1995 Almanac, p. 11–87*)

That sort of success was never replicated on high-profile budget issues, although a centrist Senate group led by Breaux and Sen. John H. Chafee, R-R.I., came tantalizingly close. In May of this year, the Senate rejected a budget proposal by the Chafee-Breaux group on a surprisingly narrow 46–53 vote, as 22 Republicans joined 24 Democrats to support it. (*1996 Weekly Report, p. 1449*)

The plan had smaller tax cuts and smaller spending cuts than the Republican budget resolution, but it also contained a controversial proposal to save money by scaling back the Consumer Price Index (CPI), the measurement that sets the size of Social Security cost-of-living adjustments and the rate at which income taxes are indexed against inflation. "We were pleasantly surprised at how well we did," said Breaux. "We'd counted and thought we'd get 35–36 [votes] at the most."

In the House, a similar bipartisan effort headed by centrist Reps. Fred Upton, R-Mich., and Tim Roemer, D-Ind., collapsed without producing a budget for reasons that are still murky. Meanwhile, "Blue Dog" conservative Democrats produced a plan similar to the Chafee-Breaux budget, except that it dictated no tax cuts until the budget was balanced and did not rely on CPI changes to the degree the Senate alternative did.

To their surprise, the Blue Dogs drew more than half the House Democrats in losing 130–295 on May 16. The trouble was that they could lure only 20 Republicans away from the hard-line GOP insistence on tax cuts and major changes in entitlement programs such as Medicare and Medicaid. (*1996 Weekly Report, p. 1379*)

"If the Democrats . . . had offered this budget two years ago," said Rep. Nick Smith, R-Mich., during the 1996 debate, "everybody on this side of the aisle would have voted for it."

In what could turn out to be a pivotal test of the House's new moderate streak, Blue Dog centrists hope to give Smith and the rest of the GOP a chance to vote for a similar plan in 1997. ∎

Battle Over Gingrich Probe May Cast a Long Shadow

Self-policing by House in doubt as divisions leave work of ethics panel at a standstill

The political war raging over the ethics investigation of House Speaker Newt Gingrich, R-Ga., has severely weakened the self-policing process in the House, with potential long-term consequences for the institution.

The House ethics committee, which for years has depended on bipartisanship and consensus-building to do its work, has ground to a near standstill in the Gingrich case, beset by partisan divisions, infighting and personal animosity among its 10 members.

Republicans on the panel view the charges against the Speaker as politically motivated and have taken a go-slow approach, even as the committee has come under intense criticism for unusually long delays at every step of the investigation, according to people knowledgeable about the secretive committee's internal workings.

"The Republicans are not up to it," acknowledged one frustrated Republican close to the panel. "They are the problem."

But Democrats have been equally partisan in their activities on the panel, driven by what one observer described as a "pathological hatred" of Gingrich.

Neither side seems capable of carrying on the traditions of the Committee on Standards of Official Conduct, as it is formally known. Although it has been criticized over the years for dealing too gently with lawmakers' ethical lapses, its members generally have taken their mandate to heart and overcome partisanship for the sake of protecting the ethics process, and thereby, the House.

"The committee has absolutely repudiated all of its precedents and procedures," said Stanley Brand, a Washington ethics attorney and former House counsel.

"For 30 years it was a consensus committee. There have been strong dis-

CQ Weekly Report Sept. 21, 1996

SCOTT J. FERRELL

Johnson leaves a meeting about Gingrich ethics charges Sept. 19.

agreements, but it was always able to move forward one way or another."

The last time the ethics committee dealt with a major investigation of a House Speaker, it brought the case to an advanced stage in little under a year. Former Speaker Jim Wright, D-Texas, resigned in 1989 after the panel concluded there was reason to believe he had broken House rules. This time, it took the committee about that long to hire an outside counsel, which is an early step in the process. It has had the case under its wing for two years, and now has run out of time to finish it by the target Oct. 4 adjournment date. *(Box, p. 61)*

Ethics attorney William Canfield, a former counsel to the Senate Ethics Committee, said, "The committee, for the first time I can recall, has come to an impasse based on what I think are

partisan considerations rather than the facts underlying the complaint."

The panel's crippling partisan divides are symptomatic of the acrimony and incivility that have pervaded the House itself. Its troubles bring to mind Wright's prophetic lament in 1989, when he warned in his resignation speech that a new brand of base partisanship was driving the institution to "mindless cannibalism."

If the process self-destructs and it becomes impossible to credibly resolve questions of ethical behavior internally, political pressure from the outside for reform is sure to grow.

Dennis F. Thompson, a Harvard professor and ethics expert who advocates the creation of an outside commission to handle ethics complaints against lawmakers, said that the committee's treatment of the Gingrich investigation "is a prime example of the problems of self-policing in an increasingly partisan legislature."

He added, "A case that involves the Speaker brings out the worst in everybody."

Internal Bad Blood

Nowhere are the committee's problems more manifest than in the relationship between Chairman Nancy L. Johnson, R-Conn., and ranking minority member Jim McDermott, D-Wash.

The committee, the only one in the House that is evenly split among Republicans and Democrats, cannot rely on a tiebreaker to resolve disputes. So it has depended heavily in the past on a good working relationship between the people in the two top posts to lead it to agreement.

That kind of rapport has not developed between Johnson and McDermott. Their relationship has been marked by loss of mutual respect, and each has taken unilateral steps that angered the other.

In open defiance of committee protocol, McDermott on Sept. 20 called a

Two Probes, Two Approaches

In recent years, two House Speakers have come under the scrutiny of the Committee on Standards of Official Conduct: former Speaker Jim Wright, D-Texas, and Speaker Newt Gingrich, R-Ga.

The ethics committee took different approaches to the two probes, taking much longer at every step in the process in the Gingrich investigation than in the Wright case.

Wright

The committee took one year to bring the investigation to completion.

In May 1988, Gingrich filed a complaint alleging several violations of House rules. The watchdog group Common Cause urged the committee to investigate and to appoint an outside counsel.

The next month, on June 9, the committee opened a preliminary inquiry into six allegations.

A month later, on July 26, the committee hired Chicago lawyer Richard J. Phelan as outside counsel.

The committee announced April 17, 1989, that it had found "reason to believe" that Wright violated the rules in 69 instances, saying that he used bulk sales of a book he wrote to evade limits on lawmakers' outside income and that he improperly accepted gifts from a Fort Worth real estate developer.

The committee dismissed a host of other charges that Phelan had recommended, and it dropped all the allegations raised by Gingrich.

On May 31, Wright, his political support in the House drained, resigned rather than face a disciplinary hearing, a trial-like phase of the process. *(1989 Almanac, p. 36)*

Gingrich

The committee has been working on the Gingrich case for two years and does not appear close to resolution.

Former Democratic Rep. Ben Jones of Georgia filed a complaint Sept. 7, 1994, alleging that Gingrich improperly financed a college course he taught. On Dec. 8, 1994, House Minority Whip David E. Bonior of Michigan called for appointment of an outside counsel.

Several months later, throughout the summer of 1995, the committee remained deadlocked over whether to appoint an outside counsel. On Dec. 6, 1995, the committee announced that it found Gingrich guilty of violating House rules in three instances, but imposed no punishment. It dismissed two other complaints and turned the one involving the funding of the college course over to independent counsel James M. Cole. *(1995 Almanac, p. I-20)*

In December 1995, House Democrats filed additional charges seeking to expand the investigation into the financing of Gingrich's political activities. The committee has not commented on the status of those allegations.

The committee on March 29 ruled on another complaint, saying Gingrich broke House rules by allowing telecommunications executive Don Jones to work as a volunteer in his office. It recommended no punishment. A Democrat asked the committee on April 22 to re-examine the complaint, but it declined to do so on Sept. 19.

Last month, Cole gave an ethics subcommittee his report, but the panel announced no other developments.

---

press briefing without Johnson present and accused Republicans of deliberately delaying release of an investigatory report completed in August by James M. Cole, the special counsel investigating a portion of the complaints against Gingrich.

"It's outrageous that it would be buried at the end of this session," McDermott said.

McDermott said that he tried repeatedly to persuade Johnson to wrap up the Gingrich case before the 1996 political season, but was unsuccessful.

In a prepared response, Johnson shot back a warning that McDermott was violating House rules with his outspokenness. "If any member of the House ethics committee wants to comment publicly about pending cases and

publicy urge support of a specific course of action . . . then he or she should resign from the committee."

McDermott has publicly criticized Johnson for a lack of leadership. If the Gingrich case cannot be resolved because of the panel's perpetual deadlocks, he said in a highly unusual floor statement in July, "the chair of the committee will have destroyed the ethics committee by failing to lead the committee to resolution of an issue of major importance."

McDermott says the problem, as he sees it, is Johnson's inability to rally the panel's Republicans behind her. "If the chair wants to drive the committee to consensus, at some point, you have to be able to deliver some votes," he said.

For her part, Johnson did not inform

McDermott of her decision in early September to consult Majority Leader Dick Armey, R-Texas, after Cole submitted his report. Armey later claimed that the two of them never discussed the Cole report.

Johnson, asked about her relationship with McDermott, declined to address it, saying only, "We both have a strong commitment to this committee and to the House."

She noted that the committee has had an extraordinarily large workload, including interpreting the new House gift ban.

The strains between the two are a marked contrast to the leadership of previous committees.

Rep. Julian C. Dixon, D-Calif., who chaired the panel during the Wright investigation, said that he and then ranking member Rep. John T. Myers, R-Ind., frequently met together to work out compromises and agreements on major issues. Then they took them to the full committee, where they were often ratified.

"Ninety-nine out of one hundred times, we reached agreement," he said. "There was a degree of collegiality on the committee that doesn't seem to be there now."

Myers said: "We did not tolerate partisanship."

Myers recalled that he and Dixon agreed quickly on the need for an outside counsel in the Wright case, that both concurred in the selection of Chicago attorney Richard J. Phelan and that they then traveled around the country together with the committee's attorneys to interview witnesses.

By contrast, Johnson and McDermott sometimes appoint other members, one from each side, to try to find consensus. But issues often wind up being debated by the full committee in hours-long and often fruitless discussions ending in deadlock.

According to one participant, committee member Rep. Benjamin L. Cardin, D-Md., once complained that Johnson and McDermott "should come to us with a resolution." Cardin declined to be interviewed.

Outside Pressures

Outside pressures have exacerbated the committee's internal problems. The panel has attempted to do some of the most sensitive work in the House with bullets flying overhead.

Democrats led by Minority Whip David E. Bonior, Mich., have repeatedly accused it of stonewalling the Gingrich investigation. They have tried to force it to disclose its progress with a series of privileged resolutions, which have failed on party-line votes.

The latest round came the week of Sept. 16. Democrats brought to the floor a resolution (H Res 526) on Sept. 19 demanding the release of the Cole report, even though the committee has yet to formally act on it. The measure was tabled 225–179 along party lines.

Earlier the same day, Republicans offered their own resolution (H Res 524) by Rep. John Linder, R-Ga., Gingrich's chief defender, calling for an independent counsel to investigate Mi-

nority Leader Richard A. Gephardt, Mo., who also is the target of a pending ethics complaint. The House approved, 395–9, a motion to table it.

Committee members also are being buffeted by criticism back home. In Connecticut, Johnson's Democratic opponent, Charlotte Koskoff, has been calling her "Stonewall Johnson," and

REUTERS

McDermott arrives at Sept. 19 meeting.

newspaper editoral boards in her district have pounded her relentlessly for not making the Cole report public. In New Mexico, Republican Rep. Steven H. Schiff's Democratic opponent has similarly accused him of protecting Gingrich.

Johnson issued a statement on Sept. 19 saying the committee would not be bullied into releasing the report until an investigative subcommittee in charge of reviewing the Gingrich allegations finishes its work.

There is precedent for Johnson's position. In the Wright case, the ethics committee did not release the investiga-

tory report by outside counsel Phelan until it announced it was bringing formal charges.

The committee also on Sept. 19 dismissed a complaint unrelated to the bulk of the Gingrich charges. In a letter to the Speaker, the committee criticized Gingrich for "lax administration and poor judgment" for letting telecommunications executive Don Jones work as a volunteer in his office in 1995. But it said it would take no further action, citing an earlier decision on a similar complaint also involving Jones.

(On March 29, the committee ruled that Gingrich's arrangement with Jones violated House rules governing the use of volunteers. But it recommended no punishment.)

The rest of the allegations deal with other complaints, all brought by Democrats: that the Speaker misused tax-exempt foundations for a college course he taught, which his critics claim was political and not educational in purpose, and that a political action committee he once ran called GOPAC broke several tax and election laws.

Cole was assigned to investigate the charge concerning the college course. The committee has not commented for several months about the status of the other allegations.

The panel's investigatory subcommittee, which acts as a kind of grand jury, is weighing whether to dismiss the college course allegations or bring formal charges, called a statement of alleged violations. A formal charge would set in motion a 30-day response period for Gingrich and then possibly a disciplinary hearing, which is the trial-like stage of the process.

But those events would have to be held over to the new Congress, complicating matters considerably for the committee.

Some members desperately want to be relieved of their service in the 105th Congress. That opens the question whether they will have to be compelled to stay to finish the Gingrich case, or whether the leadership will have to find some creative solution.

"They're stuck again, or, do you appoint two ethics committees?" Dixon said. "It's a very awkward situation coming at the end of the session."

Dixon said he has concluded: "This thing is dead in this Congress in my judgment." ∎

THE SECOND TERM

President Expected To Travel Center Lane to 21st Century

In bid to woo Republican-led Congress, Clinton likely to propose more modest change

For all his ambitious rhetoric about building a bridge to the 21st century, President Clinton has laid the groundwork for a modest second-term agenda that seeks to make incremental changes in federal policy without offending powerful interests.

Unlike the liberal initiatives he pursued in his first two years in office, Clinton is expected to stress centrist priorities such as producing a balanced-budget plan, crafting targeted tax cuts and boosting education programs. He also will likely try to seek changes to the welfare overhaul bill enacted this year (PL 104-193) by trying to promote job programs for welfare recipients. *(1996 Weekly Report, p. 3148)*

In his election-night victory speech, Clinton emphasized putting aside partisan differences and working with the Republican-led Congress.

"The challenges we face — they're not Democratic or Republican challenges. They're American challenges," he said. "What we have achieved as Americans of lasting good, we have achieved by working together."

GOP leaders in Congress, with narrow majorities in both chambers, also indicated that they will adopt a more moderate approach than in 1995, when they faced widespread criticism for their role in temporarily closing down the federal government. "I think you'll see us try to reach out and find a common ground with President Clinton," House Speaker Newt Gingrich, R-Ga., said in an interview Nov. 6 on CBS.

But Clinton begins his second term as a weakened president in many respects. Although he is the first Democratic president to win re-election since Franklin D. Roosevelt in 1944, he fell just short of winning 50 percent of the vote and can hardly claim an electoral mandate.

More ominously, his administration is dogged by a growing number of ethical questions. Congressional Republicans are expected to investigate matters ranging from Democratic fundraising tactics to the FBI files improperly obtained by White House aides. And special prosecutor Kenneth W. Starr may try to bring indictments against administration officials on

REUTERS

The president embraces his wife, Hillary, and daughter, Chelsea, as they watch fireworks in Little Rock, Ark., on Nov. 6 after Clinton's victory speech.

Whitewater-related charges.

"You would suspect that it would be distracting and preoccupying for the White House, and therefore have an effect on the agenda," said Charles O. Jones, a political science professor at the University of Wisconsin at Madison. "But what that will be, I don't know."

Clinton also faces some rocky shoals in foreign policy, with potential crises looming in China, Korea, Bosnia and the Middle East.

If the economy slows significantly, that would create additional headaches, increasing pressure for social program spending and making it extremely difficult to reach the goal of a balanced budget by 2002.

However, such potential problems were barely mentioned in the campaign. As a result, some political scientists said they were hard-pressed to predict the direction of Clinton's second term.

"Normally, a second term is a ratification," said Richard C. Wade, a historian at the graduate center of the City University of New York. "This time, there's nothing in that at all. I don't think this election is a mandate for anything."

A Tight Budget

To a large degree, the president's agenda will be driven by a Republican priority that he has reluctantly adopted: balancing the federal budget.

Clinton is expected to unveil a budget plan in February that would seek to erase the deficit by 2002 through a combination of smaller spending and tax cuts than the GOP plan last year.

A major sticking point between Clinton and Republican leaders may be whether to retain the federal guarantee of Medicaid's health care coverage — a top priority of the president. *(1996 Weekly Report, p. 3134)*

Another budget issue will be whether political leaders are willing to tackle the soaring growth of entitlement programs, such as Social Security and Medicare. The Medicare trust fund is expected to become insolvent in 2001 without a change in policy, and Social Security will be out of money 30 years later, according to trustees of those trust funds. *(1996*

CQ Weekly Report November 9, 1996

Cabinet Turnover Tops Agenda

With the election won, nearly half of the members of President Clinton's Cabinet and other top aides announced that they were planning to leave, and Clinton rushed to put together a team for his second term.

Saying he wants to govern from the "vital center," Clinton said he would cast a wide net in looking for replacements and would consider Republicans and Independents as well as Democrats.

Christopher

Perry

"I think we ought to try to have a government that can unify the country," Clinton said at a press conference Nov. 8. "It has become more apparent than ever since the election that the American people want us to fulfill our responsibilities as Democrats, Republicans and Independents second, and Americans first — to set aside our differences and join hands to make the most of this moment of possibility."

Several current and former members of Congress are under consideration to fill Cabinet vacancies. White House aides said Clinton had delayed the start of a trip to Hawaii, Australia and Asia to consider possible appointments. He had been scheduled to depart Nov. 12.

The most significant change at the White House — from the point of view of Congress — is the departure of White House Chief of Staff Leon E. Panetta. A former chairman of the House Budget Committee, Panetta drew on his many contacts on Capitol Hill to help complete deals on the 1997 appropriations bills, as well as on immigration and an overhaul of the welfare system. Panetta said he will return to California, where he is expected to run for governor.

Clinton on Nov. 8 named North Carolina businessman and former White House deputy chief of staff Erskine Bowles to replace Panetta. While he is well liked by conservative Democrats on the Hill, Bowles lacks Panetta's depth of congressional experience and his fluency on budget issues.

Departing Cabinet officers include:

• **Pentagon**: Defense Secretary William J. Perry, who combined a strong background in advanced technology with concern for the quality of life of junior enlisted officers, says he wants to spend more time with his grandchildren. Possible replacements include retiring Sens. William S. Cohen, R-Maine, and Sam Nunn, D-Ga., though people close to Nunn say he wants to return to private life.

Central Intelligence Director John M. Deutch has also been mentioned for the job; that could open up a slot at CIA for Cohen, who served on the Senate Intelligence Committee.

• **State**: Secretary Warren Christopher is leaving after traveling almost nonstop for four years and scoring diplomatic successes in Bosnia and North Korea. A leading contender for the job is former Senate Majority leader George J. Mitchell, D-Maine. Also said to be under consideration are United Nations ambassador Madeleine K. Albright and possibly former Vice President Walter F. Mondale, who said he will leave his post as ambassador to Japan.

• **Transportation**: Secretary Federico F. Peña is planning to leave following suggestions that the White House was unhappy with his performance after the Valujet crash in the Everglades in May. His likely replacement is Bill Daley of Chicago, a Democratic activist and brother of Chicago Mayor Richard Daley.

Also leaving the Transportation Department is Federal Aviation Administration Director David Hinson.

• **Labor:** Secretary Robert B. Reich, after playing a strong role in pushing key Democratic issues such as an increase in the minimum wage, wants to return to Harvard University and his family in Boston. No immediate candidates were named.

• **Commerce:** Secretary Mickey Kantor wants to return to practicing law in California, opening up one of the political plums that presidents often give to friends who have helped their election efforts. However, few clear heirs have emerged.

• **Energy:** Secretary Hazel R. O'Leary, whose frequent overseas trips drew criticism from Republicans, is leaving. Two New Mexico Democrats, Sen. Jeff Bingaman and Rep. Bill Richardson, are being floated as possible successors.

• **Housing**: Secretary Henry G. Cisneros has won kudos from Republicans in Congress as well as some urban constituencies for his work, but he is expected to leave in the face of investigation by an independent counsel for allegedly concealing information about payments to a former mistress. Possible replacements include Cisneros' deputy Andrew Cuomo, son of former New York Gov. Mario M. Cuomo, and mayors Dennis W. Archer of Detroit, Norm Rice of Seattle and Kurt L. Schmoke of Baltimore.

• **Education**: Secretary Richard W. Riley, a close friend of Clinton's, has not announced his plans, although it is rumored that he is ready to depart.

Other members of the Cabinet, including Health and Human Services Secretary Donna E. Shalala and Treasury Secretary Robert E. Rubin, are expected to stay, at least through the inauguration.

Attorney General Janet Reno declared her interest in staying despite oft-repeated complaints from White House aides that she is not enough of a team player. Although she is popular in the law enforcement community and respected on Capitol Hill, she has frustrated the White House by signing off on the appointment of several independent counsels who are investigating either White House personnel or Cabinet appointees.

Weekly Report, p. 3055)

The longer the government waits to tackle such issues, the more drastic steps it will have to take, analysts warn. Possible options include requiring higher-income retirees to pay more for their Medicare benefits, increasing the retirement age for Social Security and increasing payroll taxes.

Clinton has not spelled out his plans for those programs. Instead, he has proposed naming a commission to make recommendations.

Complicating the fiscal issues, Clinton has proposed tax cuts that would cost the Treasury about $100 billion over the next six years, according to the Joint Committee on Taxation. Among the proposals are a tax cut for low- and middle-income parents with pre-teenage children and expanded eligibility for Individual Retirement Accounts.

Republicans have proposed larger tax cuts, including a broader per-child tax credit and capital gains tax cuts.

Either way, Clinton would be faced with very little extra money for discretionary programs, putting him under further pressure to thread a moderate course.

> **"Normally, a second term is a ratification. This time, there's nothing in that at all. I don't think this election is a mandate for anything."**
>
> —Historian Richard C. Wade

Domestic Programs

For that reason, Clinton is stressing low-cost and politically popular programs to help more children read, make education more affordable, make changes to the welfare system, cut crime rates, clean up the environment and overhaul the system of financing political campaigns.

In his campaign, the president proposed a $2.8 billion "America Reads" program to make sure every child will be able to read by the third grade. The program would mobilize 1 million volunteer tutors and provide $300 million in grants to help parents teach their children to read. *(1996 Weekly Report, p. 2462)*

The president also has proposed to offer a $1,500 annual tax credit for the first two years of higher education courses, in a bid to make at least a community college education affordable to all Americans. And, to boost computer literacy, he wants to spend about $100 million to help universities and libraries get access to the Internet.

Another top Clinton priority will be to modify the new welfare law in order to help recipients find and keep jobs.

In his Aug. 29 speech accepting the Democratic presidential nomination, he proposed a $3.4 billion "welfare-to-work" program designed to find jobs for up to 1 million people facing the loss of government benefits. The proposal would provide $3 billion in direct aid to cities that create jobs for welfare recipients, and would provide about $400 million in tax breaks to companies that hire former welfare recipients. *(Weekly Report, p. 2485)*

In a bid to stave off GOP charges that Democrats are soft on crime, Clinton has proposed several initiatives to stem drug use and violent crimes. These include giving the government broader authority to bar armor-piercing bullets and requiring teenagers to pass a drug test before getting driver's licenses.

He supports a constitutional amendment to guarantee the rights of crime victims — a position shared by many Republicans.

Clinton also has proposed modest environmental programs, including a $2 billion plan to grant tax incentives to businesses that clean up and redevelop mildly polluted sites, known as "brownfields." He wants to expand the power of prosecutors in cases of environmental violations.

Amid allegations that the Democratic National Committee accepted illegal contributions from foreign interests, Clinton has proposed tightening campaign finance rules. Among the possible changes would be to limit spending on congressional races, restrict or eliminate contributions by political action committees (PACs) and restrict so-called "soft money" contributions to political parties.

"Everybody knows the problems with campaign money," Clinton said in a Nov. 1 speech on campaign finance. "There's too much of it."

However modest, some of Clinton's initiatives may face a rough reception in Congress. Republicans, for example, are critical of his education proposals as duplicating existing programs; a proposal to broaden restrictions on armor-piercing bullets foundered in the 104th Congress; and past legislative efforts to curb campaign spending have reached a partisan impasse.

Foreign Policy

Although the campaign focused almost entirely on domestic issues, foreign policy could pose a severe challenge for Clinton's second term.

The administration is keeping an especially wary eye on China, which has repeatedly clashed with the United States on issues ranging from trade to human rights. With 92-year-old Chinese leader Deng Xiaoping likely to pass from the scene, Clinton could find himself faced with changes in Sino-American relations, and possibly considerable upheaval in China.

Heavily armed North Korea, teetering on the edge of economic collapse, also could emerge as a flash point.

Another potential crisis revolves around the future of peace talks in the Middle East, where tensions are running so high that there has been talk of war between Israel and Syria.

And Bosnia, also, continues as a major concern. The administration has not set a date to withdraw American military personnel, who are serving with other NATO troops in an attempt to pacify the troubled country.

Despite the expected departures of Secretary of State Warren Christopher and Secretary of Commerce Mickey Kantor, the administration likely will continue to emphasize trade, as well as assistance to emerging democracies.

But it is not clear whether Congress will act with traditional deference to the president on foreign policy matters. To an unusual degree, Clinton found himself under criticism by Dole and other Republicans during recent foreign policy crises, including fighting between Iraq and Kurdish factions.

Overall, however, analysts said they expected Clinton and the Republican Congress to make a real effort to cooperate in coming months. That probably means both sides will emphasize a moderate approach.

"Clinton's going to have to reach out, build a coalition in the middle somehow," said James A. Thurber, a political science professor at American University in Washington. "I think the Republicans have learned they have to be moderate, which will help." ∎

Presidential Race Resuscitates Campaign Finance Debate

Proponents of overhaul hope that issue's newfound currency will ignite long-sought legislation

As the fall campaign began, the issue of campaign finance had been left to die along with the other unfinished business of the 104th Congress.

Reform proposals had gone nowhere in the 104th. The two chambers and the two parties had remained as far apart as ever in their priorities, each jealously guarding its prerogatives.

A pledge to bring a bipartisan compromise to Congress, made jointly by President Clinton and House Speaker Newt Gingrich, R-Ga., in the summer of 1995 had come to nothing.

The electoral races of the 1996 cycle were expected to generate more spending than ever — at least $1.6 billion — 37 percent higher than the $1.2 billion spent in the last presidential election cycle, 1991–92. Yet voters seemed no more focused on the issue than usual.

Then, in the closing weeks of the campaign, an explosion of news stories about foreign contributions to the Democratic National Committee suddenly brought the issue to life.

By Election Day, no topic had more currency in the presidential campaign than fundraising and the laws that attempt to govern it.

Supporters of efforts to change the way federal campaigns are paid for now hope to harness that energy in the 105th Congress to pass long-sought legislation.

Few would dispute that the spark that ignited the issue was the connotation of influence-buying by foreign interests with connections to the Clinton administration.

But despite the attention focused on such donations, the amount of money from such sources represents a relatively small portion of the total amounts of unregulated "soft money" raised in this cycle.

"Soft money" goes to party committees that can accept unlimited amounts for "party building activities" — in contrast to "hard money" contributions that go directly to a given candidate's campaign. Between Jan. 1, 1995, and Oct. 16, 1996, Democrats raised $102 million in soft money, a 232 percent increase over what they had raised in the comparable period of 1991–92.

And the Democrats were not even the leaders in this field.

Democratic Party fundraiser John Huang figures prominently in questions about the legality of campaign contributions.
REUTERS

The Republicans raised $121 million, an increase of 166 percent. *(Chart, next page)*

Foreign Connection

Nonetheless, it took the so-called Asian connection aspect to capture the imagination of the media and the public.

"It becomes an issue because of the foreign contributions," said James A. Thurber, director of American University's Center for Congressional and Presidential Studies. "Most Americans are pretty cynical about politics. They think people are bought by specialized interests. When they see money from foreign interests coming into the system, they think it's even worse, so it becomes a potent campaign issue."

The fact that the foreign element has been so potent has raised eyebrows among those who sense a double standard in the sudden tide of disapproval.

"There's a certain xenophobic aspect to it," said Anthony Corrado, a professor of government at Colby College in Waterville, Maine. "Politically, it's a more dramatic statement to say there are foreigners providing money to our presidential campaign. The real issue is not foreign contributions. It is the entire soft money system which has really gone out of control."

Until recently, foreign contributions have not been prominent in the campaign finance debate. The campaign finance bill (S 1219) that failed in the 104th Congress would have eliminated soft money but was silent on the subject of foreign contributions.

But scholars and other observers who have long tried to call attention to the soft money system in general have seized on the Huang story as an opportunity to air the larger issue. "The [foreign] contributions raised many of the questions that have been at the center of the campaign finance debate, particularly in terms of the size of these gifts and what were they getting in return," Corrado said. "The amount of money being raised and spent is so far beyond anything we've seen before that it has raised finally the question in the public of how did we get here."

The issue dominated the closing weeks of the presidential campaign, becoming a staple of stump speeches by both Republican Bob Dole and Reform Party candidate Ross Perot.

Pollster John Zogby said Clinton's failure to top 50 percent in the popular vote can be blamed on the fall-out from the

CQ Weekly Report November 9, 1996

Haley Barbour

Federal Campaign Financing

(in millions of dollars raised)

	1992	1994	1996
Presidential	$110	$ 0	$124
Congressional	412	518	558
Democratic Party	85	77	140
"Soft money"	31	43	102
Republican Party	164	160	278
"Soft money"	46	38	121

"Presidential" funds are public dollars earmarked by taxpayers for the presidential campaign and distributed to the major parties. All other figures cover the period Jan. 1, 1995, through Oct. 16, 1996. Democratic and Republican columns include the national party, senatorial and congressional committees. "Soft money" refers to unlimited contributions for "party building activities."

SOURCE: Federal Election Commission

Christopher J. Dodd

campaign finance controversy. Exit polls showed that Dole defeated Clinton, 47 percent to 35 percent, among voters who made up their minds in the last week of the campaign.

"The No. 1 thing that the undecideds were citing to us was Clinton's character," Zogby said. "Undecideds started to really pay attention during the week he was hammered the most."

Still, despite Dole and Perot's best efforts, the brouhaha did not alter the fundamental course of the campaign. Exit polls by Voter News Service did not find campaign finance or ethics among the top seven issues listed by voters.

And a late October CBS poll found that 62 percent of respondents felt the foreign contributions were nothing more than politics as usual. Only 35 percent said it was a serious issue.

"Those were not the issues that defined this election," White House spokesman Michael McCurry said. "This election was about the future of the American economy, the future of the health care system, whether or not we're going to improve education in America."

The Status Quo

Throughout the campaign, both political parties eagerly reaped contributions from American subsidiaries of foreign companies, as federal election law allows. Any immigrant with a green card who has been admitted for permanent residence also can contribute to federal campaigns.

The Democrats wound up returning a $325,000 contribution from Yogesh K. Gandhi of California, head of the Gandhi Memorial International Foundation, saying they could not verify the source of the money, and returned a $250,000 contribution from Cheong Am America because the money came from the parent Korean company rather than the U.S. subsidiary.

But the Democrats took in 19 soft-money contributions larger than Gandhi's, according to Common Cause. And Cheong Am's contribution was only the 31st largest the party had received.

Federal election law allows American subsidiaries of foreign companies to contribute to political campaigns if the money was earned in the United States. And the Democrats raised their most soft money in the 1995–96 election cycle ($720,000), from Joseph E. Seagram and Sons and MCA Inc., two companies controlled by a Canadian family, the Bronfmans.

Seagram and MCA also contributed $435,000 to the Republicans, ranking seventh. And the GOP's 10th-biggest soft money contributor also has foreign ties, British-owned Brown

& Williamson Tobacco.

On the Republican list at No. 14 was an Australian company, News Corporation, headed by media mogul Rupert Murdoch. That is the same company whose HarperCollins subsidiary initially offered Gingrich a $4.5 million book advance.

News Corporation owns television and cable television stations and was directly affected by the telecommunications deregulation bill (PL 104-104) passed by the Republican-controlled Congress and signed by Clinton. *(1995 Almanac, pp. 4–3)*

"Maybe the Republicans have as much to be embarrassed about as the Democrats," Thurber said.

Republican National Committee Chairman Haley Barbour argued that the GOP raised its money within current rules and regulations, while the Democrats broke the law. "The subject here is they're violating the law as it exists now," Barbour said Nov. 3 on NBC's "Meet the Press."

'Soft' Sources

Soft money had its origins in a 1979 campaign finance law (PL 96-187), the same measure that banned future members of the House from keeping their unspent campaign funds after leaving office.

Political party leaders complained that public financing of presidential campaigns and limits on outside fundraising relegated them to the sidelines in presidential elections. The 1979 law allowed the parties to raise unlimited amounts of money for voter registration drives and get-out-the-vote efforts. *(1979 Almanac, p. 558)*

Instead, the political parties began using that money to air commercials supporting or opposing a particular candidate or issue. The Supreme Court, in a series of decisions, ruled that advertisements that did not specifically urge a vote for or against a candidate were not subject to the restrictions and limits imposed by federal election laws, giving the parties carte blanche to raise millions of unregulated dollars for their campaigns. *(1996 Weekly Report, p. 996)*

"The issue advertising is a misuse of soft money, which was not intended for that purpose," said Herbert Alexander, a professor of political science at the University of Southern California and the director of the Citizens' Research Foundation. "It was intended for local registration, get-out-the-vote drives."

Even so, the Supreme Court continued to expand the parameters by which political parties could get involved in campaigns unfettered by federal law. In June, the justices ruled that the parties could spend unlimited amounts of money in support of a particular candidate, as long as those efforts were independent of the person running for office. *(1996 Weekly Report, p. 1857)*

The money chase spilled over to the national conventions. Though the quadrennial gatherings were to be funded with $25 million in taxpayer dollars, both parties raised millions more from corporations with a direct stake in legislation before Congress.

And while the presidential campaigns were funded with $123 million in taxpayer funds, both political parties continued to raise millions more.

"It's pretty broken down," said Candice Nelson, an assistant professor of government at American University. "We're really seeing that in this cycle. Back in '76, you didn't see the presidential candidates out raising money. Once they got the nomination, that was it. They got their checks and they went about getting their message out."

Not this year. And this huge emphasis on fundraising led to such contributions as the $250,000 from Cheong Am America and $425,000 from Arief and Soraya Wiriadinata, an Indonesian couple who lived in Virginia before returning to their native country.

The Wiriadinatas were associates of the Riady family of Indonesia, who head the Lippo Group. Lippo's American subsidiaries and executives have given $754,365 to Democrats and Republicans between 1979 and 1996, according to the Center for Responsive Politics.

John Huang, the former Commerce Department and Democratic National Committee official who solicited these contributions, is a former Lippo executive.

"The pursuit of victory led [the Democrats] to try to collect absolutely as much money as they could and therefore not pay attention to the rules," said Robert Schiff, a staff attorney with Public Citizen's Congress Watch, a group affiliated with consumer advocate Ralph Nader. "They still ended up raising a lot less money than the Republicans did. They felt that they were behind and had to tap all possible sources and the niceties be damned."

Sen. Christopher J. Dodd, D-Conn, the Democratic National Committee chairman, said Nov. 6 that the party would set up a compliance committee to review contributions when they are received.

Looking to 105th

Campaign finance is expected to top the agenda when the 105th Congress convenes. But it may not be in the form of legislation.

Senate Majority Leader Trent Lott, R-Miss., said he wanted

"If foreign corporate money can allegedly buy access and influence, what about domestic corporate money?"

—Ellen Miller, executive director, Center for Responsive Politics.

Congress to investigate the foreign contributions to the Democrats. "I think we have to find out what happened there," Lott said Nov. 6. "Congress does have a responsibility to look into those matters. I think we should talk about having some early hearings on what happened in this campaign. "

Sens. John McCain, R-Ariz., and Russell D. Feingold, D-Wis., the sponsors of the campaign finance legislation in the last Congress, said they would reintroduce the bill on the first day of the next one. Feingold said the focus on campaign finance during the election shows that its time may have come.

"It's just like the deficit issue," Feingold said. "It just kept going up the ladder. Perot made it an issue in the '92 campaign and it came of age."

Just like his predecessor, Dole (before his campaign conversion), Lott said he opposes McCain-Feingold.

"I don't think that bill is exactly what we're looking for," Lott said. "I know that the sponsors have done good work. And I worked with them to make sure they had an opportunity to offer their proposal. I think we ought to sort of take a look at what happened this year, and have some hearings and try to learn from what happened, and develop a bill."

Besides looking at ways to change the way campaigns are funded, Lott suggested Congress may want to look at the way campaigns are run.

"Should we look at the broader prospect of campaign reform?" he said. "I think maybe we should. Campaigns are so long. Can we shorten them? Does the primary system now selecting the party nominees work? Do we need the national party conventions? I'm talking about bigger questions than just the financing."

Supporters of changing the way federal campaigns are funded say that the Dole presidential campaign may have given them the boost they needed. Dole argued on the campaign trail that these foreign contributions were buying influence. "Our actions are not for sale to some foreign influence or some foreign interest," Dole said Oct. 18.

That is the same argument made for years by proponents of overhauling the campaign finance system. And if a $250,000 contribution, such as that from Cheong Am America, can buy influence, they asked, what of the $1.9 million that Philip Morris contributed to the Republicans? Or the $532,000 that went to the Democrats from Walt Disney Co., whose ABC television network and ESPN cable network fall under the telecommunications deregulation bill?

"If foreign corporate money can allegedly buy access and influence, what about domestic corporate money?" asked Ellen Miller, executive director of the Center for Responsive Politics. "The bells and whistles that have surfaced in this election cycle have put a point on it." ∎

CQ ROUNDTABLE
By Ronald D. Elving

A Chance To Overhaul Campaign Financing?

Given the portentous events that closed the 1996 electoral cycle, many now believe the moment has arrived for campaign finance reform. Reasons can be summoned to support that belief. But no one need jostle just yet for Rose Garden standing room at the signing ceremony for the Clean Campaign Practices Act of 1997.

To be sure, a strong whiff of scandal emanating from the fundraising practices of the Democratic Party soured the air just before the Nov. 5 election.

The exploits of John Huang, the Commerce Department official who took his multinational Rolodex with him to the Democratic National Committee (DNC), may be to campaign finance what the infamous $600 toilet seat was to Pentagon spending in the 1980s. It may focus the national mind on a concrete example people can understand and stay mad about.

The DNC fiasco may well have cost President Clinton a majority in the popular vote and damaged his party's chances for a more persuasive showing in the congressional elections.

It may also have helped pass a reform initiative in California that will limit contributions in state and local races. The state measure won by a ratio of 3 to 2, borne on what Ruth Holton, executive director of Common Cause in California, called "a high level of public disgust."

Beyond that, we can now expect probe-minded Republicans in the 105th Congress to make their adversaries' aggressive fundraising the new point of attack. Just as predictable is the Democratic defense, pointing right back at Republicans' own means of collecting cash from wealthy individuals and powerful corporations.

This back-and-forth might generate enough public dismay to make a difference in a way previous bouts of financial excess since Watergate have not.

But then, as the winter weeks wear on and the public is distracted again by other political concerns (not to mention daily life), the issue could well fade.

And in the meantime the lessons of 1996 gleaned by candidates and campaign professionals may be quite different from those urged on them by academics, reformers and editorialists.

Congress, as always, will find legislating reform far less fun than investigating abuses. And merely wanting a better system is worlds apart from accepting the tedious details, compromises and sacrifices entailed in an overhaul.

Most important, incumbents and challengers alike will soon be planning the campaigns of 1998 and 2000. They will surely recall the furor over current fundraising excesses, but they will also note that the wages of inadequate financing are political death.

In the 1996 cycle, the better financed House candidate won in more than nine cases out of ten (according to a survey of results and Federal Election Commission filings conducted by the Associated Press).

For prospective White House candidates, the lesson of 1996 is likely to be the iron rule of financial dominance. President Clinton and his Republican challenger, former Sen. Bob Dole, won their respective nominations largely by having the most money when it mattered.

Clinton inoculated himself against the dread effects of a primary challenge by vacuuming up every Democratic dollar available in 1995. Dole prevailed in the March GOP primaries largely because his rivals who had survived February politically were exhausted financially.

It also will be noted that Clinton established his lead for the fall campaign by having a huge dollar advantage in the late spring and early summer, when Dole was tapped out from the primaries and the president still had his full complement of federal matching funds.

These are the lessons that hard-eyed political operatives comprehend most quickly and find hardest to forget.

Perhaps there would be political points for those willing to take risks on campaign finance reform in the 105th Congress. But will such points pay the bills for the television and radio, the mailings and the polling? The answer is what stands between momentary high hopes for reform and the realization of such hopes.

Still, to let such a moment as this pass would be historically unfortunate. We find ourselves with a second-term president and a congressional majority that is reasonably secure about retaining control of both House and Senate in the next electoral cycle.

Clinton is in the market for a policy monument. He also needs more than ever to shore up his position on the ethics front, particularly with regard to political money.

Congressional Republicans profess to be confident of gaining seats in 1998, a second-term midterm cycle in which the president's party has always suffered. This combination of circumstances alone may not be enough to overcome the practical imperatives of politics. But at least it offers a season of possibility for what Abraham Lincoln once called "the better angels of our nature." ∎

> **Merely wanting a better system is worlds apart from accepting the tedious details, compromises and sacrifices entailed in an overhaul.**

High-Profile Cases Set Busy Pace for Court

Agenda may include First Amendment challenges to provisions of 1996 telecommunications act

The Supreme Court opened its new term Oct. 7 and has already agreed to take 52 cases, well ahead of its pace last year. And its docket includes several cases that have attracted the attention of legal scholars and court watchers. But it is a case the court has not yet formally agreed to take (although it almost certainly will) that may have the broadest implications.

The sweeping telecommunications overhaul law (S 652—PL 104-104) that Congress cleared in February included a provision banning the use of the Internet or online computer services to disseminate indecent or patently offensive material to minors. That raised a significant First Amendment free speech issue for a burgeoning new medium, and Congress requested expedited judicial review of its new law, putting it on a fast track to the Supreme Court.

The court could simply affirm lower court rulings striking down the provision. Or it could send it back down for another trial. Or it could issue a narrow ruling. But few people expect this to happen with so much at stake in the case, *Reno v. ACLU.*

"We're talking about the application of the First Amendment to the 21st century," says Elliot Mincburg, legal director of People For the American Way, one of the litigants. "It's going to have enormous significance."

Chris Hansen, senior staff counsel for the American Civil Liberties Union, says: "It's really as if we are in the Gutenberg era, or the era when the Constitution was written, trying to figure out what the rules should be for this new medium."

The case could highlight a term already full of First Amendment cases—

SCOTT J. FERRELL

James S. Brady speaks Oct. 10 about the court's upcoming consideration of the Brady law.

including some that could reverse several federal laws that Congress passed with much fanfare in the last few years. The court, for example, has agreed to take a case involving the free speech rights of cable television operators and a case challenging buffer zones around patients at abortion clinics. It also took a First Amendment case challenging an Arizona requirement that state employees speak English while performing official duties. *(1996 Weekly Report, p. 2926)*

Besides First Amendment questions, a second key theme this year is the relative power of the federal government compared with states. Topping the list

is a challenge to the 1993 Brady law (PL 103-159), which stipulates a waiting period for handgun purchases and requires that local officials conduct background checks. *(1996 Weekly Report, p. 2925)*

Court watchers say the term could be one of the most significant in many years—depending, in part, on how broad the court's rulings are and what additional cases the justices agree to take. Many are impressed with what the court already has on its plate.

"A typical term starts off slowly and eventually you realize how important it is," says A. E. Dick Howard, law professor at the University of Virginia. "But this one begins with a real ability to capture the public's attention."

Indecency on the Internet

It is the *Reno v. ACLU* case that has the potential for the most expansive ruling. Unlike most cases on the docket, it involves something the court has never before considered.

At issue is Congress' attempt to keep people from using the Internet and online services such as CompuServe and Prodigy to distribute objectionable material to minors. In drafting the law, Congress considered several wordings for the statute, settling on one that includes restricting "indecent" material.

Indecency, which is applied almost exclusively to the broadcast medium, can mean simple profanity. Humorist George Carlin's monologue, "The Seven Words You Can Never Say on Television," is the most famous example of indecency. Carlin meant it as a satire of the Federal Communications Commission's (FCC) standards. But it became a test case when a radio station aired a recording of it. A New York court upheld the FCC's restrictions in the 1978 case, *FCC v. Pacifica Foundation.*

Gun Law Challenged

The Second Amendment right to bear arms was at the center of the debate in 1993 when Congress passed the Brady law (PL 103-159). But as the Supreme Court prepares to review the law, it is the 10th Amendment—restricting the powers of the federal government—that is front and center.

The Brady law, which requires that people wait five business days to purchase a handgun and that police make a reasonable effort to check their backgrounds, has not been challenged directly. Rather, it is under attack on grounds that the background check is a federal mandate in violation of the 10th Amendment, which says: "The powers not delegated to the United States by the Constitution, nor prohibited by it to the States, are reserved to the States respectively, or to the people."

"The policy issue aside, the question is whether the federal government can order [the background check] be done," says conservative activist Thomas L. Jipping of the Free Congress Research and Education Foundation. "The court could say that the division of power does mean something."

This court has demonstrated an interest in re-examining the 10th Amendment and other issues related to states' rights. In *United States v. Lopez*, it struck down a federal statute banning guns near schools, and in *New York v. United States*, it struck down part of a statute requiring states to dispose of low-level nuclear waste. It also barred Congress, in *Seminole Tribe of Florida v. Florida*, from authorizing suits by Indian tribes against states.

Brady law proponents will argue that the background check is flexible, routine, and of mutual interest to states and the federal government. Furthermore, they say, striking it down could have a broad impact on noncontroversial programs—such as those that track missing children or determine highway fatality patterns—in which states are told to cooperate with federal authorities.

"The court would have to essentially say that under no circumstances could the federal government require state or local officials to do anything pursuant to a federal policy," says Dennis Henigan, general counsel of Handgun Control Inc., a Washington group that advocates gun restrictions.

The issue will be examined in two cases brought by sheriffs, one from Montana, *Printz v. United States* and one from Arizona, *Mack v. United States*. Lower courts are divided on the constitutionality of the background check.

Courts historically have been much more willing to uphold content restrictions on broadcasts than on the print media, because of limited space—and limited channels—on the airwaves. Besides indecency, the FCC in the last few decades has enforced requirements that broadcast stations air "public service" programs and, until recently, that they adhere to "fairness" standards. None of these have ever been applied to books, newspapers or magazines.

Opponents of the new statute argue that computer communications are more like print than broadcast, and should not be restrained by a broadcast standard. Their argument has prevailed so far in separate opinions by three-judge panels in Philadelphia and New York. The chief judge in the Philadelphia case, *Reno v. ACLU*, said that cyberspace was, if anything, more deserving of First Amendment protections than print, because virtually anyone can set up shop as an electronic publisher.

Proponents of the statute argue that cyberspace is so interactive that it is less like a medium than like a giant store, and that laws keeping offensive matter away from minors in cyberspace are akin to laws keeping adult magazines behind store counters or X-rated movies off limits to children. "Just like in the real world, you cannot have a child rent [an adult] video, we cannot have them do so in cyberspace," says Colby May, a lawyer with the American Center for Law and Justice, a conservative legal foundation.

New Medium

Organizations that oppose the statute approach the potential Supreme Court case with measured optimism. What worries them most is the newness of the medium and the Supreme Court justices' unfamiliarity with it.

"Talk about *terra incognita*," says the University of Virginia's Howard. "Take a group of nine individuals whose average age is about 60—not one of them grew up with a computer—and thrust a computer case like this at them."

The Supreme Court does not hear evidence, so both sides tried to explain the potential and pitfalls of the new medium in the trial courts. Statute opponents believe they scored big in Philadelphia. The ruling supports their position and begins with a lengthy factual description of cyberspace that will be read by the Supreme Court justices.

"It's a wonderful First Amendment decision; we couldn't be happier," says Deborah Liebow of the American Library Association, also a litigant. "They took a lot of time learning about this."

Daniel J. Weitzner, of the Center for Democracy and Technology, a computer civil liberties group, is a bit less optimistic about the ruling, which included three opinions from the three judges employing different lines of reasoning, all concluding that cyberspace deserved printlike First Amendment protections.

But he agrees that the factual findings, which highlight the user's role in choosing what to read, were a major coup.

Groups like Liebow's and Weitzner's hope the justices focus on this lower court ruling, rather than on their ruling this June in *DAETC v. FCC*, a case that grappled with similar questions in the context of cable television. In that case, involving television in Denver, the court split into three camps and issued a narrow ruling. No five members could agree on a broad framework for applying the First Amendment to cable, and it remains unclear whether cable should be treated more like print, more like broadcasting, or fit into some new category. Justice Anthony M. Kennedy wrote in a partial dissent that the plurality opinion, written by Justice Stephen G. Breyer, was remarkable for its refusal to define the constitutional standard applicable.

Reno v. ACLU also could set important precedents beyond First Amendment and pornography issues, because the court has never before ruled on a cyberspace issue.

"What are the rules that we are going to apply to the Internet?" asks the ACLU's Hansen. "The question is arising in terms of indecency, but it could arise in . . . lots of other contexts."

A broad ruling could settle or raise

Questions of Supreme Importance

The Supreme Court began its new term Oct. 7 with a docket many analysts believe could produce decisions of sweeping importance. Here are the questions raised by key cases:

• **Gun control.** Does the Brady Law constitute a violation of the 10th Amendment? The 1993 Brady law (PL 103-159) requires a waiting period of five business days for the purchase of a handgun, during which time local law enforcement agents are supposed to check the purchaser's background. The 10th Amendment says all powers not delegated to the federal government by the Constitution are generally reserved for the states and the people. The court will hear two cases brought by two local sheriffs, *Printz v. U.S.* and *Mack v. U.S.*

• **English only.** Are First Amendment rights to free speech violated by an Arizona constitutional amendment requiring state employees to speak in English while performing their official duties? The court will hear *Arizonans for Official English v. Arizona.*

• **Abortion.** Does a court injunction that requires protesters at abortion clinics to provide at least a 15-foot buffer zone around clinic patients and staff violate the protesters' First Amendment rights to assemble? The court upheld a buffer zone around clinics in 1994 in *Madsen v. Women's Health Center.* Now, in *Schenck v. Pro Choice Network of Western New York*, it will consider the constitutionality of a mandatory floating buffer zone around people.

• **Cable television.** Does a provision in the 1992 cable law (PL 102-385) requiring cable providers to carry most local broadcast channels infringe on the providers' free speech rights? The case may determine whether cable is to be considered more like print or more like broadcasting in terms of First Amendment rights. Traditionally, the court has been reluctant to restrict the content of printed matter. In contrast, laws restricting broadcast material have received a more sympathetic review because access to the

SCOTT J. FERRELL

The Supreme Court will hear several cases involving First Amendment rights.

medium is restricted by limited space on the airwaves. The court opened the term Oct. 7 hearing *Turner Broadcasting v. FCC.*

• **Right to die.** Do the Constitution's clauses guaranteeing due process of law and equal protection under the law include an implicit right of the terminally ill to end their own lives? The court will hear *Vacco v. Quill* and *Washington v. Glucksberg.*

• **Presidential immunity.** Can a sitting president, in this case Bill Clinton, be tried while in office on civil sexual harassment charges stemming from alleged activities before he was president? The case pits an individual's right to sue against the government's interest in protecting the office of the presidency. The court will hear *Clinton v. Jones.*

• **Sexual predators.** Does a state law allowing certain sexual predators to be indefinitely confined in mental institutions after they have completed their prison sentences violate due process rights? The court will hear *Kansas v. Hendricks.*

• **Cyberspace.** Does a provision in the 1996 telecommunications overhaul law (S 652—PL 104-104) banning the use of the Internet or online services to disseminate indecent or patently offensive material to minors violate the First Amendment? Indecency, the broader of the two standards, is used to restrict broadcast content. It can mean simple profanity, such as comedian George Carlin's recorded monologue, "The Seven Words You Can Never Say on Television," which has been banned from radio and television during certain hours.

Opponents of the statute say content restrictions from the broadcast world have no place in cyberspace. The court has not yet formally agreed to hear the case, *Reno v. ACLU.* But most legal experts believe it will take it. In writing the law, Congress requested expedited judicial review. The case was sent to the Supreme Court after a three-judge panel in Philadelphia struck down the law earlier this year.

---

fundamental questions about Internet use that could spill into areas such as copyright law and privacy.

Even beyond *Reno v. ACLU*, the new term is noted for the number of issues the court will consider that resonate beyond legal circles.

It includes two cases on the legality of assisted suicide, *Vacco v. Quill* and *Washington v. Gluksberg.* And *Clinton v. Jones* could have enormous political consequences for President Clinton. The court will examine whether the

president can put off a sexual harassment case brought by Paula Corbin Jones until after he leaves office.

The term is equally laden with cases involving recently enacted high-profile federal laws. A cable television case, *Turner Broadcasting v. FCC*, involves a 1992 law (PL 102-385) to "reregulate" the cable industry. The 102nd Congress, controlled by Democrats, enacted it in its first successful veto override over the objections of President George Bush.

The Brady handgun law is often cited by Clinton and other Democrats as one of their more significant achievements in crime control. (Republicans deride it with equal vehemence.)

And the long-sought 1993 "motor voter" law (PL 103-31), which requires states to let people register to vote when they get their driver's licenses, is up for review in *Young v. Fordice.* Mississippi says the law applies only to federal elections, but the Justice Department says it applies to all elections. ∎

Politics and Public Policy

The term *public policy making* refers to action taken by the government to address issues on the public agenda; it also refers to the method by which a decision to act on policy is reached. The work of Congress, the president and the federal bureaucracy, and the judiciary is to make, implement, and rule on the policy decisions. Articles in this section discuss major policy issues that will likely be before the federal government in 1997.

Perhaps the most sweeping legislation passed in Congress in 1996 was welfare reform, which ended the 61-year-old guarantee of federal assistance to all eligible low-income mothers and children. The new law, devised to save $54 billion over six years, will covert federal funding to the states into predetermined lump-sum payments known as block grants, giving states almost complete control over eligibility and benefits. Most welfare recipients must now find work within two years and are limited to five years of benefits. Some see the new law as moving people to jobs; others feel that it will eventually throw more people into poverty. Congress and the president will most likely be reviewing and adjusting provisions of it during the coming years.

The electrical power industry is the last major regulated monopoly in the United States. This huge industry is critical to the country, supplying electricity to most businesses and residences. Congress will soon consider deregulating the industry, which could lead to lower electric rates for consumers. Opponents of deregulation question the need to tinker with a system that is perhaps the best in the world. Opening the industry to competition means answering some tough questions: Is having cheaper electrical power more important than creating less pollution? Who will pay for maintaining the nation's costly nuclear power plants?

The last group of articles, written by the CQ staff a month before the November elections, looks at eleven key policy areas that are likely to present the toughest dilemmas to President Bill Clinton as he heads toward his second term and Congress as it starts its 105th session. Immediately after his re-election, President Clinton said that his top priority will be balancing the budget. How will the president be able to do this and keep the economy moving and fix entitlements programs? For example, Medicaid is projected to become insolvent within five years. How do tax cuts or tax reform fit in? How much should the United States spend on defense in the post–Cold War era? Should federal investment in new technology be directed to defense or civilian use?

The president and Congress must also address looming social policy issues and challenges from abroad. Should the rise in juvenile crime be addressed with punishment or prevention? How should the government deal with the increase in legal and illegal immigration? Does the federal government having any role in bettering education? How should the Superfund and Endangered Species Acts be revised? Are the states or the federal government best capable of handling the nation's big problems? How should the United States respond to the growing economic might of China? These articles examine these questions and others and provide detailed background information on the issues.

WELFARE

After 60 years, Most Welfare Control Is Passing to States

Clinton will sign measure requiring recipients to work and setting time limit on benefits

Legislation that would sweep away six decades of federal welfare policy gained bipartisan congressional approval after President Clinton announced that he would overlook his objections and sign it.

The bill (HR 3734) would give states broad authority over their own welfare programs, while requiring recipients to work within two years and limiting them to five years of benefits.

The House adopted the conference agreement, 328–101, on July 31. The Senate cleared the legislation the next day, 78–21. Republicans supported the legislation nearly unanimously, while Democrats were split.

Clinton seemed to be leaning toward signing the bill for days, but did not make the decision until after a dramatic meeting with top advisers the morning of July 31.

The meeting occurred as the House prepared for its final debate with many Democrats still uncertain how to vote. Attention shifted from the Capitol to the White House as members from both parties focused on Clinton's televised announcement.

"Today, we have a historic opportunity to make welfare what it was meant to be: a second chance, not a way of life," Clinton said. "So, I will sign this bill — first and foremost because the current system is broken."

The legislation enables Clinton to keep his 1992 campaign promise to "end welfare as we know it." But it goes far beyond anything he envisioned at the time and far beyond what he proposed two years later.

The measure was heavily influenced by the House GOP's "Contract With America" and by the efforts of influential Republican governors who suggested limiting federal welfare spending in exchange for more state control. Democrats and moderate Republicans forced several significant changes in

CQ Weekly Report August 3, 1996

Clinton announces July 31 that he will sign the welfare overhaul bill.

the proposal in the past year. But it remains in many respects a Republican bill wholeheartedly embraced by conservative lawmakers.

It will affect not only the welfare checks of low-income people, but whether and how they get jobs and obtain child care. The measure would save $54.1 billion through fiscal 2002, mostly by cutting the food stamp program and denying a variety of federal benefits to legal immigrants.

Clinton's objections centered primarily on these savings and he expressed his determination to overturn them in future legislation. Aides later conceded that the outlook for doing so any time soon was dim.

In the meantime, welfare policy will be determined in a largely piecemeal fashion by states and localities.

Throughout the final debate, Republicans placed less emphasis on the savings — now the only pieces remaining from their 1995 effort to balance the federal budget by 2002 — than on their

revolutionary prescription for a new welfare policy.

"This legislation is the best hope we have today to provide some real hope for a future for those families and children in our society who, in many instances, are totally without hope," said Senate Budget Committee Chairman Pete V. Domenici, R-N.M.

The outcome inflamed passions of advocates for the poor. As the Senate vote began, about 10 protesters shouted "Shame! Shame!" and blew whistles from the visitors' gallery until police removed them.

Earlier in the day, Sen. Daniel Patrick Moynihan, D-N.Y., a veteran of several national welfare battles, invoked sentiments similar to the protesters', though in much quieter tones. Moynihan said the legislation's premise was that "the behavior of certain adults can be changed by making the lives of their children as wretched as possible. This is a fearsome assumption."

Narrowing and Moderating

During the 18-month congressional debate on welfare, lawmakers had narrowed the scope of the Republicans' bill and moderated some provisions. They made a few more changes in the House-Senate conference that began July 25, borrowing enough from the generally more moderate Senate version to make Clinton and many congressional Democrats comfortable. *(Story, p. 75)*

The centerpiece has remained unchanged since Republicans unveiled their revised version of the contract proposal in February 1995: to end the 61-year-old federal guarantee to provide welfare checks to all eligible low-income mothers and children. Federal funding would be sent to states in predetermined lump-sum payments known as block grants, giving states almost complete control over eligibility and benefits.

Main Issues Resolved

These are the main issues resolved by House and Senate conferees on welfare overhaul legislation (HR 3734). The agreement (H Rept 104-725) would:

• **Food stamps work requirement.** Limit able-bodied, 18-to-50-year olds who have no dependents to three months of food stamp benefits every three years, unless they work at least 20 hours a week. Those who are laid off could receive an additional three months of food stamps. The House bill would have let them receive only three months of benefits, up to age 50. The Senate bill had allowed food stamps for four months each year.

SCOTT J. FERRELL

During July 25's welfare conference, Sens. Exon and Kasich shake hands as Domenici (seated, middle) and Levin talk.

• **Food stamps block grant.** Drop a House-passed provision that would have let states that meet certain criteria to gain control over their food stamp program by receiving their federal money in a block grant.

• **Family cap.** Let states decide whether to deny cash assistance to children born to welfare recipients. This was the Senate position. The House version would have prohibited federal welfare funds from being used for children born to welfare recipients, unless states passed legislation exempting them.

• **Medicaid work requirement.** Permit states to deny Medicaid to adults who are dropped from the welfare rolls because they did not meet work requirements. This was the House position. The Senate had no comparable provision.

• **Medicaid for legal immigrants.** Let states decide whether to deny Medicaid coverage to legal immigrants. This was the Senate position. The House version would have denied Medicaid to legal immigrants.

• **Child nutrition for illegal immigrants.** Prohibit illegal immigrants from receiving low-income child nutrition programs, a provision contained only in the House bill. Republicans say states would decide whether and how to enforce this ban.

• **Child care guarantee.** Prohibit states from penalizing a single parent who proves she cannot work because she cannot find care for a child under age 6. Both chambers' versions would have prohibited sanctioning those who could not find child care for a child under age 11.

• **Child protection.** Drop a House-proposed block grant for 11 child protection programs.

• **Adoption.** Drop a House-passed provision that would end delays in adoption related to trying to match children with adults of the same race.

• **Illegal drugs.** Deny cash assistance and food stamps to most individuals convicted of a felony for using, possessing or distributing illegal drugs. Other family members could continue to receive benefits. States could opt out of this prohibition. The House version had no comparable provision. The Senate version would have denied a much broader array of federal benefits to those convicted of a drug misdemeanor or felony.

• **State funds.** Require states to continue to spend at least 80 percent of their own funds on welfare programs, if they fail to meet work participation rates for welfare recipients. States that meet the work participation requirements would need to spend 75 percent of their funds. This is the House-passed requirement; the Senate would have required 80 percent of all states.

The federal government has never before transformed a major individual entitlement program into a block grant to the states.

Because of the savings, Republicans designated it as a deficit-reducing budget-reconciliation bill, which gave it procedural protections in the Senate.

About $23.3 billion of the $54.1 billion in savings would come from scaling back food stamp benefits by cutting individual allotments and making other adjustments. The other major savings would come from denying an array of federal benefits — including food stamps and Supplemental Security Income (SSI) — to most legal immigrants. Under the legislation, food stamp spending would be reduced by 13 percent when changes are fully effective in 2002. SSI, which provides cash to the low-income aged, blind and disabled, would be reduced by 12 percent.

The nation's poorest households, with incomes below half of the federal poverty level, would lose an average of $650 a year in food stamp benefits, according to the Center on Budget and Policy Priorities, a liberal public research group. Half of the poverty line is $6,250 for a family of three.

Still, the measure revamps fewer social policy programs than previous GOP welfare bills would have.

Republicans, especially in the House, had previously sought to give states almost complete control over Medicaid, foster care and adoption programs, school meals, and nutritional assistance for pregnant women and young children. They also wanted to give states the option to control their food stamp programs and to sharply reduce the number of people eligible for the earned-income tax credit, which provides tax relief to the working poor.

In the end, the legislation did none of that.

Provisions of Welfare Bill

The welfare overhaul legislation (HR 3734 — Conference report, H Rept 104-725) cleared by Congress on Aug. 1 would end the 61-year-old guarantee of providing federal welfare checks to all eligible mothers and children. It would save $54.1 billion over six years, mostly by scaling back food stamps and aid to legal immigrants. The House-Senate agreement includes highlights as follows:

Welfare

• **Benefits and eligibility.** The bill would create a block grant for Temporary Assistance for Needy Families to replace Aid to Families with Dependent Children (AFDC), the nation's main cash welfare program, and several related programs.

As a result, poor people who meet the existing eligibility criteria for AFDC would no longer automatically be entitled to cash benefits. Instead, states would have wide discretion in determining eligibility.

• **Federal funding.** Federal funding for the new block grant would be $16.4 billion annually from fiscal 1996 through fiscal 2001. States must convert to block grants by July 1, 1997, and can choose to do so earlier.

Money would be distributed to each state based on its federal funding for AFDC and related programs in either fiscal 1995, fiscal 1994 or the average of fiscal 1992–94, whichever was higher.

Several additional funds would be available for states, including:

• $800 million over four years beginning in fiscal 1998 for states with growing populations and low welfare benefits per recipient.

• $2 billion over five years beginning in fiscal 1997 for matching grants to states with high unemployment or rapidly growing food stamp rolls.

• $1.7 billion over five years beginning in fiscal 1997 for a revolving loan fund. States would have to repay the loans, with interest, within three years.

• $1 billion over five years beginning in fiscal 1999 for states that were most successful in moving welfare recipients into the workplace.

Financial incentives also would be provided to states that reduced their out-of-wedlock births, beginning in fiscal 1998. States that reduced such births by 1 percentage point in any year, compared with 1995, would get an additional 5 percent of their block grant.

States that reduced such births by 2 percentage points would receive a 10 percent bonus. Abortions would be disregarded in calculating each state's "illegitimacy ratio."

• **State funding.** To receive their full share of federal welfare funds, states would have to spend at least 75 percent of the state funds they previously spent on AFDC and related programs. States that did not place the required percentage of welfare recipients into the work force would have to spend at least 80 percent. States would lose $1 in federal funding for each $1 they fell short of this requirement.

• **Work requirements.** Adults receiving welfare benefits would be required to begin working within two years of receiving aid. States could exempt from this work requirement a parent of a child under age 1. However, a parent could receive this exemption only for a total of 12 months, regardless of whether they were consecutive.

States would be required to have at least 25 percent of their welfare caseload engaged in work in fiscal 1997, rising to 50 percent by 2002.

Single parents would be required to work at least 20 hours a week in fiscal 1996, rising to 30 hours in 2000, to count toward the work requirement. States could allow parents with a child under 6 to work 20 hours a week. Two-parent families would have to work 35 hours a week.

States that failed to meet the work requirements would have their block grant reduced by 5 percent. Subsequent failures would result in an additional 2 percent reduction per year, so that it would reach 7 percent the second year and 9 percent the third year, rising to a maximum deduction of 21 percent.

• **Restrictions on aid.** Block grant funds could not be used for adults who had received welfare for more than five years, although state and local funds could be used. States could exempt up to 20 percent of their caseload from this time limit. States could also opt to impose a shorter time limit on benefits.

None of the funds could be used for adults who do not work after receiving welfare for two years.

Adults who do not cooperate in assisting a child support enforcement agency or in establishing paternity would have their family's benefit reduced by at least 25 percent. States could choose to eliminate it.

Individuals convicted of a felony offense for possessing, using or distributing an illegal drug would be denied welfare benefits and food stamps. States could opt out of this prohibition if they passed legislation to do so.

In addition, states would have the option to:

• Deny welfare assistance to children born to welfare recipients.

• Deny welfare to unwed parents under age 18. They could only provide aid to unmarried parents under age 18 who live with an adult and attend school.

• Provide newcomers from another state the same benefits the families would have received from their former state for up to 12 months.

• **Medicaid.** States would be required to continue to offer Medicaid coverage for one year to welfare recipients who lose their welfare benefits because of increased earnings.

States also would have to continue to provide Medicaid to those who would have been eligible for AFDC if that program were still in effect.

• **Federal waivers.** States that previously received waivers of federal laws and regulations to conduct experimental welfare programs could continue those programs until the waivers expired.

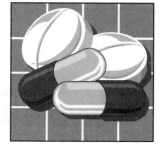

Supplemental Security Income

• **Disabled children.** The bill would make it harder for children to be considered disabled to qualify for Supplemental Security Income (SSI), a cash benefit program for the low-income aged, blind and disabled.

A child under age 18 with an impairment of "comparable severity" to what would be considered a work disability in an adult would no longer be considered disabled and eligible for SSI benefits.

Under current law, the child is considered disabled if mental, physical and social functioning is substantially lower than children of the same age. The bill would add a new definition of a childhood disability saying the child must have a medically proven physical or mental disability "which results in marked and severe functional limitations." As in current law, this disability must be expected to cause death or to last more than 12 months.

The Congressional Budget Office estimates that about 300,000 children — or 22 percent — who would be receiving SSI in 2002 would lose their eligibility as a result of this change.

• **Prisoners.** State and local jails would receive financial incentives to report to the Social Security Administration any information on inmates who are fraudulently receiving SSI.

Child-Support Enforcement

• **Registries.** States would be required to create a central case registry to track the status of all child-support orders created or modified after Oct. 1, 1998. Information would be regularly updated and shared with other entities such as a federal case registry.

States would also be required to establish a "new hire" registry by Oct. 1, 1997, to which employers would have to send the name, address and Social Security number of new hires. States would have to compare information on new hires with the registry of child-support orders and direct businesses to withhold the wages of employees who owe child support.

Similar federal registries would be created to help track deadbeat parents nationwide.

• **Collections and disbursements.** The bill would change the way child support payments — and overdue payments known as arrearages — are disbursed to welfare recipients. For example,

the bill would repeal the requirement that the first $50 collected of monthly child support payments be given to the family, without affecting the family's welfare eligibility or benefits.

• **Enforcement.** States would have the authority to suspend driver's licenses, professional licenses, occupational licenses and recreational licenses of anyone who owed past due child support.

Immigration

• **Illegal aliens and legal non-immigrants.** Illegal aliens and legal non-immigrants — such as travelers and students — would be denied most federal benefits. Exceptions would include short-term disaster relief and emergency medical care.

• **Legal immigrants.** Legal immigrants generally would be ineligible for SSI and food stamps until they became citizens or had worked in the United States for at least 10 years. States could also choose to deny them federal welfare, Medicaid and social services block grant funds.

Non-citizens who arrived in the United States after the bill was enacted would also be denied most other low-income federal social services for five years. The ban includes SSI, food stamps, cash welfare, Medicaid and social services block grants.

Refugees, veterans and those granted asylum would be exempt from these restrictions.

• **Sponsors.** The bill would increase the circumstances under which an immigrant's sponsor would be considered financially responsible for that individual.

Currently, when an immigrant applies for AFDC, food stamps or SSI, the sponsor's income and other resources are taken into account or "deemed" when determining the applicant's eligibility. The sponsor's finances are generally considered for three years after the immigrant arrives in the United States, and for five years for SSI. This would still apply to legal immigrants already in the United States.

The bill would consider the sponsor's finances for most federal programs to which future immigrants applied. Exceptions would include emergency medical services, emergency disaster relief, school meals, Head Start, and various education and training programs.

Child Care

The sponsor's financial responsibility would extend until the immigrant had worked for 10 years in the United States or had become an American citizen.

• **Block grant.** Major federal child care programs would be folded into the existing Child Care and Development block grant to the states. That block grant provides child care services for low-income families and activities to improve the quality and availability of child care. Other child care programs to be consolidated include those used to help move current welfare recipients into the work force and to enable former welfare recipients and those at risk of needing welfare to keep working.

PROVISIONS

• **Funding.** Mandatory, or guaranteed, federal funding would be set at $1.1 billion in fiscal 1996, rising to $2.7 billion in fiscal 2002, for a total of $15 billion. An additional $1 billion in discretionary funding also would be authorized for each of those years.

At least 70 percent of the funds are supposed to be spent to help welfare recipients, those attempting to leave the welfare rolls, and those at risk of needing welfare.

Food Stamps

• **Benefits and eligibility.** The bill would continue to give benefits to anyone who meets eligibility requirements, so the program would expand with demand. It would continue to link benefits to inflation. However, it would cut individual allotments to 100 percent of the Agriculture Department's "Thrifty Food Plan," rather than 103 percent. The Thrifty Food Plan, established by the Agriculture Department, is intended to reflect the benefits needed to purchase food for minimal nutrition requirements.

Benefits would be reduced by changing various deductions that recipients are allowed to count against their income — which is used to calculate benefits. For instance, the standard deduction — applied to all food stamp applications to help determine benefit levels — would be kept at $134.

It is now indexed to inflation. And state and local energy assistance would be counted as income.

The threshold above which the fair market value of a vehicle is counted as an asset would be raised to $4,650 and frozen at that level. The housing deduction would be limited to $300 a month by fiscal 2001 and frozen at that level.

Welfare recipients who did not comply with work requirements would also be denied food stamps.

Penalties would be increased for food stamps fraud and abuse.

• **Work requirements.** Able-bodied recipients between the ages of 18 and 50 who did not have dependents would have to work an average of 20 hours or more per week or par-

The bill would continue to give food stamps to anyone who meets eligibility requirements. But welfare recipients who did not comply with work requirements would be denied food stamps, and penalties would be increased for fraud and abuse.

ticipate in a work program. Otherwise, they would not be eligible to receive more than three months of food stamps out of every three years, plus an additional three months if they had been laid off.

The bill would gradually increase federal funding for food stamp employment and training programs from $79 million in fiscal 1997 to $90 million in fiscal 2002.

• **State flexibility.** States would be permitted to align their food stamp program with other revamped welfare programs. They could establish a single set of eligibility and work requirements for food stamps, welfare checks and other welfare programs.

States could also convert food stamp benefits to wage subsidies for employers who hire stamp recipients. The recipients would then receive wages instead of food stamps.

Social Services

The social services block grant, which provides money to states for services such as child care, would be reduced by 15 percent. States would be permitted to use funds from this block grant to provide noncash vouchers for children whose parents exceed the five-year time limit on benefits.

Earned Income Tax Credit

The bill would make modest changes to scale back the Earned Income Tax Credit, which provides tax relief for low-income workers. The provisions generally aim to tighten compliance with tax rules and make it harder for some people to qualify for the credit. The measure would:

• Require use of a valid taxpayer identification number to allow the Internal Revenue Service to more closely track claimants' identity and income.

• Include additional categories of income — such as capital gains — to disqualify a taxpayer for the credit.

• Exclude certain losses — such as net capital losses — that are now considered when determining whether a worker's adjusted gross income is low enough for them to qualify for the credit. ■

Among the most recent changes made in conference were those that denied states the chance to take over their food stamp programs through block grants. Negotiators also modified provisions that would limit food stamps for able-bodied, 18-to-50-year-olds without dependents who do not work.

After some dispute, they guaranteed that Medicaid would remain available for anyone who meets the current welfare eligibility requirements. And they gave states the option to deny Medicaid to current legal immigrants.

They rebuffed Clinton's call to permit states to use federal welfare block grant money to give non-cash benefits to children whose parents exceed the five-year time limit on benefits. But they allowed states to provide the vouchers from federal social services block grant funds.

For the first time, Republicans included Democrats in deliberations to reconcile the House and Senate versions of the welfare bill. But they left little doubt who was in charge. No Democrats were invited to a July 30 news conference called to reveal details of the conference agreement.

"This is a Republican Congress," said House Budget Committee Chairman John R. Kasich, R-Ohio, "and we feel an obligation to show leadership."

Liberal groups lined up for one last push against the legislation. Representatives of more than a dozen organizations, including civil rights, religious and low-income advocacy groups, urged Clinton to veto the bill July 29.

"It appears that Congress has wearied of the war on poverty and decided to wage war against poor people instead," said Hugh B. Price, president of the National Urban League.

But as details of the conference agreement emerged, more Democrats — eager to satisfy the public's yearning to change the welfare system, especially in an election year — found themselves drawn to it even as they acknowledged its shortcomings.

Rep. Sander M. Levin, D-Mich., noting the vouchers as well as the Medicaid and food stamp changes, said, "I think we were able to press the Republicans in improving the bill as relates to children."

Clinton Under Pressure

Nobody was on the spot more than Clinton. He was eager to fulfill his campaign promise, especially one so central to building his image as a moderate Democrat. It was an issue that he had been familiar with as governor of Arkansas

and in his involvement in shaping the 1988 welfare reform effort (PL 100-485).

As president, Clinton had twice vetoed GOP welfare proposals, branding them as harsh and more likely to hurt children than to help welfare recipients get jobs.

Some top aides suggested that he use his veto pen a third time. They argued that the new bill was similar to the earlier efforts and that the president had suffered little political damage from his previous vetoes.

Let's work together over the next few years to be sure this works."

— Rep. E. Clay Shaw Jr., R-Fla.

But Clinton had repeatedly urged Republicans to send him an improved version of their earlier legislation and to include Democrats in the process. Clinton thought they had done that, to some extent.

Faced with a choice of continuing the status quo or lurching into the unknown, Clinton said he ultimately decided in favor of an overhaul.

He expressed concern that the bill would cut deeply into food stamps and aid to legal immigrants, but he acknowledged that in other respects, Congress "has made many of the changes I sought."

And, he said, "even though serious problems remain in the non-welfare reform provisions of the bill, this is the best chance we will have for a long, long time to complete the work of ending welfare as we know it, by moving people from welfare to work, demanding responsibility and doing better by children."

While the endorsement may help cement Clinton's portrayal of himself as a "New Democrat," it quickly led to charges of betrayal from the left.

Children's Defense Fund President Marian Wright Edelman, a prominent friend and supporter of Clinton's during the 1992 campaign, said Clinton's signature "makes a mockery of his pledge not to hurt children. It will leave a moral blot on his presidency and on our nation."

House Speaker Newt Gingrich, R-Ga., said he did not believe Clinton was keeping children in mind either. He said Clinton would sign the bill "because he

can't avoid it and get re-elected. That is the only reason."

Clinton's decision was not necessarily welcomed by his likely GOP presidential opponent, former Senate Majority Leader Bob Dole, R-Kan.

"The first 100 days of the Dole administration have begun 97 days before the election," Dole said. "I'm pleased that the president has finally decided to support the Dole welfare reform proposal."

But Dole, as majority leader, had resisted sending Clinton another free-standing bill. He insisted on linking welfare to a Medicaid overhaul that Clinton had promised to veto. In July, a month after Dole left the Senate, GOP leaders bowed to pressure from within their ranks and dropped the Medicaid provisions.

Dole now loses his ability to slam Clinton for his earlier welfare vetoes, a potentially effective issue. Despite efforts of GOP congressional leaders to include him, Dole now appears to be an outsider in the effort to enact the legislation.

Final Debate

Clinton's announcement made both chambers' debate on the conference agreement anticlimatic, though it also made apparent that the far-reaching plan they were about to approve would become law.

Some Democrats had decided beforehand how they would vote — many liberals in particular opposed ending the federal entitlement to welfare — but others waited avidly for word from the White House. Like Clinton, they did not want to be seen as supporting the current system but had concerns about the bill's potential impact on the poor.

House Democrats used procedural maneuvers to stall action July 31, awaiting a signal from Clinton and details of the conference report that had been filed late the night before. Many Democrats wanted to make sure they were on the same side as the president.

The election-year desire to revamp an unpopular welfare system was obvious to the bill's opponents. "This is a kind of defining moment in terms of what it might do to children," said Rep. Robert T. Matsui, D-Calif. "I think we shouldn't be bringing it up on even-numbered years, so close to an election."

The legislation was opposed by top Democrats in both chambers — Senate Minority Leader Tom Daschle of South Dakota, House Minority Leader Richard A. Gephardt of Missouri and House Minority Whip David E. Bonior of Michigan.

Many Democrats who opposed the

legislation spoke fervently against it. They often alluded to estimates by the liberal-leaning Urban Institute that the measure would add nearly 2.6 million people, including 1.1 million children, to the poverty ranks.

Rep. Charles B. Rangel, D-N.Y., said it would be a "big political victory" for many politicians, including Clinton, though he expressed disgust that "my president will boldly throw 1 million into poverty."

Democrats who supported the bill, some of whom were swayed by Clinton, typically explained that they were willing to take a chance with a new, untested approach.

"Yes, we are going to take a risk to get people off of welfare to work," said Rep. Benjamin L. Cardin, D-Md. "But the current system is not fair either to the welfare recipient or the taxpayer."

House Democrats split their votes, 98–98. Only two of the party's 34 black members, two of its 12 Hispanic members and nine of its 31 women voted for the conference report.

Rep. John Lewis, D-Ga., a strong Clinton supporter in 1992, called the bill "mean" and "downright lowdown." He said later it struck at the heart of Democratic support among minorities, women and labor, and could have political implications. "It tends to depress our base in key states, in key congressional races," he said.

Only two Republicans opposed the measure — Reps. Lincoln Diaz-Balart and Ileana Ros-Lehtinen, both Cuban-Americans from South Florida who objected to provisions cutting aid to legal immigrants.

Paul Wellstone, D-Minn., was the only senator seeking re-election this year who voted against the legislation, as he did last September on the previous bill. "This legislation, once enacted into law, will create more poverty and hunger among children in America," he said. "This is not reform."

Among Republicans, many members spoke of their compassion.

"We change this system, not because we want to hurt people, but because we want to help people help themselves," said House Majority Whip Tom DeLay, R-Texas.

Said Kasich: "The American people feel fundamentally that if somebody's disabled, we're going to help them. But if somebody's able-bodied and can

work, then they need to go to work."

Some Republicans said success in enacting the law was theirs alone. "This is a Republican victory," said House Majority Leader Dick Armey, R-Texas.

There was also a sense that Congress and the president were about to embark on a historic change, and that its impact would affect millions of people — for better or worse — long after current officeholders leave the scene.

Kasich spoke of Republicans' desire to shift federal control of public and subsidized housing to state and local authorities.

More immediately, the GOP may need follow-up legislation to make clear that states operating welfare programs with waivers of federal rules still must meet the work participation rates in the bill.

Just how Congress follows through in the long term will depend largely on

SCOTT J. FERRELL

Protesting the welfare overhaul bill outside the White House Aug. 1 are Eleanor Smeal of the Feminist Majority, Rev. Jesse Jackson and NOW President Patricia Ireland.

"We all need a certain level of humility today," Clinton said.

Rep. E. Clay Shaw Jr., R-Fla., chairman of the House Ways and Means Human Resources Subcommittee, said, "Let's be patient with each other. And let's work together over the next few years to be sure this works."

More Challenges

What next? Shaw suggested that Congress might consider "the mother of all technical corrections bills" next year.

He has frequently said that lawmakers have to do more to make sure that jobs are available for welfare recipients and other low-income families, especially in inner cities.

who is in control after the November election.

But several factors, including the budget deficit, make it unlikely that Democrats could reverse the end to the welfare entitlement or the cuts in food stamps and SSI.

Said Matsui: "How do you move to the left in a period when the country's moving to the right?"

The biggest challenge by far awaits the states and local governments. They will now shoulder most of the responsibilities, financial and otherwise, of turning welfare offices into job placement centers and moving people from welfare to work. And they will also be the first to feel the consequences if those efforts fail. ■

GOVERNMENT & COMMERCE

Drive To Open Power Industry To Competition Gains Steam

Backers envision lower costs and higher efficiency; foes fear pollution and diminished reliability

They have gathered in New Hampshire, 33 of them now, to woo the Granite State's finicky folk with offers of strange gifts, appeals to conscience and promises of money in citizens' pockets.

They are not politicians vying for the next presidential nominations. They are electric power companies.

The marketing free-for-all sweeping New Hampshire could be the shape of things to come nationally for an industry considered the last government-sanctioned monopoly: electric power. It also portends a long, costly battle in the next Congress over the form energy deregulation should take and the role the federal government should play in molding competition on a national scale.

"This is the biggest deregulatory fight Congress could possibly wrestle with," said Jerry Taylor, director of natural resource studies at the libertarian Cato Institute. "Of all the others — trucking, telecommunications, airlines — there has been nothing like this."

Deputy Secretary of Energy Charles B. Curtis called it "the fundamentally important public policy issue of the day."

Talk of introducing competition into the electricity industry has been around since the 1970s, but it has only recently caught fire. The Federal Energy Regulatory Commission — the regulatory body responsible for monitoring interstate electricity transmission — issued a long-awaited order in April forcing utilities to open their transmission lines to competing wholesale electric generators. That cleared the major technical impediment to true competition.

Opponents of a sweeping restructur-

SCOTT J. FERRELL

Supporters of a sweeping deregulation of the electric power industry envision customers having a wide array of choices for their electricity needs.

ing of the electrical industry note that U.S. electric prices are among the lowest in the Western world, that there is no public clamor to fix a system most Americans do not consider broken. But economists, power producers and many energy experts see competition as the key to lower energy costs and dramatic efficiency improvements at complacent utilities. Large industrial users who pay a significant price for their electrical power stand to benefit hugely. Besides, electricity is the last major regulated monopoly; Congress has made breaking up monopolies virtually a crusade.

On May 28, New Hampshire set the stage, launching a pilot program to open the state's retail electric market to competition. Since then, marketing companies have flooded in, promising the 17,000 pilot-project customers big discounts, free electricity, environmentally friendly power, even free bird feeders. Electricity prices, among the highest in the country, have fallen as much as 18 percent, said George McCluskey, director of the New Hampshire Public Utility Commission's restructuring division.

The passions the state's grand experiment is eliciting will surely infect Capitol Hill when the 105th Congress is sworn in this January. Forty-five other states and the District of Columbia are at least studying retail competition in their electricity markets. Since August, two of them — California and Rhode Island — have enacted groundbreaking competition laws.

"It took a year or so, but in the last few months, the .[flex].[flex]. states have gone nuts," McCluskey said. "It's almost a race to get competition enacted."

That activity has attracted Capitol Hill's attention, as state legislators confront federal impediments to their efforts. More than a half-dozen bills to partially deregulate electricity and introduce retail competition were introduced in the 104th Congress, many of them in the waning days of the session. President Clinton — should he be re-elected — plans to submit comprehensive energy restructuring legislation as soon as Congress returns, Curtis said.

"This is our most vital industry. It's important to get it right," said Curtis, who served as the first chairman of the Federal Energy Regulatory Commission from 1977 to 1981.

Powerful House Republicans, from Majority Whip Tom DeLay of Texas to Commerce Committee Chairman Thomas J. Bliley Jr. of Virginia, have signaled that retail electricity competition will be a top priority of the next Congress. Even if the Democrats take over, the issue will get top billing, said Rep. Edward J. Markey, D-Mass., who has introduced two competition bills.

"This is going to be big," said Rep. Dan Schaefer, R-Colo., the chairman of the Commerce Committee's Subcommittee on Energy and Power and the man leading the charge toward retail competition. "It's probably bigger than the telecom debate. Everybody in this country has power into their house."

The Magnitude of Change

At stake is the fate of a $208 billion electric generating, transmission and marketing industry, larger than the automotive industry, larger than telecommunications. Add to that the power of big-business electricity users and activist consumer groups, and Congress could have a protracted fight.

"This is not a simple situation that can be addressed with a stroke of a pen," said Thomas R. Kuhn, president of the Edison Electric Institute, the lobbying arm of the nation's largest investor-owned utilities.

With so much money involved, lobbyists have already begun to blanket Capitol Hill, painting retail competition as either a pending cataclysm or national salvation. Kenneth L. Lay, chairman of natural gas giant Enron Corp., calls it a $60 billion to $80 billion tax cut for electric power consumers, with no offsetting spending cuts needed.

Proponents, brandishing a new study by the business-backed group Citizens for a Sound Economy, will argue that retail electric power competition will be the greatest boon to the U.S. economy since World War II, sparking a $107.6 billion cut in consumers' annual electric bills, providing up to 3 million new jobs and producing a 2.6 percent, or $191 billion, boost to the nation's gross domestic product.

"I do not think this is going to be that big a boon to the economy. On net, it will be an improvement," cautioned Peter S. Fox-Penner, who had been one of the Energy Department's point people on retail competition before departing this fall for an economic and environmental consulting firm, The Brattle Group.

The issues are complex and myriad, breaking down more along regional lines than partisan ones. They include:

• Whether federal legislation should

mandate nationwide electricity competition, even in states where energy is cheap and residents fear that competition will increase their costs.

• Whether large utilities should be compensated for old investments, such as nuclear power plants, that were undertaken with the consent of state and federal regulators but that will prove unprofitable in a free market.

• How a competitive market can protect costly programs, such as renewable energy research and development and aid to the poor, that may have societal benefits but will raise electricity prices.

• How to safeguard the reliability of electric power in a new era of cost-cutting and streamlining.

• And whether increasing demand for cheap electricity will trigger more air pollution.

Western delegations representing states with cheap hydropower will square off against delegations representing the interests of California and Northeastern consumers with high electricity bills. Midwesterners are likely to demand new life for obsolete coal-fired power plants while Northeasterners insist on environmental protection from the coal-generated pollution expected to drift their way.

Members with utilities saddled with costly, uncompetitive nuclear power plants will probably be receptive to corporate pleas for financial help, while Texans with cheap natural gas will push for a more unfettered market. The Senate, led by Frank H. Murkowski, R-Alaska, chairman of the Energy and Natural Resources Committee, will urge caution while Republican House leaders urge full steam ahead. Rep. John D. Dingell of Michigan, the ranking Democrat on the House Commerce Committee, has expressed reservations about federal involvement in electricity restructuring, but it is not clear how big a role he will play if the Republicans maintain control of the House.

If the legislation is ultimately to pass, it must temper all these passions into a broad, bipartisan bill similar to the Telecommunications Act of 1996 (PL 104-104) and the Energy Policy Act of 1992 (PL 102-486), which opened the legal avenue toward wholesale electricity competition.

Advocates are confident that that can be done. Markey called legislation "inexorable and inevitable."

Shopping for Electricity

Apostles of competition envision a world where customers can shop for

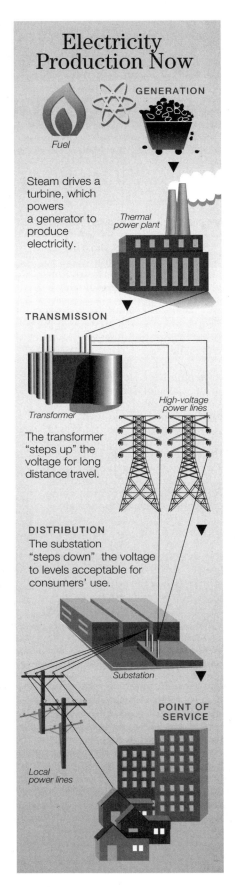

Electricity Production Now

GENERATION

Fuel

Steam drives a turbine, which powers a generator to produce electricity.

Thermal power plant

TRANSMISSION

Transformer

High-voltage power lines

The transformer "steps up" the voltage for long distance travel.

DISTRIBUTION

The substation "steps down" the voltage to levels acceptable for consumers' use.

Substation

POINT OF SERVICE

Local power lines

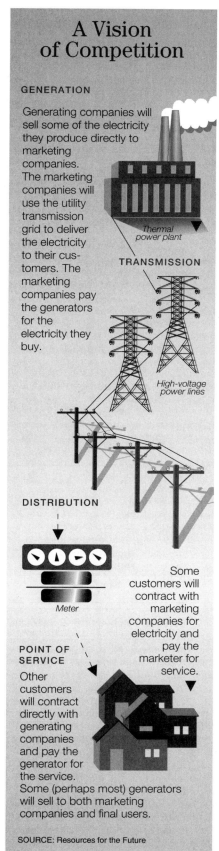

A Vision of Competition

GENERATION

Generating companies will sell some of the electricity they produce directly to marketing companies. The marketing companies will use the utility transmission grid to deliver the electricity to their customers. The marketing companies pay the generators for the electricity they buy.

Thermal power plant

TRANSMISSION

High-voltage power lines

DISTRIBUTION

Meter

Some customers will contract with marketing companies for electricity and pay the marketer for service.

POINT OF SERVICE

Other customers will contract directly with generating companies and pay the generator for the service. Some (perhaps most) generators will sell to both marketing companies and final users.

SOURCE: Resources for the Future

MARILYN GATES DAVIS

electricity packages just as they choose long-distance telephone service. Energy service companies could turn appliances off during peak hours. Large business customers could work out deals to buy electricity from independent generators, or they could set up their own generating systems without facing legal obstacles now being erected by utilities. Homeowners would likely hook up with newfangled power marketing companies that would negotiate their own deal with generators. California's competition legislation, enacted in September, will make this vision a reality in that state, beginning in 1998, and could prove to be the template for many other states. *(Graphic, p. 82)*

All of this became possible April 24, when the Federal Energy Regulatory Commission issued a landmark ruling, Order 888, requiring public utilities to open their power lines to any electric generating company willing to pay a fair transmission cost. The order implements provisions in the 1992 Energy Policy Act, which allowed power generators to compete to sell large quantities of electricity to utilities. The utilities still control distribution to retail customers.

Even before wholesale competition can take hold, states and members of Congress are pushing toward retail competition, in which even homeowners could choose their electricity supplier. Advocates such as the free-market group Citizens for a Sound Economy (CSE) predict that robust competition would drive down electricity bills by as much as 43 percent, cutting costs dramatically for such energy-intensive industries as automobile manufacturing. Increased energy consumption on the order of 25 percent would in turn spur dramatic productivity gains; a firm's production would not be limited by the amount of energy it could afford.

But Curtis, along with independent analysts in the Energy Department's Energy Information Administration, said those "heroic analyses of benefits" — now in wide currency on Capitol Hill — are overstated. The Citizens for a Sound Economy analysis reached its conclusions by inferring that competition will cause regions with excess and unused generating capacity to stoke up their plants to supply more power to other regions. That glut of energy would drive prices down, which in turn would allow energy use to rise dramatically at no net additional cost to the consumer.

Other analysts suggest problems with this scenario. Contrary to what the study reports, energy experts agree that a coal-fired generator in Ohio cannot really ship electricity to California. Too much energy would be lost in transmission. The CSE study does not factor in transition costs that may be paid to investor-owned utilities to ease them into a free market.

Moreover, the study assumes all Americans will radically increase their energy usage. In fact, residential electric consumers do not dramatically curb their electricity usage because of large electric bills, said Douglas R. Bohi, director of the energy and natural resources division at the nonpartisan research group Resources for the Future. Nor, Bohi said, would consumers rush to use more electricity if prices dropped. There are just not that many people who want to get up in the middle of the night to watch TV or run the air conditioning in October.

Nevertheless, many economists say that in the long run, the gains envisioned by the CSE study will become real. Residential consumers may not increase their demand much, but industrial users — 34 percent of the retail market — will, said Douglas Houston, an economist at the University of Kansas School of Business.

A Federal Role

The problems that must be worked out are broad and tricky, going to the heart of the noisiest issues in Washington: federalism and states' rights, environmental protections and "corporate welfare." They boil down to the role the federal government should take in a traditional local issue, how to protect the environment from pollution generated by increasing electricity demand, whether greater societal benefits like clean energy should be insulated from market forces, and whether the government should provide financial help for regulated monopolies facing competition for the first time.

The monopoly utilities are demanding the recovery of their "stranded costs," the difference between the prices utilities are now allowed to charge to cover operations and profits, and the price their electricity will be able to fetch on the open market. *(Story, p. 84)*

But the first issue that must be tackled is the federal role. Curtis, a top candidate to be the next Energy secretary if Clinton is re-elected, says restructuring legislation should be "the first thing out of the box this Congress." But that legislation should be limited to clearing the decks for state action.

Plea for Utility 'Bailout' May Spark . . .

Some of the nation's largest corporations will soon be heading to Washington, cap in hand, pleading for a $300 billion bailout to cover their own bad investments.

If the 1980s were about savings and loans, the late 1990s could be about utilities and an obscure concept known as "stranded costs."

Technically, stranded costs are the monetary difference between what regulators allow utilities to charge now to turn a reasonable profit and what the market will bear once competition is introduced. Free-marketeers and consumer groups call stranded costs a term of art popularized by the electricity industry more than an economic concept. It is a loaded way of saying "unprofitability margin" or "uneconomic costs," said Kenneth Rose, the senior economist at the National Regulatory Research Institute in Columbus, Ohio.

"Every time you see 'stranded cost' in text, it would pay to cross it out and write 'losses,'" said Jerry Taylor, director of natural resource studies at the libertarian Cato Institute. "It's no different from WalMart buying too many purple shirts, than asking to be bailed out for the ones they couldn't sell."

The issue has its roots in the 1970s. As oil prices soared, investor-owned utilities began building colossal nuclear power plants that cost billions of dollars and will almost certainly not be competitive in a free market. Some utilities also signed long-term contracts with alternative energy suppliers at the behest of state governments and public utility commissions. At the time, it seemed safe. The utilities needed only to show the local public utility commission that their costs were "prudently incurred," and they would be reimbursed with a tidy profit.

With competition looming, it is no longer safe. Natural gas is selling at as little as 2 cents a kilowatt hour; renewable and nuclear power can cost several times that.

Currently, ratepayers pay for these unprofitable invest-

SCOTT J. FERRELL

Utilities will likely seek assistance to deal with nuclear plants like the one at Calvert Cliffs, Md.

ments through hidden costs in their utility bills, costs they have no choice but to bear with a monopoly supplier. In a totally free market, nimble utilities and new independent generators — unburdened by past bad investments — could very well bankrupt some of the nation's largest utilities by enticing customers to "strand" the utilities with large nuclear and renewables burdens. Out of 114 investor-owned utilities, 57 have enough old debt to put them at risk in a competitive economy, according to a 1995 report by Moody's Investors Service.

Those utilities, represented by the Edison Electric Institute, argue for federal help with these "stranded costs." They say all of these investments were approved by government regulators; therefore, the government bears responsibility. Legislation should mandate that all customers, even those choosing competitors, must pay for investments incurred originally on their behalf.

The Public Utilities Holding Company Act of 1935 (PUHCA) — enacted to prevent the U.S. power supply from being concentrated in a few corporate hands — hamstrings the ability of major investor-owned utilities to compete in a free market. The Public Utility Regulatory Policies Act of 1978 (PURPA), designed to spark the development of alternative energy supplies, is saddling utilities with unprofitable generating facilities. A federal hand will likely be needed to govern competitive interstate electricity transmission and to monitor pricing.

Moreover, it is not legally clear that states can order retail competition in their electricity markets. Some utilities, seeking to block or slow state efforts,

contend that the Federal Energy Regulatory Commission's transmission access ruling gives federal regulators control over all electricity distribution.

All of these issues should be clarified through federal legislation, said Curtis, whose department began a series of public meetings Oct. 10, preparing to draft the administration's restructuring legislation. The White House would also like to ensure that the development of renewable energy resources, such as solar and wind power, will continue, that deregulation does not trigger increased air pollution, and that low-income Americans are not left out in the cold.

What the Energy Department does not want is a mandate on states to open their markets to competition. That man-

date, thus far, has been the Republican bottom line. Schaefer's bill (HR 3790) — now considered the most likely to move toward enactment — would give the states until Dec. 15, 2000, to implement retail competition. If they failed, the Federal Energy Regulatory Commission would do it for them. DeLay's bill (HR 4297), introduced Sept. 28, moves that deadline forward to Jan. 1, 1998.

"The bottom line is to provide all consumers choice in electricity," Schaefer said.

The conflict over mandated competition will be regional. Western states with cheap hydropower fear that allowing their utilities to send electricity to high-cost states may raise their bills.

. . . Charges of 'Corporate Welfare'

One problem is determining how much stranded costs are out there. Estimates range from as little as $20 billion to as much as $300 billion. Moody's put the cost at $135 billion. It is obviously in the utilities' interest to inflate the stranded-cost estimates, then push for 100 percent reimbursement.

'Corporate Welfare'

The resolution of the issue could determine just how large an economic boon retail energy competition will be. George McCluskey, director of the New Hampshire Public Utilities Commission's restructuring division, said customers in a state pilot project testing retail electricity competition are realizing savings largely because investor-owned utilities consented to forgo up to 45 percent of their stranded costs to entice customers to the program. The utilities will not do so when all-out retail competition begins in 1998. Full stranded-cost recovery would nullify every cent of consumer savings, McCluskey said.

That bolsters the arguments of independent generators, consumer groups and some investor-owned utilities that never invested heavily in nuclear power. They want little or no stranded-cost recovery, arguing it amounts to a colossal piece of corporate welfare. An electricity restructuring bill by House Majority Whip Tom DeLay, R-Texas, (HR 4297) would have banned all stranded-cost recovery.

"We the ratepayers saw no benefits when the nuclear industry shareholders were laughing all the way to the bank" in the 1970s, said Anna Aurilio, a staff scientist with the liberal U.S. Public Interest Research Group. "We're not going to bail them out now."

The utilities will not go down without a fight. Edison Electric Institute levied a $3 million assessment on its members in 1996 to lobby for the deregulation it wants. Another $3 million will be raised in 1997, and it could continue as long as the issue is unresolved. In California, the state's three giant utilities ponied up $1.5 million in lobbying and an additional $300,000 in campaign donations to influence the stranded-cost debate, according to the consumer group Toward Utility Rate Normalization. The result was legisla-

tion that would give the utilities up to $28.5 billion in stranded-cost reimbursement over the next five years.

The federal deregulation Edison wants includes a repeal of energy legislation that curbs utilities' business ambitions while mandating the purchase of expensive power from renewable energy sources. Edison is also demanding some kind of assurances on stranded costs. At least it wants a federal backstop in case the states are less than forthcoming with stranded-cost reimbursement.

If President Clinton is reelected, the utilities will gain a sympathetic ear. The president's Council of Economic Advisers, the Energy Department and the Federal Energy Regulatory Commission have all weighed in for reasonable stranded-cost recovery.

If utilities are rushed into a competitive market with no help, the administration fears widespread economic dislocation. Thousands could be thrown out of work by utilities that employed 466,453 workers in 1994. Shareholders, including large pension funds, could be left with next to nothing. Severe utility cost-cutting could impact efforts to decontaminate old nuclear power plants. And tremors in the capital markets, caused by utility bankruptcies, could make it difficult for surviving energy companies to raise the funds they need to enter the competitive market.

If large businesses flee the utilities in droves, small consumers — frozen in the headlights of electricity choices they have never seen before — could be the only ones left to pay off their electric companies' debts.

Kenneth L. Lay, chairman of natural gas giant Enron Corp., dismissed that concern as a red herring.

"They're about 180 degrees wrong," he said. "The big guys have already made their deals. They've gotten the big price breaks on their electricity. The little user doesn't have any choice. The little user is the captive customer."

But taken together, Energy Department officials say concern over the fate of the utilities is warranted.

"If the big utilities go into some kind of cataclysmic collapse, that's not going to be good for anyone," a top agency official said, speaking on condition of anonymity.

"Electricity is a little different from setting up a hamburger stand or a gas station. There's a lot at stake and there's going to be winners and losers," said Dennis Hansen, an Idaho public utility commissioner. "With our congressional delegation, we're going to be voicing our concerns, . . . trying to protect the interests in this state."

Proponents of deregulation say that attitude is just why a federal mandate is needed. If all low-cost states seal their electricity borders, the benefits of interstate competition will be greatly diminished.

Environmental Concerns

Two other big issues will be environmental. Ironically, competition was first pushed in the 1970s by environmentalists such as Amory Lovins, research director of the Rocky Mountain Institute in Colorado, who saw it as a way of moving from large, inefficient, polluting power plants to dispersed, small-scale generators more conducive to alternative energy sources.

Now, Lovins is concerned about competition pushed by "a curious coalition of large industries eager to grab the cheapest power at everyone else's expense, free-market ideologues with a limited knowledge of utility reality and history, anti-environmentalists who think "retail wheeling" is a neat way of avoiding environmental accountability or expenditures . . . and consultants who see chaos as a profit opportunity."

(Terms, p. 86)

The first environmental issue is the fear that cheaper energy will spur increased consumption, which in turn will stoke Midwestern coal production plants. A study by Resources for the Future foresees an increase in annual emissions by 2000 of 349,000 tons of nitrogen oxide, a key component of smog, and 113.5 million tons of carbon dioxide, the biggest culprit in global warming.

The emissions issue looms large for Northeastern representatives who believe coal-generated pollution will drift their way from the Ohio Valley. Rep. Frank Pallone Jr., D-N.J., introduced a bill (HR 4316) late in the 104th Congress that would predicate any restructuring

Terms of Debate

- **Wheeling** — The practice of a utility using its own transmission network to take in and pass along electricity produced by another utility or generator.
- **Retail wheeling** — The use of a local utility's transmission lines by electricity marketing firms to provide retail customers with a choice of electric generators beyond their traditional utility.
- **Wholesale wheeling** — The process of allowing local utilities to buy energy from competing electric generators, then sell it to retail markets still under monopoly control.
- **Stranded costs** — The monetary difference between the costs a regulated utility now is allowed to charge to cover its operations and profits, and the price it will be able to fetch for power on the competitive market. Current costs are inflated by past investments in nuclear power plants and other long-term contractual obligations that will no longer be profitable on the open market. Stranded costs are also known as transition costs, or uncompetitive costs.
- **Stranded benefits** — Aspects of the electricity market — such as renewable energy generation and subsidies for the poor — that are seen as a public good but that increase the price of energy. Currently, the provision of such benefits is often mandated by federal and state regulators, but such

legislation on changes to the Clean Air Act to bring old coal-fired plants under tighter federal air quality standards. Reopening the Clean Air Act just as members are trying to enact sweeping energy legislation would make the task that much more daunting.

The other environmental issue concerns the fate of renewable energy. Wind, solar and geothermal power may cost more than coal or gas, but there are societal benefits to these energy sources that go beyond price, such as cleaner air and less dependence on foreign oil. As price becomes a critical issue to consumers, some fear these more expensive power sources will be left in the lurch. New energy marketing companies racing toward the bottom line could also abandon their commitments to research, development and aid for poor households, what Curtis has dubbed "stranded benefits."

In this arena, environmentalists have a key ally in Rep. Schaefer, whose suburban Denver district includes the Energy Department's National Renewable Energy Laboratory. Schaefer's bill would require all electric power genera-

tors to maintain "renewable energy credits" equal to 2 percent of their generation, increasing to 4 percent by 2010. They could get those credits by actually generating renewable energy, or they could buy credits from companies that generate more than 2 percent of their energy through such renewable means.

Though they would like to see those percentages set higher, alternative energy groups and environmentalists like the idea. "The market doesn't take into account environmental benefits," said Randy Swisher, executive director of the American Wind Energy Agency. "We want a renewables portfolio standard to ensure that in the transition to a competitive market, renewables don't get lost."

But independent generators and big utilities do not want such requirements. They dispute Schaefer's contention that generators will produce 2 percent of their power from alternative energy by 2000. The Energy Information Administration says renewable resources like geothermal, wood, waste, wind and solar energy currently supply less than 1 percent of electric utility energy. And

Schaefer's detractors say such heavy-handed mandates defeat the purpose of competition. If alternative energy companies want to survive, they must market their products to niche consumers willing to pay more for clean power.

If New Hampshire is any indication, the market may exist. Green Mountain Energy Partners has joined the fray with a "green" portfolio of wind and hydropower. Working Assets is promising a 1 percent donation to an environmental group the customer chooses.

With few allies and opposition from both the utilities and the independent generators, the environmental community is gearing for a fight. "It's going to be a battle," said Alan Nogee, a senior energy analyst with the Union of Concerned Scientists in Cambridge, Mass. "We don't have any illusions."

The Pace of Overhaul

Competition advocates say all these issues can be worked through relatively quickly. Telecommunications deregulation sensitized most members to the issues of competition and the ploys that may be used to slow it down, Schaefer said.

But opponents, primed with utility money or strong ideological convictions, caution that members of Congress evincing a fait accompli attitude are in for a rude awakening once the debate moves beyond the Beltway.

Amory Lovins warned in a recent essay that the apostles of retail wheeling will be proved embarrassingly wrong.

There is no public outcry for a radical overhaul of the nation's electric power system, considered by many to be the best in the world. And with so much at stake, the kind of fear-mongering raised in past deregulatory debates may just ring true with the American people.

"There is obviously a tremendous risk here," said Robert K. Johnson, executive director and general counsel of the Electric Consumers Alliance in Indianapolis, a group formed with start-up money from the utilities. "People appreciate the notion that everybody doesn't win. And the fear is that the people who won't win are the small consumers, the little guys."

SOCIAL ISSUES

The Next President's Burdens

*They may not play prominently on the campaign trail,
but 11 inescapable issues await in the Oval Office*

The decisions by which history will judge a president often are not decided or even debated in an election campaign. Sometimes an unforeseen crisis erupts; sometimes the contending candidates share similar ideas. But often the problem is evident; it is just not ripe for resolution.

Thus in 1932, Franklin D. Roosevelt advocated conventional tactics, such as a 25 percent reduction in federal expenditures, to combat a virulent Depression. It took a bank panic on the eve of his inauguration for the country to contemplate — and FDR to embrace — more ambitious steps.

More recently, Bill Clinton learned the hard way that the nation was not ready to reinvent the health care system.

When Congressional Quarterly's editors gathered to survey the issues that will face the next president, they found the docket crowded with problems that are inexorably marching toward the Oval Office.

Some issues — tax policy, crime, the environment, Medicare — resonate in sound-bite slogans in the campaign between Clinton and his Republican rival, Bob Dole. But a closer look shows an inchoate cluster of devilish choices. Some — such as the population trends that will inevitably squeeze education, health and pension programs — have not quite reached crisis proportions. Others — foreign policy, defense, the economy — lack only the spark of a defining event to set off a full-bore tumult in the media and Congress.

These are not hypothetical situations. They are a matter of "when," not "if." During the next four years, the president will be able to duck these 11 problems only by extraordinary luck, or by risking his place in history.

In foreign policy, for instance, China is muscling its way into world markets at a pace that will eventually reduce the United States to the No. 2 economy. But while Clinton and Dole share the same stance of free trade tinged with moral pressure, the real determinant of U.S. policy will be what hap-

The Issues

■ ■ ■

pens after 92-year-old leader Deng Xiaoping disappears.

Presidents love to take credit for economic prosperity, and they are the first to be blamed when the economy sours. The problem facing any president is how and when to respond when the inevitable recession occurs.

It will be extraordinary if the next president leaves office without the nation enduring a recession. The most recent peacetime expansion — and the longest in the nation's history — lasted 91 months. The current period of uninterrupted growth has run 67 months, and though it shows no serious signs of faltering, eventually it surely will.

The challenge will be to tailor a response to the situation — each business cycle displays different characteristics — and to neither overreact nor project the false buoyancy that cost George Bush credibility in 1992.

The die is already cast on several issues for which demographics are destiny. As more people reach the age of 65, Social Security and Medicare costs will skyrocket. Children of baby boomers and a wave of immigrants are about to flood the schools, creating more pressure to address a topic that ranks No. 1 among public concerns. The rising teenage population also will exacerbate the No. 2 concern, crime.

Deadlines loom on environmental programs that demand choosing winners and losers. The budget deficit, shrunk by more than 60 percent in the past four years, will resume its upward spiral next year. Although the federal government is devolving welfare to the states, the public clamors for a stronger federal role in education, crime and telecommunications.

Each of the issues on the following pages presents excruciating dilemmas for the next president. Each needs to be translated, by events or leadership, into a well-defined set of alternatives. But the act of defining alternatives is one of the most important ways in which a president can claim power.

"No easy problems ever come to the president of the United States," Dwight D. Eisenhower told President John F. Kennedy. "If they are easy to solve, somebody else has solved them."

CQ Weekly Report October 5, 1996

How to Keep the Economy Rolling Along?

■ **The fiscal 1996 deficit is expected to be about $116 billion; measured as a percentage of gross domestic product, that is the lowest since 1974.**

■ **The "misery index" (inflation plus unemployment) is lower than at any time during the 12 years of the Reagan and Bush administrations.**

■ **Inflation is running at the lowest it has been since the 1960s.**

Sources: Commerce and Labor departments; Blue Chip Economic Indicators

What a difference a term makes. When Bill Clinton was running against then-President George Bush four years ago, the economy seemed stuck in an agonizingly slow recovery from the 1990 recession.

How much credit Clinton deserves for the turnaround since then is debatable, but the economy is much improved. Measured by indices such as inflation and unemployment, in fact, the economy is about as good as it has been in a generation. Average inflation is lower than at any time since the 1960s, and unemployment has dropped to levels that as little as a year ago were thought to be too low, with so much of the labor force at work that a renewed bout of inflation was virtually certain — which has not happened.

All this has produced the lowest "misery index" (inflation plus unemployment) since Jimmy Carter coined the term for his 1976 campaign against President Gerald R. Ford, when the index measured 13.4. In 1992, when Clinton beat Bush, the misery index was 10.4; it has now dropped to 8.2, with inflation at about 3 percent and unemployment at just over 5 percent. That's lower than anything recorded during all 12 Reagan-Bush years.

Add a stock market that keeps hitting record highs, a falling crime rate, diminishing welfare rolls, the lowest federal budget deficit (relative to the economy) in more than two decades and slow but steady economic growth, and whoever wins the election on Nov. 5 is likely to have one question on his mind:

How do I keep the good times going?

'First, Do No Harm'

Actually, most economists say that is not the question the next president ought to be asking himself, or perhaps not the first one.

That is because economists generally agree that there are other, more pressing economic challenges the new president ought to be thinking about: naggingly slow growth, persistently stagnant wages and the looming explosion in entitlement spending on such programs as Social Security and Medicare. It is also because there isn't much a president can do to keep the current economic expansion going besides minding his own business.

"First, do no harm," advises David Wyss, chief financial economist for DRI-McGraw Hill Inc., invoking the physician's creed. "You've got to keep it going slow. Don't get greedy, because holding the inflation rate down is critical to keeping the expansion going."

That means don't jawbone or otherwise try to lean on the Federal Reserve Board, the anti-inflation watchdog that has raised interest rates at key junctures to keep inflation — and the economy — from overheating.

The temptation to jawbone the Fed into keeping rates low is nearly irresistible, since rising interest rates can cool off and and even help kill expansions. Steady anti-inflationary pressure was one of the factors that helped end the long Reagan-Bush expansion in 1990, leading to the recession that contributed to Bush's loss of the presidency in 1992.

Economists give Clinton good marks for staying silent.

"Clinton deserves credit mostly because of what he did not do, which was nag the Fed," says William Niskanen, president of the Cato Institute and a former economic adviser to President Ronald Reagan. "He basically has kept his mouth shut."

Clinton did more than that. Acceding to Republican demands, he nominated Fed Chairman Alan Greenspan to a third term in a package deal with two Democratic appointees, Alice M. Rivlin and Laurence H. Meyer.

It was not always easy to leave Greenspan alone. The Fed raised rates after the economy took off during Clinton's first year in office, and some economists expected a recession during the winter of 1994-95. Instead, the economy appeared to get the much hoped-for "soft landing" in 1995, when inflation cooled without triggering a downturn. Wyss says that probably bought another three to five years of expansion, holding off a recession until at least 1998, possibly longer.

Indeed, a recent survey of 45 economists by the influential "Blue Chip Economic Indicators" newsletter found that none of them is predicting a recession this year. Only nine of them think a recession will occur in 1997, and the rest are about evenly split between predicting a downturn in 1998 and betting it will happen in 1999 or later. Getting all the way through the next presidential term without a recession would set a record — 10 years without a significant downturn.

So, thinks the next president to himself as he savors his breakfast on Nov. 6, things are good.

Storm Clouds Ahead

Don't get complacent, warn the economists. Had he invited them to dine with him, here are some of the things they would warn the president he should be worrying about:

● **Entitlements explosion.** A hair-raising report from the usually staid Congressional Budget Office (CBO) projects economic catastrophe early in the next century unless the nation comes to grips with the way the cost of the nation's two biggest entitlement programs — Social Security and Medicare — will accelerate when Baby Boomers begin to retire.

If no changes are made, the widening mismatch between a smaller work force and a huge and growing retiree population will make it impossible to pay retiree benefits without enormous new deficit spending.

That would cause deficits and the national debt to explode to "unsustainable — indeed, unthinkable — levels," potentially triggering a "severe recession," a stock market collapse and even global economic chaos, CBO warns.

"Policymakers would surely take action before the economy was driven into such dire straits," CBO declares. But in the most recent Congress, Republicans and Democrats left Social Security changes off the table altogether and gridlocked over proposals to make changes to Medicare. The parties are so polarized and the entitlement issues so politically poisonous that there is no obvious way to make progress.

Former CBO Director Rudolph G. Penner says the entitlements problem "just overwhelmingly overshadows all others" in urgency for the next president.

While economic meltdown is still years away — the first Baby Boomers become eligible for early retirement Social Security benefits 12 years from now, in 2008, and deficits and the debt do not begin to soar for some years after that — it is already too late to painlessly phase in changes the way past Congresses and presidents have been able to do.

"When we changed the Social Security retirement age [to 67] in 1983, we gave 17 years of notice," Penner noted. "It's too late to give 17 years of notice now."

Penner is hardly alone in sending up a dire warning. The 45 "Blue Chip" economists who thought a recession was unlikely this year rated the "growth in government spending/entitlements" as the most serious economic problem facing the United States today. Inflation was way down the list at No. 18, and recession was No. 20.

• **The budget deficit.** Right now, the news on the deficit is startlingly good. Clinton more than fulfilled his 1992 campaign pledge to cut the federal deficit in half: When he took office, the red ink had just set an all-time dollar record at $290 billion; projections for this year show it dropping to about $116 billion, the lowest since Jimmy Carter's last deficit of $79 billion, in 1981.

The news is even better when the deficit is measured as a percentage of the gross domestic product (GDP), as economists usually prefer (it adjusts for inflation and allows comparisons across the years). In those terms, the estimated 1996 deficit would equal 1.5 percent of GDP, the lowest since Richard M. Nixon pushed the deficit down to just 0.4 percent of GDP in 1974.

All that is expected to change quickly, however. CBO predicts that the deficit will tick back up again next year and rise to as much as 2.5 percent of GDP by 1999. Further, it forecasts the deficit to increase to as much as 3 percent of GDP by 2003 — big enough to be worrisome, though still a full percentage point less than the average deficit of the 1980s.

The return to rising deficits is likely to put new pressure on Congress and the next president to make good on pledges by both parties to balance the budget by 2002.

• **Slow growth, stagnant wages.** The anomaly that underlies all the generally positive news about the economy is that economic growth is relatively weak by postwar standards. A related phenomenon is that inflation-adjusted wages have generally stalled or even fallen for some workers.

GOP presidential candidate Bob Dole has built his campaign around the notion that Clinton's economic "boom" is actually quite weak, and that GOP supply-side remedies — chiefly a 15 percent reduction in individual tax rates and a halving of the capital gains tax rate — would dramatically boost growth.

Here opinions diverge radically. How fast the economy can grow and whether and how much fiscal policy changes can affect the growth rate are complex areas where economists often disagree, and where the truth sometimes seems more a matter of faith or political stripe than of empirical proof.

There is no disagreement that today's inflation-adjusted growth rate — barely more than 2 percent a year — seems wimpy compared with what it was in the 1960s (4.4 percent), the 1970s (3.2 percent) or the 1980s (2.8 percent).

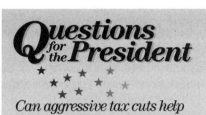

Questions for the President

Can aggressive tax cuts help propel economic growth from its current 2.2 percent to more than 3 percent a year?

Is the deficit now so low that the president and Congress can, in effect, safely ignore it?

Should the next president focus only on balancing the budget by 2002 or take on the much tougher job of warding off long-term disaster for Medicare and Social Security?

■ ■ ■

A Magic Bullet?

Politicians love to talk about magic bullets such as lower taxes or the transfer of power, money and influence back to state and local governments. But there is wide agreement that there is no economic bullet more magical than robust growth.

Charles L. Schultze, a senior fellow at the Brookings Institution and former economic adviser to President Carter, says that raising GDP growth a single percentage point and keeping it there for 10 years would add $4,000 a year to the $40,000 annual income of the average family. Over that same 10-year period, 1-point higher GDP growth would raise federal revenues and lower interest payments on the national debt, literally "growing the economy" enough to painlessly balance the budget.

That sounds fabulous, but economists disagree over whether it is possible, and, if so, how to do it. Whoever is elected as the next president will have to wrestle with these questions.

There are some areas of rough accord. Economists generally agree that changing the current tax system to reward savings and discourage consumption would help boost investment. They agree that regulations and litigation have, in some cases, become a counterproductive drag on business activity. They think that stimulating research and development and raising the quality of the nation's educational system could help boost productivity.

All of these could help boost the growth rate and improve America's standing in the face of foreign competition. (The U.S. trade deficit — American exports versus imports, seasonally adjusted — stood at just under $7.9 billion in January 1993, the month Clinton took office. In July, it stood at nearly $15.65 billion, according to Census Bureau's Foreign Trade Division.)

But economists differ sharply over how far to go in any of these areas, and how much of a difference it would make to the nation's bottom line.

The Dole campaign has projected that its policies would boost growth rates to 3.5 percent or more, an increase of more than 1 percentage point beyond the current rate of 2.2 percent to 2.3 percent.

Economist John H. Makin of the American Enterprise Institute says Dole's proposed 15 percent cut in individual tax rates would raise personal income enough to entice more workers into the labor force and get more hours of work out of those already working. Over five years, Makin concludes, this could raise growth from the current 2.0 to 2.5 percent range to 2.5 to 3.0 percent.

Other economists strongly disagree. "Nothing that is realistically possible, not tax cuts, nor public investments nor regulatory reform, will generate the large gains that many politicians are . . . promising," writes Schultze in The Brookings Review.

Echoes his Brookings colleague Robert D. Reischauer, a former CBO director, "A majority of economists would say a plan like Bob Dole's would increase the growth rate by 0.1 percent to 0.2 percent. . . . The notion that some president can take actions that will cause the economy to leap from an underlying rate of 2.3 percent to 3.5 percent is pure nonsense."

It's been called the "crime bomb," "the baby boomerang," the "nightmare of the future." To be sure, the issue of juvenile crime is not going away. Indeed it may well be the most nettlesome problem to confront the next president.

"Youth crime is the issue. It's the issue now, and it's the issue in the future," said James Alan Fox, dean of the Northeastern University's College of Criminal Justice. It's an issue because of the anticipated surge in the number of children expected to hit puberty in the next administration.

And there are two perspectives on how to cope with the problem. Some say more prisons, stiffer penalties and less tolerance for repeat offenders. Others advocate prevention.

"There are a growing number of disaffected young people in our society and the fact is, we won't be able to incarcerate our way out of this," said J. David Hawkins, director of the Social Development Research Group at the University of Washington in Seattle. "We simply can't afford it in dollar figures, and we can't take the toll as a society."

Despite yo-yo statistics, despite the most recent Department of Justice data showing that violent crime actually declined by 9 percent last year, there is a widespread perception across the country that crime is on the rise and the level of violence is escalating. A recent Washington Post survey, for example, ranked crime second among the top 20 worries confronting voters, right behind education.

And at a time when the federal government appears to be reducing its responsibility for social programs such as welfare, it is stepping up its role in fighting crime. The Department of Justice, the main purveyor of crime fighting, is set to get about four times the amount of money it received a decade ago.

The next president will also confront a federal prison population where nearly two-thirds of the prisoners are drug offenders; a racial disparity between blacks and whites in the prison population that is as high as 20 to 1; and a parole and probation system so overburdened that agents are assigned an average load of 260 cases.

Juvenile Crime

When compared to other industrialized nations, the United States has the highest homicide rate for males aged 15 to 24. That is five times greater than the second highest nation, Scotland.

From 1990 to 1994, the overall rate of murder in America declined by 4 percent. At the same time, the rate of murder committed by teenagers aged 14 to 17 increased 22 percent. That continued a trend that began in 1985 and continued until 1994, during which time the homicide rate for teenagers rose by 172 percent.

However, last year the number of juveniles arrested for violent offenses dropped — for the first time in a decade — by 2.9 percent. The murder arrest rate dropped for the second year in a row, declining by 15.2 percent. U.S. Attorney General Janet Reno attributed that drop to law enforcement effectively cracking down on the problem. But crime experts tell a different story.

"This may be the calm before the crime storm," said Fox, who chalked up the decline to a statistical blip. He predicts the juve-

Crime Debate: Punishment or Prevention?

- The number of juvenile murder victims increased by 82 percent between 1984 and 1994. The number of murders committed by teens aged 14-17 increased 172 percent.

- Of federal prisoners, 59.2 percent are serving time for drug-related crimes.

- The incarceration rate of blacks is eight times that of whites.

Sources: Alfred Blumstein, Carnegie Mellon University; James Alan Fox, Northeastern University; U.S. Department of Justice.

nile offender rate will worsen with the upcoming generation of teens — children of the baby boomers.

"They will become teenagers before you can say juvenile crime wave," Fox said. "The future may be so bad that unless we act now in a preventive way, we will look back at the 90s and call them good old days."

Some 39 million children are now under the age of 10. By the year 2005 the teen population is expected to increase by 20 percent, with the largest increase in the African-American population. The most current statistics from the U.S. Census indicate that 46 percent of black teenagers live below the federal poverty level. Criminologists expect that number to increase. Studies show, in varying degrees, a strong correlation between living in poverty and entering a life of crime.

"With the population of juveniles about to surge and with many of those children living in poverty, the United States could confront a tide of youth violence more deadly than we have seen yet," concluded Fox.

But others are not so certain that a tidal wave is on its way.

"It's 'Star Trek' stuff," said Franklin E. Zimring, the director of the Earl Warren Legal Institute at the University of California at Berkeley.

As the juvenile population increases, so too will the overall population, said Zimring. In 1994, teenagers made up 5.4 percent of the population. By 2010, they will hover around 5.9 percent.

What they do agree on is that the level of violence is escalating as more youths are apparently becoming desensitized to violent behavior. As one Justice Department official put it, "Instead of fists, youths today are settling their battles with bullets."

Since 1984, the number of juveniles killing with a firearm has quadrupled, while the number of killings with all other weapons combined has remained virtually unchanged, according to Fox.

Compounding the increase in gun use is the issue of race. Between 1985 and 1990, the juvenile homicide rate for white youths doubled, while it tripled among African-American youths.

"It's not the number of kids we have in the population, it's the lethal crime rate that is the problem," Zimring said.

"Young people are more impulsive than older ones, and thus distant penalties are less likely to make a difference," said James Q. Wilson, a professor at the University of California at Los Angeles, speaking at a recent crime forum. Because many inner-city neighborhoods are not much different from Bosnia or Beirut, Wilson said, "gun ownership has become necessary in the eyes of many juveniles for reasons of self-defense."

Drugs, Racial Disparity and Prison

The state and federal prisons are bursting at the seams. But the rate of new prison construction is keeping the capacity rate fairly stable. What isn't stable is the racial makeup of the prison system, which could be a time bomb for the next president.

"One of the most distressing and troublesome aspects of the criminal justice system is the disparity between blacks and whites," wrote Alfred Blumstein, a professor of urban systems and operations research at Carnegie Mellon University. In Minnesota, Blumstein found the ratio of blacks to whites in prison to be as high as 20 to 1.

When compared to total population figures, African-Americans are being incarcerated at a rate eight times that of whites, according to the Bureau of Justice Statistics. Between 1980 and 1994, the number of blacks in prison tripled to 489,200, representing 3.2 percent of the total African-American male population. That compares with 0.4 percent of all white males, according to Allen J. Beck, chief of corrections statistics at the bureau.

Why is the disparity so great?

Of the 100,250 prisoners in the federal system, 59.2 percent were there for drug-related crimes, according to the Bureau of Justice Statistics. Of the 1.03 million in the state system, roughly a quarter were there for drug crimes. African-American males make up about 50 percent of convicted drug offenders.

Most of the drug offenders are serving federally mandated sentences, which tend to be harsher for drugs used in the African-American community. For example, in 1991, the Minnesota Supreme Court struck down a state law which mandated two years for posessing three grams of crack cocaine but just one year for possessing three times as much powder cocaine. The ruling, based on equal protection grounds, found that the legislative distinction was racially discriminatory in impact because a study had found that 100 percent of those sentenced under the crack cocaine statute were black and 66 percent of those sentenced under the powder cocaine statute were white.

While the prevailing tendency is to fight the drug war with stiffer sentences, Blumstein and other experts say that prison should not be the only solution.

"The demand side is where you have to put your attention," Blumstein said. "You take a dealer off the street, another one is sure to crop up in his place. On the other hand, when you lock up a pathological rapist or say, a murderer, you lock up their traits."

Despite falling crime rates, there will be one violent crime committed this year for every 130 citizens, said Peter W. Greenwood of the California-based Rand Corporation. Preventing crime is a critical issue for the next president to reckon with.

But how?

While the number of inmates in state prisons tripled during the 1980s, Greenwood said, few dollars were allocated toward programs that keep youths from pursuing the criminal life.

Greenwood and a team of researchers found that a combination of incentives to graduate from school and parental training could reduce the crime rate and cost one-fifth what it would take to implement California's Three Strikes Law. By locking up repeat offenders under the new law, Greenwood predicted, the state's overall crime rate would drop by 21 percent. It would cost taxpayers $5.5 billion. When Greenwood returned to the issue and studied the effects of a multi-layered prevention program, he reported the crime rate would drop about the same amount, but the price tag would be much less — $1 billion.

The trick is reaching out to youths before they hit their "peak criminal years," said Hawkins of the University of Washington. His research found that only 20 percent of those who commit violent crimes before 18 actually become violent later in life, he said.

If youths are given the chance to feel bonded to their community, are encouraged to produce in school and have family members who establish clear standards of proper behavior, they are less likely to turn to a life of crime, according to Hawkins. Youths who get help generally have a more positive self-image and a more positive attitude toward school and are less likely to become career criminals, Hawkins said.

Questions for the President

Some say the answer to juvenile crime is to lock them up at younger ages. Some say prevention is the way. What is the best way to handle the anticipated juvenile 'crime bomb'?

How can the growing racial disparity in the state and federal prison system be addressed?

Nearly two-thirds of the prisoners in the federal system are there for drug crimes. Is incarceration the best answer to the drug war?

■ ■ ■

Federalization

At the core of the crime debate are fundamental questions of what role each level of government should play.

"There are constant complaints of overfederalization, yet politicians want to do more and more," said Gerald B. Lefcourt, president-elect of the National Association of Defense Attorneys. "It's a dangerous time, particularly since the Democrats have tried to co-opt the Republicans on the crime issue."

Dangerous, because with the federal government acting like the sheriff of Dodge City comes hysterical overreaction to criminals and thus the loss of defendants' rights, in Lefcourt's opinion.

Local prosecutors say that line of reasoning is absurd. But they too feel the federal posse coming through what they consider their territory. Prior to the 1994 Crime Control Law Enforcement Act, three federal crimes were punishable by death — espionage, aircraft piracy and murder associated with a criminal enterprise such as the Mafia. Now there are more than 60, and they include cases once considered the domain of state prosecutors, such as drug-related drive-by shootings and killing a law enforcement official. Of the 11 people now on death row, six were sentenced following the crime bill, and the federal government is responding to an anticipated bulge of prisoners sentenced to death by building a new 50-bed death row at their facility in Terre Haute, Ind.

"The problem [of crime] is local, local, local," said William L. Murphy, the District Attorney of Staten Island, N.Y. Instead of federalizing crimes, he said, more money should be funneled to the front lines of local government to combat crime.

Over the last five years, the caseload in his largely suburban office has doubled, and local police have started a narcotics division to deal with a surge of drug arrests. As the president-elect of the National District Attorney Association, Murphy thinks juvenile crime will be the most critical problem to face the president because it touches not only the criminal justice system but the future of the country. If the next generation of youths are not harnessed and youth offenders not deterred, the long-term effects will reverberate in the economy.

There are nearly twice as many felons being supervised in local communities than in prison, according to the Bureau of Justice Statistics. Despite the high caseload and parole officers complaining that they are unable to keep track of their cases, 62 percent of all felons are rearrested within three years of their release from prison.

In practical terms, a president's decisions about defense policy are bound by assumptions about money: How much does the American political system want to spend each year on the U.S. military establishment?

Five years after the collapse of the only rival superpower, the answer seems to be: around $265 billion. And barring a sweeping shift in Capitol Hill's partisan lineup, the next president likely will find that this most fundamental of defense policy decisions already has been made — at least for a few years to come.

For the four most recent fiscal years, after some pushing and shoving between President Clinton and congressional Republicans, the defense budget has hovered between $261 billion and $266 billion.

Those budgets are roughly 90 percent of the average U.S. defense budget during 1985-92, the climactic years of the Cold War standoff between the United States and the Soviet Union. Inflation, of course, has eroded the value of those dollars, so that the current budget provides about two-thirds of the purchasing power of the fiscal 1985 defense budget, the largest since the Korean War.

Spending for new weapons and equipment has been cut much more dramatically than the defense budget as a whole. In inflation-adjusted terms, the Pentagon's procurement appropriation for fiscal 1997 has about one-third the purchasing power of the fiscal 1985 hardware accounts.

Even so, the size of the current budget, as well as the narrow scope and perfunctory character of mainstream political debate over that amount — all are striking. Now that the Soviet threat, which paced the Pentagon for half a century, is defunct, one might have expected a more vigorous debate over military spending, if only because it accounts for roughly half the portion of the federal budget Congress can adjust from year to year.

That debate has been muted, in part, because the military forces and its supporting industrial base still mean lots of jobs in vote-rich states. But another reason is that the post-Soviet world has turned out to be nastier and more uncertain than many had hoped.

There had been a single adversary — massively armed and opportunistic, but relatively cautious and predictable. Now U.S. interests around the world face an array of actual or potential threats, each much less predictable than the old Soviet empire, and some evidently convinced that they have much less to lose if they overreach.

In a category by themselves stand the Soviet empire's Russian remnant and China, each large enough to aspire to superpower status in a decade or two, each armed with nuclear weapons (and, in Russia's case, with thousands of long-range ballistic missiles), and each embroiled in wrenching social change.

Then there is a pariah caste of expansionist regional powers — Iran, Iraq, Libya, North Korea and Syria, all armed to the teeth and apparently more or less intent on acquiring nuclear, chemical and biological weapons.

Finally, there are countless small states, tribes, sects and ter-

Should Defense Budget Remain the Same?

- **The fiscal 1997 defense budget is 40 percent below peak Reagan years, after inflation.**

- **Congressional Republicans proposed spending 0.68 percent more than President Clinton for fiscal 1998-2002.**

- **Active service strength of 1.4 million is designed to win two major regional wars at once.**

Source: Department of Defense

rorist cabals, trivial by traditional military calculus, but able to use violence as leverage on a military superpower that is economically interdependent and electronically interconnected with the rest of the globe.

To deal with that chaotic environment, conservative pundits William Kristol and Robert Kagan urge "a neo-Reaganite foreign policy of military supremacy and moral confidence," for which they would increase annual defense budgets by $60 billion to $80 billion. On the other hand, Brookings Institution analyst Lawrence Korb has called for a reduction in defense spending of about $20 billion. But both proposals are far outside the range of $10 billion or so within which the Washington defense debate has been focused since Bill Clinton moved into the White House.

Nor do either the Clinton administration or the GOP congressional majority promise any radical shift in the near future. Both have called for the defense budget to gradually increase over the next five years to between $280 billion and $288 billion annually. Over that period (fiscal 1998-2002), Clinton's projected defense budgets would total $1.36 billion, and the Republicans' plan would total $1.37 billion — a difference of $9.3 million (0.68 percent).

What Missions?

One point of departure in deciding how that defense budget should be spent is to decide what kinds of jobs the president wants the military to perform and how large a force those missions would require. Indeed, Congress has mandated just such a review as part of the fiscal 1997 defense authorization bill signed into law in September. *(1996 Weekly Report, p. 2256)*

Clinton has set the bar pretty high, aiming at a force that could win two nearly simultaneous wars with regional powers such as Iraq and North Korea. An active-duty force of 1.4 million members to meet that standard also is expected to deal with lesser contingencies such as peacekeeping missions or humanitarian efforts. But if one major war breaks out, forces involved in such peripheral missions would be withdrawn to be ready for a second war.

This two-war standard has a dual rationale: (1) providing a base from which the U.S. force could be expanded if Russia or China showed signs of becoming a global competitor; (2) having enough forces to deter any one of the rogue states from capitalizing on the fact that U.S. forces have gotten involved in combat with another.

Clinton's program is designed to meet additional criteria that drive up the size and technological prowess — and thus the cost — of the two-war force. The victories are to be swift and decisive with U.S. casualties kept to very low levels. And while it would be preferable to fight in a coalition, U.S. forces are to be able to go it alone, if need be.

Republican defense leaders have tried to spark a public debate over the urgency of one other mission: They have demanded an immediate commitment to deploy by 2003 a "thin" anti-missile defense that could protect U.S. territory against a few dozen nuclear warheads — the kind of attack that might be launched by one of the pariah states or by a rogue Russian military unit. But the issue has gained no political traction, partly because Clinton claims that his program, too, could field an anti-missile defense by 2003 but that a decision to meet that deadline can be deferred to see whether new missile threats materialize.

Among defense policy experts, Clinton's assumptions about the mission and size of the force have triggered several other debates, none of which have drawn much notice in the broader political arena.

One is whether the "two-war" standard is appropriate. Kristol and Kagan call for a larger force, partly to persuade potential superpowers and regional troublemakers that it would be futile to try to build up their forces to a level that could challenge U.S. interests — defined in expansive terms — around the world. But John D. Steinbruner of the Brookings Institution warns that the Clinton policy may rest on a self-fulfilling prophecy, since it might provoke Russia, China and the potential regional troublemakers to maintain larger forces than they otherwise would.

A second issue is whether Clinton's goal of a 1.4 million member force, fully modernized and ready for war on short notice, meets the two-war standard. Noting that U.S. troops have been deployed on peacekeeping and humanitarian missions much more often than had been anticipated, Army Chief of Staff Gen. Dennis L. Reimer contends that the Pentagon needs a force large enough to fight two regional wars without assuming that less vital — but manpower-intensive — missions would be abandoned.

On the other hand, Brookings' Korb contends that the administration has overdrawn the two-war requirement. He discounts the combat effectiveness of Iraq and other potential predators and argues that an active duty force of 1.3 million would suffice. Moreover, he says, many units in that smaller force could be kept at a more relaxed (and less expensive) state of readiness and could forego some high-tech weapons they are slated to receive.

A third question is whether Clinton's projected defense budgets adequately fund his planned two-war force. The General Accounting Office (GAO) and the Congressional Budget Office (CBO) both have warned that Clinton's budgets would fall short. Heritage Foundation defense specialists Kim R. Holmes and John Hillen contend that it would cost an additional $20 billion to $30 billion annually just to fund Clinton's own force — which, they go on to argue, really is only large enough to handle one major regional war and one lesser conflict while maintaining skeletal forces in Europe and the Western Pacific.

But Defense Secretary William J. Perry discounts the GAO and CBO warnings, saying they ignore recent, far-reaching management changes. Already, Perry argues, the Defense Department is starting to realize savings from the closure of unneeded bases under a 1990 law and from simplifications in the procurement process. Perry also is counting on further cutting the Pentagon's overhead costs by contracting with private companies for equipment overhauls, base operations and some other activities. Those plans face fierce opposition from members of Congress representing large groups of federal employees who would be displaced.

Dividing Up the Pie

Whatever the size of the force, a president also faces some broad choices about how the Pentagon budget should be divvied up — choices that beg further questions about the types of combat U.S. forces are likely to face.

One of these fundamental issues is the scope and direction of the Pentagon's investment in new weapons. Each service currently has at least one new, big-ticket program — the Air Force's F-22 fighter, the Army's Comanche helicopter, the Navy's new submarine — that is touted as a quantum leap over its current counterpart. But Korb and others contend that U.S. personnel, with their superior training, could easily defeat any plausible opponent using their current arsenal. The Pentagon's response is that U.S. personnel deserve the equipment that would give them overwhelming supremacy, both to dissuade potential troublemakers from going to war and to keep U.S. casualties to the very low level the public has come to expect.

Former Pentagon analyst Andrew Krepinevich represents another school of thought, which views the services as too slow to exploit technology that might perform old missions more cheaply or more effectively. For instance, predicting that the Navy will not be able to afford its planned fleet of 12 aircraft carriers, Krepinevich has called for replacing a few of those big ships with their 5,500-member crews with highly automated "arsenal ships" carrying crews of perhaps 100 and armed with hundreds of long-range cruise missiles that could strike many of the same targets as a carrier.

Another priorities question is the trade-off between "stand-off" air and naval forces and "muddy boots" ground troops. In general, air and naval forces can arrive at a distant trouble spot more quickly and are more isolated from local residents, thus reducing political friction. Moreover, using stealthy and very precise (but also very expensive) weapons, they expose few U.S. personnel to hostile fire.

How serious a national interest is required to justify sending U.S. ground troops into danger?

Does a large U.S. military provoke potential adversaries to build up their own forces?

Should high-tech weapons due for full-scale production be shelved in favor of either current weapons or radical new weapons ideas?

But that same mobility also limits their credibility as guarantors of a U.S. commitment to an imperiled ally. Forces that can quickly move into a troubled region can move out just as fast, while a deployment of ground forces is more difficult to reverse. Also, troops on the ground often are the only way to bring U.S. military force to bear on murky and ambiguous conflicts — although they carry an inherently higher risk of casualties.

Four years ago, it seemed likely that senior military leaders, seared by the evaporation of public support for the Vietnam War, would form a solid phalanx of opposition to U.S. involvements in such "low-end" conflicts. Retired Joint Chiefs of Staff Chairman Gen. Colin L. Powell spoke for a generation of officers who were leery of using force except in a full-bore response to an unambiguous threat against vital national interests.

But the three top-ranking U.S. ground combat officers in today's Pentagon take a different view. Army chief Reimer, Joint Chiefs Chairman Gen. John M. Shalikashvili (also an Army officer), and Marine Corps Commandant Gen. Charles C. Krulak all contend that important — if not vital — U.S. interests sometimes will require the use of force for more subtle purposes than a blitzkrieg response to a pariah state's cross-border invasion, and that their forces must have the manpower, training and equipment to carry them out.

The first American policy on immigration was set in 1607, when three boatloads of Englishmen landed at Jamestown and never left. Since then, immigration has been a defining element of the nation — fueling economic growth and creating a mosaiclike and changing culture unlike that in other countries.

Today, the United States is experiencing what most experts consider the second great wave of legal immigration (the first was from about 1840 to World War I) and the first great wave of illegal immigration — prompting many to rethink U.S. openness to outsiders.

Congress just spent two years debating new restrictions on legal and illegal entrants, pushed by longtime proponents of the idea that America is losing control of its borders and even its identity. But lawmakers emerged with considerably less to show for their efforts than proponents had hoped.

And that means the issue is not going away. Increased worldwide mobility, unrest, and America's attraction as a place to find a better life will

Can the U.S. Regain Control Of Its Borders?

- About 4 million illegal immigrants reside in the United States and about 300,000 arrive each year.

- The number of legal immigrants can vary dramatically, from 724,000 in 1995 to 1.8 million in 1991. It has averaged about 1 million people per year over the last decade.

- Between 1982 and 1989, 1.3 million legal immigrants settled in California.

Sources: Immigration and Naturalization Service; U.S. Commission on Immigration Reform.

(FAIR), the principal group advocating more restrictive immigration policies. Large numbers of unskilled immigrants, legal and illegal, can help drive down wages by creating competition for work.

"The next president will have to come to terms with the immigration-related wage gap," Stein says.

Areas along the southern border and most large urban areas are receiving so many legal and illegal immigrants that many wonder how much assimilation is going on.

On the financial front, state and local governments already have said the services they must provide — including free public schooling and health care for the uninsured — are bankrupting them. California spends $2 billion a year educating illegal immigrants. It cost the state $1.2 million per day to pay for school lunches for students in the country illegally.

But stemming immigration — particularly illegal immigration — does not lend itself to simplistic solutions. Experts say no increase in the number of Border Patrol agents will keep people out for long; the only way to really

continue to draw millions of people. This will continue to put pressure on social services, raise questions about how much melting is going on in the melting pot, and spark intense debate about limiting future immigration.

Polls consistently show Americans are concerned with the number of people (about 1 million) who legally immigrate to the United States each year. In a February Roper Poll, for instance, 83 percent of respondents said a million was too many. And a majority said the number should be lower than 300,000.

The public is even more troubled by the nation's seeming inability to enforce laws against illegal immigration. Estimates are that about 4 million illegal immigrants reside in the country now and the ranks are growing by about 300,000 a year. The public's anger has been perhaps most vivid in its desire to cut off even the most basic of services to illegal immigrants. California's Proposition 187 — to deny benefits to illegal aliens — passed with 59 percent of the vote. A Times Mirror poll found that it would pass nationwide as well.

Americans have found other ways to show they are not satisfied with immigration policies. The "English-only" movement, naming English as the official language, has gone from a fringe movement to the center of political debate in a few short years. Politicians, such as Patrick J. Buchanan, Ross Perot and numerous local candidates, have thrived on nativist themes that directly or indirectly question the size of the immigrant population.

"I can tell you that backlash is still out there," says Sen. Dianne Feinstein, D-Calif. Feinstein argues that whenever lawmakers fail to act on immigration issues, the public expresses its dissatisfaction at the polls.

One potential area for a backlash is from the labor movement. Labor unions have adamantly opposed trade pacts, such as the General Agreement on Tariffs and Trade (GATT), enacted in 1994, and the North American Free Trade Agreement (NAFTA), enacted in 1993, but have not become a force against large numbers of immigrants. That could change, says Daniel A. Stein, director of Federation for American Immigration Reform

stop illegal entrants is to switch off the main attraction: jobs. That takes extreme measures — such as national I.D. cards, barbed wire fences, and massive computer verification systems.

And that raises a legal and political challenge for the next president, who must lead the nation in determining who should be allowed in, who pays, and how far the nation is willing to go to stem civil liberties to keep out undesirables.

Illegal Immigration

The recently enacted legislation (HR 3610, formerly HR 2202) restricting illegal immigration may take the immediate pressure off lawmakers to "do something," but few experts believe it will stem the flow of immigrants. *(1996 Weekly Report, p. 2755)*

That's because the measure, while attempting to be tough on people who enter the United States illegally through such means as enhanced deportation measures, does little to tackle illegal immigration in the workplace.

In 1994, the Commission on Immigration Reform, known as the "Jordan Commission" after its chairman, the late Rep. Barbara Jordan, D-Texas, concluded that the centerpiece of any effort to stop illegal entrants should be to turn off the jobs magnet that attracts them. As long as illegal immigrants could expect to find work in the United States, the commission concluded, attempts to stop them at the border would not work.

The commission recommended a nationwide data base of Social Security numbers that would allow employers to check the legal status of every job applicant.

But the immigration measure includes only three pilot programs to test the effectiveness of electronic workplace verification systems. The systems are voluntary for employers, with no added sanctions for hiring illegal immigrants — hardly the type of measure likely to have an impact, says Mark Krikorian, executive director of the Center for Immigration Studies, which favors more restrictive immigration policies.

"If, as a country, we are serious about controlling illegal immigration, some kind of verification system is inevitable," he said.

But attempts to deal with illegal immigration run up against business and civil liberties issues. Any attempts to go beyond the pilot programs could face stern opposition from the left and right.

Employers, who successfully kept meaningful workplace verification provisions out of this year's effort, would be equally resistant in the future. Some employers, particularly larger agriculture interests and some small businesses, have a stake in continuing the flow of cheap, illegal labor.

Verification programs can mean additional paperwork and a responsibility by employers to play the role of immigration officers. An employer in South Texas might see the need for such a program, while one in Seattle might see it as an inconvenience. Perhaps most important, a meaningful program would have to include penalties against employers the government believes are not sufficiently vigilant.

Civil liberties groups are equally wary of workplace identification systems. The Jordan Commission only recommended maintaining a data base of information that people already provide for routine matters, but these groups fear the worker verification system will eventually evolve into something more sinister.

They envision the government gathering vast amounts of information about people to find who is in the country legally. They also see the system involving some sort of national identification card, a concept that has long spawned an emotional debate. A requirement that U.S. citizens and legal residents present I.D. cards on request is seen as a tremendous violation of civil liberties. Some critics fear it might become something police ask for when stopping a suspicious individual, making it required carrying at all times.

"Are we willing to have a nationwide verification system? That probably involves a card," said Frank Sharry, executive director of the National Immigration Forum, a pro-immigration group. "You can almost hear the opposition now: 'A national I.D. card, how dare we?' That will be the rallying cry of the libertarian left and right."

In the end, some analysts believe, illegal immigration as an issue will become a perennial one like the crime issue — with Washington unable to solve the problem, but unable for political reasons to leave it alone.

Legal Immigration

The next president will find himself facing immigration policy issues that Congress abandoned when it dropped provisions on legal immigration from HR 2202. Among them are whether the overall number of legal immigrants (now about 1 million a year) should be reduced, whether to seek more skilled workers and fewer unskilled ones, and whether certain family preference visas (such as for siblings and adult children of permanent residents) should be curtailed.

Immigration levels are now at all-time highs in absolute numbers, but not as a percentage of the population. Immigrants between 1900 and 1910 made up a little under 10 percent of the nation's population. Immigrants of the 1980s made up 3.5 percent of the population.

The United States grants immigrant visas in three main categories: for family members, workers, and refugees and other special cases. Most efforts to cut legal immigration center on family visas because it is the largest group and America needs skilled workers.

The Jordan Commission recommended cutting total legal immigration back from about a million to 555,000 a year by eliminating family visas covering adult children and parents of citizens and permanent residents, as well as siblings of citizens.

Congressional liberals, however, are not likely to abide immigration cuts based solely on cutting family-based immigration. One area they might target is temporary employment visas for skilled and unskilled workers.

"Democrats are not going to allow the temporary visas to be left alone, and while we go after family immigration," says Rick Swartz, an immigration lawyer and former director of the National Immigration Forum.

The extent to which these issues come up during the next president's term could depend on who is elected to Congress in 1996 and 1998, and who chairs the House and Senate immigration panels.

The next president faces a political calculus as well: Should he court immigrant voters or the growing, largely untapped voters in the restrictionist movement?

Restrictionist groups like FAIR failed to make much headway in the 104th Congress in part because they did not have a solid position in either party.

Democrats have long been the party of the working class and immigrants who naturalize often become Democratic voters. The GOP certainly has a restrictionist wing that wants to cut legal immigration. But it is offset by an unabashedly pro-immigration wing driven in part by business interests that thrive on imported workers. From unskilled farm workers to computer engineers hired by high-tech companies, hundreds of thousands of workers help staff American companies.

The result is that the pro-immigration faction includes liberals such as Sen. Edward M. Kennedy, D-Mass., and conservatives such as GOP vice presidential candidate Jack F. Kemp, former Education Secretary William J. Bennett, and House Speaker Newt Gingrich, R-Ga.

This liberal-conservative alliance has successfully fought major changes in legal immigration policy and has frustrated groups like FAIR, which has not had much success in forming alliances. "We have a very hard time building coalitions because everyone wants to ignore the issue, or pander to it politically," says FAIR's Stein.

One scenario envisioned by immigration policy experts is that restrictionists, not feeling accepted in either party, will try to find a home in Ross Perot's Reform Party. This idea was fueled when former Colorado Gov. Richard D. Lamm, a restrictionist and longtime FAIR board member, sought the nomination.

It would not be the first time that a third party captured the nativist vote. In the mid-19th century, the "Know-Nothing" movement, known officially as the American Party, emerged to challenge the established parties on the immigration issue.

Questions for the President

How far should the government go in restricting individual liberties to prevent illegal immigrants from getting jobs?

Should the government reduce the number of legal immigrant visas granted each year?

Should the distribution of visas — with about 60 percent going to family members and 20 percent to people with needed job skills — be changed to accommodate a competitive high-tech economy?

■ ■ ■

Few decisions the next president makes will be more significant than what — if anything — he does to the government programs that are on autopilot.

Left alone, entitlements such as Social Security, Medicare and Medicaid will make up nearly two-thirds of all federal spending by early in the next century. If that happens, discretionary spending will have to be tightly squeezed — on everything from Head Start to submarines — or a huge tax increase will need to be imposed. And probably some of both.

But restraining the growth of these entitlements will be difficult. Their growth is determined by the number of people who need them, not by congressional appropriation. Each has a strong constituency.

A generation or more of Americans have come to rely on Social Security, the largest of them, as a personal guarantee that the federal government will provide a basic pension when they retire. They also depend on Medicare, the second largest, as a guarantee of health insurance for the elderly. Others rely on Medicaid, which guarantees health care for the poor and those in nursing homes.

The biggest problem with maintaining the current level of benefits is demographic. The ranks of retirees are growing compared with those who are working and paying taxes, and the retirees are living longer.

What seemed to be a reasonable expectation of assistance in 1960, when there were five workers for every Social Security beneficiary, seems tougher now, when there are slightly more than three. By 2030 there will be two workers for every beneficiary.

The implications are clear: There will not be enough revenue to fund these programs and provide benefits for retiring baby boomers.

Many economists believe that relatively modest changes now will avert the need for a dramatic overhaul later. "We basically have a demographic holiday right now," said Robert D. Reischauer, a senior fellow at the Brookings Institution and former director of the Congressional Budget Office. "By taking small steps now we avoid giant leaps later."

Among the possible solutions: increasing the retirement age, lowering benefits, steering more Medicare recipients into managed care and permitting some privatization for Social Security.

But tackling these cherished entitlements carries enormous political risk. Few think it can be done without strong presidential leadership and bipartisan congressional support. Will the next president be spurred to act?

Social Security and perhaps Medicaid can go for several more years without prompting louder fiscal alarms, though as each year passes the price of inaction increases. By contrast, Medicare's finances present a more immediate threat and will be virtually impossible to ignore in the next four years. Even so, the president could opt for a short-term fix and leave the broader questions for another day.

The shelves are stacked with proposed solutions. The problem with any of the serious ones is that they involve sacrifice, a notion that is hard to sell to the public and that can easily be used against anyone who suggests it.

The challenge: asking people to take a measurable reduction

Managing the Costs of Entitlements

- In 1995, one in eight Americans was age 65 or older. By 2025, it will be one in five Americans. By 2040, it may be one in four.

- Social Security was the major source of income for 66 percent of beneficiaries in 1994.

- Benefits for Medicare Part A amounted to $116.4 billion in 1995, a 13 percent increase over 1994.

Sources: Congressional Budget Office; Social Security Administration; Medicare Board of Trustees

in their benefits in exchange for shoring up the long-term health of these vital entitlements. "That's a tough sell," said Martha Phillips, executive director of the Concord Coalition, which advocates making tough choices to eradicate the federal deficit.

Whoever wins the presidential election would be in a position to make some of them. Democrat Bill Clinton cannot seek a third term. Republican Bob Dole might not seek re-election. Either could expend some political capital to burnish his legacy as the man who "saved" cherished entitlement programs for future generations.

At this point, though, neither is talking much about it.

Dramatic Change

It is easy to understand why talk of reducing entitlement benefits is incendiary. Clinton has lambasted Republicans for proposing deeper cuts in Medicare benefits than he thought necessary to ensure its solvency. Bipartisan actions on entitlements, such as the sweeping 1983 law (PL 98-21) that improved Social Security's long-term solvency by increasing tax rates and reducing benefits, among other things, are rare and delicately stitched together.

The 104th Congress did set a precedent for ending an entitlement when it enacted a law (HR 3734 — PL 104-193) this summer that eliminated Aid to Families with Dependent Children (AFDC) and the 61-year-old federal guarantee of welfare checks to all eligible low-income women and children. The action raised the profile of entitlement programs and the notion that dramatic change is possible.

But welfare is hardly comparable to the big three entitlements. That legislation was driven by widespread agreement that the welfare system was broken — and the realization that welfare recipients had relatively little political clout. A far different response can be expected from tampering with Social Security, whose public support inspired the cliche that it is the "third rail" of American politics: touch it and die.

Even so, several factors might prompt the next president to propose far-reaching changes.

For one thing, most Democrats — and a growing number of Republicans — are frustrated about the lack of federal money to satisfy their priorities for domestic discretionary spending. With entitlement programs growing rapidly, tax increases virtually off limits and defense spending already in retreat, discretionary programs continue to get pinched. This is particularly difficult for Clinton, who wants to emphasize the federal role in education and the environment while protecting money for medical research, crime fighting and job training.

A different perspective among generations might also spur the next president to act. Baby boomers — those born between 1946 and 1964 — and especially the "Generation X" group that followed them, may look at the social compact a little differently from current retirees.

"The younger you are, the less confidence you have that Social Security or Medicare will be there for you," said Martin Corry, director of federal affairs at the American Association of Retired Persons (AARP). An AARP poll shows that only 35 percent have confidence in Social Security's future — 46 percent of retirees and 27 percent of non-retirees; 51 percent have confidence in Medicare. Current workers might be somewhat more amenable than their elders to changes that would protect future entitlements.

There is also the lure of achieving a historical legacy. Reischauer said this could be especially appealing to Clinton, of whom "historians will say he saved the New Deal and the Great Society for the baby boom generation."

Besides the president, arguably few would benefit more from a popular, decisive plan to ensure the long-term health of leading entitlements than the vice president. Whether it is Democrat Al Gore or Republican Jack F. Kemp, either would surely be relieved if he did not have to confront the issue if he sought the presidency four years from now.

Medicare

Medicare is the most vulnerable but also one of the most politically sensitive of the federal entitlement programs. It is divided into two parts. Medicare Part A, funded through a payroll tax that goes into the Hospital Insurance Trust Fund, generally pays for inpatient hospital care. Part B generally covers doctors services and is funded through patient premiums and general revenues.

The crisis in Medicare is the pending insolvency of the trust fund — by law the only source of Part A funding. It began draining reserves in 1995 by paying out more than it received in tax revenues. The trust fund is expected to be exhausted by 2001, maybe sooner. This can be explained by inflation in health costs — the short-term problem — and demographic changes, which project a smaller ratio of workers paying for a growing number of beneficiaries. There are now roughly four workers for every Medicare beneficiary — 37 million beneficiaries with 144 million workers to support them in 1995. As baby boomers retire, that ratio will gradually change, leveling off in 2030 at about 2-to-1.

Clinton and the GOP-led Congress offered somewhat similar proposals in 1995 to shore up Medicare, but the efforts died in the budget stalemate at the end of the year. Medicare is expected to cost $1.62 trillion from 1997 to 2002, and Clinton's proposal would have slowed its growth by $116 billion. Republicans aimed for $158 billion. Both restructuring proposals avoided raising the Part A payroll tax, instead opting to reduce payments to Medicare providers such as hospitals and doctors. They also aimed to cut costs by creating incentives to draw more beneficiaries into managed care.

But the plans differed in several key ways, including a GOP proposal to make wealthier seniors pay more in premiums for the voluntary Part B insurance that helps pay doctors bills. Democrats exploited these differences, accusing Republicans of seeking deep cuts in health care for the elderly mainly to finance a tax cut for the rich. Wounded, Republicans left the worsening Medicare problem for another day.

The next president will not have that luxury. He will at least need a short-term fix to shore up the trust fund — something like the competing GOP and Clinton proposals.

A long-term fix would include stronger doses of the same

proposals, with perhaps an increase in the payroll tax — something considered politically impossible. Some advocates of a Medicare overhaul have suggested forming a commission similar to the one that made sensitive decisions about which U.S. military bases to close. Such a bipartisan panel could make recommendations that would give political cover to lawmakers backing unpopular proposals.

Social Security

Like Medicare, Social Security is funded through a payroll tax. Unlike Medicare, its trust fund is flush at the moment. Through 2013, more tax revenues will come in than benefits will be paid out. But by 2020, taxes and fund earnings will no longer meet demand, and the fund itself will have to be tapped. By 2030, it will be depleted.

Like Medicare, Social Security involves long-term commitments that people are counting on when they retire. Americans contribute to the program while they work and feel strongly that it is their due to help make ends meet in retirement.

Changing the program now, before the crisis arrives, would lessen the need for drastic action later, and give people more time to plan for their retirement accordingly.

Among the options, many of them advanced by Sens. Alan K. Simpson, R-Wyo., and Bob Kerrey, D-Neb., are raising the retirement age to 70, adjusting downward the annual cost-of-living allowance, and allowing workers to invest part of their Social Security payroll contributions in a personal investment plan in return for somewhat lower Social Security benefits.

Medicaid

Double-digit increases in the annual growth rate of Medicaid, the state-federal health insurance program for the poor, have made it a prime target for saving. Between 1990 and 1995, federal Medicaid spending grew an average of nearly 17 percent a year. It cost the federal government $40.9 billion in 1990 and $90.7 billion in 1995. State costs rose from $31.3 billion to $68.8 billion.

Recent Medicaid spending figures have shown a remarkable slowdown. In the first 10 months of 1996, federal spending grew only 3.6 percent over the same 10 months of 1995. That may make the next president less likely to propose restructuring, or make it more difficult for him to sell lawmakers on such a plan.

"If the slowdown persists, it's going to take a lot of pressure off of the president and Congress to make fundamental reforms in the Medicaid program," Reischauer said.

Still, no one feels confident that the program has been cured. The aging of America will become a growing problem for Medicaid, which pays for nursing home care for the elderly who qualify. In 1994, 25 percent of Medicaid spending went to skilled nursing care — when the aged accounted for only 11.4 percent of the Medicaid population.

And pressure from the nation's governors may prod the next president to restructure Medicaid. The average state spent 19.2 percent of its budget on Medicaid in 1995, compared with 12.5 percent in 1990. Governors have lobbied aggressively for a major Medicaid overhaul.

Questions for the President

★ ★ ★ ★
★ ★ ★

Should the guarantee of health care to the poor through Medicaid be eliminated while states largely determine eligibility and benefits?

Should workers be permitted to invest part of their Social Security payroll contributions in a personal investment plan?

Should wealthier seniors pay higher premiums than others for Medicare's optional Part B insurance, which covers doctor care?

■ ■ ■

Seeking Middle Ground on the Environment

- **The current fee for grazing cattle on public lands is $1.35 per animal unit month, which is the amount of acreage needed to feed a cow and her calf for one month.**

- **In 1980, 198 million people visited the national parks. In 1995, 270 million visited.**

- **Number of superfund sites: 1,227. Number of sites cleaned up or taken off the superfund priority list: 403.**

Sources: Interior Department, Environmental Protection Agency

Whether the issue is protecting endangered species or cleaning up toxic dumps, the next president will confront no shortage of unfinished environmental business.

The 1980 superfund program badly needs revamping and has failed to clean up many of the nation's worst toxic waste dumps. The 1973 Endangered Species Act, which awaits reauthorization, pits developers against environmentalists. And federal land management in general is increasingly the subject of perennial harsh criticism over its failure to broker competing recreational and industrial pressures on public land.

Whatever the problem, the solution will have to conform to ever-tightening budgets, which will provide any administration less leeway in such areas as much-needed renovations of popular National Parks sites.

Budgets aside, however, the biggest hurdle for the next president will most likely be contending with a public and a Congress that often send mixed political signals. Gone — at least for now — are the days of cries to protect the bald eagle or the fears sparked by the Love Canal disaster that mobilized the public behind bold moves to place stringent new requirements on industry.

Instead, a growing consensus exists that regulations need to be more flexible and that regulators should be given more authority to weigh costs and benefits in writing regulations. But translating such principles into action is a delicate balancing act.

Many voters favor protecting the environment but are skittish about regulations that go too far or mean personal sacrifice, such as spending hours in line at car emissions testing centers.

"People care about the environment, so you can't play fast and loose with it," said Paul R. Portney, president of Resources for the Future, an environmental research company. "But if anybody pushes too far in either direction, the public is going to be riled up."

One need only examine the past four years to see how difficult that task will likely prove. Both parties registered stunning success and colossal failures at appealing to the competing impulses.

In 1994, Westerners hung in effigy President Clinton's Interior secretary, Bruce Babbitt, over a decision that pleased many environmentalists but angered ranchers whose land the Babbitt-backed policy addressed. And less than one year after the Republicans rode a 1994 wave of anti-government anger to majority status in Congress, then-Senate Majority Leader Bob Dole, R-Kan., was vilified on editorial pages as a protector of polluters because of his effort to move legislation that would have eased regulatory policy.

Noting the swings in policy and politics since 1992, Michael J. Bean, chairman of the wildlife program at the Environmental Defense Fund, observed "that there are impulses in the American public that tug in different directions."

Bridging the gap between competing interests will not be easy for the next president. Many of the solutions that have been test driven in congressional debates have not performed well enough to become law. Witness Dole and the regulatory debate and Clinton on range policy.

Moreover, the potential punch carried by environmental themes underscores how a debate that in recent memory seemed as bipartisan in Congress and as popular with the electorate as motherhood and apple pie has turned as partisan as a barroom brawl.

That means, Bean argued, that in such contentious areas as revising the Endangered Species Act, the next administration will have to consider new approaches, especially given the tight-fisted fiscal environment.

"If the next president wants to find a way to reconcile these competing interests, he's going to have to come up with some new, creative ideas," said Bean.

Formula for Success

Meeting such a challenge could mean that a president will have to chart a new course in some areas of environmental policy and risk angering entrenched constituencies — or duck the issues altogether, which itself is fraught with potential for long-term, negative effects.

It is apparent then, because the major environmental issues often find themselves among the most contentious of any legislative session, that the president will have to look to bipartisan coalitions as a formula for success.

Two major environmental bills of the 104th Congress, the safe drinking water bill and the rewrite of pesticide regulations, grew out of agreements that reached across the aisle. In contrast, efforts to revamp the badly broken superfund program, rewrite the clean water act or overhaul the Endangered Species Act lacked such broad-based support and sank under their own weight.

The degree of success the next administration will have in dealing with the unfinished business will depend on the ability to stitch together warring interest groups from environmentalists to allies of industry, as well as with combatants in both chambers.

A case in point is overhauling the superfund program, which would be a significant achievement for a program that has been defined more by its shortcomings than signs of success.

Both the Democratic-controlled 103rd Congress and the Republican-controlled 104th failed to produce legislation, and the taxes that flow into the program's trust fund were allowed to expire at the end of 1995 when Congress declined to reauthorize them.

The 1980 law was aimed as a limited cleanup of the nation's worst toxic dump sites, such as the Love Canal in New York, but the number of sites grew beyond expectations and cleanup bogged down in litigation over who should foot the bill for the cleanups.

Developing a formula on how to reduce the number of lawsuits without completely unraveling the program's requirement that polluters pay for cleanup has proved elusive.

As a result, relatively few sites have been cleaned up, and while the Clinton administration says it is making improvements on its own, only congressional action can bring about a permanent fix by enacting changes in cleanup standards and polluter liability.

A challenge of equal proportion is revising the endangered species law, which has come under scrutiny from both environmentalists and property owners. Passed in 1973 with the support of many of its present-day critics, the act was seen as a bold step toward stemming extinction of the nation's most threatened species.

But even environmentalists have come to see the act's shortcomings: Instead of protecting habitats needed for the long-term survival of animals and plant life, the act too often focuses on threatened species in isolation.

Property rights advocates say environmentalists often use the act to bar development and restrict them from timber harvesting and other commercial enterprises. A further criticism of the law is that it discourages landowners from protecting endangered species. Landowners fear that once an endangered species is found on their property, federal regulators implement undue restrictions.

One key question for the next president will be the degree to which any revision includes tax incentives or other monetary sweeteners to encourage protection of habitats.

Although superfund and the species rewrite may attract early attention, other public land issues could move to the front burner.

Robert H. Nelson, a senior fellow at the pro-business Competitive Enterprise Institute, and others argue that the flurry of major land-use laws signed in the 1970s have failed to live up to their promise.

Despite such laws as the 1976 Federal Land Policy Management Act, aimed at giving managers the tools they needed to broker rival interests on public rangelands, ranchers, recreational users and environmentalists are locked in combat.

"There is a lot of agreement that the public lands system is gridlocked and polarized," said Nelson. But Democrats and Republicans, and Easterners and Westerners, disagree on what to do: whether grazing fees should be increased; recreational users should pay more or the land should be turned over to the states.

Similarly, overhaul of the 1872 mining law to increase the fees charged to prospectors has become a perennial battle — and so far has shown little chance of being easily resolved.

As Western fires frequently flare, means the "forest health" issue could also arise as land-use policy. Foresters throughout the West contend that the fires are a result of nearly a century of mismanagement, particularly by landowners and forest managers who decided to try to prevent fire, a natural environmental process, in timber stands.

Timber interests argue for more logging, saying it is the best method for protecting forests without sacrificing valuable timber to disease or fires. Environmentalists contend other practices are called for, such as reintroducing fire to clear out fire-prone undergrowth and to help rejuvenate soils.

Revamping land policy could prove as difficult as revising clean air regulations. Throughout the 104th Congress, Republi-

cans pushed to alter provisions of the Clean Air Act, and efforts to revisit the 1990 amendments regarded as too stringent are likely to be on the agenda of pro-business Republicans, particularly Rep. Tom DeLay, R-Texas.

And a potential sleeper is climate change. A December 1997 meeting is scheduled in Kyoto, Japan, to hash out an international agreement to stem global warming, and an agreement could impact American industry by imposing new limits on emissions.

Park Cutbacks

Looming over almost any of the major environmental and land use issues is the promise of increasingly tight budgets. In theory, both major parties would likely agree, any program could be run more efficiently and fat trimmed.

For example, there is broad agreement that the nation's parks are in some cases crumbling and at the very least are facing a $4 billion maintenance backlog. While the parks have so far been protected from the kind of cuts seen at other agencies, the paucity of available federal funding has forced the parks to consider politically controversial alternatives to deal with the shortfall.

One of the alternatives is a proposal to allow corporate sponsorship. Attempts to move in that direction spurred charges that the good name of the parks were being auctioned off to corporate interests, and the provision was dropped from the Omnibus Parks bill.

A similar fiscal challenge faces public land policy in general. Private groups, such as the Nature Conservancy, are increasingly concluding that they cannot carry the burden of protecting critical habitats on their own. A number of such environmental groups have tried to buy land on their own to save it from development, but are finding that their own budgets cannot begin to meet the needs of protecting habitats threatened by development.

Bean, of the Environmental Defense Fund, said that the federal government needs to consider consolidating its environmental programs to better husband its resources. One example is the conservation easement program in the farm bill, which he says could be refocused to include habitat protection.

"More money can be spent on the Endangered Species program, and better results will occur," said Bean.

A far more immediate question, said Bean, is the degree to which the increasing partisanship of the past four years will subside to permit the kind of cooperation that produced pesticide changes and the safe drinking water revisions.

After all, a president often tries to satisfy the desires of his own most vocal constituencies, both on and off Capitol Hill. For example, Dole has drummed up support from property rights activists while Clinton courts environmentalists.

"Both parties have to deal with wings of their party that are more ideologically driven than pragmatically driven," said Bean. "To the degree to which environmental policy continues to be partisan in nature, the future of environmental policy will continue to be in doubt."

Questions for the President

How can the superfund hazardous waste program be revamped to reduce litigation and speed the pace of cleanups?

Can the Endangered Species Act balance species protection with the rights of property owners?

Is it time to revise federal land management laws, and if so, what changes should be undertaken?

■ ■ ■

When Foreign Policy magazine recently published an optimistic piece on Asia's future, titled "The Rising East," it symbolized the region's immense economic power with a huge statue of a smiling Buddha, tapping away on a laptop computer.

Contrast that with The Economist's cover for an August feature on Asia, which had the vaguely ominous title "China Looming." The British magazine portrayed a fierce-looking panda towering menacingly behind some modern office buildings.

Those contradictory images underscore the promise and peril that Asia holds for the next president.

On the one hand, the region stands to be the most important market for U.S. goods well into the next century. According to a recent estimate, Asia will soon be home to five of the world's six leading economies — the United States being the sixth. Democracy is on the rise as well. Democratic governments have replaced authoritarian regimes in South Korea, Thailand and Taiwan.

Yet Asia is also rife with geopolitical risk. No foreign policy challenge is more vexing or important than China, which has repeatedly clashed with the United States on issues ranging from trade to human rights to Taiwan.

With 92-year-old Chinese leader Deng Xiaoping about to pass from the scene, the next American president is likely to face a new and perhaps very different regime in Beijing. Political change could further strain Sino-American relations, and some Asia analysts see the prospect for internal chaos.

North Korea, armed to the teeth and presumably in possession of a nuclear weapon, teeters on the brink of collapse. In Japan, the most important U.S. military ally in the region, popular opposition to American military bases is increasing. On the Asian subcontinent, India and Pakistan are locked in a bitter struggle to achieve nuclear weapons superiority.

Even Asia's greatest asset — its booming economies — will pose problems for the next president. As trade imbalances with China and Japan threaten to spiral out of control, the president will face tremendous pressure to retaliate with stiff countermeasures.

Whoever occupies the Oval Office on Jan. 20 will not possess a magic formula for dealing with the panoply of Asian issues. While he surely will be blamed if any of the region's hot spots blows up, his ability to influence events will be limited.

For instance, President Clinton and Bob Dole agree on the need to remain diplomatically and economically engaged with China. But the policy of engagement, pursued by every president since Richard M. Nixon, has yet to bring much in the way of democratic reform to China. Nor has it given the United States much leverage over Chinese behavior.

Dole would take a tougher line than Clinton against North Korea, one of the most isolated regimes in the world. Yet neither candidate has stated what he would do if the bankrupt government of Kim Jong Il simply implodes — an increasingly likely scenario.

"There is a 50-50 chance for a 'hard landing,' in which the regime just falls to pieces," said James Shinn, a senior fellow for

Asia: Critical Area for Foreign Policy?

■ Of the 1995 U.S. trade deficit of $159.6 billion, Japan accounted for $59.3 billion, China for $33.8 billion.

■ Of the eight fastest growing markets for U.S. exports, six are in Asia. Between 1990 and 1995, U.S. exports to China grew by 275 percent.

■ U.S. policy calls for maintaining about 100,000 troops in East Asia and the Pacific for the foreseeable future.

Sources: U.S. Commerce Department, Brookings Institution, Department of Defense

Asia at the Council on Foreign Relations. Such a crisis would almost certainly drag in neighboring South Korea, Shinn said, which could in turn trigger intervention by the Chinese.

At that point, the United States would face pressure to enter the fray in behalf of South Korea, a close ally. The chain reaction could ultimately ignite a new Korean war.

Return to Rivalry?

As frightening as that scenario is, the most pressing foreign policy question facing the next president may be the one suggested by The Economist: Given the downturn in Sino-American relations during the past few years, is a renewed military rivalry between Beijing and Washington inevitable?

By virtue of its size and military potential, China stands at the top of the list of possible threats to the United States. While Americans have long been intrigued by the size of the Chinese market, they have been equally repelled by persistent reports of China repressing its citizens, violating trade agreements and ignoring U.S. concerns about arms proliferation.

Some conservatives harbor particular animus toward China's communist leaders and have never quite forgiven Nixon for setting the nation on a path to full ties with Beijing.

But Clinton and Dole, along with many leading politicians of both parties, firmly reject the notion that China is the once-and-future enemy. While Dole has slammed the president for past vacillations on China, the candidates are on the same page concerning future policy.

Both strongly favor continuing Beijing's preferential trade status and support more frequent high-level contacts with Chinese officials. It is an open secret that Clinton, should he win re-election, will visit China in early 1997. For their part, Chinese leaders have sent conciliatory signals in recent weeks.

The degree of consensus between Clinton and Dole is striking, particularly since the rationale advanced during the Cold War for maintaining close ties with China — Beijing's role as a crucial bulwark against Soviet expansionism — collapsed along with the Soviet Union in 1991.

That confluence of views came about relatively recently. Clinton arrived in office on a promise to link China's most-favored-nation (MFN) trade status to improvements in human rights. But the policy proved politically unsustainable, and Clinton abandoned it in 1994, arguing that China's MFN status should not be tied to its human rights record. In doing so, he reversed the stance he took in the 1992 presidential campaign and implicitly endorsed Dole's long-held position. (1994 Almanac, p. 137)

Clinton and Dole now accept the premise that China is too strategically and economically important to isolate. Yet both men acknowledge that China, not the United States, holds the key to future relations. When Dole ticked off U.S. objectives in China during a major policy address in May, he could easily have been speaking for the administration:

"Our strategic goals should be clear: a China which does not threaten its neighbors, and a China which plays by the rules of the international system on non-proliferation and trade, a

China which is peaceful, prosperous and free."

All well and good. But the reality is that Beijing is a threatening presence to its neighbors, if only because of its size. And as the Clinton administration has discovered, Beijing doesn't always play by accepted rules of international behavior, particularly when those rules conflict with China's perceived national interest.

That was demonstrated during this year's blowup over Taiwan. China regards Taiwan as a renegade province and has threatened military action to prevent Taiwan from taking steps toward independence. In March, as Taiwan prepared for its first direct presidential election, China delivered that message with unmistakable clarity by test-firing missiles into the seas around Taiwan's main ports.

The United States responded with its own show of force, dispatching a pair of aircraft carrier battle groups to the region. Taiwan's election went off smoothly and the crisis soon abated. But there is no reason to believe that China wouldn't again move to the brink of war, if it perceives that Taiwan is seeking independence.

Taiwan, a key U.S. ally and trading partner, presents special difficulties for U.S. presidents. The nation enjoys considerable domestic support, owing to its historical anti-communism and contemporary status as an emerging democracy. It also is backed by a formidable Washington lobby.

Thus in any future showdown between China and Taiwan, the next president will face intense pressure to intervene militarily on Taiwan's behalf. In addition, by dispatching a naval task force to counter China's campaign of military intimidation, Clinton made it hard for Dole or himself to do any less if China threatens Taiwan again.

Less than six months after the next president is inaugurated, China will fulfill its historic destiny by reasserting sovereignty over the British territory of Hong Kong. CNN and every major global television network will be on hand when Britain formally relinquishes control over its tiny, prosperous colony, on July 1, 1997.

Despite Deng's vow that China and Hong Kong will be "one country, two systems," some tensions are inevitable. It remains to be seen whether they will rise to the level that would warrant a U.S. response.

Trade and Tension

As in 1992, foreign policy has been relegated to the periphery of the presidential campaign. Dole and his aides have sharply criticized Clinton's Middle East policy, following the U.S. attack on Iraq and the recent outbreak of violence between Israelis and Palestinians. But for the most part, international matters have taken a back seat to issues like crime, drugs and taxes.

Still, Dole and independent candidate Ross Perot seized on the trade statistics for July, which showed the largest monthly deficit in goods in nearly 11 years, to blast the administration's performance on that front. And even if trade does not emerge as a major campaign theme, it appears likely to occupy a prominent place on the president's agenda next year.

The next president, like his predecessors, will confront the challenge of trying to rein in the huge U.S. trade deficits with

Questions for the President
★ ★ ★ ★ ★

Should the United States intervene militarily if China attacks Taiwan?

Does free trade with Asian nations hurt the United States?

Should the United States try to prevent a North Korean collapse, or give that nation's hard-line communist government a final push?

■ ■ ■

Japan and China. But Clinton and Dole, both free traders, are not likely to prescribe the strong medicine of high tariffs favored by Perot and conservative commentator Patrick J. Buchanan.

Other trade controversies are likely to arise next year. China wants to join the World Trade Organization (WTO), but has yet to meet economic criteria set by the United States and European nations. China is certain to step up pressure to join the global trade regime, but on its own terms. Shortly before Congress adjourned, House Minority Leader Richard A. Gephardt, D-Mo., introduced a bill (HR 4065) requiring the president to seek congressional approval before supporting China's admission to the WTO. With the U.S. trade deficit with China running at nearly $35 billion annually, the next president will have a fight on his hands if he supports China's WTO bid.

Pro-business lobbies would like to eliminate the annual congressional review of China's MFN trade status, which affords lawmakers an opportunity to assess China's actions on trade, human rights and other issues for the preceding year. Vietnam is pressing to earn MFN status, which may trigger another highly charged debate over expanding relations with that former U.S. adversary.

But for the next president, those matters will be dwarfed by Asian security concerns. And the most serious of those — China, North Korea, India and Pakistan — may not even win a mention during this year's presidential debates.

Dole has taken the president to task for the U.S. nuclear agreement with North Korea, under which the United States and its allies promised to provide Pyongyang with oil and safe nuclear energy in exchange for North Korea's commitment to freeze its nuclear weapons program. Dole has urged suspending bilateral contacts with North Korea, although he has not called for abrogating the agreement.

But the more urgent question — whether the United States should take actions to prevent a North Korean collapse, or give the reeling communist dictatorship one final push — has yet to arise. The crisis has been made more complicated by Pyongyang's bizarre behavior. At a time when North Korea desperately needs Western food aid to stave off widespread famine, its decision to dispatch a submarine in a clumsy attempt to infiltrate the South alienated potential donors.

Given the array of flash points in Asia, the next president will be fortunate just to keep things from exploding. Some past presidents have not been so lucky. Americans have fought in Asia five times in the past 100 years — most recently in Vietnam.

Writing in Foreign Policy, former New York Times correspondent Richard Halloran blames both parties for giving short shrift to Asian policy. Even is this era of expanding U.S. economic ties with Asia, U.S. officials acknowledge they look to Europe first.

By now, U.S. policymakers should be well aware of the dangers of neglecting Asia. Halloran quotes Robert S. McNamara, who writes in his controversial memoir "In Retrospect": "When it came to Vietnam, we found ourselves setting policy for a region that was terra incognita."

Education: A Quest for Performance

■ **This school year, 51.7 million students are enrolled in public and private elementary and secondary schools, an all-time high. (By 2006, enrollment is projected to reach 54.6 million.)**

■ **The costs of tuition, room and board at private colleges rose 71 percent between 1980 and 1994.**

■ **Public college costs during the same period rose 45 percent.**

Source: U.S. Department of Education's National Center for Education Statistics

---

Education presents the president with a dilemma unmatched in other policy arenas.

More than $286 billion worth of taxpayers' money will flow into the public education system this school year, providing funds for pre-kindergarten through high school. That's more than what taxpayers will pay for national defense — more, in fact, than for the federal government's entire civilian discretionary budget.

In opinion polls, schools rank first or second on the priority list of voters, as they anxiously eye a changing economy, surging enrollment, soaring college tuition and persistent questions over educational quality.

Yet many Americans, especially those with a conservative bent, are clamoring for less federal involvement in their schools, not more. The federal share of education funding is already small, 6.9 percent of the total amount spent nationally on education in 1993. And efforts to mandate programs from national achievement tests to national academic standards have proven politically impossible. But the cry for educational improvement will only increase over the next decade.

If candidates for the White House in 1992 scrambled for the mantle of "the education president," today they tiptoe over a political terrain that has grown much more complex and dangerous.

"We don't want an education president," says Jennifer A. Marshall, an education policy analyst at the conservative Family Research Council. "We want local leaders."

The presidential role in education, if there is one, just may be fostering those local leaders. But there are also many other factors to consider.

Declining Quality?

The panic over education that marked the 1980s and early '90s has died down to quiet anxiety. Alarms sounded as the landmark 1983 report, "A Nation At Risk" reverberated through the past decade, and built up strength before the last presidential .election as the nation remained mired in recession. The oft-repeated assertion that a lackluster educational system was behind the United States' dwindling international competitiveness seemed borne out by reality. Test scores were down. Unemployment was up.

But over the past four years, the external indicators have been less clear. National test scores are up, if only slightly, in math and science. The gap between minority and white academic achievement has narrowed. Scores on the Scholastic Assessment Test in 1995 were the best since 1974, although assessors warn that might be due to changes in the test itself. U.S. students ranked well behind other large nations in math and science in 1991, the most recent statistics available, yet the U.S. economy is outperforming its international rivals.

"People question now whether there was an educational crisis synonymous with war, like 'A Nation At Risk' indicated," says Arnold F. Fege, director of government relations for the National Congress of Parents and Teachers, the umbrella organization of local Parent-Teacher Associations. "Students aren't doing any worse today, taking into consideration so many more are taking tests and so many more of those are minorities and English-deficient, than they were in 1965."

"But," he added, "we've got to do better than that to meet the employment needs of the 21st century."

Future Crises

Doing better may be easier said than done. Questions of educational quality, economic productivity, and school finances are unavoidable, says Diane Ravitch, assistant secretary for educational research under President Bush. Fundamental, non-ideological issues like rising enrollment and school repairs will be difficult enough to resolve. The restructuring of the education system to offer more choice and more competition will be even tougher.

"In some ways, it doesn't matter how the election turns out in terms of what the educational issues are going to be," Ravitch says. "These are the issues that will face us for the next 10 to 20 years."

A crisis mentality over education might return as early as this November, when the Education Department releases a 55-country analysis of math and science achievement. If that does not do it, a downturn in the natural business cycle could. Out of 45 top economists recently polled by the newsletter, "Blue Chip Economic Indicators," 62 percent said they expected a recession to begin by 1998.

Even if the economy stays healthy, demographics will pinch the schools and taxpayers.

A flood of baby boomer children and immigrants has already begun to swamp the schools. Elementary and secondary school enrollment hit an all-time high of 51.7 million students this year, and increases are expected to continue until the national student body, public and private, reaches 54.6 million in 2006, according to projections by the Department of Education's National Center on Education Statistics. Those extra students will tax the infrastructure of a school network that already faces a $112 billion backlog of basic repairs and a growing demand for rewiring to accommodate new technologies, according to the General Accounting Office.

There will also be a growing demand for teachers. The classroom teacher corps is expected to increase 16 percent by 2006, to 3.43 million from 2.96 million in 1994. Already, demand for teachers is luring into the field poorly educated, poorly trained instructors, a September report by the National Commission on Teaching and America's Future warned.

In recent years, more than 50,000 people who lacked required training have entered the field each year. In the 1990-91 school year, 14.9 percent of newly hired teachers came in on a provisional, temporary or emergency license.

Education spending will also tax available resources. Expenditures increased 43 percent, in constant dollars, between the 1980-81 school year and the 1992-93 school year. The $286.1 billion expected to be raised this year for pre-kindergarten through 12th grade education is up more than $18 billion just from last year. In 1982, expenditures totaled just $118.4 billion.

Changes in federal welfare programs, the stagnation of

wages, and the shrinkage of the industrial sector have also brought into sharp relief the demand for a highly trained work force. Education means better jobs.

But education attainment has become another source of anxiety, perhaps one of the biggest. Between 1980 and 1994, tuition, room and board rose 45 percent at public colleges, in constant dollars, and a staggering 71 percent at private schools. In 1982, it cost $4,582 on average to send a student to a public university and $10,766 to attend a private institution, in 1995 dollars. By 1994, those figures had surged to $6,053 for public school and $16,470 for private.

Potential Roadblocks

Faced with such problems, it would be tempting for a president to begin drafting programs to solve them. President Clinton has tried to do so — with grant programs for states and school districts, new financial aid proposals, and the pushing of educational standards. But no consensus exists regarding the president's role in meeting any of these challenges. And without consensus, Clinton has faced opposition at every turn.

The federal role in education has been traditionally circumscribed: equity — improving the disparities in educational spending between poor and rich districts — and access — the ability of poor, minority, or disabled students to attain an education. The federal share of education funding has actually declined of late, from a high of 9.8 percent in the 1979-80 school year to 6.9 percent in 1993. Yet critics and fans alike say President Clinton has expanded the federal role from equity and access to educational quality.

"Clearly, the government is always going to have a role in civil rights, access and equity. But those were the problems of the '60s. It's not the '60s anymore," Ravitch said.

Clinton has paid the political price for shifting the federal role in education. Cries of a federal takeover have polarized the debate like never before, Fege says. And it extends far beyond concerns over federal programs. Political arguments seem to lurk behind every educational delivery technique, from outcomes-based education, which stresses achievement over curriculum content, to phonics.

"What used to be educational decisions has now become part of the political realm," Fege said. "And phonics looks very different in the political realm than it does in the educational realm."

Undaunted, Clinton has continued to champion new programs. Administration initiatives have included:

• Grants worth hundreds of million of dollars for educators, employers and labor representatives to set up apprenticeship and on-the-job training programs for high school juniors and seniors not intending to go to college. (1994 Almanac, pp. 400-402)

• A grant program to encourage states to set up Charter Schools, public schools under contract with parents, teachers or school administrators and run independently of central school district mandates.

• The Eisenhower math and science grant program to develop more minority math and science teachers and improve math

What is the appropriate role for the federal government in setting and enforcing national educational standards?

As the children of baby boomers swell school enrollment, should districts and states be allowed to bar the children of illegal immigrants from competing for scarce resources?

Why do U.S. students rank so far behind other nations in math and science performance?

■ ■ ■

and science instruction. (1994 Almanac, p. 383)

• A proposed, $5 billion interest subsidy for districts struggling to fund new school construction and renovation.

But the tensions over the federal role in education have centered on one Clinton program: Goals 2000. The notion of establishing voluntary national standards and using grants and research to help state and local governments meet them was considered modest reform on the cheap during the Bush administration. The 1994 Goals 2000 education reform law (PL 103-227) was meant to do just that, formally establishing eight national education goals, six of which had been drafted by Bush.

Some of the goals — such as making U.S. students No. 1 in math and science by the turn of the century and ensuring students would leave grades four, eight and 12 with demonstrated competence in English, math, science, foreign languages, civics and government, economics, arts, history and geography — begged the question of who would set academic standards for those subjects and who would ensure those goals were actually met. To answer it, Goals 2000 set up the presidentially appointed National Education Standards and Improvement Council. Democrats expressed concerns that all students would be held to the same standards, regardless of how effective their schools were. That led to voluntary Opportunity-to-learn standards for educational delivery. Goals 2000 would also offer hundreds of millions of dollars in grants to states and local governments to help them meet the goals. (1994 Almanac, pp. 397-399)

These programs, while praised as vital and even modest by some educators and education advocates, have led to sometimes-vehement charges from conservatives of a creeping federal takeover of education. Ultimately, the most controversial parts of Goals 2000 were dismantled.

The debate over national standards and Goals 2000 has focused attention on the president's role in education. Conservatives say that role should be largely confined to the bully pulpit, using the presidency to advance education issues and talk up voluntary national standards and issues of educational organization, like school choice and charter schools.

The U.S. Department of Education's primary task should be research, they say, to see how local educational experiments are working on the local level and to disseminate information with no strings attached, Ravitch says. Other conservatives believe the Education Department should be abolished.

Anne Bryant, the executive director of the National School Boards Association, sees the prime focus of the government resting on troubled urban school districts, where the problems are most pressing and political resistance might be less contentious.

"If you ask what big issues are going to be on the agenda of the next president, it leads to urban education," Bryant said. "That's not an acknowledgment that we're perfect in the suburbs, so let's focus on the cities, no. It's a realization there is a serious disequilibrium."

Even though President Clinton and Republican challenger Bob Dole are campaigning for the top job in the federal government, both say they want to move power from Washington to the states.

Clinton, who battled for states rights as governor of Arkansas, has downplayed the role of a centralized bureaucracy ever since declaring in his State of the Union speech this year: "The era of big government is over."

And Dole touts states rights so often on the campaign trail that he keeps a copy of the Tenth Amendment, which guarantees states constitutional powers that are not reserved for the federal government.

No wonder state officials are bracing for some changes in their relationship with Washington.

"There's a general feeling that there's going to be more responsibility coming to the states," said Scott DeFife, who oversees budget and taxation issues for the National Conference of State Legislatures.

The question, however, is which areas Washington will hand over to the states — and in which ways it will expand its own jurisdiction.

Advocates of "devolution" — moving more power out of Washington — say that state and local governments are in the best position to respond to the needs of their constituents. The federal government, in contrast, often runs into criticism when it tries to mandate a prescriptive, "one-size-fits-all" approach.

But many environmentalists and public health advocates worry that devolution in some cases can undercut federal laws intended to safeguard the public health and safety. That's because states can cut costs, or please powerful business interests, by paring back some regulations.

Such political philosophies aside, the next president will face complex crosscurrents that actually could lead to some increased federal powers.

On one hand, the president will be under continued pressure from the budget deficit to cut funding for expensive programs and give states more responsibility for administering them. The controversial new welfare law (HR 3734 — PL 104-193), which will give states greater control over benefits and will save the federal government an estimated $54 billion between now and 2002, may be a prelude to similar changes in Medicaid, environmental initiatives and other programs.

On the other hand, both Clinton and Dole have talked about at least some federal expansion into areas traditionally left to the states. Public opinion polls show strong concern over issues such as crime and education — and federal policymakers may feel obliged to take action.

"Fiscal realities are pushing the national government toward devolution slowly," said John Shannon, senior fellow at the Urban Institute. "But there's still a lot of ready willingness on the part of both Democrats and Republicans to forget all about federalism when they think it will be a vote-gathering position."

Spurring debate over federal-state relations will be the planned reauthorizations of several major laws.

For example, one issue on the administration's radar next year will be the reauthorization of a major highway measure, the Intermodal Surface Transportation and Efficiency Act

Reshaping the Federal-State Relationship

■ The federal government is giving states $251 billion in major grants in fiscal year 1997, an increase of about $15 billion over fiscal 1996.

■ At least 34 states have raised their speed limits since Congress ended the national speed limit last year.

■ States will receive a record $18 billion in highway funding in fiscal 1997.

Source: National Conference of State Legislatures.

(ISTEA) of 1991 (PL 102-240). A key consideration will be whether to give states more or less flexibility over their transportation spending.

Also on the agenda will be the reauthorization of laws governing clean water regulations and hazardous waste cleanup — and the role that states will assume when enforcing those laws.

The debate over federal-state relations also may surface in such areas as energy deregulation and job training.

Shaping the Federal Role

Debate on these bills is likely to take place against the backdrop of continued public unease about centralized authority and federal spending. Although polls decades ago showed high public regard for the federal government — possibly because of its role during the Great Depression and World War II — public opinion in recent years appears to have swung sharply against federal institutions.

In fact, Clinton's ambitious health care initiative was stopped in 1994 largely because of fears that Washington would be unable to run an efficient health care system.

In many ways, Washington's influence crested during the "Great Society" days of President Lyndon B. Johnson in the 1960s. The federal government sent many billions of dollars to state and local governments for urban renewal and social service programs. All the programs operated on the same premise: to receive the massive infusions of federal aid, the states and cities had to march to Washington's tune.

But in the 1980s, President Ronald Reagan embraced the "New Federalism," an idea fostered by President Richard M. Nixon. Under Reagan's stewardship, this course involved giving far more control to the states and cities — and also slashing federal funds by the billions.

As a result, even as many governors welcomed the chance to show what they could do when unfettered by federal rules and regulations, they found their own coffers increasingly bare.

This fiscal squeeze intensified in the 1980s and early 1990s, as Congress passed a series of expensive state requirements, such as expanded Medicaid benefits, without appropriating the funds to pay for them. Governors and mayors of both parties began lobbying for relief from these requirements, known as "unfunded mandates."

When Republicans swept the 1994 elections, they promised to give states greater autonomy. One of the first acts of the 104th Congress was to clear a bill (S 1 — PL 104-4), supported by both Clinton and Dole, to restrict Washington from imposing new mandates on state or local governments without providing funds to pay for them. *(1995 Almanac, p. 3-15)*

In another nod to the states, lawmakers ended the national speed limit, which had prevented states from allowing people to drive at 70 mph or faster even on lightly trafficked Western highways. *(1995 Almanac, p. 3-60)*

Similarly, in legislation passed this year overhauling the Safe Drinking Water Act (S 1316 — PL 104-182), Congress ended requirements that the federal government create new regulations every three years. Instead, it gave local governments more flexibility to target water contaminants, and gave states more flexibility over the use of federal funds. *(1996 Weekly Report, p. 2622)*

Perhaps the most far-reaching legislation to affect federal-state relations was the welfare overhaul bill (HR 3734 — PL 104-193). Clinton reluctantly signed the legislation, which ended the federal government's 61-year-old guarantee of providing welfare checks to all eligible low-income mothers and children, and instead gave states considerable leeway over eligibility and benefits.

Generally, these efforts to give states greater authority have been spearheaded by conservatives in both parties. They say state governments are better able to address their problems than the large and sometimes unresponsive federal bureaucracy.

"We can still set national standards, but the administration of the standards can be directed to the state level," said Sen. Dirk Kempthorne, R-Idaho, a sponsor of the unfunded mandates legislation. "You'll get better decisions, because they [state officials] are closer to the problem. Washington, D.C. does not corner the market on wisdom."

However, Republicans and Democrats alike have also expanded federal power in several significant ways.

In the new telecommunications law (S 652 — PL 104-104), for example, the federal government requires states to allow competition in local telephone service. The new pesticides law (HR 1627 — PL 104-170) sets national standards for food safety and limits the degree to which a state could set stricter standards. *(Telecommunications, 1996 Weekly Report, p. 2438; pesticides, 1996 Weekly Report, p. 2546)*

Amid concerns about public safety, lawmakers also have moved more criminal cases to the federal courts by expanding the number of federal offenses.

Some experts question whether the federal government really has shifted as much power to the states as the rhetoric would indicate.

"If you look at the situation over the last year or two, I would say that it's very ambivalent," said Shannon.

Future Issues

The next president will have ample opportunity to redefine federal-state relations. Here are some issues to watch:

• **Highway funding.** When reauthorizing road funding in the ISTEA bill, the administration and Congress will consider giving states greater flexibility over their highway funding. Such transportation debates generally cut across regional, rather than partisan, lines.

At issue will be whether to continue to penalize states that fail to follow such guidelines as establishing a 21-year-old drinking age and restricting billboards along designated roads. Another issue will be whether to expand "sub-allocations" — federal requirements that states earmark a percentage of their federal funds to certain areas, such as cities.

The federal gas tax also may come under fire. Some states want to do away with most of the federal levy, thereby making it easier to increase their own gas taxes, and spend the money directly instead of getting it from the federal government. If the federal gas tax stays, many state officials would like to see more of the proceeds go to infrastructure, rather than the current pol-

Questions for the President
★ ★ ★ ★
★ ★ ★ ★
★ ★ ★

What current federal programs should be turned over to the states for management and funding?

Is there a danger that public health and safety programs could be weakened if they are overseen by the states instead of the federal government?

Should states be prevented from imposing regulations that are stricter than Washington's?

■ ■ ■

icy of holding back a percentage to reduce the budget deficit.

• **Environmental programs.** The next administration will almost certainly push for reauthorization of the federal hazardous waste cleanup program, or "superfund." Revamping the program has been a top Clinton environmental priority, but Democratic and Republican lawmakers have been at odds over cleanup standards and funding.

A major superfund issue will be whether states can set different cleanup standards than the federal government. Some states would like to go even further, and essentially take over the cleanup operations with federal funding.

A battle also may break out over reauthorization of the clean water act. Federal officials are expected to consider new environmental standards for non-point source pollution, which generally is run-off from fields, farms and urban areas. They will have to decide how much leeway to give states to establish and enforce the new standards.

Another possible issue may be whether to give states greater flexibility over protecting wetlands.

• **Health care.** The federal government is expected again to wrestle with ways to reduce Medicaid and Medicare costs. State officials will be watching the debate closely.

Republican lawmakers in the 104th Congress, including Dole, wanted to make substantial changes to the Medicaid program, a joint federal-state effort that provides health insurance for the poor. But they ran into unyielding opposition from Clinton. Their plan called for giving states much greater authority over the program by ending the federal guarantee of coverage, and giving states Medicaid block grants. *(1996 Weekly Report, p. 2446)*

Even if such a sweeping proposal is not revived next year, the next president may consider changes to the Medicaid waiver process, which states use to seek federal approval to make changes in their programs. If the waiver requirements are scaled back, states could find themselves with more flexibility over administering benefits.

A secondary debate could take place over limits on the ability of states to tax health care providers.

Medicare, a federal program that provides health insurance for the elderly, affects the states fiscally because of a requirement that states pay the premiums and other health care expenses of residents who are eligible for both Medicaid and Medicare. As a result, state officials may lobby Washington against proposed changes that could increase their costs.

• **Job training.** With sharp new limits on welfare benefits, the next administration is likely to scrutinize the effectiveness of the estimated 160 federal job training programs.

State organizations, such as the National Governors Association, would like the programs consolidated, with states getting more flexibility over whether to focus on job training for young people, dislocated workers or other populations.

• **Utility deregulation.** States are beginning to move toward deregulating electric utilities, which could lower electric rates for consumers. Although the federal government so far has played a minor role on this issue, the administration next year may consider whether to carve out a bigger Washington role, possibly by creating deadlines for the deregulation.

This being an election year, the presidential candidates are filling the air with talk of tax cuts, but the reality is that there is little money to pay for them. A tax code overhaul — another often-mentioned goal — looks even less likely.

The next president also faces the surprising paradox that, despite the clamor inside the Washington Beltway to cut taxes, polls show that people across the country do not expect a tax cut and consider "high taxes" a less important problem than crime, illegal drugs or poverty.

Indeed, the late 1990s are strikingly different from the period 15 years ago, when Ronald Reagan pushed the politics of tax cuts to a new high. Now, budget rules — enacted in 1990 — require tax cuts to be paid for, meaning that each tax reduction engenders a fight over which programs will be eliminated or which taxes raised to offset it.

A tax system overhaul presents its own difficulties. In the past decade, Congress has moved away from the basic tenet of keeping the base broad and the marginal tax rates low. Instead, many recent tax changes have narrowed the base and increased marginal rates, and there is no sign of a reversal.

Furthermore, as money for domestic spending dries up, politicians increasingly are turning to targeted tax cuts to cope with a variety of social and economic problems. After the Los Angeles riots, for instance, lawmakers proposed an enterprise zone for South-Central Los Angeles. And when gas prices were high this past summer, lawmakers proposed removing a portion of the federal gas tax.

Even though tax cuts must be paid for just like new spending programs, it is still possible to find offsets within the tax system; in contrast, domestic discretionary spending accounts already have been squeezed. A tax system overhaul would require eliminating many if not all tax preferences, and that in turn would require a sea change in the political culture of giving tax breaks as a way of dispensing largess.

"The presidential campaign has done grievous damage to a good debate on tax reform," said Rudolph G. Penner, a former director of the Congressional Budget Office who is now a managing director of the Barents Group, an affiliate of the accounting firm KPMG Peat Marwick.

"Both candidates [Democratic incumbent Bill Clinton and Republican Bob Dole] put the emphasis on tax cutting instead of tax reforming, and both candidates have these proposals — tuition deductions or . . . IRAs [individual retirement accounts] and such — and those go against moving towards simplicity and flatness. It's just a hodgepodge of special items being developed," he said.

There is little agreement within the Republican party, let alone the nation, on how to replace the income tax code, said Rep. Bill Archer, R-Texas, chairman of House Ways and Means Committee. "Such a massive undertaking will have to have a broad, bipartisan consensus in the country, and that consensus is not there yet," said Archer, adding that he planned to put off indefinitely his effort to overhaul the tax code.

Taxation: Reductions or Overhaul ?

- **Payroll taxes have increased steadily since 1965, from 3.2 percent of gross domestic product (GDP) to 6.7 percent.**

- **Three revenue sources declined as a percentage of GDP: corporate income taxes from 3.7 to 2.3 percent; excise taxes from 2.1 to 0.8 percent; estate and gift taxes from 0.4 to 0.2 percent.**

- **Federal, state and local taxes total 30 percent of GDP. Among 24 developed nations, only Japan, Australia and Turkey have lower overall taxes.**

Source: Congressional Budget Office

Whether next year will bring a substantial tax cut or major changes in the tax system will depend above all on which candidate wins, and whether Republicans or Democrats control the Congress.

For a tax cut to become law, the executive branch would have to work closely with Congress, and the two would have to agree on both the size of the tax cut and how to pay for it.

Such a scenario is hard to imagine given the experience of the past two years, in which Republicans ran Congress and a Democrat was in the White House. The reverse — Democrats running Congress and a Republican in the White House — would be just as unlikely to yield an agreement.

Of course, if either party dominates both Congress and the presidency, prospects might be quite different. A Democratic-led government would likely be able to agree on a relatively small tax cut targeted at middle-income workers that would be paid for largely by eliminating tax preferences for business. A Republican-led government would likely agree on a far larger tax cut paid for with more cuts on the spending side of the budget.

Little Public Outcry

Whoever wins the presidency will face the striking paradox that, despite the outcry within Washington for lower taxes, the issue is not a top priority right now for the general public.

That is not to say that if people are offered a tax cut, they will return the check to the Internal Revenue Service (IRS). But in many polls, Americans rank tax cuts as less important than an array of other problems. Among key domestic concerns, "high taxes" ranked below crime and drug problems, public education, unemployment, and poverty and homelessness, in a January 1996 poll by Princeton Research Associates. By a margin of almost 2-to-1, the public said it wanted to balance the budget rather than cut taxes, according to a *New York Times* poll taken in October of 1995.

One reason for the lukewarm interest may be that for the majority of taxpayers the portion of income that they pay in federal taxes has been static or even dropped slightly in the past few years. Nearly three-fourths of all taxpayers have adjusted gross incomes of less than $50,000 a year. At the same time, there has been a slight increase in real income, according to the Census Bureau.

While both Presidents George Bush and Clinton raised taxes as part of budget-balancing efforts, most of the increases hit wealthy taxpayers and businesses. Additionally, both presidents expanded the earned-income tax credit, which reduced the tax liability of the 45 percent of taxpayers who earn less than $30,000 a year.

In contrast, politicians have gotten considerable mileage for pledges to "end the IRS as we know it." The IRS has become a symbol for all that the public hates about government bureaucracy. After the recent passage of two "taxpayer bills of rights," it looks increasingly likely that in the next couple of years there will be efforts to make the IRS more customer-friendly and to simplify the tax filing and reporting process. A bipartisan commission is studying ways to restructure the IRS.

Long-term Trends

Overall, federal tax revenues have risen slightly since Clinton became president — from 17.7 percent of gross domestic product in 1992 to 18.9 percent in 1995. They are slated to rise another two-tenths of a percentage point in 1996 and then, assuming no policy changes, drop to 18.5 percent of gross domestic product (GDP) by 2002, according to the Congressional Budget Office (CBO).

Part of the increase is due to growth in the overall economy — tax receipts rise slightly faster than the economy as a whole because of the system's progressive marginal rates. But most of the increase is due to the tax hike that Clinton advocated in 1993.

In contrast, 10 years ago when Ronald Reagan was president, taxes were 17.6 percent of GDP. However, the deficit then was three to four times higher than it is today — 5.1 percent of GDP in 1986, compared with the 1.6 percent of GDP it is now — and government spending as a percentage of the economy was also higher.

Another possible reason for the limited excitement about the tax reduction plans proposed during the presidential campaigns and by Congress is that the plans do nothing to reduce payroll taxes — the most burdensome tax for most Americans. Nearly 78 percent of taxpayers pay more in payroll taxes than they do in income taxes, according to the CBO.

Small Tax Cuts or None

The past two years present a telling case study of why a substantial tax cut — such as the $551 billion one proposed by candidate Dole — would be so difficult to enact.

Flush with their victory in the 1994 election, GOP House members proposed cutting taxes by about $350 billion over seven years as part of an effort to balance the budget. To pay for it, they proposed reductions in spending for domestic programs including Medicare and Medicaid, the federal health care programs for the aged, poor and disabled. *(1994 Almanac, p. 81)*

Initially, the Senate refused to reduce taxes at all because it made the job of eliminating the deficit harder. The two chambers finally agreed on a tax cut of $245 billion over seven years. It was to be paid for by controversial cuts in health care programs and welfare, as well as a tax increase on low-income workers who receive the earned-income tax credit. A sliver of the cut — about $25 billion — was to be offset with an increase in corporate taxes by ending certain tax breaks.

Clinton vetoed the 1995 reconciliation bill (HR 2491), which contained the tax cuts and the spending reductions.

In 1996, Congress tried a smaller tax cut: $123 billion over seven years with the understanding that more cuts could be done if lawmakers were willing to end more corporate tax breaks. The more modest tax cut was to be paid for with smaller reductions in Medicare and Medicaid as well as the earned-income tax credit. But the depth of cuts was still too great to win support from Democrats.

The only tax cuts Congress and Clinton ultimately agreed on

Are lawmakers willing to eliminate more corporate tax preferences in order to pay for tax cuts?

To what extent does the public's desire to reduce the deficit conflict with the appetite for future tax cuts?

To achieve a major overhaul of the tax code, are lawmakers willing to give up the leverage of using tax changes to influence economic behavior?

■ ■ ■

were small ones attached to a health care bill and to the bill raising the minimum wage (HR 3103 — PL 104-191 and HR 3448 — PL 104-737), and to the debt limit bill (HR 3136 — PL 104-121). The last bill effectively reduced taxes on retirees by increasing the Social Security earnings limit. These tax cuts — about half of them targeted at business — cost about $50 billion over 10 years and were largely paid for by ending business tax preferences.

Most Congress watchers expect such small-scale fights to be the bread and butter of tax legislation for the next few years. For example, influential Budget Committee Chairman John R. Kasich, R-Ohio, ardently seeks to end corporate tax breaks as part of budget-balancing efforts. Most recently, Kasich proposed using the termination of corporate tax preferences as a way to pay for additional tax breaks for contributions to charities.

"The money is just not there any more for substantial tax cuts," said Alan Auerbach, an economist at the University of California at Berkeley and former chief economist for Congress' Joint Committee on Taxation. "Sure, we will continue to have small refinements in the tax system — a billion here and a billion there — that can continue ad infinitum, but those aren't going to allow a major tax cut."

If Congress is unwilling to make deep cuts in spending entitlements such as Medicare, Social Security and Medicaid to pay for a tax cut, then the only other way to enact a broad-based tax cut is to end large tax preferences.

The problem is lawmakers are leery of going after the remaining tax preferences in the code because they are broadly popular. According to the Office of Management and Budget, more than $262 billion in tax breaks in fiscal 1996 benefited middle-income taxpayers. They include the mortgage interest deduction ($51 billion), the exclusion for employer-provided health insurance ($65 billion), the exclusion for fringe benefits such as pensions ($70 billion), the deduction for state and local taxes ($45.3 billion) and the charitable deduction ($21 billion).

"The largest tax entitlements go to the broad rank and file of middle America, and they are as tightly lodged as many of the spending entitlements such as Medicare," said Martha Phillips, executive director of the Concord Coalition, a bipartisan group that promotes balancing the budget.

Tax Reform

Without a willingness to take on tax preferences — both for middle-income taxpayers and businesses — the chances for a tax system overhaul are poor indeed.

Economists who have compared the current legislative and political climate with the one that prevailed before the 1986 overhaul of the code find few parallels.

Randy Weiss, a partner at the accounting firm of Deloitte & Touche, points out two catalysts before the 1986 action: a series of prior tax bills that began the process of ending some tax preferences, and "visible and consistent abuses in the tax system" to which lawmakers felt they had to respond.

"If the experience of the early 1980s, and its relationship to the 1986 tax reform act is any clue at all to whether we will see tax reform in 1997, the answer is no," Weiss said.

The federal government has long primed the technology pump in the United States, spending prodigiously on research and development since World War II. Although its share of the load has fallen, Washington still supplies $1 of every $3 spent on R&D in America.

While technology has changed, however, some critical federal policies have not. For example, Cold War priorities continue to dictate where the federal government invests much of the roughly $70 billion it spends annually on R&D.

The next president will have to decide whether to keep those priorities, find new targets for federal dollars or simply cut the spending. A cut would accelerate a trend that began in the late 1980s, when federal investments in R&D started falling behind the rate of inflation.

Although Congress controls the purse strings, White House budget proposals have a major influence on the debate over how to spend science and technology dollars. The survival of the expensive and embattled space station project, for example, is due in part to the support of the last three presidents.

The decision about spending priorities will be joined on the next administration's technology agenda by troubling issues related to the coming revolution in telecommunications. As competition takes the place of regulated monopolies in telecommunications, market forces could unleash a flood of new services, advanced technologies and innovation. Will these benefits reach all Americans, or only a well-positioned few?

The new law that promoted competition in telephone and cable services (S 652 — PL 104-104) also removed some of the ownership limits on broadcast stations and cable systems. The result has been a rapid consolidation by media outlets, particularly among radio stations. The next administration and its Justice Department will play a key role in determining how far this process will go, and how few independent media voices will be left standing after the dust settles.

The explosive growth of the Internet web of computer networks, meanwhile, has been cited by many policymakers as a prime example of the good things that can happen when the government stays out of the way. Still, the next administration will be tempted to intervene on several Internet-related issues.

The promise of the Internet is that it can be a great unifying medium, providing all regions and classes access to vast resources and opportunity. The same technologies that open these doors, however, also can unlock electronic secrets and steal intellectual property. These are issues that the White House and Congress have struggled with and will continue to address over the next four years.

Billions for R&D

The most important and enduring contribution that the federal government makes to U.S. technology is the money it provides for research at universities, industry consortia, Energy Department laboratories and other R&D programs. According to the National Science Foundation, federal funding has grown fairly steadily in recent decades, reaching $69.6 billion in fiscal

Technology: For Defense Or 'Dual Use'?

- Federal government spending on R&D (1995): $69.4 billion

- Industry put up roughly 60 percent of all R&D dollars in 1995; the federal government contributed 36 percent.

- Ratio of R&D spending to Gross Domestic Product: 2.4 percent, down from 2.8 percent in the late 1980s.

Sources: National Science Foundation, Science & Engineering Indicators 1996

1994 before dipping to $69.4 billion in fiscal 1995.

Both Republicans and Democrats strongly support this spending. Still, tightening budgets in the 1990s have taken their toll, and the federal subsidies for R&D have not kept pace with inflation. By the National Science Foundation's calculation, federal spending on R&D in fiscal 1995 was the lowest in real terms since 1983.

Given the belt-tightening, the federal government has come under increasing pressure to spend each technology dollar more effectively. The debate has focused on two areas: whether to shift dollars away from defense-oriented research and whether to place more emphasis on applied research that makes a quicker payoff in the marketplace.

National security has always been one of the primary rationales for federal spending on R&D, and the share of research devoted to defense grew from roughly 50 percent of the federal dollars in 1980 to more than 60 percent in 1990. Presidents George Bush and Clinton both worked to reverse that trend, putting more emphasis on "dual use" technologies that could benefit both the military and civilians.

Congress, however, insisted that the Pentagon's needs remain the top priority. Nowhere was this more evident than in the battles over redirecting the Department of Energy's research at approximately 700 laboratories around the country. Legislation to give the labs a new, post-Cold War mission was stymied by opposition from defense hawks, who insisted that nuclear weapons projects and other military work remain Job No. 1.

David Y. Peyton, director of technology policy for the National Association of Manufacturers, said that the need to reorient the labs was made abundantly clear by an Aug. 7, 1996, report from the National Science Foundation. A survey of 1,000 U.S. companies found that government labs were among the least important sources of leads for new products and among the least likely to be chosen as a partner for cooperative R&D efforts. The challenge, Peyton said, is making the government's investment more valuable to industry.

Most of the federal dollars for research go to basic science projects that are not tied to a product or manufacturing process. Many policymakers, particularly Republicans, argue that the government needs to stick to these long-term efforts, rather than seeking the quicker results of applied R&D.

When Washington gets into the business of developing products, said Chairman Robert S. Walker, R-Pa., of the House Science Committee, "then government has wandered off into an area where it has little competence and little to contribute." By contrast, Walker said, the federal support for basic research in past decades has led to the United States dominating the world in computers and software.

Arati Prabhakar, director of the National Institute of Science and Technology, puts a different spin on the competitiveness argument. "To spend $70 billion on R&D . . . without an explicit strategy for how we connect it to the economy, it's a bad way to spend $70 billion of the taxpayers' money," she said.

Although the United States has one of the richest pools of science in the world, the fruits of that knowledge are flowing increasingly to foreign industries that transform U.S. breakthroughs into their products. Thus, the basic research done in the United States no longer translates directly into U.S. technological growth, Prabhakar said. That is why she wants the government to invest both in performing basic research and in capturing its benefits for U.S. industry.

Telecommunications Unleashed

Shaped in part by the current administration, the new telecommunications law will pose several challenges for the next president.

The first task will be to fill two of the five seats on the Federal Communications Commission (FCC), the independent regulatory panel that is implementing the new law. The FCC will play a critical role in the transition to competition, settling disputes between competitors, setting rules to preserve low-cost phone service and deciding when to let the powerhouse regional Bell telephone companies into long-distance service.

The move to competition comes at a time when telecommunications is a growing part of the nation's economy. The Internet is the leading edge of a wave of interactive technologies that could transform the phone lines and video cables into pipelines for commerce, education, civic functions and medicine.

"If the benefits of this information society are to be realized," said Andrew Jay Schwartzman of the Media Access Project, a group that promotes public access to communications networks, "people like myself believe it can happen only if all Americans are connected and literate, capable of using these technologies. We are already seeing a tremendous gap in the availability of these technologies, and it threatens to divide us and further segment Americans into a class of people with access and a class of people without access to the tools of information society."

"This is more than 'information haves' and 'information have-nots.' This is literacy, this is the ability to participate in the democratic process . . . the ability to participate in commerce at all."

Although both Republicans and Democrats say that telephone service should be made available to all Americans at an affordable price — a policy known as universal service — there is a considerable split over how advanced that phone service should be. The next administration will have an important voice in the debate over whether and how to bring the Internet and other cutting-edge information services to the communities that the market would ignore.

Through the Justice Department, the administration also will determine how vigorously the federal antitrust laws will be enforced as broadcasters and telephone companies form increasingly powerful media conglomerates. At stake is whether competition is snuffed out by a handful of giant communications and information companies before it has a chance to flourish, Schwartzman said. He added, "It potentially decreases the diversity of viewpoints and opinions available to voters to use when they are deciding how to govern themselves."

Schwartzman's fear is shared more by Democrats than Republicans, who argued during the debate over the telecom-

munications bill that big was not necessarily bad. On the other hand, opposition to monopolies runs deep in both parties. After all, it was Assistant Attorney General William F. Baxter, a Republican appointee in the Reagan Justice Department, who successfully fought to break up AT&T in the early 1980s.

The federal government has little authority over what programs the broadcasters and cable companies carry. Nevertheless, the next president is likely to pressure programmers to air less violent and sexually graphic material, as both Republican presidential nominee Bob Dole and Clinton have tried to do in recent years.

Clinton has also urged broadcasters to carry more educational programs for children, a mandate championed by Reed Hundt, Clinton's appointee as chairman of the FCC.

Regulating the Computer Industry?

The federal government has taken a hands-off approach to the computer industry, keeping regulation to a minimum as it poured money into the Internet and related research projects. On at least two issues critical to the industry's fortunes, however, the next administration will be deeply involved.

The first is encryption, or the ability to protect computer files against unauthorized use. Fearful of terrorists being able to conceal their plans in uncrackable code, the government has classified all powerful encryption software as munitions and restricted their export. This declaration not only forbids exchange of such software on the Internet, a global medium, but also deters U.S. industry from building encryption into its products.

After a lengthy standoff between government and industry, the Clinton administration in October proposed to allow strong encryption to be exported so long as law enforcement officials had access to keys that could unlock the coded files. The proposal was supported by one computer-industry giant, IBM, as a workable compromise. But many other industry and computer-user groups continued to object to the use of keys, particularly if foreign governments were given access to them.

The next administration will be under increasing pressure to end the dispute, said Peyton of the National Association of Manufacturers, because of the evolution in the manufacturing process. More companies are keeping smaller inventories and filling orders on a "just in time" basis. This approach requires a lot of data to be exchanged over the phone lines between manufacturers, suppliers and customers, and encryption is needed to secure these communications both at home and abroad, Peyton said.

A second issue is intellectual property. Although the Internet makes it easy to gain a wide audience, publishers and other copyright holders have been reluctant to make valuable material available there. The problem is that digital technology makes duplication fast, easy and undetectable.

The copyright situation also has hindered the efforts of public libraries to make more resources available online. The Clinton administration and Congress have tried in vain to resolve the issue, and the next administration can be expected to try again.

Questions for the President

★ ★ ★ ★ ★
★ ★ ★ ★

Should the government spend less on defense-related research and more on projects that help civilian industries?

Should all Americans have access to the Internet and other advanced communications tools?

Should the computer industry be allowed to export powerful security software that cannot be unlocked by law enforcement agents?

■ ■ ■

Appendix

1996 Election Results

Here are nearly complete, unofficial 1996 vote returns for House, Senate and gubernatorial races from the Associated Press. In some cases, there will be significant changes in the final, official returns.

The box below is a key to party designation.

Other symbols:
- • incumbent
- x candidate without major-party opposition
- AL at-large district
- * runoff Dec. 10

	Vote Total	%
ALABAMA		
Senate		
Jeff Sessions (R)	779,415	51.9
Roger Bedford (D)	685,556	45.7
Mark Thornton (LIBERT)	27,633	1.8
Charles Hebner (NL)	8,983	.6
House		
1 • Sonny Callahan (R)	132,086	64.5
Don Womack (D)	69,322	33.9
Bob Burns (LIBERT)	3,302	1.6
2 • Terry Everett (R)	132,596	63.3
Bob E. Gaines (D)	74,330	35.5
Michael Probst (LIBERT)	2,659	1.3
3 Bob Riley (R)	102,923	50.9
T.D. "Ted" Little (D)	94,927	46.9
Lucy Lawrence (NL)	2,366	1.2
Ralph "R.E." Stokes (LIBERT)	1,992	1.0
4 Robert Aderholt (R)	102,879	50.0
Robert T. "Bob" Wilson (D)	99,356	48.3
Alan Barksdale (LIBERT)	3,596	1.7
5 • Robert E. "Bud" Cramer (D)	126,705	56.1
Wayne Parker (R)	94,334	41.8
Shirley Madison (NL)	2,665	1.2
Craig Goodrich (LIBERT)	1,973	.9
6 • Spencer Bachus (R)	181,313	70.9
Mary Lynn Bates (D)	70,072	27.4
T. Franklin Harris (LIBERT)	2,309	.9
Diane Vogel (NL)	2,130	.8
7 • Earl F. Hilliard (D)	136,634	71.2
Joe Powell (R)	52,084	27.1
Ken Hager (LIBERT)	3,167	1.7
ALASKA		
Senate		
• Ted Stevens (R)	149,475	77.4
Jed Whittaker (GREEN)	24,219	12.5
Theresa Nangle Obermeyer (D)	19,402	10.0
House		
AL • Don Young (R)	115,480	59.1
Georgianna Lincoln (D)	72,448	37.1
William J. Nemec II (AKI)	3,911	2.0
John J.G. "Johnny" Grames (GREEN)	3,503	1.8

	Vote Total	%
ARIZONA		
House		
1 • Matt Salmon (R)	123,527	59.9
John Cox (D)	82,547	40.1
2 • Ed Pastor (D)	78,090	64.7
Jim Buster (R)	37,486	31.1
Alice Bangle (LIBERT)	5,053	4.2
3 • Bob Stump (R)	159,939	66.4
Alexander "Big Al" Schneider (D)	80,980	33.6
4 • John Shadegg (R)	137,639	66.6
Maria Elena Milton (D)	69,176	33.4
5 • Jim Kolbe (R)	171,629	68.7
Mort Nelson (D)	64,964	26.0
John C. Zajac (LIBERT)	6,982	2.8
Ed Finkelstein (REF)	6,312	2.5
6 • J.D. Hayworth (R)	113,545	47.2
Steve Owens (D)	112,955	46.9
Robert Anderson (LIBERT)	14,090	5.9
ARKANSAS		
Senate		
Tim Hutchinson (R)	441,705	52.7
Winston Bryant (D)	396,008	47.3
House		
1 Marion Berry (D)	102,567	52.8
Warren Dupwe (R)	86,028	44.3
Keith Carle (REF)	5,703	2.9
2 Victor F. Snyder (D)	113,786	52.3
Bud Cummins (R)	103,793	47.7
3 Asa Hutchinson (R)	135,970	55.7
Ann Henry (D)	102,244	41.9
Tony Joe Huffman (REF)	5,928	2.4
4 • Jay Dickey (R)	125,568	63.5
Vincent Tolliver (D)	72,066	36.5
CALIFORNIA		
House		
1 • Frank Riggs (R)	96,622	49.0
Michela Alioto (D)	86,997	44.1
Emil Rossi (LIBERT)	13,701	6.9

	Vote Total	%
2 • Wally Herger (R)	131,749	60.5
Roberts A. Braden (D)	73,965	34.0
Patrice Thiessen (NL)	6,629	3.0
William Brunner (LIBERT)	5,308	2.4
3 • Vic Fazio (D)	112,590	53.6
Tim LeFever (R)	86,204	41.0
Timothy R. Erich (REF)	7,271	3.5
Erin D. Donelle (LIBERT)	4,025	1.9
4 • John T. Doolittle (R)	147,879	60.2
Katie Hirning (D)	89,178	36.3
Patrick Lee McHargue (LIBERT)	8,489	3.5
5 • Robert T. Matsui (D)	134,802	70.5
Robert S. Dinsmore (R)	49,820	26.1
Joseph B. Miller (LIBERT)	2,408	1.3
Gordon Mors (AMI)	2,110	1.1
Charles Kersey (NL)	1,983	1.0
6 • Lynn Woolsey (D)	145,364	62.0
Duane C. Hughes (R)	79,317	33.8
Ernest K. Jones Jr. (PFP)	5,982	2.6
Bruce B. Kendall (NL)	3,849	1.6
7 • George Miller (D)	128,249	71.9
Norman H. Reece (R)	39,514	22.2
William C. Thompson (REF)	6,411	3.6
Bob Liatunick (NL)	4,150	2.3
8 • Nancy Pelosi (D)	158,533	84.5
Justin Raimondo (R)	22,828	12.2
David Smithstein (NL)	6,142	3.3
9 • Ronald V. Dellums (D)	140,638	77.2
Deborah Wright (R)	33,201	18.2
Tom Condit (PFP)	5,104	2.8
Jack Forem (NL)	3,143	1.7
10 Ellen O. Tauscher (D)	126,868	49.0
• Bill Baker (R)	121,332	46.8
John Place (REF)	5,861	2.3
Valerie Janlois (NL)	2,801	1.1
Gregory K. Lyon (LIBERT)	2,222	.9
11 • Richard W. Pombo (R)	100,404	59.2
Jason Silva (D)	61,573	36.3
Kelly Rego (LIBERT)	4,738	2.8
Selene L. Bush (NL)	2,831	1.7
12 • Tom Lantos (D)	133,583	71.8
Storm Jenkins (R)	43,809	23.5
Christopher V.A. Schmidt (LIBERT)	5,495	3.0
Richard Borg (NL)	3,151	1.7

Abbreviations for Party Designations

AF	— America First	I	— Independent	NL	— Natural Law	S	— Socialist
AKI	— Alaskan Independence	IA	— Independent American	NON	— Non-Partisan	SE	— Socialist Equality
AM	— American	IG	— Independent Grassroots	P	— Prohibition	SM	— Save Medicare
AMI	— American Independent	INDC	— Independence	PAC	— Politicians Are Crooks	SW	— Socialist Workers
C	— Conservative	IP	— Independent Party	PACIFIC	— Pacific Party	TAX	— Taxpayers
CC	— Concerned Citizens	IPC	— Independent Peoples	PF	— Protecting Freedom	TLL	— Truth, Life, Liberty
CONSTL	— Constitutional		Coalition	PFP	— Peace and Freedom	USA	— Undauntable Stalwart
D	— Democratic	JPR	— Jobs, Property Rights	PS	— Protect Seniors		Allegiance
FDM	— Freedom Party	L	— Liberal	PTC	— Property Tax Cut	USTAX	— U.S. Taxpayers
FN	— Future Now Party	LIBERT	— Libertarian	R	— Republican	VG	— Vermont Grassroots
FWC	— Francis Worley Congress	LU	— Liberty Union	REF	— Reform	VREF	— Virginia Reform
GCP	— Green Coalition Party	NJC	— New Jersey Conservative	RES	— Resource Party	WC	— Working Class
GR	— Grassroots		Party	ROP	— Running On Principles	WSN	— West Side Neighbors
GREEN	— Green	NJI	— New Jersey Independents	RTL	— Right to Life	WW	— Workers World

		Vote Total	%
13 •	Pete Stark (D)	106,467	65.4
	James S. Fay (R)	49,141	30.2
	Terry C. Savage (LIBERT)	7,211	4.4
14 •	Anna G. Eshoo (D)	131,595	65.1
	Ben Brink (R)	62,334	30.8
	Timothy Thompson (PFP)	3,277	1.6
	Joseph W. Dehn III (LIBERT)	3,103	1.5
	Robert Wells (NL)	1,936	1.0
15 •	Tom Campbell (R)	115,434	57.8
	Dick Lane (D)	70,691	35.4
	Valli Sharpe-Geisler (REF)	5,602	2.8
	Ed Wimmers (LIBERT)	4,867	2.4
	Bruce Currivan (NL)	2,993	1.5
16 •	Zoe Lofgren (D)	85,082	66.1
	Chuck Wojslaw (R)	38,205	29.7
	David R. Bonino (LIBERT)	3,748	2.9
	Abaan Abu-Shumays (NL)	1,703	1.3
17 •	Sam Farr (D)	100,658	58.5
	Jess Brown (R)	65,648	38.1
	John H. Black (NL)	5,820	3.4
18 •	Gary A. Condit (D)	98,517	65.6
	Bill Conrad (R)	47,890	31.9
	James B. Morzella (LIBERT)	2,059	1.4
	Page Roth Riskin (NL)	1,660	1.1
19 •	George P. Radanovich (R)	114,211	67.0
	Paul Barile (D)	47,565	27.9
	Pamela J. Pescosolido (LIBERT)	5,012	2.9
	David P. Adalian Sr. (NL)	3,756	2.2
20 •	Cal Dooley (D)	46,427	55.2
	Trice Harvey (R)	33,939	40.3
	Jonathan Richter (LIBERT)	3,770	4.5
21 •	Bill Thomas (R)	111,105	65.7
	Deborah A. Vollmer (D)	45,230	26.7
	John Evans (REF)	7,159	4.2
	Jane Bialosky (NL)	3,020	1.8
	Mike Hodges (LIBERT)	2,716	1.6
22	Walter Holden Capps (D)	102,915	49.3
•	Andrea Seastrand (R)	90,374	43.3
	Steven Wheeler (I)	8,308	4.0
	Richard D. "Dick" Porter (REF)	3,429	1.6
	David L. Bersohn (LIBERT)	1,948	.9
	Dawn Tomastik (NL)	1,569	.8
23 •	Elton Gallegly (R)	98,369	58.5
	Robert R. Unruhe (D)	60,388	35.9
	Gail Lightfoot (LIBERT)	7,328	4.4
	Stephen Hospodar (NL)	1,967	1.2
24 •	Brad Sherman (D)	96,641	50.4
	Rich Sybert (R)	81,428	42.5
	Ralph Shroyer (PFP)	5,749	3.0
	Erich Miller (LIBERT)	5,162	2.7
	Ron Lawrence (NL)	2,791	1.5
25 •	Howard P. "Buck" McKeon (R)	110,998	62.2
	Diane Trautman (D)	59,602	33.4
	Bruce Acker (LIBERT)	5,638	3.2
	Justin Charles Gerber (PFP)	2,300	1.3
26 •	Howard L. Berman (D)	61,963	66.0
	Bill Glass (R)	26,734	28.5
	Scott K. Fritschler (LIBERT)	3,275	3.5
	Gary Hearne (NL)	1,962	2.1
27	James E. Rogan (R)	84,642	49.9
	Doug Kahn (D)	73,679	43.4
	Elizabeth Michael (LIBERT)	6,062	3.6
	Walt Contreras Sheasby (GREEN)	3,769	2.2
	Martin Zucker (NL)	1,623	1.0
28 •	David Dreier (R)	103,939	60.4
	David Levering (D)	63,972	37.2
	Ken Saurenman (LIBERT)	4,183	2.4
29 •	Henry A. Waxman (D)	132,206	68.1
	Paul Stepanek (R)	46,667	24.1
	John Peter Daly (PFP)	8,046	4.1
	Mike Binkley (LIBERT)	4,299	2.2
	Brian Rees (NL)	2,803	1.4
30 •	Xavier Becerra (D)	52,673	72.7
	Patricia Jean Parker (R)	13,216	18.2
	Pam Probst (LIBERT)	2,464	3.4
	Shirley Mandel (PFP)	2,264	3.1
	Rosemary Watson-Frith (NL)	1,805	2.5
31 •	Matthew G. Martinez (D)	63,553	67.7
	John V. Flores (R)	26,041	27.7
	Michael B. Everling (LIBERT)	4,252	4.5
32 •	Julian C. Dixon (D)	114,584	82.7
	Larry Ardito (R)	16,712	12.1
	Neal Donner (LIBERT)	5,870	4.2
	Rashied Jibri (NL)	1,435	1.0

		Vote Total	%
33 •	Lucille Roybal-Allard (D)	43,788	82.4
	John P. Leonard (R)	7,308	13.8
	Howard Johnson (LIBERT)	2,030	3.8
34 •	Esteban E. Torres (D)	87,803	68.7
	David G. Nunez (R)	33,677	26.3
	J. Walter Scott (AMI)	3,846	3.0
	David Argall (LIBERT)	2,528	2.0
35 •	Maxine Waters (D)	86,878	85.8
	Eric Carlson (R)	11,930	11.8
	Gordon Michael Mego (AMI)	2,433	2.4
36 •	Jane Harman (D)	107,738	52.8
	Susan Brooks (R)	88,909	43.6
	Bruce Dovner (LIBERT)	4,505	2.2
	Bradley McManus (NL)	3,001	1.5
37 •	Juanita Millender-McDonald (D)	81,695	85.3
	Michael E. Voetee (R)	14,115	14.7
38 •	Steve Horn (R)	81,372	52.6
	Rick Zbur (D)	65,882	42.6
	William A. Yeager (GREEN)	4,282	2.8
	Paul N. Gautreau (LIBERT)	3,020	2.0
39 •	Ed Royce (R)	110,201	62.5
	R.O. "Bob" Davis (D)	56,723	32.2
	Jack Dean (LIBERT)	9,416	5.3
40 •	Jerry Lewis (R)	93,750	64.8
	Robert "Bob" Conaway (D)	42,117	29.1
	Hale McGee (AMI)	4,686	3.2
	Joseph T. Kelley (LIBERT)	4,131	2.9
41 •	Jay C. Kim (R)	77,578	58.1
	Richard L. Waldron (D)	44,425	33.3
	Richard G. Newhouse (LIBERT)	6,736	5.0
	David F. Kramer (D)	4,765	3.6
42 •	George E. Brown Jr. (D)	49,907	50.6
	Linda M. Wilde (R)	48,757	49.4
43 •	Ken Calvert (R)	85,172	54.2
	Guy C. Kimbrough (D)	60,516	38.5
	Annie Wallack (NL)	5,860	3.7
	Kevin Akin (PFP)	2,971	1.9
	Gene L. Berkman (LIBERT)	2,713	1.7
44 •	Sonny Bono (R)	97,522	57.2
	Anita Rufus (D)	66,750	39.1
	Donald Cochran (AMI)	3,475	2.0
	Karen Wilkinson (NL)	2,806	1.6
45 •	Dana Rohrabacher (R)	113,827	60.7
	Sally J. Alexander (D)	62,569	33.4
	Mark F. Murphy (LIBERT)	8,150	4.3
	Rand McDevitt (NL)	2,834	1.5
46 •	Robert K. Dornan (R)	41,308	46.4
	Loretta Sanchez (D)	41,075	46.1
	Lawrence J. Stafford (REF)	2,907	3.3
	Thomas E. Reimer (LIBERT)	2,094	2.4
	J. Carlos Aguirre (NL)	1,693	1.9
47 •	Christopher Cox (R)	143,383	65.3
	Tina Louise Laine (D)	63,877	29.1
	Iris Adam (NL)	6,186	2.8
	Victor A. Wagner Jr. (LIBERT)	5,991	2.7
48 •	Ron Packard (R)	128,066	65.4
	Dan Farrell (D)	53,381	27.3
	Sharon K. Miles (NL)	7,158	3.7
	William Dreu (REF)	7,083	3.6
49 •	Brian P. Bilbray (R)	94,850	52.0
	Peter Navarro (D)	77,482	42.5
	Ernie Lippe (LIBERT)	3,745	2.1
	Kevin Philip Hambsch (REF)	3,320	1.8
	Peter Sterling (NL)	2,915	1.6
50 •	Bob Filner (D)	65,246	62.1
	Jim Baize (R)	33,722	32.1
	Dan Clark (REF)	2,896	2.8
	Earl M. Shepard (NL)	1,900	1.8
	Philip Zoebisch (LIBERT)	1,249	1.2
51 •	Randy "Duke" Cunningham (R)	127,961	64.7
	Rita Tamerius (D)	57,917	29.3
	Miriam E. Clark (PFP)	4,768	2.4
	J.C. "Jack" Anderson (LIBERT)	4,624	2.3
	Eric Hunter Bourdette (NL)	2,640	1.3
52 •	Duncan Hunter (R)	103,231	65.1
	Darity Wesley (D)	47,676	30.0
	Janice Jordan (PFP)	3,284	2.1
	Dante Ridley (LIBERT)	3,159	2.0
	Peter Robert Ballantyne (NL)	1,317	.8

COLORADO

Senate

	Vote Total	%
Wayne Allard (R)	748,516	50.7
Tom Strickland (D)	677,151	46.3
Randy MacKenzie (NL)	42,972	3.0

House

		Vote Total	%
1	Diana DeGette (D)	112,555	56.9
	Joe Rogers (R)	79,536	40.2
	Richard Combs (LIBERT)	5,656	2.9
2 •	David E. Skaggs (D)	145,894	57.0
	Pat Miller (R)	97,865	38.3
	Larry E. Johnson (I)	6,304	2.5
	W. Earl Allen (LIBERT)	5,721	2.2
3 •	Scott McInnis (R)	183,062	68.9
	Al Gurule (D)	82,544	31.1
4 •	Robert W. Schaffer (R)	136,580	56.1
	Guy Kelley (D)	92,680	38.1
	Wes McKinley (AM)	7,375	3.0
	Cynthia Parker (NL)	6,681	2.7
5 •	Joel Hefley (R)	188,795	71.9
	Mike Robinson (D)	73,654	28.1
6 •	Dan Schaefer (R)	146,018	62.2
	Joan Fitz-Gerald (D)	88,600	37.8

CONNECTICUT

House

		Vote Total	%
1 •	Barbara B. Kennelly (D)	159,312	73.8
	Kent Sleath (R)	53,678	24.9
	John F. Forry III (CC)	1,888	.9
	Daniel A. Wasielewski (NL)	1,035	.5
2 •	Sam Gejdenson (D)	114,453	51.5
	Edward W. Munster (R)	100,008	45.0
	Dianne G. Ondusko (I)	6,346	2.9
	Thomas E. Hall (NL)	1,316	.6
3 •	Rosa DeLauro (D)	149,212	71.2
	John Coppola (R)	59,093	28.2
	Gail J. Dalby (NL)	1,126	.5
4 •	Christopher Shays (R)	121,658	60.6
	Bill Finch (D)	75,181	37.5
	Edward H. Tonkin (LIBERT)	2,755	1.4
	Terry M. Nevas (NL)	1,075	.5
5	James H. Maloney (D)	110,844	52.1
•	Gary A. Franks (R)	97,725	45.9
	Rosita Rodriguez (CC)	2,985	1.4
	Walter F. Thiessen Jr. (L)	1,353	.6
6 •	Nancy L. Johnson (R)	113,022	49.8
	Charlotte Koskoff (D)	110,840	48.8
	Timothy A. Knibbs (CC)	3,303	1.5

DELAWARE

Governor

	Vote Total	%
• Thomas R. Carper (D)	188,323	69.5
Janet C. Rzewnicki (R)	82,653	30.5

Senate

	Vote Total	%
• Joseph R. Biden Jr. (D)	165,241	60.0
Raymond J. Clatworthy (R)	104,982	38.1
Mark Jones (LIBERT)	3,333	1.2
Jacqueline Kossoff (NL)	1,693	.6

House

		Vote Total	%
AL •	Michael N. Castle (R)	185,341	69.5
	Dennis E. Williams (D)	73,177	27.5
	George A. Jurgensen (LIBERT)	3,991	1.5
	Felicia B. Johnson (P)	3,006	1.1
	Robert E. "Bob" Mattson (NL)	985	.4

FLORIDA

House

		Vote Total	%
1 •	Joe Scarborough (R)	175,382	72.6
	Kevin Beck (D)	66,243	27.4
2	Allen Boyd (D)	137,213	59.5
	Bill Sutton (R)	93,519	40.5
3 •	Corrine Brown (D)	97,972	61.2
	Preston James Fields (D)	62,128	38.8
4 •	Tillie Fowler (R)	x	x
5 •	Karen L. Thurman (D)	161,027	61.7
	Dave Gentry (R)	100,023	38.3
6 •	Cliff Stearns (R)	161,461	67.2
	Newell O'Brien (D)	78,886	32.8
7 •	John L. Mica (R)	143,503	62.0
	George Stuart Jr. (D)	87,773	38.0
8 •	Bill McCollum (R)	136,133	67.5
	Al Krulick (D)	65,528	32.5
9 •	Michael Bilirakis (R)	161,649	68.7
	Jerry Provenzano (D)	73,779	31.3

	Vote Total	%
10 • C.W. Bill Young (R)	114,418	66.6
Henry Green (D)	57,359	33.4
11 Jim Davis (D)	108,454	58.0
Mark Sharpe (R)	78,680	42.0
12 • Charles T. Canady (R)	122,531	61.6
Mike Canady (D)	76,490	38.4
13 • Dan Miller (R)	173,570	64.4
Sanford Gordon (D)	96,049	35.6
14 • Porter J. Goss (R)	176,961	73.5
Jim Nolan (D)	63,833	26.5
15 • Dave Weldon (R)	138,965	51.4
John L. Byron (D)	115,952	42.9
David Golding (I)	15,350	5.7
16 • Mark Foley (R)	176,670	64.1
Jim Stuber (D)	98,823	35.9
17 • Carrie P. Meek (D)	114,170	88.8
Wellington Rolle (R)	14,428	11.2
18 • Ileana Ros-Lehtinen (R)	x	x
19 Robert Wexler (D)	188,693	65.6
Beverly "Bev" Kennedy (R)	99,015	34.4
20 • Peter Deutsch (D)	159,053	65.0
Jim Jacobs (R)	85,620	35.0
21 • Lincoln Diaz-Balart (R)	x	x
22 • E. Clay Shaw Jr. (R)	136,967	61.9
Kenneth D. Cooper (D)	84,451	38.1
23 • Alcee L. Hastings (D)	102,063	73.5
Robert Paul Brown (R)	36,881	26.5

GEORGIA

Senate

	Vote Total	%
Max Cleland (D)	1,103,492	48.8
Guy Millner (R)	1,075,628	47.6
John Cashin (LIBERT)	81,833	3.6

House

	Vote Total	%
1 • Jack Kingston (R)	108,557	68.2
Rosemary Kaszans (D)	50,516	31.8
2 • Sanford D. Bishop Jr. (D)	88,253	53.8
Darrel Ealum (R)	75,686	46.2
3 • Mac Collins (R)	120,254	61.1
Jim Chafin (D)	76,537	38.9
4 • Cynthia A. McKinney (D)	127,157	57.8
John Mitnick (R)	92,985	42.2
5 • John Lewis (D)	x	x
6 • Newt Gingrich (R)	174,152	57.8
Michael Coles (D)	127,132	42.2
7 • Bob Barr (R)	112,008	57.8
Charlie Watts (D)	81,763	42.2
8 • Saxby Chambliss (R)	93,432	52.6
Jim Wiggins (D)	84,175	47.4
9 • Nathan Deal (R)	130,516	65.4
McCracken "Ken" Poston (D)	69,011	34.6
10 • Charlie Norwood (R)	94,683	51.8
David Bell (D)	88,108	48.2
11 • John Linder (R)	145,813	64.3
Tommy Stephenson (D)	81,030	35.7

HAWAII

House

	Vote Total	%
1 • Neil Abercrombie (D)	86,732	50.4
Orson Swindle (R)	80,053	46.5
Mark Duering (NON)	4,126	2.4
Nicholas Bedworth (NL)	1,295	.8
2 • Patsy T. Mink (D)	109,178	57.0
Tom Pico Jr. (R)	55,729	29.1
Amanda "Mandy" Toulon (NL)	13,985	7.3
Nolan Crabbe (NON)	7,723	4.0
James M. Keefe (LIBERT)	4,769	2.5

IDAHO

Senate

	Vote Total	%
• Larry E. Craig (R)	283,530	57.0
Walt Minnick (D)	198,415	39.9
Mary J. Charbonneau (I)	10,137	2.0
Susan Vegors (NL)	5,140	1.0

House

	Vote Total	%
1 • Helen Chenoweth (R)	132,340	50.0
Dan Williams (D)	125,893	47.5
Marion Ellis (NL)	6,530	2.5
2 • Michael D. Crapo (R)	157,643	68.8
John D. Seidl (D)	67,620	29.5
John Butler (NL)	3,976	1.7

ILLINOIS

Senate

	Vote Total	%
Richard J. Durbin (D)	2,340,655	55.8
Al Salvi (R)	1,718,856	41.0
Steven H. Perry (REF)	60,579	1.4
Robin J. Miller (LIBERT)	40,758	1.0
Chad Koppie (USTAX)	17,420	.4
James E. Davis (NL)	13,553	.3

House

	Vote Total	%
1 • Bobby L. Rush (D)	164,163	85.1
Noel Naughton (R)	25,335	13.1
Tim M. Griffin (LIBERT)	3,330	1.7
2 • Jesse Jackson Jr. (D)	168,086	94.0
Frank H. Stratman (LIBERT)	10,706	6.0
3 • William O. Lipinski (D)	134,846	65.2
Jim Nalepa (R)	66,365	32.1
George Skaritka (REF)	3,613	1.7
Robert R. Prazak (LIBERT)	1,882	.9
4 • Luis V. Gutierrez (D)	81,298	93.6
William Passmore (LIBERT)	5,602	6.4
5 Rod R. Blagojevich (D)	111,608	64.1
• Michael Patrick Flanagan (R)	62,588	35.9
6 • Henry J. Hyde (R)	131,962	64.3
Stephen de la Rosa (D)	68,573	33.4
George Meyers (LIBERT)	4,726	2.3
7 • Danny K. Davis (D)	139,973	82.3
Randy Borow (R)	26,088	15.3
Chauncey L. Stroud (I)	1,836	1.1
Toietta Dixon (LIBERT)	1,475	.9
Charles A. Winter (NL)	741	.4
8 • Philip M. Crane (R)	127,763	62.2
Elizabeth Ann "Betty" Hull (D)	74,068	36.1
H. Daniel Druck (LIBERT)	3,474	1.7
9 • Sidney R. Yates (D)	120,354	63.3
Joseph Walsh (R)	69,785	36.7
10 • John Edward Porter (R)	145,626	69.1
Philip R. Torf (D)	65,144	30.9
11 • Jerry Weller (R)	109,135	51.7
Clem Balanoff (D)	101,839	48.3
12 • Jerry F. Costello (D)	150,005	71.6
Shapley R. Hunter (R)	55,690	26.6
Geoffrey S. Nathan (LIBERT)	3,824	1.8
13 • Harris W. Fawell (R)	141,120	59.9
Susan W. Hynes (D)	94,277	40.1
14 • Dennis Hastert (R)	134,432	64.4
Doug Mains (D)	74,332	35.6
15 • Thomas W. Ewing (R)	121,019	57.3
Laurel Lunt Prussing (D)	90,065	42.7
16 • Donald Manzullo (R)	137,523	60.3
Catherine M. Lee (D)	90,575	39.7
17 • Lane Evans (D)	120,008	51.9
Mark Baker (R)	109,240	47.3
William J. Herrmann (LIBERT)	1,925	.8
18 • Ray LaHood (R)	143,110	59.3
Mike Curran (D)	98,413	40.7
19 • Glenn Poshard (D)	158,668	66.7
Brent Winters (R)	75,751	31.8
Patricia Riker (NL)	2,269	1.0
James R. Lacher (LIBERT)	1,242	.5
20 John M. Shimkus (R)	120,749	50.3
Jay C. Hoffman (D)	119,496	49.7

INDIANA

Governor

	Vote Total	%
Frank O'Bannon (D)	1,075,342	51.5
Steven Goldsmith (R)	977,505	46.8
Steve Dillon (LIBERT)	35,261	1.7

House

	Vote Total	%
1 • Peter J. Visclosky (D)	132,430	69.1
Michael Edward Petyo (R)	56,205	29.3
Michael Crass (LIBERT)	3,122	1.6
2 • David M. McIntosh (R)	122,288	58.1
R. Marc Carmichael (D)	83,478	39.7
Paul E. Zimmerman (LIBERT)	4,662	2.2
3 • Tim Roemer (D)	114,381	57.9
Joe Zakas (R)	80,748	40.9
Bernie Taylor (LIBERT)	2,331	1.2
4 • Mark E. Souder (R)	118,344	59.4
Gerald L. Houseman (D)	76,152	38.2
Ken Bisson (LIBERT)	4,743	2.4
5 • Steve Buyer (R)	133,604	64.9
Douglas L. Clark (D)	67,125	32.6
Tom Lehman (LIBERT)	5,253	2.6

	Vote Total	%
6 • Dan Burton (R)	189,461	74.9
Carrie J. Dillard-Trammell (D)	58,362	23.1
Fred Peterson (LIBERT)	5,295	2.1
7 • Ed Pease (R)	130,010	62.0
Robert F. Hellmann (D)	72,705	34.6
Barbara Bourland (LIBERT)	7,125	3.4
8 • John Hostettler (R)	109,582	49.9
Jonathan Weinzapfel (D)	106,134	48.3
Paul Hager (LIBERT)	3,799	1.7
9 • Lee H. Hamilton (D)	128,885	56.3
Jean Leising (R)	97,747	42.7
Diane Feeney (LIBERT)	2,315	1.0
10 • Julia M. Carson (D)	80,869	52.6
Virginia Blankenbaker (R)	69,248	45.1
Kurt St. Angelo (LIBERT)	3,505	2.3

IOWA

Senate

	Vote Total	%
• Tom Harkin (D)	629,162	51.8
Jim Ross Lightfoot (R)	568,329	46.8
Sue Atkinson (I)	9,369	.8
Fred Gratzon (NL)	4,079	.3
Shirley E. Pena (SW)	1,741	.1
Joe Sulentic (I)	1,619	.1

House

	Vote Total	%
1 • Jim Leach (R)	128,684	52.9
Bob Rush (D)	111,190	45.7
Thomas W. Isenhour (I)	2,227	.9
Michael J. Cuddehe (NL)	1,341	.6
2 • Jim Nussle (R)	127,418	53.5
Donna L. Smith (D)	109,420	45.9
Albert W. Schoeman (LIBERT)	756	.3
Peter Lamoureaux (NL)	621	.3
3 • Leonard L. Boswell (D)	113,811	49.2
Mike Mahaffey (R)	110,507	47.8
Jay B. Marcus (NL)	3,145	1.4
Edward T. Rusk (WC)	2,480	1.1
Dick Kruse (LIBERT)	1,215	.5
4 • Greg Ganske (R)	132,397	52.1
Connie McBurney (D)	118,912	46.8
Rogers Badgett (NL)	1,166	.5
Carl E. Olsen (LIBERT)	1,126	.4
Richard McBride (SW)	678	.3
5 • Tom Latham (R)	146,955	65.4
MacDonald Smith (D)	75,709	33.7
Michael C. Dimick (NL)	1,954	.9

KANSAS

Senate — Full Term

	Vote Total	%
Pat Roberts (R)	647,612	62.0
Sally Thompson (D)	359,474	34.4
Mark S. Marney (REF)	23,812	2.1
Steven Rosile (LIBERT)	12,981	1.2

Senate — Short Term

	Vote Total	%
Sam Brownback (R)	569,304	53.9
Jill Docking (D)	457,646	43.3
Donald Klaasen	28,880	2.7

House

	Vote Total	%
1 Jerry Moran (R)	191,050	73.5
John Divine (D)	63,537	24.5
Bill Earnest (LIBERT)	5,189	2.0
2 Jim Ryun (R)	130,927	52.2
John Frieden (D)	114,051	45.5
Art Clack (LIBERT)	5,775	2.3
3 Vince Snowbarger (R)	137,598	49.9
Judy Hancock (D)	125,389	45.4
Randy Gardner (REF)	9,338	3.4
Charles Clack (LIBERT)	3,687	1.3
4 • Todd Tiahrt (R)	127,166	50.0
Randy Rathbun (D)	118,689	46.6
Seth L. Warren (LIBERT)	8,722	3.4

KENTUCKY

Senate

	Vote Total	%
• Mitch McConnell (R)	722,525	55.4
Steven Beshear (D)	558,621	42.9
Dennis L. Lacey (LIBERT)	8,647	.7
Patricia Metten (NL)	8,312	.6
Mac McElroy (USTAX)	5,343	.4

	Vote Total	%
House		
1 • Edward Whitfield (R)	111,483	53.6
Dennis L. Null (D)	96,640	46.4
2 • Ron Lewis (R)	125,430	58.2
Joe Wright (D)	90,208	41.8
3 • Anne Northup (R)	126,625	50.3
• Mike Ward (D)	125,326	49.7
4 • Jim Bunning (R)	147,997	68.3
Denny Bowman (D)	68,661	31.7
5 • Harold Rogers (R)	x	x
6 • Scotty Baesler (D)	125,908	55.7
Ernest Fletcher (R)	100,234	44.3

LOUISIANA

Senate

	Vote Total	%
Mary Landrieu (D)	852,622	50.4
Louis "Woody" Jenkins (R)	840,342	49.6
House		
1 • Robert L. Livingston (R)	Won in primary	
2 • William J. Jefferson (D)	Won in primary	
3 • W.J. "Billy" Tauzin (R)	Won in primary	
4 • Jim McCrery (R)	Won in primary	
5 • John Cooksey (R)	135,699	58.4
Francis Thompson (D)	96,717	41.6
6 • Richard H. Baker (R)	Won in primary	
7 • Chris John (D)	128,263	53.1
Hunter Lundy (D)	113,235	46.9

MAINE

Senate

	Vote Total	%
Susan Collins (R)	294,401	49.2
Joseph E. Brennan (D)	262,800	43.9
John C. Rensenbrink (I)	22,683	3.8
William P. Clarke (I)	18,881	3.2
House		
1 Tom Allen (D)	166,851	55.4
• James B. Longley Jr. (R)	134,539	44.6
2 • John Baldacci (D)	200,754	71.8
Paul R. Young (R)	69,720	24.9
Aldric Saucier (I)	9,121	3.3

MARYLAND

House

	Vote Total	%
1 • Wayne T. Gilchrest (R)	124,687	61.3
Steven R. Eastaugh (D)	78,865	38.7
2 • Robert L. Ehrlich Jr. (R)	137,746	61.7
Connie Galiazzo DeJuliis (D)	85,526	38.3
3 • Benjamin L. Cardin (D)	123,237	67.0
Patrick L. McDonough (R)	60,655	33.0
4 • Albert R. Wynn (D)	137,100	85.4
John B. Kimble (R)	23,373	14.6
5 • Steny H. Hoyer (D)	116,611	57.0
John S. Morgan (R)	88,111	43.0
6 • Roscoe G. Bartlett (R)	127,415	56.9
Stephen Crawford (D)	96,592	43.1
7 • Elijah E. Cummings (D)	110,473	83.2
Kenneth Kondner (R)	22,386	16.8
8 • Constance A. Morella (R)	144,125	61.3
Don Mooers (D)	91,173	38.7

MASSACHUSETTS

Senate

	Vote Total	%
• John Kerry (D)	1,329,447	52.2
William F. Weld (R)	1,140,472	44.8
Susan C. Gallagher (C)	69,926	2.7
Robert C. Snowe (NL)	7,179	.3
House		
1 • John W. Olver (D)	129,020	52.7
Jane Swift (R)	115,712	47.3
2 • Richard E. Neal (D)	162,890	71.7
Mark Steele (R)	49,858	22.0
Scott Andrichak (I)	9,182	4.0
Richard Kaynor (NL)	5,118	2.3
3 • Jim P. McGovern (D)	134,780	53.1
• Peter I. Blute (R)	115,477	45.5
Dale E. Friedgen (NL)	3,357	1.3
4 • Barney Frank (D)	183,629	71.6
Jonathan Raymond (R)	72,670	28.4

	Vote Total	%
5 • Marty T. Meehan (D)	x	x
6 John F. Tierney (D)	132,880	48.3
• Peter G. Torkildsen (R)	132,298	48.1
Martin J. McNulty (I)	4,194	1.5
Randal C. Fritz (C)	2,429	.9
Benjamin A. Gatchell (I)	2,042	.7
Orrin Smith (NL)	1,355	.5
7 • Edward J. Markey (D)	176,592	69.8
Patricia Long (R)	76,275	30.2
8 • Joseph P. Kennedy II (D)	145,949	84.3
R. Philip Hyde (R)	27,271	15.7
9 • Joe Moakley (D)	171,749	72.4
Paul Gryska (R)	65,608	27.6
10 William D. Delahunt (D)	160,486	54.5
Edward Teague (R)	123,261	41.8
A. Charles Laws (Green)	10,892	3.7

MICHIGAN

Senate

	Vote Total	%
• Carl Levin (D)	2,137,668	58.3
Ronna Romney (R)	1,463,639	39.9
Kenneth L. Proctor (LIBERT)	36,781	1.0
William Roundtree (WW)	12,055	.3
Joseph S. Mattingly (NL)	10,895	.3
Martin P. McLaughlin (SE)	6,022	.2
House		
1 • Bart Stupak (D)	180,389	70.6
Bob Carr (R)	69,970	27.4
Michael C. Oleniczak (LIBERT)	2,828	1.1
Wendy Conway (NL)	2,460	1.0
2 • Peter Hoekstra (R)	165,330	65.5
Dan Kruszynski (D)	82,562	32.7
Bruce A. Smith (LIBERT)	3,032	1.2
Henry Ogden Clark (NL)	1,313	.5
3 • Vernon J. Ehlers (R)	169,021	68.6
Betsy J. Flory (D)	72,685	29.5
Erwin J. Haas (LIBERT)	2,993	1.2
Eric Anderson (NL)	1,734	.7
4 • Dave Camp (R)	158,816	65.5
Lisa A. Donaldson (D)	79,333	32.7
Ben Steele III (LIBERT)	2,395	1.0
Susan Arnold (NL)	1,928	.8
5 • James A. Barcia (D)	162,531	70.0
Lawrence H. Sims (R)	65,513	28.2
Mark Owen (LIBERT)	2,903	1.3
Brian D. Ellison (NL)	1,270	.5
6 • Fred Upton (R)	145,056	67.7
Clarence J. Annen (D)	65,814	30.7
Scott Beavers (LIBERT)	3,342	1.6
7 • Nick Smith (R)	107,552	53.4
Kim H. Tunnicliff (D)	89,487	44.5
Robert F. Broda Jr. (LIBERT)	2,929	1.5
Scott K. Williamson (NL)	1,342	.7
8 • Debbie Stabenow (D)	136,781	54.2
• Dick Chrysler (R)	110,307	43.7
Doug MacDonald (LIBERT)	3,615	1.4
Patricia Rayfield Allen (NL)	1,591	.6
9 • Dale E. Kildee (D)	136,129	59.1
Patrick M. Nowak (R)	89,522	38.9
Malcolm Johnson (LIBERT)	3,464	1.5
Terrence Daryl Shulman (NL)	1,122	.5
10 • David E. Bonior (D)	117,894	54.5
Susy Heintz (R)	93,848	43.4
Stuart E. Scott (LIBERT)	3,506	1.6
John D. Litle (NL)	1,167	.5
11 • Joe Knollenberg (R)	170,083	61.3
Morris Frumin (D)	99,210	35.8
Dick Gach (LIBERT)	5,061	1.8
Stuart J. Goldberg (NL)	3,044	1.1
12 • Sander M. Levin (D)	116,007	58.4
John Pappageorge (R)	78,153	39.4
Albert J. Titran (LIBERT)	2,934	1.5
Gail Petrosoff (NL)	1,397	.7
13 • Lynn Rivers (D)	119,144	56.3
Joe Fitzsimmons (R)	87,979	41.6
James F. Montgomery (LIBERT)	3,070	1.5
Jane Cutter (WW)	963	.5
Jim Hartnett (SE)	491	.2
14 • John Conyers Jr. (D)	136,148	84.0
William A. Ashe (R)	22,114	13.6
Scott Boman (LIBERT)	1,692	1.0
Richard R. Miller (NL)	730	.5
Willie M. Reid (I)	706	.4
Helen Halyard (SE)	653	.4

	Vote Total	%
15 Carolyn Cheeks Kilpatrick (D)	143,498	87.9
Stephen Hume (R)	16,002	9.8
Kevin Carey (WW)	1,683	1.0
Raymond H. Warner (LIBERT)	1,357	.8
Gregory F. Smith (NL)	656	.4
16 • John D. Dingell (D)	132,556	62.1
James R. DeSana (R)	76,003	35.6
Bruce W. Cain (LIBERT)	3,067	1.4
Noha F. Hamze (NL)	1,005	.5
David Sole (WW)	852	.4

MINNESOTA

Senate

	Vote Total	%
• Paul Wellstone (D)	1,093,734	50.4
Rudy Boschwitz (R)	897,305	41.3
Dean Barkley (REF)	151,738	7.0
Tim Davis (GR)	13,980	.6
Roy Ezra Carlton (LIBERT)	5,307	.2
Howard B. Hanson (RES)	4,301	.2
Steve Johnson (NL)	4,245	.2
Thomas A. Fiske (SW)	1,540	.1
House		
1 • Gil Gutknecht (R)	137,247	52.8
Mary Rieder (D)	122,933	47.2
2 • David Minge (D)	144,186	55.0
Gary B. Revier (R)	107,533	41.0
Stan Bentz (REF)	10,288	3.9
3 • Jim Ramstad (R)	202,348	70.2
Stanley J. Leino (D)	85,766	29.8
4 • Bruce F. Vento (D)	146,611	57.0
Dennis Newinski (R)	94,725	36.8
Richard J. Gibbons (REF)	9,408	3.7
Phil Willkie (GR)	3,642	1.4
Dan R. Vacek (IG)	2,721	1.1
5 • Martin Olav Sabo (D)	156,633	64.5
Jack Uldrich (R)	68,994	28.4
Erika Anderson (GR)	13,001	5.4
Jennifer Benton (SW)	4,249	1.7
6 • William P. "Bill" Luther (D)	164,915	55.9
Tad Jude (R)	129,986	44.1
7 • Collin C. Peterson (D)	170,278	68.1
Darrell McKigney (R)	79,901	31.9
8 • James L. Oberstar (D)	183,522	68.5
Andy Larson (R)	64,219	24.0
Stan "The Man" Estes (REF)	16,563	6.2
Larry Fuhol (LIBERT)	3,664	1.4

MISSISSIPPI

Senate

	Vote Total	%
• Thad Cochran (R)	616,160	71.2
James W. "Bootie" Hunt (D)	235,990	27.3
Ted C. Weill (I)	13,616	1.6
House		
1 • Roger Wicker (R)	122,554	67.7
Henry Boyd Jr. (D)	55,200	30.5
John A. "Andy" Rouse (LIBERT)	2,220	1.2
Luke Lundemo (NL)	956	.5
2 • Bennie Thompson (D)	99,754	59.4
Danny Covington (R)	63,989	38.1
William Chipman III (LIBERT)	4,256	2.5
3 • Charles W. "Chip" Pickering Jr. (R)	114,379	61.4
John Arthur Eaves Jr. (D)	67,957	36.5
Lamen Clemons (I)	2,481	1.3
C.T. Scarborough (LIBERT)	1,525	.8
4 • Mike Parker (R)	110,895	61.6
Kevin Antoine (D)	64,823	36.0
Kenneth "K.W." Welch (I)	2,236	1.2
Eileen Mahoney (NL)	1,119	.6
William F. Fausek (LIBERT)	952	.5
5 • Gene Taylor (D)	101,832	58.3
Dennis Dollar (R)	69,990	40.1
Le'Roy C. Carney (I)	1,772	1.0
Dan Rogers (LIBERT)	470	.3
Jordan N. Gollub (I)	419	.2
Philip Mayeux (NL)	168	.1

MISSOURI

Governor

	Vote Total	%
• Mel Carnahan (D)	1,223,315	57.1
Margaret Kelly (R)	865,932	40.5
J. Mark Oglesby (LIBERT)	51,414	2.4

	Vote Total	%
House		
1 • William L. Clay (D)	131,125	70.0
Daniel F. O'Sullivan Jr. (R)	51,969	27.8
Tamara Millay (LIBERT)	4,132	2.2
2 • James M. Talent (R)	165,984	61.3
Joan Kelly Horn (D)	100,539	37.1
Anton Charles Stever (LIBERT)	2,738	1.0
Judith Clessler (NL)	1,619	.6
3 • Richard A. Gephardt (D)	136,869	59.0
Deborah Lynn "Debbie" Wheelehan (R)	89,951	38.8
Michael H. Crist (LIBERT)	3,956	1.7
James E. Keersemaker (NL)	1,286	.6
4 • Ike Skelton (D)	153,555	63.8
Bill Phelps (R)	81,646	33.9
Edwin "Ed" Hoag (LIBERT)	5,573	2.3
5 • Karen McCarthy (D)	143,903	67.4
Penny Bennett (R)	61,773	28.9
Kevin Hertel (LIBERT)	4,111	1.9
Tom Danaher (NL)	3,846	1.8
6 • Pat Danner (D)	168,935	68.6
Jeff Bailey (R)	72,039	29.3
Karl H. Wetzel (LIBERT)	5,208	2.1
7 • Roy Blunt (R)	162,529	64.9
Ruth Bamberger (D)	79,298	31.6
Mike Harman (LIBERT)	6,546	2.6
Sharalyn Harris (NL)	2,176	.9
8 • Jo Ann Emerson (R)	112,473	50.5
Emily Firebaugh (D)	83,074	37.3
Richard A. Kline (R)	23,459	10.5
Greg Tlapek (LIBERT)	2,496	1.1
David R. Zimmer (NL)	1,318	.6
9 Kenny Hulshof (R)	123,579	49.4
• Harold L. Volkmer (D)	117,684	47.0
Mitchell J. Moore (LIBERT)	7,153	2.9
Douglas Rexford (NL)	1,827	.7

MONTANA

	Vote Total	%
Governor		
• Marc Racicot (R)	272,013	79.6
Judy Jacobson (D)	69,925	20.4
Senate		
• Max Baucus (D)	200,549	49.5
Dennis Rehberg (R)	180,863	44.7
Becky Shaw (REF)	19,203	4.7
Stephen Heaton (NL)	4,129	1.0
House		
AL Rick Hill (R)	211,014	52.4
Bill Yellowtail (D)	173,771	43.2
Jim Brooks (NL)	17,894	4.4

NEBRASKA

	Vote Total	%
Senate		
Chuck Hagel (R)	372,142	56.2
Ben Nelson (D)	276,088	41.7
John W. DeCamp (LIBERT)	9,229	1.4
Bill Dunn (NL)	4,667	.7
House		
1 • Doug Bereuter (R)	153,794	70.1
Patrick J. Combs (D)	65,741	29.9
2 • Jon Christensen (R)	122,017	56.8
James Martin Davis (D)	86,702	40.4
Patricia A. Dunn (NL)	4,244	2.0
Phillip E. Torrison (LIBERT)	1,867	.9
3 • Bill Barrett (R)	164,782	77.4
John Webster (D)	48,047	22.6

NEVADA

	Vote Total	%
House		
1 • John Ensign (R)	84,958	50.1
Bob Coffin (D)	73,925	43.6
Ted Gunderson (IA)	4,481	2.6
James Dan (LIBERT)	3,266	1.9
Richard Eidson (NL)	3,108	1.8
2 Jim Gibbons (R)	161,633	58.6
Thomas "Spike" Wilson (D)	97,241	35.2
Dan Hansen (IA)	8,743	3.2
Lois Avery (NL)	4,544	1.6
Louis R. Tomburello (LIBERT)	3,711	1.3

NEW HAMPSHIRE

	Vote Total	%
Governor		
Jeanne Shaheen (D)	283,592	57.3
Ovide Lamontagne (R)	195,903	39.6
Fred Bramante (I)	9,712	2.0
Robert Kingsbury (LIBERT)	5,584	1.1
Senate		
• Robert C. Smith (R)	241,862	49.4
Dick Swett (D)	226,616	46.3
Ken Blevens (LIBERT)	21,366	4.4
House		
1 John E. Sununu (R)	123,616	50.2
Joseph F. Keefe (D)	114,930	46.6
Gary A. Flanders (LIBERT)	7,858	3.2
2 • Charles Bass (R)	122,931	50.6
Deborah "Arnie" Arnesen (D)	105,764	43.5
Carole Lamirande (I)	10,626	4.4
Roy Kendel (IA)	3,637	1.5

NEW JERSEY

	Vote Total	%
Senate		
Robert G. Torricelli (D)	1,469,086	52.5
Dick Zimmer (R)	1,192,695	42.6
Richard J. Pezzullo (NJC)	50,207	1.8
Mary Jo Christian (NL)	24,229	.9
Paul A. Woomer (GCP)	14,735	.5
Olga L. Rodriguez (SW)	14,164	.5
Mark Wise (FN)	13,676	.5
Wilburt Kornegay (IPC)	10,768	.4
Steven J. Baeli (PF)	7,605	.3
House		
1 • Robert E. Andrews (D)	154,486	76.2
Mel Suplee (R)	42,500	21.0
Michael Edmondson (LIBERT)	2,588	1.3
Patricia A. Bily (NL)	1,803	.9
Norman E. Wahner (NJC)	1,456	.7
2 • Frank A. LoBiondo (R)	128,308	60.4
Ruth Katz (D)	81,141	38.2
David Roger Headrick (TLL)	986	.5
Andrea Lippi (JPR)	922	.4
Judith Lee Azaren (NL)	921	.4
3 • H. James Saxton (R)	151,748	64.1
John Leonardi (D)	78,756	33.3
Janice Presser (LIBERT)	2,945	1.2
Agnes A. James (NJC)	1,332	.6
Eugene B. Ashworth (NL)	1,121	.5
Ken Feduniewicz (AF)	791	.3
4 • Christopher H. Smith (R)	143,412	63.7
Kevin John Meara (D)	75,851	33.7
Robert Figueroa (LIBERT)	2,903	1.3
J. Morgan Strong (NJC)	1,918	.9
Arnold Kokans (NL)	1,087	.5
5 • Marge Roukema (R)	178,243	71.3
Bill Auer (D)	61,601	24.6
Lorraine L. La Neve (NJC)	3,888	1.6
Dan Karlan (LIBERT)	2,102	.8
Helen Hamilton (NL)	1,840	.7
Barry Childers (ROP)	1,371	.5
E. Gregory Kresge (USA)	871	.3
6 • Frank Pallone Jr. (D)	125,448	61.6
Steven J. Corodemus (R)	73,035	35.8
Keith Quarles (LIBERT)	2,009	1.0
Richard Sorrentino (NJC)	1,439	.7
Susan H. Normandin (NL)	1,236	.6
Stepanie C. Trice (SW)	624	.3
7 • Bob Franks (R)	125,952	55.1
Larry Lerner (D)	96,367	42.1
Dorothy De Laura (NJC)	4,084	1.8
Nicholas W. Gentile (NL)	1,660	.7
Robert G. Robertson (SW)	694	.3
8 William J. Pascrell Jr. (D)	94,086	51.0
• Bill Martini (R)	88,683	48.1
Jeffrey M. Levine (NL)	1,549	.8
9 Steve R. Rothman (D)	102,810	54.6
Kathleen A. Donovan (R)	81,715	43.4
Arthur B. Rosen (NJI)	2,498	1.3
Leon Myerson (LIBERT)	1,441	.8
10 • Donald M. Payne (D)	121,684	83.8
Vanessa Williams (R)	21,612	14.9
Harley Tyler (NL)	1,160	.8
Toni M. Jackson (SW)	745	.5

	Vote Total	%
11 • Rodney Frelinghuysen (R)	160,067	66.0
Chris Evangel (D)	75,350	31.1
Ed De Mott (NJC)	2,761	1.1
Austin S. Lett (LIBERT)	2,485	1.0
Victoria S. Spruiell (NL)	1,767	.7
12 Mike Pappas (R)	134,452	49.9
David N. Del Vecchio (D)	125,111	46.5
Virginia A. Flynn (LIBERT)	3,929	1.5
Phillip G. Cenicola (NL)	2,926	1.1
Joseph M. Mercurio (NJC)	2,826	1.0
13 • Robert Menendez (D)	112,957	78.9
Carlos E. Munoz (R)	25,313	17.7
Mike Buoncristiano (LIBERT)	2,165	1.5
Herbert H. Shaw (PAC)	2,129	1.5
Rupert Ravens (NL)	633	.4

NEW MEXICO

	Vote Total	%
Senate		
• Pete V. Domenici (R)	326,053	64.3
Art Trujillo (D)	152,742	30.1
Abraham J. Gutmann (GREEN)	22,406	4.4
Bruce Bush (LIBERT)	5,656	1.1
House		
1 • Steven H. Schiff (R)	82,694	54.9
John Wertheim (D)	57,745	38.4
John A. "Jack" Uhrich (GREEN)	6,428	4.3
Betty Turrietta-Koury (I)	3,705	2.5
2 • Joe Skeen (R)	94,546	56.0
E. Shirley Baca (D)	74,294	44.0
3 • Bill Richardson (D)	123,894	67.4
Bill Redmond (R)	55,893	30.4
Ed Nagel (LIBERT)	4,070	2.2

NEW YORK

	Vote Total	%
House		
1 • Michael P. Forbes (R,C,INDC,RTL,PTC)	113,330	55.0
Nora Bredes (D,SM)	92,767	45.0
2 • Rick A. Lazio (R,C,PTC)	107,875	63.9
Kenneth J. Herman (D,INDC)	56,347	33.4
Alice Cort Ross (RTL)	4,555	2.7
3 • Peter T. King (R,C,FDM)	124,941	55.6
Dal LaMagna (D,INDC)	94,208	41.9
John O'Shea (RTL)	3,992	1.8
John A. DePrima (L)	1,758	.8
4 Carolyn McCarthy (D,INDC)	123,228	57.2
• Daniel Frisa (R,C,FDM)	87,695	40.7
Vincent P. Garbitelli (RTL)	3,181	1.5
Robert S. Berkowitz (L)	1,145	.5
5 • Gary L. Ackerman (D,L,INDC)	120,739	63.4
Grant M. Lally (R,C,FDM)	67,105	35.2
Andrew J. Duff (RTL)	2,566	1.3
6 • Floyd H. Flake (D)	94,626	85.0
Jorawar Misir (R,C,INDC,FDM)	16,714	15.0
7 • Thomas J. Manton (D)	72,351	70.6
Rose Birtley (R,C,INDC)	30,135	29.4
8 • Jerrold Nadler (D,L)	115,476	81.8
Michael Benjamin (R,FDM,WSN)	23,359	16.5
George A. Galip Jr. (C)	2,330	1.7
9 • Charles E. Schumer (D,L)	99,450	74.0
Robert J. Verga (R,INDC,FDM)	29,378	21.9
Michael Mossa (C)	5,587	4.2
10 • Edolphus Towns (D,L)	91,848	90.7
Amelia Smith Parker (R,C,FDM)	8,056	8.0
Julian M. Hill Jr. (RTL)	1,358	1.3
11 • Major R. Owens (D,L)	81,950	91.5
Claudette Hayle (R,C,INDC,FDM)	7,606	8.5
12 • Nydia M. Velazquez (D,L)	54,851	84.0
Miguel I. Prado (R,C,RTL)	9,241	14.1
Eleanor Garcia (SW)	1,226	1.9
13 • Susan Molinari (R,C,FDM)	89,884	61.6
Tyrone G. Butler (D,L)	50,464	34.6
Kathleen Marciano (RTL)	3,296	2.3
Anita Lerman (INDC)	2,357	1.6
14 • Carolyn B. Maloney (D,L)	113,433	72.4
Jeffrey E. Livingston (R)	36,978	23.6
Thomas N. Leighton (INDC,GREEN)	3,122	2.0
Joseph A. Lavezzo (L)	2,035	1.3
Delco L. Cornett (RTL)	1,127	.7
15 • Charles B. Rangel (D,L)	102,840	90.9
Edward R. Adams (R)	5,526	4.9
Ruben Dario Vargas (C,INDC)	3,457	3.1
Jose Suero (RTL)	1,352	1.2

		Vote Total	%
16 •	Jose E. Serrano (D,L)	89,227	96.4
	Rodney Torres (R)	2,662	2.9
	Owen Camp (C)	707	.8
17 •	Eliot L. Engel (D,L)	95,966	84.7
	Denis McCarthy (R,C,RTL)	15,392	13.6
	Dennis Coleman (INDC)	1,944	1.7
18 •	Nita M. Lowey (D)	110,327	63.3
	Kerry J. Katsorhis (R,C)	56,343	32.3
	Concetta M. Ferrara (INDC)	4,101	2.4
	Florence T. O'Grady (RTL)	3,615	2.1
19 •	Sue W. Kelly (R,FDM)	97,383	46.2
	Richard S. Klein (D,L)	83,251	39.5
	Joseph J. DioGuardi (C,RTL)	26,452	12.6
	William E. Haase (INDC)	3,573	1.7
20 •	Benjamin A. Gilman (R)	115,066	56.9
	Yash P. Aggarwal (D,L)	76,324	37.7
	Robert F. Garrison (RTL)	5,934	2.9
	Ira W. Goodman (INDC)	4,861	2.4
21 •	Michael R. McNulty (D,C,INDC)	150,938	66.3
	Nancy Norman (R,FDM)	61,016	26.8
	Lee H. Wasserman (L)	15,809	6.9
22 •	Gerald B.H. Solomon (R,C,RTL,FDM)	97,911	61.2
	Steve James (D)	62,005	38.8
23 •	Sherwood Boehlert (R,FDM)	115,053	64.2
	Bruce W. Hapanowicz (D)	46,875	26.1
	Thomas E. Loughlin Jr. (INDC)	10,284	5.7
	William Tapley (RTL)	7,114	4.0
24 •	John M. McHugh (R,C)	118,680	71.2
	Donald Ravenscroft (D)	41,276	24.8
	William H. Beaumont (INDC)	6,776	4.1
25 •	James T. Walsh (R,C,INDC,FDM)	123,441	55.3
	Marty Mack (D)	99,860	44.7
26 •	Maurice D. Hinchey (D,L)	116,333	54.9
	Sue Wittig (R,C,RTL,FDM)	89,956	42.4
	Douglas Walter Drazen (INDC)	5,673	2.7
27 •	Bill Paxon (R,C,RTL,FDM)	137,292	60.0
	Thomas M. Fricano (D,SM)	91,404	40.0
28 •	Louise M. Slaughter (D)	125,425	57.0
	Geoffrey Rosenberger (R,C,FDM)	94,647	43.0
29 •	John J. LaFalce (D,L)	128,272	61.9
	David B. Callard (R,C,RTL,FDM)	78,938	38.1
30 •	Jack Quinn (R,C,INDC,FDM)	117,414	54.9
	Francis Pordum (D,PS)	96,435	45.1
31 •	Amo Houghton (R,C,FDM)	132,896	71.5
	Bruce D. MacBain (D)	47,327	25.5
	LeRoy Stewart Wilson (RTL)	5,729	3.1

NORTH CAROLINA

Governor
•	James B. "Jim" Hunt Jr. (D)	1,423,351	56.0
	Robin Hayes (R)	1,088,113	42.8
	Scott D. Yost (LIBERT)	17,304	.7
	Julia Van Witt (NL)	14,527	.6

Senate
•	Jesse Helms (R)	1,331,457	52.6
	Harvey B. Gantt (D)	1,160,449	45.9
	Ray Ubinger (LIBERT)	25,965	1.0
	J. Victor Pardo (NL)	11,229	.4

House
1 •	Eva Clayton (D)	104,867	65.7
	Ted Tyler (R)	53,216	33.3
	Todd Murphrey (LIBERT)	1,058	.7
	Joseph Boxerman (NL)	536	.3
2	Bob Etheridge (D)	113,371	52.6
•	David Funderburk (R)	98,317	45.6
	Mark D. Jackson (LIBERT)	2,873	1.3
	Robert Argy Jr. (NL)	962	.4
3 •	Walter B. Jones Jr. (R)	117,641	63.0
	George Parrott (D)	67,647	36.2
	Edward Downey (NL)	1,510	.8
4	David E. Price (D)	155,164	54.4
•	Fred Heineman (R)	124,983	43.8
	David Allen Walker (LIBERT)	4,063	1.4
	Russell Wollman (NL)	1,184	.4
5 •	Richard M. Burr (R)	129,578	62.1
	Neil Grist Cashion Jr. (D)	73,961	35.4
	Barbara J. Howe (LIBERT)	4,141	2.0
	Craig Berg (NL)	993	.5
6 •	Howard Coble (R)	166,846	73.4
	Mark Costley (D)	57,701	25.4
	Gary Goodson (LIBERT)	2,665	1.2

		Vote Total	%
7 •	Mike McIntyre (D)	86,489	52.9
	Bill Caster (R)	74,883	45.8
	Chris Nubel (LIBERT)	1,543	.9
	Garrison King Frantz (NL)	548	.3
8 •	W.G. "Bill" Hefner (D)	101,777	54.9
	Curtis Blackwood (R)	81,487	44.0
	Thomas W. Carlisle (NL)	2,073	1.1
9 •	Sue Myrick (R)	143,040	62.7
	Michel C. "Mike" Daisley (D)	81,297	35.7
	David L. Knight (LIBERT)	2,217	1.0
	Jeannine Austin (NL)	1,460	.6
10 •	Cass Ballenger (R)	156,875	69.9
	Ben Neill (D)	64,653	28.8
	Richard Kahn (NL)	2,775	1.2
11 •	Charles H. Taylor (R)	132,203	58.3
	James Mark Ferguson (D)	90,758	40.0
	Phil McCanless (LIBERT)	2,272	1.0
	Milton Burrill (NL)	1,568	.7
12 •	Melvin Watt (D)	123,899	71.5
	Joseph A. "Joe" Martino Jr. (R)	46,406	26.8
	Roger L. Kohn (LIBERT)	1,849	1.1
	Walter Lewis (NL)	1,247	.7

NORTH DAKOTA

Governor
•	Edward T. Schafer (R)	174,337	66.2
	Lee Kaldor (D)	89,078	33.8

House
AL •	Earl Pomeroy (D)	144,305	55.1
	Kevin Cramer (R)	113,225	43.2
	Kenneth R. Loughead (I)	4,457	1.7

OHIO

House
1 •	Steve Chabot (R)	116,003	54.3
	Mark P. Longabaugh (D)	92,197	43.2
	John G. Halley (NL)	5,275	2.5
2 •	Rob Portman (R)	183,167	72.1
	Thomas R. Chandler (D)	57,548	22.6
	Kathleen M. McKnight (NL)	13,498	5.3
3 •	Tony P. Hall (D)	141,469	63.6
	David A. Westbrock (R)	74,127	33.4
	Dorothy H. Mackey (NL)	4,935	2.2
	James Lawrence (I)	1,750	0.8
4 •	Michael G. Oxley (R)	143,706	64.6
	Paul McClain (D)	67,747	30.5
	Michael McCaffery (NL)	10,847	4.9
5 •	Paul E. Gillmor (R)	143,276	61.1
	Annie Saunders (D)	79,704	34.0
	David J. Schaffer (NL)	11,372	4.9
6	Ted Strickland (D)	114,961	51.2
•	Frank A. Cremeans (R)	109,626	48.8
7 •	David L. Hobson (R)	155,067	67.9
	Richard K. Blain (D)	60,234	26.4
	Dawn Marie Johnson (NL)	13,151	5.8
8 •	John A. Boehner (R)	161,938	70.3
	Jeffrey D. Kitchen (D)	60,115	26.1
	William Baker (NL)	8,325	3.6
9 •	Marcy Kaptur (D)	166,671	77.1
	Randy Whitman (R)	44,846	20.7
	Elizabeth A. Slotnick (NL)	4,649	2.2
10	Dennis J. Kucinich (D)	107,986	49.0
•	Martin R. Hoke (R)	102,149	46.4
	Robert B. Iverson (NL)	10,050	4.6
11 •	Louis Stokes (D)	148,346	81.1
	James J. Sykora (R)	28,143	15.4
	Sonja Glavina (NL)	6,437	3.5
12 •	John R. Kasich (R)	199,361	66.5
	Cynthia L. Ruccia (D)	91,493	30.5
	Barbara Ann Edelman (NL)	8,852	3.0
13 •	Sherrod Brown (D)	144,198	60.5
	Kenneth C. Blair Jr. (R)	85,807	36.0
	David Kluter (NL)	8,503	3.6
14 •	Tom Sawyer (D)	121,650	54.3
	Joyce George (R)	93,725	41.8
	Terry E. Wilkinson (NL)	8,797	3.9
15 •	Deborah Pryce (R)	164,208	71.1
	Cliff Arnebeck (D)	66,626	28.9
16 •	Ralph Regula (R)	156,034	68.7
	Thomas E. Burkhart (D)	63,593	28.0
	Brad Graef (NL)	7,385	3.3

		Vote Total	%
17 •	James A. Traficant Jr. (D)	215,114	91.0
	James M. Cahaney (NL)	21,378	9.0
18 •	Bob Ney (R)	115,153	50.1
	Robert L. Burch (D)	106,583	46.4
	Margaret Chitti (NL)	7,907	3.4
19 •	Steven C. LaTourette (R)	131,624	54.8
	Tom Coyne Jr. (D)	98,023	40.8
	Thomas A. Martin (NL)	10,562	4.4

OKLAHOMA

Senate
•	James M. Inhofe (R)	670,609	56.7
	Jim Boren (D)	474,161	40.1
	Bill Maguire (I)	15,092	1.3
	Agnes Marie Regier (LIBERT)	14,595	1.2
	Chris Nedbalek (I)	8,691	.7

House
1 •	Steve Largent (R)	143,415	68.2
	Randolph John Amen (D)	57,996	27.6
	Karla Condray (I)	8,996	4.3
2 •	Tom Coburn (R)	112,272	55.5
	Glen D. Johnson (D)	90,120	44.5
3	Wes Watkins (R)	98,525	51.4
	Darryl Roberts (D)	86,646	45.2
	Scott Demaree (I)	6,331	3.3
4 •	J.C. Watts (R)	106,923	57.7
	Ed Crocker (D)	73,950	39.9
	Robert T. Murphy (LIBERT)	4,499	2.4
5 •	Ernest Istook (R)	148,362	69.7
	James L. Forsythe (D)	57,594	27.1
	Ava Kennedy (I)	6,835	3.2
6 •	Frank D. Lucas (R)	113,499	63.9
	Paul M. Barby (D)	64,173	36.1

OREGON

Senate
	Gordon Smith (R)	334,171	48.9
	Tom Bruggere (D)	318,232	46.5
	Brent Thompson (REF)	10,808	1.6
	Gary Kutcher (PACIFIC)	7,669	1.1
	Paul "Stormy" Mohn (LIBERT)	7,128	1.0
	Christopher Phelps (S)	3,083	.5
	Michael L. Hoyes (NL)	2,566	.4

House
1 •	Elizabeth Furse (D)	69,469	54.6
	Bill Witt (R)	53,691	42.2
	Richard Johnson (LIBERT)	3,540	2.8
	David Princ (S)	631	.5
2 •	Bob Smith (R)	99,128	59.1
	Mike Dugan (D)	65,374	39.0
	Frank Wise (LIBERT)	3,317	2.0
3 •	Earl Blumenauer (D)	74,779	68.2
	Scott Bruun (R)	27,321	24.9
	Joe Keating (PACIFIC)	4,337	4.0
	Bruce Alexander Knight (LIBERT)	2,084	1.9
	Victoria P. Guillebeau (S)	1,202	1.1
4 •	Peter A. DeFazio (D)	104,302	68.6
	John D. Newkirk (R)	40,435	26.6
	Tonie Nathan (LIBERT)	2,874	1.9
	William "Bill" Bonville (REF)	2,486	1.6
	David G. Duemler (S)	1,088	.7
	Allan Opus (PACIFIC)	850	.6
5	Darlene Hooley (D)	59,013	51.6
•	Jim Bunn (R)	51,462	45.0
	Lawrence Knight Duquesne (LIBERT)	2,761	2.4
	Trey Smith (S)	1,140	1.0

PENNSYLVANIA

House
1 •	Thomas M. Foglietta (D)	142,304	87.4
	James D. Cella (R)	20,584	12.6
2 •	Chaka Fattah (D)	166,626	88.1
	Larry G. Murphy (R)	22,533	11.9
3 •	Robert A. Borski (D)	120,106	68.9
	Joseph M. McColgan (R)	54,334	31.1
4 •	Ron Klink (D)	142,207	64.2
	Paul T. Adametz (R)	79,217	35.8
5 •	John E. Peterson (R)	116,072	60.2
	Ruth C. Rudy (D)	76,605	39.8

		Vote Total	%
6	• Tim Holden (D)	114,977	58.6
	Christian Y. Leinbach (R)	79,714	40.6
	Thomas List (NL)	1,457	.7
7	• Curt Weldon (R)	165,692	67.0
	John Innelli (D)	79,864	32.3
	John Pronchik (NL)	1,689	.7
8	• James C. Greenwood (R)	133,183	59.1
	John P. Murray (D)	79,410	35.3
	Richard J. Piotrowski (LIBERT)	6,928	3.1
	David A. Booth (CONSTL)	5,661	2.5
9	• Bud Shuster (R)	141,676	73.7
	Monte Kemmler (D)	50,572	26.3
10	• Joseph M. McDade (R)	124,711	59.4
	Joe Cullen (D)	76,771	36.6
	Thomas J. McLaughlin (REF)	8,416	4.0
11	• Paul E. Kanjorski (D)	127,253	68.5
	Stephen A. Urban (R)	58,586	31.5
12	• John P. Murtha (D)	136,406	69.9
	Bill Choby (R)	58,628	30.1
13	Jon D. Fox (R)	120,297	48.9
	Joseph M. Hoeffel (D)	120,287	48.9
	Thomas Patrick Burke (LIBERT)	4,942	2.0
	Bill Ryan (NL)	517	.2
14	• William J. Coyne (D)	122,440	60.6
	Bill Ravotti (R)	78,800	39.0
	Paul Scherrer (SE)	646	.3
15	• Paul McHale (D)	109,377	55.3
	Bob Kilbanks (R)	80,784	40.8
	Nicholas R. Sabatine III (REF)	6,946	3.5
	Philip E. Faust (NL)	804	.4
16	Joseph R. Pitts (R)	124,560	59.4
	James G. Blaine (D)	78,572	37.5
	Robert S. Yorczyk (REF)	6,489	3.1
17	• George W. Gekas (R)	150,559	72.2
	Paul Kettl (D)	57,874	27.8
18	• Mike Doyle (D)	120,181	56.0
	David B. Fawcett (R)	86,816	40.5
	Richard Edward Caligiuri (I)	6,694	3.1
	Ralph A. Emmerich (NL)	871	.4
19	• Bill Goodling (R)	130,552	62.6
	Scott L. Chronister (D)	74,755	35.9
	Francis Worley (FWC)	3,185	1.5
20	• Frank R. Mascara (D)	113,302	53.9
	Mike McCormick (R)	97,037	46.1
21	• Phil English (R)	106,421	50.7
	Ronald A. DiNicola (D)	103,675	49.3

RHODE ISLAND

Senate

	Vote Total	%
Jack Reed (D)	215,303	63.1
Nancy J. Mayer (R)	120,436	35.3
Donald W. Lovejoy (I)	5,231	1.5

House

		Vote Total	%
1	• Patrick J. Kennedy (D)	116,235	69.1
	Giovanni D. Cicione (R)	47,624	28.3
	Michael J. Rollins (I)	1,653	1.0
	Graham R. Schwass (I)	1,402	.8
	Gregory Raposa (I)	1,263	.8
2	Robert A. Weygand (D)	112,764	64.5
	Rick Wild (R)	55,275	31.6
	Thomas J. Ricci (I)	3,106	1.8
	Gail Alison Casman (I)	2,106	1.2
	Jack D. Potter (I)	1,650	.9

SOUTH CAROLINA

Senate

	Vote Total	%
• Strom Thurmond (R)	607,616	53.3
Elliott Close (D)	502,619	44.1
Richard T. Quillian (LIBERT)	12,745	1.1
Peter J. Ashy (REF)	9,556	.8
Annette C. Estes (NL)	7,455	.7

House

		Vote Total	%
1	• Mark Sanford (R)	136,576	96.5
	Joseph F. Innella (NL)	4,999	3.5
2	• Floyd D. Spence (R)	157,667	89.9
	Maurice T. Raiford (NL)	17,633	10.1
3	• Lindsey Graham (R)	107,395	60.6
	Debbie Dorn (D)	68,080	38.4
	Linda L. Pennington (NL)	1,703	1.0
4	• Bob Inglis (R)	137,386	70.9
	Darrell E. Curry (D)	53,837	27.8

		Vote Total	%
	C. Faye Walters (NL)	2,470	1.3
5	• John M. Spratt Jr. (D)	96,390	54.0
	Larry L. Bigham (R)	80,950	45.4
	P.G. Joshi (NL)	1,147	.6
6	• James E. Clyburn (D)	120,012	68.4
	Gary McLeod (R)	52,096	29.7
	Savita P. Joshi (NL)	3,236	1.8

SOUTH DAKOTA

Senate

	Vote Total	%
Tim Johnson (D)	166,511	51.3
• Larry Pressler (R)	157,912	48.7

House

		Vote Total	%
AL	John Thune (R)	186,330	57.7
	Rick Weiland (D)	119,406	37.0
	Stacey L. Nelson (I)	10,442	3.2
	Kurt Evans (I)	6,857	2.1

TENNESSEE

Senate

	Vote Total	%
• Fred Thompson (R)	1,088,364	61.4
J. Houston Gordon (D)	652,754	36.8
John Jay Hooker (I)	14,324	.8
Bruce Gold (I)	5,828	.3
Robert O. Watson (I)	5,650	.3
Greg Samples (I)	4,155	.2
Philip L. Kienlen (I)	2,206	.1

House

		Vote Total	%
1	Bill Jenkins (R)	117,922	63.9
	Kay C. Smith (D)	61,346	33.2
	Dave Davis (I)	1,909	1.0
	James B. Taylor (I)	1,076	.6
	Bill Bull Durham (I)	862	.5
	John Curtis (I)	683	.4
	Mike Fugate (I)	440	.2
	Paul Schmidt (I)	368	.2
2	• John J. "Jimmy" Duncan Jr. (R)	149,205	70.7
	Stephen Smith (D)	60,267	28.6
	Chris G. Dimit (I)	1,289	.6
	George Njezic (I)	287	.1
3	• Zach Wamp (R)	113,411	56.4
	Charles "Chuck" Jolly (D)	85,678	42.6
	William A. Cole (I)	929	.5
	Walt "Combat" Ward (I)	661	.3
	Thomas Ed Morrell (I)	284	.1
	Richard M. "Dick" Sims (I)	268	.1
4	• Van Hilleary (R)	102,993	58.0
	Mark Stewart (D)	72,950	41.1
	S. Patrick Lyons (I)	1,035	.6
	Preston T. Spaulding (I)	529	.3
5	• Bob Clement (D)	140,025	72.4
	Steven L. Edmondson (R)	45,988	23.8
	Mike Childers (I)	7,306	3.8
6	• Bart Gordon (D)	123,786	54.4
	Steve Gill (R)	94,572	41.6
	Jim Coffer (I)	9,108	4.0
7	• Ed Bryant (R)	136,720	64.1
	Don Trotter (D)	73,752	34.6
	Steven E. Romer (I)	2,802	1.3
8	• John Tanner (D)	121,993	67.3
	Tom Watson (R)	54,499	30.1
	Donna Malone (I)	4,768	2.6
9	Harold E. Ford Jr. (D)	116,304	61.1
	Rod DeBerry (R)	70,886	37.3
	Silky Sullivan (I)	956	.5
	Mary D. Taylor (I)	498	.3
	Anthony Burton (I)	424	.2
	Greg Voehringer (I)	325	.2
	Tom Jeanette (I)	222	.1
	Del Gill (I)	199	.1
	Bill Taylor (I)	179	.1
	Johnny E. Kelly (I)	156	.1
	Don Fox (I)	146	.1

TEXAS

Senate

	Vote Total	%
• Phil Gramm (R)	3,028,504	54.8
Victor M. Morales (D)	2,428,998	43.9
Michael Bird (LIBERT)	51,539	.9
John Huff (NL)	19,482	.4

House

		Vote Total	%
1	Max Sandlin (D)	103,924	51.6
	Ed Merritt (R)	94,107	46.7
	Margaret A. Palms (NL)	3,394	1.7
2	Jim Turner (D)	102,868	52.2
	Brian Babin (R)	89,810	45.6
	Henry McCullough (I)	2,390	1.2
	David Constant (LIBERT)	1,240	.6
	Gary Hardy (NL)	592	.3
3	• Sam Johnson (R)	142,325	73.0
	Lee Cole (D)	47,654	24.4
	John Davis (L)	5,045	2.6
4	• Ralph M. Hall (D)	132,128	63.8
	Jerry Ray Hall (R)	71,065	34.3
	Steven Rothacker (LIBERT)	3,171	1.5
	Enos M. Denham Jr. (NL)	814	.4
5	Pete Sessions (R)	80,311	53.1
	John Pouland (D)	71,065	46.9
6	• Joe L. Barton (R)	160,800	77.1
	Janet Carroll "Skeet" Richardson (I)	26,713	12.8
	Catherine A. Anderson (L)	14,456	6.9
	Doug Williams (USTAX)	6,547	3.1
7	• Bill Archer (R)	151,997	81.4
	Al J.K. Siegmund (I)	28,186	15.1
	Gene Hsiao (I)	3,895	2.1
	Robert R. "Randy" Sims Jr. (I)	2,722	1.5
8	Kevin Brady (R) *	80,334	41.5
	Gene Fontenot (R) *	75,398	38.9
	Cynthia "C.J." Newman (D)	26,246	13.6
	Robert Musemeche (D)	11,698	6.0
9	• Steve Stockman (R) *	88,171	46.4
	Nick Lampson (D) *	83,781	44.1
	Geraldine Sam (I)	17,886	9.4
10	• Lloyd Doggett (D)	132,066	56.2
	Teresa Doggett (R)	97,204	41.4
	Gary Johnson (LIBERT)	3,950	1.7
	Steven Klayman (NL)	1,771	.8
11	• Chet Edwards (D)	100,107	56.8
	Jay Mathis (R)	74,712	42.4
	Ken Hardin (NL)	1,391	.8
12	Kay Granger (R)	98,349	57.8
	Hugh Parmer (D)	69,859	41.0
	Heather Proffer (NL)	1,996	1.2
13	• William M. "Mac" Thornberry (R)	115,899	67.0
	Samuel Brown Silverman (D)	55,743	32.2
	Don Harkey (NL)	1,463	.8
14	Ron Paul (R)	99,970	51.0
	Charles "Lefty" Morris (D)	93,326	47.7
	Ed Fasanella (NL)	2,543	1.3
15	• Ruben Hinojosa (D)	85,442	62.2
	Tom Haughey (R)	50,608	36.8
	Rob Wofford (NL)	1,400	1.0
16	Silvestre Reyes (D)	90,260	70.6
	Rick Ledesma (R)	35,271	27.6
	Carl Proffer (NL)	2,253	1.8
17	• Charles W. Stenholm (D)	99,458	51.7
	Rudy Izzard (R)	91,197	47.4
	Richard Caro (NL)	1,881	1.0
18	• Sheila Jackson-Lee (D)	106,097	77.1
	Larry White (R)	13,955	10.1
	Jerry Burley (R)	7,876	5.7
	George A. Young (R)	5,332	3.9
	Mike Lamson (D)	4,411	3.2
19	• Larry Combest (R)	156,845	80.4
	John W. Sawyer (D)	38,283	19.6
20	• Henry B. Gonzalez (D)	88,190	63.7
	James D. Walker (R)	47,616	34.4
	Alejandro "Alex" DePena (LIBERT)	2,156	1.6
	Lyndon Felps (NL)	447	.3
21	• Lamar Smith (R)	205,829	76.4
	Gordon H. Wharton (D)	60,338	22.4
	Randy Rutenbeck (NL)	3,138	1.2
22	• Tom DeLay (R)	126,054	68.1
	Scott Douglas Cunningham (D)	59,029	31.9
23	• Henry Bonilla (R)	101,340	61.9
	Charles P. Jones (D)	59,549	36.4
	Linda J. Caswell (NL)	2,911	1.8
24	• Martin Frost (D)	77,847	55.8
	Ed Harrison (R)	54,551	39.1
	Marion Jacob (D)	4,656	3.3
	Dale Mouton (I)	2,574	1.8

		Vote Total	%
25 •	Ken Bentsen (D) *	43,693	34.0
	Dolly Madison McKenna (R) *	21,898	17.1
	Beverley Clark (D)	21,698	16.9
	Brent Perry (R)	16,737	13.0
	John Devine (R)	9,070	7.1
	John M. Sanchez (R)	8,983	7.0
	Ken G. Mathis (R)	3,649	2.8
	Ron "RC" Meinke (R)	997	.8
	Lloyd W. Oliver (R)	826	.6
	Dotty Quinn Collins (R)	561	.4
	Jerry Freiwirth (SW)	268	.2
26 •	Dick Armey (R)	163,708	73.6
	Jerry Frankel (D)	58,623	26.4
27 •	Solomon P. Ortiz (D)	97,251	64.7
	Joe Gardner (R)	50,962	33.9
	Kevin G. Richardson (NL)	1,989	1.3
28 •	Frank Tejeda (D)	110,143	75.4
	Mark Lynn Cude (R)	34,190	23.4
	Clifford Finley (NL)	1,794	1.2
29 •	Gene Green (D)	61,872	67.4
	Jack Rodriguez (R)	28,535	31.1
	Jack W. Klinger (USTAX)	1,344	1.5
30 •	Eddie Bernice Johnson (D)	61,723	54.6
	John Hendry (R)	20,664	18.3
	James L. Sweatt (D)	9,909	8.8
	Marvin E. Crenshaw (D)	7,765	6.9
	Lisa Anne Kitterman (R)	7,761	6.9
	Lisa Hembry (I)	3,501	3.1
	Ada Jane Granado (I)	1,278	1.1
	Stevan A. Hammond (I)	468	.4

UTAH

Governor

		Vote Total	%
•	Michael O. Leavitt (R)	500,293	75.0
	Jim Bradley (D)	155,294	23.3
	Ken Larsen (IA)	4,709	.7
	Dub Richards (IP)	3,825	.6
	Robert C. Lesh (NL)	2,956	.4

House

		Vote Total	%
1 •	James V. Hansen (R)	149,216	68.3
	Gregory J. Sanders (D)	65,515	30.0
	Randall Tolpinrud (NL)	3,769	1.7
2	Merrill Cook (R)	129,339	55.0
	Ross Anderson (D)	99,689	42.4
	Arly H. Pederson (IA)	3,056	1.3
	Catherine Carter (NL)	2,971	1.3
3	Chris Cannon (R)	105,297	51.1
•	Bill Orton (D)	97,416	47.3
	Amy L. Lassen (LIBERT)	2,337	1.1
	Gerald "Bear" Slothower (I)	697	.3
	John Phillip Langford (SW)	265	.1

VERMONT

Governor

		Vote Total	%
•	Howard Dean (D)	178,032	70.6
	John L. Gropper (R)	56,993	22.6
	Mary Alice Herbert (LU)	4,121	1.6
	Dennis "Denny" Lane (VG)	3,609	1.4
	Bill Brunelle (NL)	3,310	1.3
	August St. John (I)	3,145	1.2
	Neil Randall (LIBERT)	2,872	1.1

House

		Vote Total	%
AL •	Bernard Sanders (I)	139,756	55.1
	Susan Sweetser (R)	82,351	32.5
	Jack Long (D)	23,839	9.4
	Thomas J. Morse (LIBERT)	2,641	1.0
	Peter Diamondstone (LU)	2,010	.8
	Norio Kushi (NL)	1,531	.6
	Robert Melamede (VG)	1,319	.5

VIRGINIA

Senate

		Vote Total	%
•	John W. Warner (R)	1,221,508	52.7
	Mark Warner (D)	1,098,440	47.3

House

		Vote Total	%
1 •	Herbert H. Bateman (R)	x	x
2 •	Owen B. Pickett (D)	106,208	65.2
	John Tate (R)	56,682	34.8
3 •	Robert C. Scott (D)	117,399	82.2
	Elsie Holland (R)	25,471	17.8
4 •	Norman Sisisky (D)	157,807	78.5
	A.J. "Tony" Zevgolis (R)	43,237	21.5
5	Virgil H. Goode Jr. (D)	118,949	60.1
	George C. Landrith III (R)	72,000	36.4
	George R. "Tex" Wood (VREF)	6,970	3.5
6 •	Robert W. Goodlatte (R)	132,599	66.9
	Jeffrey Grey (D)	61,398	31.0
	Jay P. Rutledge (I)	4,184	2.1
7 •	Thomas J. Bliley Jr. (R)	188,626	75.2
	Roderic H. Slayton (D)	50,839	20.3
	Bradley E. Evans (I)	11,424	4.6
8 •	James P. Moran (D)	145,140	66.5
	John E. Otey (R)	62,126	28.4
	R. Ward Edmonds (VREF)	5,585	2.6
	Sarina J. Grosswald (I)	4,876	2.2
	Charles Stanard Severance (I)	667	.3
9 •	Rick Boucher (D)	122,866	65.1
	Patrick Muldoon (R)	58,038	30.7
	Thomas I. "Tom" Roberts (VREF)	7,947	4.2
10 •	Frank R. Wolf (R)	163,593	71.8
	Robert Weinberg (D)	57,845	25.4
	Gary A. Reams (I)	6,323	2.8
11 •	Thomas M. Davis III (R)	129,807	64.2
	Tom Horton (D)	69,886	34.6
	C.W. "Levi" Levy (I)	2,557	1.3

WASHINGTON

Governor

		Vote Total	%
	Gary Locke (D)	1,038,108	59.0
	Ellen Craswell (IR)	721,944	41.0

House

		Vote Total	%
1 •	Rick White (R)	106,372	52.1
	Jeffrey Coopersmith (D)	97,711	47.9
2	Kevin Quigley (D)	99,155	48.7
•	Jack Metcalf (R)	96,826	47.5
	Karen Leibrant (NL)	7,682	3.8
3	Brian Baird (D)	102,044	50.7
•	Linda Smith (R)	99,397	49.3
4 •	Richard "Doc" Hastings (R)	87,033	52.0
	Rick Locke (D)	80,352	48.0
5 •	George Nethercutt (R)	110,338	54.9
	Judy Olson (D)	90,592	45.1
6 •	Norm Dicks (D)	123,815	68.3

		Vote Total	%
	Bill Tinsley (R)	51,179	28.2
	Ted Haley (I)	3,934	2.2
	Michael Huddleston (NL)	2,467	1.4
7 •	Jim McDermott (D)	173,668	82.3
	Frank Kleschen (R)	37,456	17.7
8 •	Jennifer Dunn (R)	121,550	63.5
	Dave Little (D)	69,757	36.5
9	Adam Smith (D)	81,029	51.4
•	Randy Tate (R)	72,367	45.9
	David Gruenstein (NL)	4,114	2.6

WEST VIRGINIA

Governor

		Vote Total	%
	Cecil Underwood (R)	320,502	51.6
	Charlotte Pritt (D)	284,398	45.8
	Wallace Johnson (LIBERT)	15,958	2.6

Senate

		Vote Total	%
•	John D. Rockefeller IV (D)	450,903	76.7
	Betty A. Burks (R)	137,240	23.3

House

		Vote Total	%
1 •	Alan B. Mollohan (D)	x	x
2 •	Bob Wise (D)	139,778	68.9
	Greg Morris (R)	63,036	31.1
3 •	Nick J. Rahall II (D)	x	x

WISCONSIN

House

		Vote Total	%
1 •	Mark W. Neumann (R)	118,397	51.0
	Lydia C. Spottswood (D)	113,850	49.0
2 •	Scott L. Klug (R)	154,553	57.4
	Paul Soglin (D)	110,560	41.0
	Ben Masel (LIBERT)	4,247	1.6
3 •	Ron Kind (D)	122,462	52.1
	Jim Harsdorf (R)	112,686	47.9
4 •	Gerald D. Kleczka (D)	134,017	57.7
	Tom Reynolds (R)	98,398	42.3
5 •	Thomas M. Barrett (D)	140,697	73.3
	Paul D. Melotik (R)	47,274	24.6
	James D. Soderna (USTAX)	3,884	2.0
6 •	Tom Petri (R)	168,941	73.1
	Alver Lindskoog (D)	55,047	23.8
	James Dean (LIBERT)	4,528	2.0
	Timothy Farness (TAX)	2,530	1.1
7 •	David R. Obey (D)	136,397	57.0
	Scott West (R)	102,807	43.0
8	Jay Johnson (D)	129,544	52.0
	David Prosser Jr. (R)	119,666	48.0
9 •	F. James Sensenbrenner Jr. (R)	197,929	74.5
	Floyd Brenholt (D)	67,744	25.5

WYOMING

Senate

		Vote Total	%
	Mike Enzi (R)	114,071	54.1
	Kathy Karpan (D)	89,056	42.2
	W. David Herbert (LIBERT)	5,261	2.5
	Lloyd Marsden (NL)	2,569	1.2

House

		Vote Total	%
AL •	Barbara Cubin (R)	115,664	55.2
	Pete Maxfield (D)	85,742	40.9
	Dave Dawson (LIBERT)	8,261	3.9

The Legislative Process in Brief

Note: Parliamentary terms used below are defined in the glossary.

Introduction of Bills

A House member (including the resident commissioner of Puerto Rico and non-voting delegates of the District of Columbia, Guam, the Virgin Islands and American Samoa) may introduce any one of several types of bills and resolutions by handing it to the clerk of the House or placing it in a box called the hopper. A senator first gains recognition of the presiding officer to announce the introduction of a bill. If objection is offered by any senator, the introduction of the bill is postponed until the following day.

As the next step in either the House or Senate, the bill is numbered, referred to the appropriate committee, labeled with the sponsor's name and sent to the Government Printing Office so that copies can be made for subsequent study and action. Senate bills may be jointly sponsored and carry several senators' names. Until 1978, the House limited the number of members who could cosponsor any one bill; the ceiling was eliminated at the beginning of the 96th Congress. A bill written in the executive branch and proposed as an administration measure usually is introduced by the chairman of the congressional committee that has jurisdiction.

Bills — Prefixed with HR in the House, S in the Senate, followed by a number. Used as the form for most legislation, whether general or special, public or private.

Joint Resolutions — Designated H J Res or S J Res. Subject to the same procedure as bills, with the exception of a joint resolution proposing an amendment to the Constitution. The latter must be approved by two-thirds of both houses and is thereupon sent directly to the administrator of general services for submission to the states for ratification instead of being presented to the president for his approval.

Concurrent Resolutions — Designated H Con Res or S Con Res. Used for matters affecting the operations of both houses. These resolutions do not become law.

Resolutions — Designated H Res or S Res. Used for a matter concerning the operation of either house alone and adopted only by the chamber in which it originates.

Committee Action

With few exceptions, bills are referred to the appropriate standing committees. The job of referral formally is the responsibility of the Speaker of the House and the presiding officer of the Senate, but this task usually is carried out on their behalf by the parliamentarians of the House and Senate. Precedent, statute and the jurisdictional mandates of the committees as set forth in the rules of the House and Senate determine which committees receive what kinds of bills. An exception is the referral of private bills, which are sent to whatever committee is designated by their sponsors. Bills are technically considered "read for the first time" when referred to House committees.

When a bill reaches a committee it is placed on the committee's calendar. At that time the bill comes under the sharpest congressional focus. Its chances for passage are quickly determined — and the great majority of bills falls by the legislative roadside. Failure of a committee to act on a bill is equivalent to killing it; the measure can be withdrawn from the committee's purview only by a discharge petition signed by a majority of the House membership on House bills, or by adoption of a special resolution in the Senate. Discharge attempts rarely succeed.

The first committee action taken on a bill usually is a request for comment on it by interested agencies of the government. The committee chairman may assign the bill to a subcommittee for study and hearings, or it may be considered by the full committee. Hearings may be public, closed (executive session) or both. A subcommittee, after considering a bill, reports to the full committee its recommendations for action and any proposed amendments.

The full committee then votes on its recommendation to the House or Senate. This procedure is called "ordering a bill reported." Occasionally a committee may order a bill reported unfavorably; most of the time a report, submitted by the chairman of the committee to the House or Senate, calls for favorable action on the measure since the committee can effectively "kill" a bill by simply failing to take any action.

After the bill is reported, the committee chairman instructs the staff to prepare a written report. The report describes the purposes and scope of the bill, explains the committee revisions, notes proposed changes in existing law and, usually, includes the views of the executive branch agencies consulted. Often committee members opposing a measure issue dissenting minority statements that are included in the report.

Usually, the committee "marks up" or proposes amendments to the bill. If they are substantial and the measure is complicated, the committee may order a "clean bill" introduced, which will embody the proposed amendments. The original bill then is put aside and the clean bill, with a new number, is reported to the floor.

The chamber must approve, alter or reject the committee amendments before the bill itself can be put to a vote.

Floor Action

After a bill is reported back to the house where it originated, it is placed on the calendar.

There are five legislative calendars in the House, issued in one cumulative calendar titled *Calendars of the United States House of Representatives and History of Legislation.* The House calendars are:

The Union Calendar to which are referred bills raising revenues, general appropriations bills and any measures directly or indirectly appropriating money or property. It is the Calendar of the Committee of the Whole House on the State of the Union.

How a Bill Becomes Law

This graphic shows the most typical way in which proposed legislation is enacted into law. There are more complicated, as well as simpler, routes, and most bills never become law. The process is illustrated with two hypothetical bills, House bill No. 1 (HR 1) and Senate bill No. 2 (S 2). Bills must be passed by both houses in identical form before they can be sent to the president. The path of HR 1 is traced by a solid line, that of S 2 by a broken line. In practice, most bills begin as similar proposals in both houses.

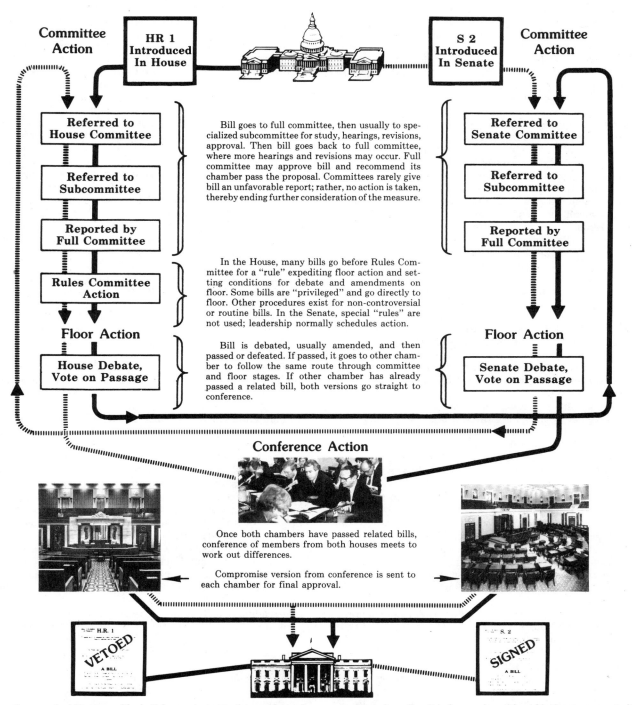

Committee Action

HR 1 Introduced In House

S 2 Introduced In Senate

Committee Action

Referred to House Committee

Referred to Subcommittee

Reported by Full Committee

Bill goes to full committee, then usually to specialized subcommittee for study, hearings, revisions, approval. Then bill goes back to full committee, where more hearings and revisions may occur. Full committee may approve bill and recommend its chamber pass the proposal. Committees rarely give bill an unfavorable report; rather, no action is taken, thereby ending further consideration of the measure.

Referred to Senate Committee

Referred to Subcommittee

Reported by Full Committee

Rules Committee Action

In the House, many bills go before Rules Committee for a "rule" expediting floor action and setting conditions for debate and amendments on floor. Some bills are "privileged" and go directly to floor. Other procedures exist for non-controversial or routine bills. In the Senate, special "rules" are not used; leadership normally schedules action.

Floor Action

House Debate, Vote on Passage

Bill is debated, usually amended, and then passed or defeated. If passed, it goes to other chamber to follow the same route through committee and floor stages. If other chamber has already passed a related bill, both versions go straight to conference.

Floor Action

Senate Debate, Vote on Passage

Conference Action

Once both chambers have passed related bills, conference of members from both houses meets to work out differences.

Compromise version from conference is sent to each chamber for final approval.

H.R. 1 VETOED A BILL

S. 2 SIGNED A BILL

Compromise bill approved by both houses is sent to the president, who may sign it into law, allow it to become law without his signature, or veto it and return it to Congress. Congress may override veto by two-thirds majority vote in both houses; bill then becomes law without president's signature.

The House Calendar to which are referred bills of public character not raising revenue or appropriating money.

The Corrections Calendar to which are referred bills to repeal rules and regulations deemed excessive or unnecessary when the Corrections Calendar is called the second and fourth Tuesday of each month. (Instituted in the 104th Congress to replace the seldom-used Consent Calendar.) A three-fifths majority is required for passage.

The Private Calendar to which are referred bills for relief in the nature of claims against the United States or private immigration bills that are passed without debate when the Private Calendar is called the first and third Tuesdays of each month.

The Discharge Calendar to which are referred motions to discharge committees when the necessary signatures are signed to a discharge petition.

There is only one legislative calendar in the Senate and one "executive calendar" for treaties and nominations submitted to the Senate. When the Senate Calendar is called, each senator is limited to five minutes' debate on each bill.

Debate. A bill is brought to debate by varying procedures. If a routine measure, it may await the call of the calendar. If it is urgent or important, it can be taken up in the Senate either by unanimous consent or by a majority vote. The majority leader, in consultation with the minority leader and others, schedules the bills that will be taken up for debate.

In the House, precedence is granted if a special rule is obtained from the Rules Committee. A request for a special rule usually is made by the chairman of the committee that favorably reported the bill, supported by the bill's sponsor and other committee members. The request, considered by the Rules Committee in the same fashion that other committees consider legislative measures, is in the form of a resolution providing for immediate consideration of the bill. The Rules Committee reports the resolution to the House where it is debated and voted on in the same fashion as regular bills. If the Rules Committee fails to report a rule requested by a committee, there are several ways to bring the bill to the House floor — under suspension of the rules, on Calendar Wednesday or by a discharge motion.

The resolutions providing special rules are important because they specify how long the bill may be debated and whether it may be amended from the floor. If floor amendments are banned, the bill is considered under a "closed rule," which permits only members of the committee that first reported the measure to the House to alter its language, subject to chamber acceptance.

When a bill is debated under an "open rule," amendments may be offered from the floor. Committee amendments always are taken up first but may be changed, as may all amendments up to the second degree; that is, an amendment to an amendment to an amendment is not in order.

Duration of debate in the House depends on whether the bill is under discussion by the House proper or before the House when it is sitting as the Committee of the Whole House on the State of the Union. In the former, the amount of time for debate either is determined by special rule or is allocated with an hour for each member if the measure is under consideration without a rule. In the Committee of the Whole the amount of time agreed on for general debate is equally divided between proponents and opponents. At the end of general discussion, the bill is read section by section for amendment. Debate on an amendment is limited to five minutes for each side; this is called the "five-minute rule." In practice, amendments regularly are debated more than ten minutes, with members gaining the floor by offering pro

forma amendments or obtaining unanimous consent to speak longer than five minutes.

Senate debate usually is unlimited. It can be halted only by unanimous consent by "cloture," which requires a three-fifths majority of the entire Senate except for proposed changes in the Senate rules. The latter requires a two-thirds vote.

The House considers almost all important bills within a parliamentary framework known as the Committee of the Whole. It is not a committee as the word usually is understood; it is the full House meeting under another name for the purpose of speeding action on legislation. Technically, the House sits as the Committee of the Whole when it considers any tax measure or bill dealing with public appropriations. It also can resolve itself into the Committee of the Whole if a member moves to do so and the motion is carried. The Speaker appoints a member to serve as the chairman. The rules of the House permit the Committee of the Whole to meet when a quorum of 100 members is present on the floor and to amend and act on bills, within certain time limitations. When the Committee of the Whole has acted, it "rises," the Speaker returns as the presiding officer of the House and the member appointed chairman of the Committee of the Whole reports the action of the committee and its recommendations. The Committee of the Whole cannot pass a bill; instead it reports the measure to the full House with whatever changes it has approved. The full House then may pass or reject the bill — or, on occasion, recommit the bill to committee. Amendments adopted in the Committee of the Whole may be put to a second vote in the full House.

Votes. Voting on bills may occur repeatedly before they are finally approved or rejected. The House votes on the rule for the bill and on various amendments to the bill. Voting on amendments often is a more illuminating test of a bill's support than is the final tally. Sometimes members approve final passage of bills after vigorously supporting amendments that, if adopted, would have scuttled the legislation.

The Senate has three different methods of voting: an untabulated voice vote, a standing vote (called a division) and a recorded roll call to which members answer "yea" or "nay" when their names are called. The House also employs voice and standing votes, but since January 1973 yeas and nays have been recorded by an electronic voting device, eliminating the need for time-consuming roll calls.

Another method of voting, used in the House only, is the teller vote. Traditionally, members filed up the center aisle past counters; only vote totals were announced. Since 1971, one-fifth of a quorum can demand that the votes of individual members be recorded, thereby forcing them to take a public position on amendments to key bills. Electronic voting now is commonly used for this purpose.

After amendments to a bill have been voted upon, a vote may be taken on a motion to recommit the bill to committee. If carried, this vote removes the bill from the chamber's calendar and is usually a death blow to the bill. If the motion is unsuccessful, the bill then is "read for the third time." An actual reading usually is dispensed with. Until 1965, an opponent of a bill could delay this move by objecting and asking for a full reading of an engrossed (certified in final form) copy of the bill. After the "third reading," the vote on final passage is taken.

The final vote may be followed by a motion to reconsider, and this motion may be followed by a move to lay the motion on the table. Usually, those voting for the bill's passage vote for the tabling motion, thus safeguarding the final passage action. With that, the bill has been formally passed by the cham-

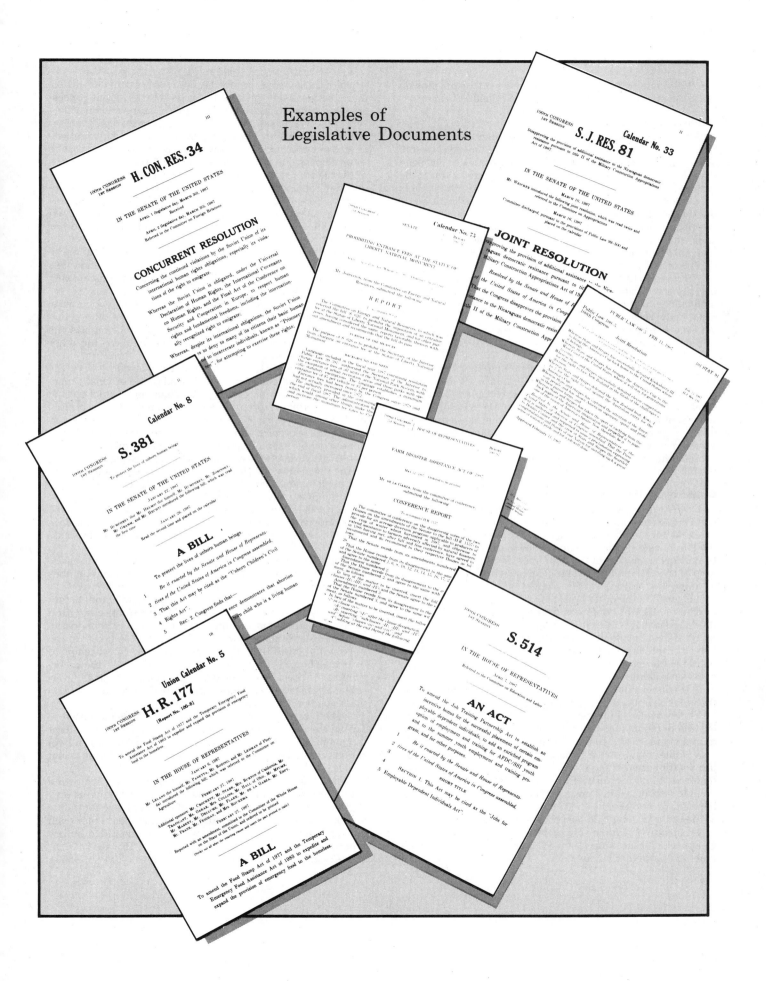

Examples of
Legislative Documents

ber. While a motion to reconsider a Senate vote is pending on a bill, the measure cannot be sent to the House.

Action in Second House

After a bill is passed it is sent to the other chamber. This body may then take one of several steps. It may pass the bill as is — accepting the other chamber's language. It may send the bill to committee for scrutiny or alteration, or reject the entire bill, advising the other house of its actions. Or it simply may ignore the bill submitted while it continues work on its own version of the proposed legislation. Frequently, one chamber may approve a version of a bill that is greatly at variance with the version already passed by the other house, and then substitute its contents for the language of the other, retaining only the latter's bill number.

A provision of the Legislative Reorganization Act of 1970 permits a separate House vote on any non-germane amendment added by the Senate to a House-passed bill and requires a majority vote to retain the amendment. Previously the House was forced to act on the bill as a whole; the only way to defeat the non-germane amendment was to reject the entire bill.

Often the second chamber makes only minor changes. If these are readily agreed to by the other house, the bill then is routed to the president. However, if the opposite chamber significantly alters the bill submitted to it, the measure usually is "sent to conference." The chamber that has possession of the "papers" (engrossed bill, engrossed amendments, messages of transmittal) requests a conference and the other chamber must agree to it. If the second house does not agree, the bill dies.

Conference, Final Action

Conference. A conference works out conflicting House and Senate versions of a legislative bill. The conferees usually are senior members appointed by the presiding officers of the two houses, from the committees that managed the bills. Under this arrangement the conferees of one house have the duty of trying to maintain their chamber's position in the face of amending actions by the conferees (also referred to as "managers") of the other house.

The number of conferees from each chamber may vary, the range usually being from three to nine members in each group, depending upon the length or complexity of the bill involved. There may be five representatives and three senators on the conference committee, or the reverse. But a majority vote controls the action of each group so that a large representation does not give one chamber a voting advantage over the other chamber's conferees.

Theoretically, conferees are not allowed to write new legislation in reconciling the two versions before them, but this curb sometimes is bypassed. Many bills have been put into acceptable compromise form only after new language was provided by the conferees. The 1970 Reorganization Act attempted to tighten restrictions on conferees by forbidding them to introduce any language on a topic that neither chamber sent to conference or to modify any topic beyond the scope of the different House and Senate versions.

Frequently the ironing out of difficulties takes days or even weeks. Conferences on involved appropriations bills sometimes are particularly drawn out.

As a conference proceeds, conferees reconcile differences between the versions, but generally they grant concessions only insofar as they remain sure that the chamber they represent will accept the compromises. Occasionally, uncertainty over how either house will react, or the positive refusal of a chamber to back down on a disputed amendment, results in an impasse, and the bills die in conference even though each was approved by its sponsoring chamber.

Conferees sometimes go back to their respective chambers for further instructions, when they report certain portions in disagreement. Then the chamber concerned can either "recede and concur" in the amendment of the other house or "insist on its amendment."

When the conferees have reached agreement, they prepare a conference report embodying their recommendations (compromises). The report, in document form, must be submitted to each house.

The conference report must be approved by each house. Consequently, approval of the report is approval of the compromise bill. In the order of voting on conference reports, the chamber which asked for a conference yields to the other chamber the opportunity to vote first.

Final Steps. After a bill has been passed by both the House and Senate in identical form, all of the original papers are sent to the enrolling clerk of the chamber in which the bill originated. He then prepares an enrolled bill, which is printed on parchment paper. When this bill has been certified as correct by the secretary of the Senate or the clerk of the House, depending on which chamber originated the bill, it is signed first (no matter whether it originated in the Senate or House) by the Speaker of the House and then by the president of the Senate. It is next sent to the White House to await action.

If the president approves the bill, he signs it, dates it and usually writes the word "approved" on the document. If he does not sign it within 10 days (Sundays excepted) and Congress is in session, the bill becomes law without his signature.

However, should Congress adjourn before the 10 days expire, and the president has failed to sign the measure, it does not become law. This procedure is called the pocket veto.

A president vetoes a bill by refusing to sign it and, before the 10-day period expires, returning it to Congress with a message stating his reasons. The message is sent to the chamber that originated the bill. If no action is taken on the message, the bill dies. Congress, however, can attempt to override the president's veto and enact the bill, "the objections of the president to the contrary notwithstanding." Overriding a veto requires a two-thirds vote of those present, who must number a quorum and vote by roll call.

Debate can precede this vote, with motions permitted to lay the message on the table, postpone action on it or refer it to committee. If the president's veto is overridden by a two-thirds vote in both houses, the bill becomes law. Otherwise it is dead.

When bills are passed finally and signed, or passed over a veto, they are given law numbers in numerical order as they become law. There are two series of numbers, one for public and one for private laws, starting at the number "1" for each two-year term of Congress. They are then identified by law number and by Congress — for example, Private Law 21, 97th Congress; Public Law 250, 97th Congress (or PL 97–250).

The Budget Process in Brief

Through the budget process, the president and Congress decide how much to spend and tax during the upcoming fiscal year. More specifically, they decide how much to spend on each activity, ensure that the government spends no more and spends it only for that activity, and report on that spending at the end of each budget cycle.

The President's Budget

The law requires that, by the first Monday in February, the president submit to Congress his proposed federal budget for the next fiscal year, which begins on October 1. In order to accomplish this, the president establishes general budget and fiscal policy guidelines. Based on these guidelines, executive branch agencies make requests for funds and submit them to the White House's Office of Management and Budget (OMB) nearly a year prior to the start of a new fiscal year. The OMB, receiving direction from the president and administration official, reviews the agencies' requests and develops a detailed budget by December. From December to January the OMB prepares the budget documents, so that the president can deliver it to Congress in February.

The president's budget is the executive branch's plan for the next year — but it is just a proposal. After receiving it, Congress has its own budget process to follow from February to October. Only after Congress passes the required spending bills — and the president signs them — has the government created its actual budget.

Action in Congress

Congress first must pass a "budget resolution" — a framework within which the members of Congress will make their decisions about spending and taxes. It includes targets for total spending, total revenues, and the deficit, and allocations within the spending target for the two types of spending — discretionary and mandatory.

Discretionary spending, which currently accounts for about 33 percent of all federal spending, is what the president and Congress must decide to spend for the next year through the thirteen annual appropriations bills. It includes money for such activities as the FBI and the Coast Guard, for housing and education, for NASA and highway and bridge construction, and for defense and foreign aid.

Mandatory spending, which currently accounts for 67 percent of all spending, is authorized by laws that have already been passed. It includes entitlement spending — such as for Social Security, Medicare, veterans' benefits, and food stamps — through which individuals receive benefits because they are eligible based on their age, income, or other criteria. It also includes interest on the national debt, which the government pays to individuals and institutions that hold Treasury bonds and other government securities. The only way the president and Congress can change the spending on entitlement and other mandatory programs is if they change the laws that authorized the programs.

Currently, the law imposes a limit or "cap" through 1998 on total annual discretionary spending. Within the cap, however, the president and Congress can, and often do, change the spending levels from year to year for the thousands of individual federal programs.

In addition, the law requires that legislation that would raise mandatory spending or lower revenues — compared to existing law — be offset by spending cuts or revenue increases. This requirement, called "pay-as-you-go" is designed to prevent new legislation from increasing the deficit.

Once Congress passes the budget resolution, it turns its attention to passing the thirteen annual appropriations bills and, if it chooses, "authorizing" bills to change the laws governing mandatory spending and revenues.

Congress begins by examining the president's budget in detail. Scores of committees and subcommittees hold hearings on proposals under their jurisdiction. The House and Senate Armed Services Authorizing Committees, and the Defense and Military Construction Subcommittees of the Appropriations Committees, for instance, hold hearings on the president's defense budget. The White House budget director, cabinet officers, and other administration officials work with Congress as it accepts some of the president's proposals, rejects others, and changes still others. Congress can change funding levels, eliminate programs, or add programs not requested by the president. It can add or eliminate taxes and other sources of revenue, or make other changes that affect the amount of revenue collected. Congressional rules require that these committees and subcommittees take actions that reflect the congressional budget resolution.

The president's budget, the budget resolution, and the appropriations or authorizing bills measure spending in two ways — "budget authority" and "outlays." Budget authority is what the law authorizes the federal government to spend for certain programs, projects, or activities. What the government actually spends in a particular year, however, is an outlay. For example, when the government decides to build a space exploration system, the president and Congress may agree to appropriate $1 billion in budget authority. But the space system may take ten years to build. Thus, the government may spend $100 million in outlays in the first year to begin construction and the remaining $900 million during the next nine years as the construction continues.

Congress must provide budget authority before the federal agencies can obligate the government to make outlays. When Congress fails to complete action on one or more of the regular annual appropriations bills before the fiscal year begins on October 1, budget authority may be made on a temporary basis through continuing resolutions. Continuing resolutions make budget authority available for limited periods of time, generally at rates related through some formula to the rate provided in the previous year's appropriation.

Monitoring the Budget

Once Congress passes and the president signs the federal appropriations bills or authorizing laws for the fiscal year, the government monitors the budget through (1) agency program managers and budget officials, including the Inspectors General, who report only to the agency head; (2) the Office of Management and Budget; (3) congressional committees; and (4) the General Accounting Office, an auditing arm of Congress.

This oversight is designed to (1) ensure that agencies comply with legal limits on spending, and that they use budget authority only for the purposes intended; (2) see that programs are operating consistently with legal requirements and existing policy; and (3) ensure that programs are well managed and achieving the intended results.

The president may withhold appropriated amounts from obligation only under certain limited circumstances — to provide for contingencies, to achieve savings made possible through changes in requirements or greater efficiency of operations, or as otherwise provided by law. The Impoundment Control Act of 1974 specifies the procedures that must be followed if funds are withheld. Congress can also cancel previous authorized budget authority by passing a rescissions bill — but it also must be signed by the president.

Glossary of Congressional Terms

Act — The term for legislation once it has passed both houses of Congress and has been signed by the president or passed over his veto, thus becoming law. *(See also Pocket Veto.)* Also used in parliamentary terminology for a bill that has been passed by one house and engrossed. *(See Engrossed Bill.)*

Adjournment Sine Die — Adjournment without definitely fixing a day for reconvening; literally "adjournment without a day." Usually used to connote the final adjournment of a session of Congress. A session can continue until noon, Jan. 3, of the following year, when, under the 20th Amendment to the Constitution, it automatically terminates. Both houses must agree to a concurrent resolution for either house to adjourn for more than three days.

Adjournment to a Day Certain — Adjournment under a motion or resolution that fixes the next time of meeting. Under the Constitution, neither house can adjourn for more than three days without the concurrence of the other. A session of Congress is not ended by adjournment to a day certain.

Amendment — A proposal of a member of Congress to alter the language, provisions or stipulations in a bill or in another amendment. An amendment usually is printed, debated, and voted upon in the same manner as a bill.

Amendment in the Nature of a Substitute — Usually an amendment that seeks to replace the entire text of a bill. Passage of this type of amendment strikes out everything after the enacting clause and inserts a new version of the bill. An amendment in the nature of a substitute also can refer to an amendment that replaces a large portion of the text of a bill.

Appeal — A member's challenge of a ruling or decision made by the presiding officer of the chamber. In the Senate, the senator appeals to members of the chamber to override the decision. If carried by a majority vote, the appeal nullifies the chair's ruling. In the House, the decision of the Speaker traditionally has been final; seldom are there appeals to the members to reverse the Speaker's stand. To appeal a ruling is considered an attack on the Speaker.

Appropriations Bill — A bill that gives legal authority to spend or obligate money from the Treasury. The Constitution disallows money to be drawn from the Treasury "but in Consequence of Appropriations made by Law."

By congressional custom, an appropriations bill originates in the House, and it is not supposed to be considered by the full House or Senate until a related measure authorizing the funding is enacted. An appropriations bill grants the actual money approved by authorization bills, but not necessarily the full amount permissible under the authorization. The 1985 Gramm-Rudman-Hollings law stipulated that the House is to pass by June 30 the last regular appropriations bill for the fiscal year starting the following Oct. 1. (There is no such deadline for the Senate.) However, for decades appropriations often have not been final until well after the fiscal year begins, requiring a succession of stopgap bills to continue the government's functions. In addition, much federal spending — about half of all budget authority, notably that for Social Security and interest on the federal debt — does not require annual appropriations; those programs exist under permanent appropriations. *(See also Authorization, Budget Process, Backdoor Spending Authority, Entitlement Program.)*

In addition to general appropriations bills, there are two specialized types. *(See Continuing Resolution, Supplemental Appropriations Bill.)*

Authorization — Basic, substantive legislation that establishes or continues the legal operation of a federal program or agency, either indefinitely or for a specific period of time, or which sanctions a particular type of obligation or expenditure. An authorization normally is a prerequisite for an appropriation or other kind of budget authority.

Under the rules of both houses, the appropriation for a program or agency may not be considered until its authorization has been considered. An authorization also may limit the amount of budget authority to be provided or may authorize the appropriation of "such sums as may be necessary." *(See also Backdoor Spending Authority.)*

Backdoor Spending Authority — Budget authority provided in legislation outside the normal appropriations process. The most common forms of backdoor spending are borrowing authority, contract authority, entitlements, and loan guarantees that commit the government to payments of principal and interest on loans — such as Guaranteed Student Loans — made by banks or other private lenders. Loan guarantees only result in actual outlays when there is a default by the borrower.

In some cases, such as interest on the public debt, a permanent appropriation is provided that becomes available without further action by Congress.

Bills — Most legislative proposals before Congress are in the form of bills and are designated by HR in the House of Representatives or S in the Senate, according to the house in which they originate, and by a number assigned in the order in which they are introduced during the two-year period of a congressional term. "Public bills" deal with general questions and become public laws if approved by Congress and signed by the president. "Private bills" deal with individual matters such as claims against the government, immigration and naturalization cases, or land titles and become private laws if approved and signed. *(See also Concurrent Resolution, Joint Resolution, Resolution.)*

Bills Introduced — In both the House and Senate, any number of members may join in introducing a single bill or resolution. The first member listed is the sponsor of the bill, and all subsequent members listed are the bill's cosponsors.

Many bills are committee bills and are introduced under the name of the chairman of the committee or subcommittee. All appropriations bills fall into this category. A committee frequently holds hearings on a number of related bills and may agree to one of them or to an entirely new bill. *(See also Report, Clean Bill, By Request.)*

Bills Referred — When introduced, a bill is referred to the committee or committees that have jurisdiction over the subject with which the bill is concerned. Under the standing rules of the House and Senate, bills are referred by the Speaker in the House and by the presiding officer in the Senate. In practice, the House and Senate parliamentarians act for these officials and refer the vast majority of bills.

Borrowing Authority — Statutory authority that permits a federal agency to incur obligations and make payments for specified purposes with borrowed money.

Budget — The document sent to Congress by the president early each year estimating government revenue and expenditures for the ensuing fiscal year.

Budget Act — The common name for the Congressional Budget and Impoundment Control Act of 1974, which established the current budget process and created the Congressional Budget Office. The act also put limits on presidential authority to spend appropriated money. *(See Impoundments, Budget Process.)*

Budget Authority — Authority to enter into obligations that will result in immediate or future outlays involving federal funds. The basic forms of budget authority are appropriations, contract authority, and borrowing authority. Budget authority may be classified by (1) the period of availability (one-year, multiple-year, or without a time limitation), (2) the timing of congressional action (current or permanent), or (3) the manner of determining the amount available (definite or indefinite).

Budget Process — Congress in 1990 made far-reaching changes in its 1974 budget process law, called the Congressional Budget and Impoundment Control Act. The law continues to provide for congressional approval of budget resolutions and reconciliation bills, two mechanisms created by the 1974 law. *(See Budget Resolution, Reconciliation.)* The 1990 changes discarded provisions of 1985 and 1987 amendments to the act that automatically cut federal spending in certain areas when pre-determined targets were exceeded. Those amendments, collectively known as Gramm-Rudman-Hollings for their congressional sponsors, were intended to balance the federal budget by fiscal year 1991. Soaring deficits made the goal unachievable, threatening federal programs with almost random and massive cuts.

Congress stepped back from that brink and provided, instead, for spending caps in three categories: defense, domestic, and international for 1991–93; for the following two years the 1990 changes set overall discretionary spending caps. Each cap will increase automatically with inflation plus — for domestic spending only — an extra $20 billion. Moreover, spending that exceeds the cap due to factors beyond the control of Congress, such as a recession, will not trigger automatic cuts. Entitlement spending, such as for Medicare, was put on a "pay as you go" basis, requiring any expansion be paid for by a corresponding entitlement cut or revenue increase. Also, any tax cut must be paid for by a compensating tax increase or entitlement cut. But if all these provisions failed, automatic spending cuts could still occur. *(See Sequestration.)*

Budget Resolution — A concurrent resolution passed by both houses of Congress, but not requiring the president's signature, establishing the congressional budget plan. The resolution sets forth various budget totals and functional allocations. Its deadline is April 15 but if missed the Budget committees must report spending limits for the Appropriations committees based on discretionary spending in the president's budget.

By Request — A phrase used when a senator or representative introduces a bill at the request of an executive agency or private organization but does not necessarily endorse the legislation.

Calendar — An agenda or list of business awaiting possible action by each chamber. The House uses five legislative calendars. *(See Corrections, Discharge, House, Private, and Union Calendar.)*

In the Senate, all legislative matters reported from committee go on one calendar. They are listed there in the order in which committees report them or the Senate places them on the calendar, but they may be called up out of order by the majority leader, either by obtaining unanimous consent of the Senate or by a motion to call up a bill. The Senate also uses one nonlegislative calendar; this is used for treaties and nominations. *(See Executive Calendar.)*

Calendar Wednesday — In the House, committees, on Wednesdays, may be called in the order in which they appear in Rule X of the House, for the purpose of bringing up any of their bills from either the House or the Union Calendar, except bills that are privileged. General debate is limited to two hours. Bills called up from the Union Calendar are considered in Committee of the Whole. Calendar Wednesday is not observed during the last two weeks of a session and may be dispensed with at other times by a two-thirds vote. This procedure is rarely used and routinely is dispensed with by unanimous consent.

Call of the Calendar — Senate bills that are not brought up for debate by a motion, unanimous consent, or a unanimous consent agreement are brought before the Senate for action when the calendar listing them is "called." Bills must be called in the order listed. Measures considered by this method usually are noncontroversial, and debate on the bill and any proposed amendments is limited to a total of five minutes for each senator.

Chamber — The meeting place for the membership of either the House or the Senate; also the membership of the House or Senate meeting as such.

Clean Bill — Frequently after a committee has finished a major revision of a bill, one of the committee members, usually the chairman, will assemble the changes and what is left of the original bill into a new measure and introduce it as a "clean bill." The revised measure, which is given a new number, then is referred back to the committee, which reports it to the floor for consideration. This often is a timesaver, as committee-recommended changes in a clean bill do not have to be considered and voted on by the chamber. Reporting a clean bill also protects committee amendments that could be subject to points of order concerning germaneness.

Clerk of the House — Chief administrative officer of the House of Representatives, with duties corresponding to those of the secretary of the Senate. *(See also Secretary of the Senate.)*

Cloture — The process by which a filibuster can be ended in the Senate other than by unanimous consent. A motion for cloture can apply to any measure before the Senate, including a proposal to change the chamber's rules. A cloture motion requires the signatures of 16 senators to be introduced. To end a filibuster, the cloture motion must obtain the votes of three-fifths of the entire Senate membership (60 if there are no vacancies), except when the filibuster is against a proposal to amend the standing rules of the Senate and a two-thirds vote of senators present and voting is required. The cloture request is put to a roll-call vote one hour after the Senate meets on the second day following introduction of the motion. If approved, cloture limits each senator to one hour of debate. The bill or amendment in question comes to a final vote after 30 hours of consideration (including debate time and the time it takes to conduct roll calls, quorum calls and other procedural motions). *(See Filibuster.)*

Committee — A division of the House or Senate that prepares legislation for action by the parent chamber or makes investigations as directed by the parent chamber. There are several types of committees. *(See Standing and Select or Special Committees.)* Most standing committees are divided into subcommittees, which study legislation, hold hearings and report bills, with or without amendments, to the full committee. Only the full committee can report legislation for action by the House or Senate.

Committee of the Whole — The working title of what is formally "The Committee of the Whole House [of Representatives] on the State of the Union." The membership comprises all House members sitting as a committee. Any 100 members who are present on the floor of the chamber to consider legislation comprise a quorum of the committee. Any legislation taken up by the Committee of the Whole, however, must first have passed through the regular legislative or Appropriations committee and have been placed on the calendar.

Technically, the Committee of the Whole considers only bills directly or indirectly appropriating money, authorizing appropriations or involving taxes or charges on the public. Because the Committee of the Whole need number only 100 representatives, a quorum is more readily attained, and legislative business is expedited. Before 1971, members' positions were not individually recorded on votes taken in Committee of the Whole. *(See Teller Vote.)*

When the full House resolves itself into the Committee of the Whole, it supplants the Speaker with a "chairman." A measure is debated and amendments may be proposed, with votes on amendments as needed. *(See Five-Minute Rule.)* The committee, however, cannot pass a bill. When the committee completes its work on the measure, it dissolves itself by "rising." The Speaker returns, and the chairman of the Committee of the Whole reports to the House that the committee's work has been completed. At this time members may demand a roll-call vote on any amendment adopted in the Committee of the Whole. The final vote is on passage of the legislation.

Committee Veto — A requirement added to a few statutes directing that certain policy directives by an executive department or agency be reviewed by certain congressional committees before they are implemented. Under common practice, the government department or agency and the committees involved are expected to reach a consensus before the directives are carried out. *(See also Legislative Veto.)*

Concurrent Resolution — A concurrent resolution, designated H Con Res or S Con Res, must be adopted by both houses, but it is not sent to the president for approval and therefore does not have the force of law. A concurrent resolution, for example, is used to fix the time for adjournment of a Congress. It also is used as the vehicle for expressing the sense of Congress on various foreign policy and domestic issues, and it serves as the vehicle for coordinated decisions on the federal budget under the 1974 Congressional Budget and Impoundment Control Act. *(See also Bills, Joint Resolution, Resolution.)*

Conference — A meeting between the representatives of the House and the Senate to reconcile differences between the two houses on provisions of a bill passed by both chambers. Members of the conference committee are appointed by the Speaker and the presiding officer of the Senate and are called "managers" for their respective chambers. A majority of the managers for each house must reach agreement on the provisions of the bill (often a compromise between the versions of the two chambers) before it can be considered by either chamber in the form of a "conference report." When the conference report goes to the floor, it cannot be amended, and, if it is not approved by both chambers, the bill may go back to conference under certain situations, or a new conference must be convened. Many rules and informal practices govern the conduct of conference committees.

Bills that are passed by both houses with only minor differences need not be sent to conference. Either chamber may "concur" in the other's amendments, completing action on the legislation. Sometimes leaders of the committees of jurisdiction work out an informal compromise instead of having a formal conference. *(See Custody of the Papers.)*

Confirmations — *(See Nominations.)*

Congressional Record — The daily, printed account of proceedings in both the House and Senate chambers, showing substantially verbatim debate, statements, and a record of floor action. Highlights of legislative and committee action are embodied in a Daily Digest section of the *Record*, and members are entitled to have their extraneous remarks printed in an appendix known as "Extension of Remarks." Members may edit and revise remarks made on the floor during debate, and therefore quotations from debate reported by the press are not always found in the *Record*.

The *Congressional Record* provides a way to distinguish remarks spoken on the floor of the House and Senate from undelivered speeches. In the Senate, all speeches, articles, and other matter that members insert in the *Record* without actually reading them on the floor are set off by large black dots, or bullets. However, a loophole allows a member to avoid the bulleting if he delivers any portion of the speech in person. In the House, undelivered speeches and other material are printed in a distinctive typeface. *(See also Journal)*

Congressional Terms of Office — Normally begin on Jan. 3 of the year following a general election and are two years for representatives and six years for senators. Representatives elected in special elections are sworn in for the remainder of a term. A person may be appointed to fill a Senate vacancy and serves until a successor is elected; the successor serves until the end of the term applying to the vacant seat.

Continuing Resolution — A joint resolution, cleared by Congress and signed by the president (when the new fiscal year is about to begin or has begun), to provide new budget authority for federal agencies and programs to continue in operation until the regular appropriations acts are enacted. *(See Appropriations Bill.)*

The continuing resolution usually specifies a maximum rate at which an agency may incur obligations, based on the rate of the prior year, the president's budget request, or an appropriations bill passed by either or both houses of Congress but not yet enacted. In recent years, most regular appropriations bills have not cleared and a full-year continuing resolution has taken their place. For fiscal 1987 and 1988, Congress intentionally rolled all 13 regular appropriations bills into one continuing resolution.

Continuing resolutions also are called "CRs" or continuing appropriations.

Contract Authority — Budget authority contained in an authorization bill that permits the federal government to enter into contracts or other obligations for future payments from funds not yet appropriated by Congress. The assumption is that funds will be available for payment in a subsequent appropriation act.

Controllable Budget Items — In federal budgeting this refers to programs for which the budget authority or outlays during a fiscal year can be controlled without changing existing, substantive law. The concept "relatively uncontrollable under current law" includes outlays for open-ended programs and fixed costs such as interest on the public debt, Social Security benefits, veterans' benefits, and outlays to liquidate prior-year obligations. More and more spending for federal programs has become uncontrollable or relatively uncontrollable.

Correcting Recorded Votes — Rules prohibit members from changing their votes after the result has been announced. But, occasionally hours, days, or months after a vote has been taken, a member may announce that he was "incorrectly recorded." In the Senate, a request to change one's vote almost always receives unanimous consent. In the House, members are prohibited from changing their votes if tallied by the electronic voting system. If the vote was taken by roll call, a change is permissible if consent is granted.

Corrections Calendar — Members of the House may place on this calendar bills reported favorably from committee that repeal rules and regulations considered excessive or unnecessary. Bills on the Corrections Calendar normally are called on the second and fourth Tuesday of each month at the discretion of the House Speaker in consultation with the minority leader. A bill must be on the calendar for at least three legislative days before it can be brought up for floor consideration. Once on the floor, a bill is subject to one hour of debate equally divided between the chairman and ranking member of the committee of jurisdiction. A vote may be called on whether to recommit the bill to committee with or without instructions. To pass, a three-fifths majority, or 261 votes if all House members vote, is required.

Cosponsor — *(See Bills Introduced.)*

Current Services Estimates — Estimated budget authority and outlays for federal programs and operations for the forthcoming fiscal year based on continuation of existing levels of service without policy changes. These estimates of budget authority and outlays, accompanied by the underlying economic and policy assumptions upon which they are based, are transmitted by the president to Congress when the budget is submitted.

Custody of the Papers — To reconcile differences between the House and Senate versions of a bill, a conference may be arranged. The chamber with "custody of the papers" — the engrossed bill, engrossed amendments, messages of transmittal — is the only body empowered to request the conference. By custom, the chamber that asks for a conference is the last to act on the conference report once agreement has been reached on the bill by the conferees.

Custody of the papers sometimes is manipulated to ensure that a particular chamber acts either first or last on the conference report.

Deferral — Executive branch action to defer, or delay, the spending of appropriated money. The 1974 Congressional Budget and Impoundment Control Act requires a special message from the president to Congress reporting a proposed deferral of spending. Deferrals may not extend beyond the end of the fiscal year in which the message is transmitted. A federal district court in 1986 struck down the president's authority to defer spending for policy reasons; the ruling was upheld by a federal appeals court in 1987. Congress can and has prohibited proposed deferrals by enacting a law doing so; most often cancellations of proposed deferrals are included in appropriations bills. *(See also Rescission.)*

Dilatory Motion — A motion made for the purpose of killing time and preventing action on a bill or amendment. House rules outlaw dilatory motions, but enforcement is largely within the discretion of the Speaker or chairman of the Committee of the Whole. The Senate does not have a rule banning dilatory motions, except under cloture.

Discharge a Committee — Occasionally, attempts are made to relieve a committee from jurisdiction over a measure before it. This is attempted more often in the House than in the Senate, and the procedure rarely is successful.

In the House, if a committee does not report a bill within 30 days after the measure is referred to it, any member may file a discharge motion. Once offered, the motion is treated as a petition needing the signatures of 218 members (a majority of the House). After the required signatures have been obtained, there is a delay of seven days. Thereafter, on the second and fourth Mondays of each month, except during the last six days of a session, any member who has signed the petition must be recognized, if he so desires, to move that the committee be discharged. Debate on the motion to discharge is limited to 20 minutes, and, if the motion is carried, consideration of the bill becomes a matter of high privilege.

If a resolution to consider a bill is held up in the Rules Committee for more than seven legislative days, any member may enter a motion to discharge the committee. The motion is handled like any other discharge petition in the House.

Occasionally, to expedite noncontroversial legislative business, a committee is discharged by unanimous consent of the House, and a petition is not required. *(Senate procedure, see Discharge Resolution.)*

Discharge Calendar — The House calendar to which motions to discharge committees are referred when they have the required number of signatures (218) and are awaiting floor action.

Discharge Petition — *(See Discharge a Committee.)*

Discharge Resolution — In the Senate, a special motion that any senator may introduce to relieve a committee from consideration of a bill before it. The resolution can be called up for Senate approval or disapproval in the same manner as any other Senate business. *(House procedure, see Discharge a Committee.)*

Division of a Question for Voting — A practice that is more common in the Senate but also used in the House, a member may demand a division of an amendment or a motion for purposes of voting. Where an amendment or motion can be divided, the individual parts are voted on separately when a member demands a division. This procedure occurs most often during the consideration of conference reports.

Division Vote — *(See Standing Vote.)*

Enacting Clause — Key phrase in bills beginning, "Be it enacted by the Senate and House of Representatives . . ." A successful motion to strike it from legislation kills the measure.

Engrossed Bill — The final copy of a bill as passed by one chamber, with the text as amended by floor action and certified by the clerk of the House or the secretary of the Senate.

Enrolled Bill — The final copy of a bill that has been passed in identical form by both chambers. It is certified by an officer of the house of origin (clerk of the House or secretary of the Senate) and then sent on for the signatures of the House Speaker, the Senate president pro tempore and the president of the United States. An enrolled bill is printed on parchment.

Entitlement Program — A federal program that guarantees a certain level of benefits to persons or other entities who meet requirements set by law, such as Social Security, farm price supports, or unemployment benefits. It thus leaves no discretion with Congress on how much money to appropriate, and some entitlements carry permanent appropriations.

Executive Calendar — This is a non-legislative calendar in the Senate on which presidential documents such as treaties and nominations are listed.

Executive Document — A document, usually a treaty, sent to the Senate by the president for consideration or approval. Executive documents are identified for each session of Congress according to the following pattern: Executive A, 97th Congress, 1st Session; Executive B, and so on. They are referred to committee in the same manner as other measures. Unlike legislative documents, however, treaties do not die at the end of a Congress but remain "live" proposals until acted on by the Senate or withdrawn by the president.

Executive Session — A meeting of a Senate or House committee (or occasionally of either chamber) that only its members may attend. Witnesses regularly appear at committee meetings in executive session — for example, Defense Department officials during presentations of classified defense information. Other members of Congress may be invited, but the public and press are not to attend.

Expenditures — The actual spending of money as distinguished from the appropriation of funds. Expenditures are made by the disbursing officers of the administration; appropriations are made only by Congress. The two are rarely identical in any fiscal year. In addition to some current budget authority, expenditures may represent budget authority made available one, two, or more years earlier.

Federal Debt — The federal debt consists of public debt, which occurs when the Treasury or the Federal Financing Bank (FFB) borrows money directly from the public or another fund or account, and agency debt, which is incurred when a federal agency other than Treasury or the FFB is authorized by law to borrow money from the public or another fund or account. The public debt comprises about 99 percent of the gross federal debt.

Filibuster — A time-delaying tactic associated with the Senate and used by a minority in an effort to prevent a vote on a bill or amendment that probably would pass if voted upon directly. The most common method is to take advantage of the Senate's rules permitting unlimited debate, but other forms of parliamentary maneuvering may be used. The stricter rules of the House make filibusters more difficult, but delaying tactics are employed occasionally through various procedural devices allowed by House rules. *(Senate filibusters, see Cloture.)*

Fiscal Year — Financial operations of the government are carried out in a 12-month fiscal year, beginning on Oct. 1 and ending on Sept. 30. The fiscal year carries the date of the calendar year in which it ends. (From fiscal year 1844 to fiscal year 1976, the fiscal year began July 1 and ended the following June 30.)

Five-Minute Rule — A debate-limiting rule of the House that is invoked when the House sits as the Committee of the Whole. Under the rule, a member offering an amendment is allowed to speak five minutes in its favor, and an opponent of the amendment is allowed to speak five minutes in opposition. Debate is then closed. In practice, amendments regularly are debated more than 10 minutes, with members gaining the floor by offering pro forma amendments or obtaining unanimous consent to speak longer than five minutes. *(See Strike Out the Last Word.)*

Floor Manager — A member who has the task of steering legislation through floor debate and the amendment process to a final vote in the House or the Senate. Floor managers usually are chairmen or ranking members of the committee that reported the bill. Managers are responsible for apportioning the debate time granted supporters of the bill. The ranking minority member of the committee normally apportions time for the minority party's participation in the debate.

Frank — A member's facsimile signature, which is used on envelopes in lieu of stamps, for the member's official outgoing mail. The "franking privilege" is the right to send mail postage-free.

Functions (Functional Classifications) — Categories of spending established for accounting purposes to keep track of specific expenditures. Each account is placed in the single function (such as national defense, agriculture, health, etc.) that best represents its major purpose, regardless of the agency administering the program. The functions do not correspond directly with appropriations or with the budgets of individual agencies. *(See also Budget Resolution.)*

Germane — Pertaining to the subject matter of the measure at hand. All House amendments must be germane to the bill being considered. The Senate requires that amendments be germane when they are proposed to general appropriation bills, bills being considered once cloture has been adopted, or, frequently, when proceeding under a unanimous consent agreement placing a time limit on consideration of a bill. The 1974 budget act also requires that amendments to concurrent budget resolutions be germane. In the House, floor debate must be germane, and the first three hours of debate each day in the Senate must be germane to the pending business.

Gramm-Rudman-Hollings Deficit Reduction Act — *(See Budget Process, Sequestration.)*

Grandfather Clause — A provision exempting persons or other entities already engaged in an activity from rules or legislation affecting that activity. Grandfather clauses sometimes are added to legislation in order to avoid antagonizing groups with established interests in the activities affected.

Grants-in-Aid — Payments by the federal government to states, local governments, or individuals in support of specified programs, services, or activities.

Hearings — Committee sessions for taking testimony from witnesses. At hearings on legislation, witnesses usually include specialists, government officials, and spokespersons for individuals or entities affected by the bill or bills under study. Hearings related to special investigations bring forth a variety of witnesses. Committees sometimes use their subpoena power to summon reluctant witnesses. The public and press may attend open hearings but are barred from closed, or "executive," hearings. The vast majority of hearings are open to the public. *(See Executive Session.)*

Hold-Harmless Clause — A provision added to legislation to ensure that recipients of federal funds do not receive less in a future year than they did in the current year if a new formula for allocating funds authorized in the legislation would result in a reduction to the recipients. This clause has been used most frequently to soften the impact of sudden reductions in federal grants.

Hopper — Box on House clerk's desk where members deposit bills and resolutions to introduce them. *(See also Bills Introduced.)*

Hour Rule — A provision in the rules of the House that permits one hour of debate time for each member on amendments debated in the House of Representatives sitting as the House. Therefore, the House normally amends bills while sitting as the Committee of the Whole, where the five-minute rule on amendments operates. *(See Committee of the Whole, Five-Minute Rule.)*

House — The House of Representatives, as distinct from the Senate, although each body is a "house" of Congress.

House as in Committee of the Whole — A procedure that can be used to expedite consideration of certain measures such as continuing resolutions and, when there is debate, private bills. The procedure only can be invoked with the unanimous consent of the House or a rule from the Rules Committee and has procedural elements of both the House sitting as the House of Representatives, such as the Speaker presiding and the previous question motion being in order, and the House sitting as the Committee of the Whole, such as the five-minute rule pertaining.

House Calendar — A listing for action by the House of public bills that do not directly or indirectly appropriate money or raise revenue.

Immunity — The constitutional privilege of members of Congress to make verbal statements on the floor and in committee for which they cannot be sued or arrested for slander or libel. Also, freedom from arrest while traveling to or from sessions of Congress or on official business. Members in this status may be arrested only for treason, felonies, or a breach of the peace, as defined by congressional manuals.

Impoundments — Any action taken by the executive branch that delays or precludes the obligation or expenditure of budget authority previously approved by Congress. The Congressional Budget and Impoundment Control Act of 1974 was enacted after frequent use of impoundments by President Richard Nixon. In addition to creating the budget process currently used, the 1974 law established procedures for congressional approval or disapproval of temporary or permanent impoundments, which are called deferrals and rescissions.

Joint Committee — A committee composed of a specified number of members of both the House and Senate. A joint committee may be investigative or research-oriented, an example of the latter being the Joint Economic Committee. Others have housekeeping duties such as the joint committees on Printing and on the Library of Congress.

Joint Resolution — A joint resolution, designated H J Res or S J Res, requires the approval of both houses and the signature of the president, just as a bill does, and has the force of law if approved. There is no practical difference between a bill and a joint resolution. A joint resolution generally is used to deal with a limited matter such as a single appropriation.

Joint resolutions also are used to propose amendments to the Constitution. They do not require a presidential signature but become a part of the Constitution when three-fourths of the states have ratified them.

Journal — The official record of the proceedings of the House and Senate. The *Journal* records the actions taken in each chamber, but, unlike the *Congressional Record*, it does not include the substantially verbatim report of speeches, debates, statements, and the like.

Law — An act of Congress that has been signed by the president or passed over his veto by Congress. Public bills, when signed, become public laws, and are cited by the letters PL and a hyphenated number. The two digits before the hyphen correspond to the Congress, and the one or more digits after the hyphen refer to the numerical sequence in which the bills were signed by the president during that Congress. Private bills, when signed, become private laws. *(See also Pocket Veto, Slip Laws, Statutes at Large, U.S. Code.)*

Legislative Day — The "day" extending from the time either house meets after an adjournment until the time it next adjourns. Because the House normally adjourns from day to day, legislative days and calendar days usually coincide. But in the Senate, a legislative day may, and frequently does, extend over several calendar days. *(See Recess.)*

Legislative Veto — A procedure, no longer allowed, permitting either the House or Senate, or both chambers, to review proposed executive branch regulations or actions and to block or modify those with which they disagreed.

The specifics of the procedure varied, but Congress generally provided for a legislative veto by including in a bill a provision that administrative rules or action taken to implement the law were to go into effect at the end of a designated period of time unless blocked by either or both houses of Congress. Another version of the veto provided for congressional reconsideration and rejection of regulations already in effect.

The Supreme Court June 23, 1983, struck down the legislative veto as an unconstitutional violation of the lawmaking procedure provided in the Constitution.

Loan Guarantees — Loans to third parties for which the federal government in the event of default guarantees, in whole or in part, the repayment of principal or interest to a lender or holder of a security.

Lobby — A group seeking to influence the passage or defeat of legislation. Originally the term referred to persons frequenting the lobbies or corridors of legislative chambers in order to speak to lawmakers.

The definition of a lobby and the activity of lobbying are matters of differing interpretation. By some definitions, lobbying is limited to direct attempts to influence lawmakers through personal interviews and persuasion. Under other definitions, lobbying includes attempts at indirect, or "grassroots," influence, such as persuading members of a group to write or visit their district's representative and state's senators or attempting to create a climate of opinion favorable to a desired legislative goal.

The right to attempt to influence legislation is based on the First Amendment to the Constitution, which says Congress shall make no law abridging the right of the people "to petition the government for a redress of grievances."

Majority Leader — The majority leader is elected by his or her party colleagues. In the Senate, in consultation with the minority leader and his colleagues, the majority leader directs the legislative schedule for the chamber. He also is his party's spokesperson and chief strategist. In the House, the majority leader is second to the Speaker in the majority party's leadership and serves as his party's legislative strategist.

Majority Whip — In effect, the assistant majority leader, in either the House or Senate. His job is to help marshal majority forces in support of party strategy and legislation.

Manual — The official handbook in each house prescribing in detail its organization, procedures, and operations.

Marking Up a Bill — Going through the contents of a piece of legislation in committee or subcommittee to, for example, consider its provisions in large and small portions, act on amendments to provisions and proposed revisions to the language, and insert new sections and phraseology. If the bill is extensively amended, the committee's version may be introduced as a separate bill, with a new number, before being considered by the full House or Senate. *(See Clean Bill.)*

Minority Leader — Floor leader for the minority party in each chamber. *(See also Majority Leader.)*

Minority Whip — Performs duties of whip for the minority party. *(See also Majority Whip.)*

Morning Hour — The time set aside at the beginning of each legislative day for the consideration of regular, routine business. The "hour" is of indefinite duration in the House, where it is rarely used.

In the Senate it is the first two hours of a session following an adjournment, as distinguished from a recess. The morning hour can be terminated earlier if the morning business has been completed. Business includes such matters as messages from the president, communications from the heads of departments, messages from the House, the presentation of petitions, reports of standing and select committees, and the introduction of bills and resolutions. During the first hour of the morning hour in the Senate, no motion to proceed to the consideration of any bill on the calendar is in order except by unanimous consent. During the second hour, motions can be made but must be decided without debate. Senate committees may meet while the Senate conducts morning hour.

Motion — In the House or Senate chamber, a request by a member to institute any one of a wide array of parliamentary actions. A member "moves" for a certain procedure, such as the consideration of a measure. The precedence of motions, and whether they are debatable, is set forth in the House and Senate manuals.

Nominations — Presidential appointments to office subject to Senate confirmation. Although most nominations win quick Senate approval, some are controversial and become the topic of hearings and debate. Sometimes senators object to appointees for patronage reasons — for example, when a nomination to a local federal job is made without consulting the senators of the state concerned. In some situations a senator may object that the nominee is "personally obnoxious" to him or her. Usually other senators join in blocking such appointments out of courtesy to their colleagues. *(See Senatorial Courtesy.)*

Obligations — Orders placed, contracts awarded, services received, and similar transactions during a given period that will require payments during the same or future period. Such amounts include outlays for which obligations had not been previously recorded and reflect adjustments for differences between obligations previously recorded and actual outlays to liquidate those obligations.

One-Minute Speeches — Addresses by House members at the beginning of a legislative day. The speeches may cover any subject but are limited to one minute's duration.

Outlays — Payments made (generally through the issuance of checks or disbursement of cash) to liquidate obligations. Outlays during a fiscal year may be for the payment of obligations incurred in prior years or in the same year.

Override a Veto — If the president disapproves a bill and sends it back to Congress with objections, Congress may try to override veto and enact the bill into law. Neither house is required to attempt to override a veto. The override of a veto requires a recorded vote with a two-thirds majority in each chamber. The question put to each house is: "Shall the bill pass, the objections of the president to the contrary notwithstanding?" *(See also Pocket Veto, Veto.)*

Oversight Committee — A congressional committee, or designated subcommittee of a committee, that is charged with general oversight of one or more federal agencies' programs and activities. Usually, the oversight panel for a particular agency also is the authorizing committee for that agency's programs and operations.

Pair — A voluntary, informal arrangement that two lawmakers, usually on opposite sides of an issue, make on recorded votes. In many cases the result is to subtract a vote from each side, with no effect on the outcome. Pairs are not authorized in the rules of either house, are not counted in tabulating the final result, and have no official standing. However, members pairing are identified in the *Congressional Record*, along with their positions on such votes, if known. A member who expects to be absent for a vote can pair with a member who plans to vote, with the latter agreeing to withhold his or her vote.

There are three types of pairs: 1) A live pair involves a member who is present for a vote and another who is absent. The member in attendance votes and then withdraws the vote, announcing that he or she has a live pair with colleague "X" and stating how the two members would have voted, one in favor, the other opposed. A live pair may affect the outcome of a closely contested vote, since it subtracts one "yea" or one "nay" from the final tally. A live pair may cover one or several specific issues. 2) A general pair, widely used in the House, does not entail any arrangement between two members and does not affect the vote. Members who expect to be absent notify the clerk that they wish to make a general pair. Each member then is paired with another desiring a pair, and their names are listed in the *Congressional Record*. The member may or may not be paired with another taking the opposite position, and no indication of how the members would have voted is given. 3) A specific pair is similar to a general pair, except that the opposing stands of the two members are identified and printed in the *Record*.

Petition — A request or plea sent to one or both chambers from an organization or private citizens' group asking support of particular legislation or favorable consideration of a matter not yet receiving congressional attention. Petitions are referred to appropriate committees.

Pocket Veto — The act of the president in withholding approval of a bill after Congress has adjourned. When Congress is in session, a bill becomes law without the president's signature if the president does not act upon it within 10 days, excluding Sundays, from the time he gets it. But if Congress adjourns sine die within that 10-day period, the bill will die even if the president does not formally veto it.

The Supreme Court in 1986 agreed to decide whether the president can pocket veto a bill during recesses and between sessions of the same Congress or only between Congresses. The justices in 1987 declared the case moot, however, because the bill in question was invalid once the case reached the Court. *(See also Veto.)*

Point of Order — An objection raised by a member that the chamber is departing from rules governing its conduct of business. The objector cites the rule violated, the chair sustaining the objection if correctly made. Order is restored by the chair's suspending proceedings of the chamber until it conforms to the prescribed "order of business."

President of the Senate — Under the Constitution, the vice president of the United States presides over the Senate. In his absence, the president pro tempore, or a senator designated by the president pro tempore, presides over the chamber.

President Pro Tempore — The chief officer of the Senate in the absence of the vice president; literally, but loosely, the president for a time. The president pro tempore is elected by the senators, and the recent practice has been to elect the senator of the majority party with the longest period of continuous service.

Previous Question — A motion for the previous question, when carried, has the effect of cutting off all debate, preventing the offering of further amendments, and forcing a vote on the pending matter. In the House, the previous question is not permitted in the Committee of the Whole. The motion for the previous question is a debate-limiting device and is not in order in the Senate.

Printed Amendment — A House rule guarantees five minutes of floor debate in support and five minutes in opposition, and no other debate time, on amendments printed in the *Congressional Record* at least one day prior to the amendment's consideration in the Committee of the Whole. In the Senate, although amendments may be submitted for printing, they have no parliamentary standing or status. An amendment submitted for printing in the Senate, however, may be called up by any senator.

Private Calendar — In the House, private bills dealing with individual matters such as claims against the government, immigration, or land titles are put on this calendar. The private calendar must be called on the first Tuesday of each month, and the Speaker may call it on the third Tuesday of each month as well.

When a private bill is before the chamber, two members may block its consideration, which recommits the bill to committee. Backers of a recommitted private bill have recourse. The measure can be put into an "omnibus claims bill" — several private bills rolled into one. As with any bill, no part of an omnibus claims bill may be deleted without a vote. When the private bill goes back to the House floor in this form, it can be deleted from the omnibus bill only by majority vote.

Privilege — Relates to the rights of members of Congress and to the relative priority of the motions and actions they may make in their respective chambers. The two are distinct. "Privileged questions" deal with legislative business. "Questions of privilege" concern legislators themselves.

Privileged Questions — The order in which bills, motions, and other legislative measures are considered by Congress is governed by strict priorities. A motion to table, for instance, is more privileged than a motion to recommit. Thus, a motion to recommit can be superseded by a motion to table, and a vote would be forced on the latter motion only. A motion to adjourn, however, takes precedence over a tabling motion and thus is considered of the "highest privilege." *(See also Questions of Privilege.)*

Pro Forma Amendment — *(See Strike Out the Last Word.)*

Public Laws — *(See Law.)*

Questions of Privilege — These are matters affecting members of Congress individually or collectively. Matters affecting the rights, safety, dignity, and integrity of proceedings of the House or Senate as a whole are questions of privilege in both chambers.

Questions involving individual members are called questions of "personal privilege." A member rising to ask a question of personal privilege is given precedence over almost all other proceedings. An annotation in the House rules points out that the privilege rests primarily on the Constitution, which gives a member a conditional immunity from arrest and an unconditional freedom to speak in the House. *(See also Privileged Questions.)*

Quorum — The number of members whose presence is necessary for the transaction of business. In the Senate and House, it is a majority of the membership. A quorum is 100 in the Committee of the Whole House. If a point of order is made that a quorum is not present, the only business that is in order is either a motion to adjourn or a motion to direct the sergeant-at-arms to request the attendance of absentees.

Readings of Bills — Traditional parliamentary procedure required bills to be read three times before they were passed. This custom is of little modern significance. Normally a bill is considered to have its first reading when it is introduced and printed, by title, in the *Congressional Record*. In the House, its second reading comes when floor consideration begins. (This is the most likely point at which there is an actual reading of the bill, if there is any.) The second reading in the Senate is supposed to occur on the legislative day after the measure is introduced, but before it is referred to committee. The third reading (again, usually by title) takes place when floor action has been completed on amendments.

Recess — Distinguished from adjournment in that a recess does not end a legislative day and therefore does not interrupt unfinished business. The rules in each house set forth certain matters to be taken up and disposed of at the beginning of each legislative day. The House usually adjourns from day to day. The Senate often recesses, thus meeting on the same legislative day for several calendar days or even weeks at a time.

Recognition — The power of recognition of a member is lodged in the Speaker of the House and the presiding officer of the Senate. The presiding officer names the member who will speak first when two or more members simultaneously request recognition.

Recommit to Committee — A motion, made on the floor after a bill has been debated, to return it to the committee that reported it. If approved, recommittal usually is considered a death blow to the bill. In the House, a motion to recommit can be made only by a member opposed to the bill, and, in recognizing a member to make the motion, the Speaker gives preference to members of the minority party over majority party members.

A motion to recommit may include instructions to the committee to report the bill again with specific amendments or by a certain date. Or, the instructions may direct that a particular study be made, with no definite deadline for further action. If the recommittal motion includes instructions to "report the bill back forthwith" and the motion is adopted, floor action on the bill continues; the committee does not actually reconsider the legislation.

Reconciliation — The 1974 budget act provides for a "reconciliation" procedure for bringing existing tax and spending laws into conformity with ceilings enacted in the congressional budget resolution. Under the procedure, Congress instructs designated legislative committees to approve measures adjusting revenues and expenditures by a certain amount. The committees have a deadline by which they must report the legislation, but they have the discretion of deciding what changes are to be made. The recommendations of the various committees are consolidated without change by the Budget committees into an omnibus reconciliation bill, which then must be considered and approved by both houses of Congress. The orders to congressional committees to report recommendations for reconciliation bills are called reconciliation instructions, and they are contained in the budget resolution. Reconciliation instructions are not binding, but Congress must meet annual deficit targets to avoid the automatic spending cuts of sequestration, which means it must also meet the goal of reconciliation. *(See also Budget Resolution, Sequestration.)*

Reconsider a Vote — A motion to reconsider the vote by which an action was taken has, until it is disposed of, the effect of putting the action in abeyance. In the Senate, the motion can be made only by a member who voted on the prevailing side of the original question or by a member who did not vote at all. In the House, it can be made only by a member on the prevailing side.

A common practice in the Senate after close votes on an issue is a motion to reconsider, followed by a motion to table the motion to reconsider. On this motion to table, senators vote as they voted on the original question, which allows the motion to table to prevail, assuming there are no switches. The matter then is finally closed and further motions to reconsider are not entertained. In the House, as a routine precaution, a motion to reconsider usually is made every time a measure is passed. Such a motion almost always is tabled immediately, thus shutting off the possibility of future reconsideration, except by unanimous consent.

Motions to reconsider must be entered in the Senate within the next two days of actual session after the original vote has been taken. In the House they must be entered either on the same day or on the next succeeding day the House is in session.

Recorded Vote — A vote upon which each member's stand is individually made known. In the Senate, this is accomplished through a roll call of the entire membership, to which each senator on the floor must answer "yea," "nay," or, if he or she does not wish to vote, "present." Since January 1973, the House has used an electronic voting system for recorded votes, including yea-and-nay votes formerly taken by roll calls.

When not required by the Constitution, a recorded vote can be obtained on questions in the House on the demand of one-fifth (44 members) of a quorum or one-fourth (25) of a quorum in the Committee of the Whole. *(See Yeas and Nays.)*

Report — Both a verb and a noun as a congressional term. A committee that has been examining a bill referred to it by the parent chamber "reports" its findings and recommendations to the chamber when it completes consideration and returns the measure. The process is called "reporting" a bill.

A "report" is the document setting forth the committee's explanation of its action. Senate and House reports are numbered separately and are designated S Rept or H Rept. When a committee report is not unanimous, the dissenting committee members may file a statement of their views, called minority or dissenting views and referred to as a minority report. Members in disagreement with some provisions of a bill may file additional or supplementary views. Sometimes a bill is reported without a committee recommendation.

Adverse reports occasionally are submitted by legislative committees. However, when a committee is opposed to a bill, it usually fails to report the bill at all. Some laws require that committee reports — favorable or adverse — be made.

Rescission — An item in an appropriations bill rescinding or canceling budget authority previously appropriated but not spent. Also, the repeal of a previous appropriation by Congress at the request of the president to cut spending or because the budget authority no longer is needed. Under the 1974 budget act, however, unless Congress approves a rescission within 45 days of continuous session after receipt of the proposal, the funds must be made available for obligation. *(See also Deferral.)*

Resolution — A "simple" resolution, designated H Res or S Res, deals with matters entirely within the prerogatives of one house or the other. It requires neither passage by the other chamber nor approval by the president, and it does not have the force of law. Most resolutions deal with the rules or procedures of one house. They also are used to express the sentiments of a single house such as condolences to the family of a deceased member or to comment on foreign policy or executive business. A simple resolution is the vehicle for a "rule" from the House Rules Committee. *(See also Concurrent and Joint Resolutions, Rules.)*

Rider — An amendment, usually not germane, that its sponsor hopes to get through more easily by including it in other legislation. Riders become law if the bills embodying them are enacted. Amendments providing legislative directives in appropriations bills are outstanding examples of riders, though technically legislation is banned from appropriations bills. The House, unlike the Senate, has a strict germaneness rule; thus, riders usually are Senate devices to get legislation enacted quickly or to bypass lengthy House consideration and, possibly, opposition.

Rules — The term has two specific congressional meanings. A rule may be a standing order governing the conduct of House or Senate business and listed among the permanent rules of either chamber. The rules deal with issues such as duties of officers, the order of business, admission to the floor, parliamentary procedures on handling amendments, and voting and jurisdictions of committees.

In the House, a rule also may be a resolution reported by its Rules Committee to govern the handling of a particular bill on the floor. The committee may report a "rule," also called a "special order," in the form of a simple resolution. If the resolution is adopted by the House, the temporary rule becomes as valid as any standing rule and lapses only after action has been completed on the measure to which it pertains. A rule sets the time limit on general debate. It also may waive points of order against provisions of the bill in question such as non-germane language or against certain amendments intended to be proposed to the bill from the floor. It may even forbid all amendments or all amendments except those proposed by the legislative committee that handled the bill. In this instance, it is known as a "closed" or "gag" rule as opposed to an "open" rule, which puts no limitation on floor amendments, thus leaving the bill completely open to alteration by the adoption of germane amendments.

Secretary of the Senate — Chief administrative officer of the Senate, responsible for overseeing the duties of Senate employees, educating Senate pages, administering oaths, handling the registration of lobbyists, and handling other tasks necessary for the continuing operation of the Senate. *(See also Clerk of the House.)*

Select or Special Committee — A committee set up for a special purpose and, usually, for a limited time by resolution of either the House or Senate. Most special committees are investigative and lack legislative authority — legislation is not referred to them and they cannot report bills to their parent chamber. *(See also Standing Committees.)*

Senatorial Courtesy — Sometimes referred to as "the courtesy of the Senate," it is a general practice — with no written rule — applied to consideration of executive nominations. Generally, it means that nominations from a state are not to be confirmed unless they have been approved by the senators of the president's party of that state, with other senators following their colleagues' lead in the attitude they take toward consideration of such nominations. *(See Nominations.)*

Sequestration — A procedure to cancel (or withhold) budgetary resources. Originally approved under the 1985 Gramm-Rudman-Hollings deficit reduction law, as amended in 1987, it threatened massive across-the-board cuts in federal programs in 1990 and later. Congress in late 1990 changed the law to provide a set of three sequesters, each of which kicks in 15 days after Congress adjourns. One offsets discretionary appropriations for the coming year that exceed statutory limitations and only affects discretionary spending. The second is triggered if Congress enacts entitlement spending increases or revenue decreases during the year and affects "non-exempt" entitlements. The third offsets an increase in the deficit above the limit set in law if the first two sequestions have not eliminated the excess deficit; it will cover all non-exempt spending. *(See Budget Process.)*

Sine Die — *(See Adjournment Sine Die.)*

Slip Laws — The first official publication of a bill that has been enacted and signed into law. Each is published separately in unbound single-sheet or pamphlet form. *(See also Law, Statutes at Large, U.S. Code.)*

Speaker — The presiding officer of the House of Representatives, selected by the caucus of the party to which he or she belongs and formally elected by the whole House.

Special Session — A session of Congress after it has adjourned sine die, completing its regular session. Special sessions are convened by the president.

Spending Authority — The 1974 budget act defines spending authority as borrowing authority, contract authority, and entitlement authority for which budget authority is not provided in advance by appropriation acts.

Sponsor — *(See Bills Introduced.)*

Standing Committees — Committees permanently established by House and Senate rules. The standing committees of the House were extensively reorganized in 1995 by the 104th Congress. The last major realignment of Senate committees was in the committee system reorganization of 1977. The standing committees are legislative committees — legislation may be referred to them and they may report bills and resolutions to their parent chambers. *(See also Select or Special Committees.)*

Standing Vote — A nonrecorded vote used in both the House and Senate. (A standing vote also is called a division vote.) Members in favor of a proposal stand and are counted by the presiding officer. Then members opposed stand and are counted. There is no record of how individual members voted.

Statutes at Large — A chronological arrangement of the laws enacted in each session of Congress. Though indexed, the laws are not arranged by subject matter, and there is no indication of how they changed previously enacted laws. *(See also Law, Slip Laws, U.S. Code.)*

Strike From the Record — Remarks made on the House floor may offend some member, who moves that the offending words be "taken down" for the Speaker's cognizance and then expunged from the debate as published in the *Congressional Record*.

Strike Out the Last Word — A motion whereby a House member is entitled to speak for five minutes on an amendment then being debated by the chamber. A member gains recognition from the chair by moving to "strike out the last word" of the amendment or section of the bill under consideration. The motion is proforma, requires no vote, and does not change the amendment being debated.

Substitute — A motion, amendment, or entire bill introduced in place of the pending legislative business. Passage of a substitute measure kills the original measure by supplanting it. The substitute also may be amended. *(See also Amendment in the Nature of a Substitute.)*

Supplemental Appropriations Bill — Legislation appropriating funds after the regular annual appropriations bill for a federal department or agency has been enacted. A supplemental appropriation provides additional budget authority beyond original estimates for programs or activities, including new programs authorized after the enactment of the regular appropriation act, for which the need for funds is too urgent to be postponed until enactment of the next year's regular appropriation bill.

Suspend the Rules — Often a time-saving procedure for passing bills in the House. The wording of the motion, which may be made by any member recognized by the Speaker, is: "I move to suspend the rules and pass the bill . . ." A favorable vote by two-thirds of those present is required for passage. Debate is limited to 40 minutes and no amendments from the floor are permitted. If a two-thirds favorable vote is not attained, the bill may be considered later under regular procedures. The suspension procedure is in order every Monday and Tuesday and is intended to be reserved for noncontroversial bills.

Table a Bill — Motions to table, or to "lay on the table," are used to block or kill amendments or other parliamentary questions. When approved, a tabling motion is considered the final disposition of that issue. One of the most widely used parliamentary procedures, the motion to table is not debatable, and adoption requires a simple majority vote.

In the Senate, however, different language sometimes is used. The motion may be worded to let a bill "lie on the table," perhaps for subsequent "picking up." This motion is more flexible, keeping the bill pending for later action, if desired. Tabling motions on amendments are effective debate-ending devices in the Senate.

Teller Vote — This is a largely moribund House procedure in the Committee of the Whole. Members file past tellers and are counted as for or against a measure, but they are not recorded individually. In the House, tellers are ordered upon demand of one-fifth of a quorum. This is 44 in the House, 20 in the Committee of the Whole.

The House also has a recorded teller vote, now largely supplanted by the electronic voting procedure, under which the votes of each member are made public just as they would be on a recorded vote.

Treaties — Executive proposals — in the form of resolutions of ratification — which must be submitted to the Senate for approval by two-thirds of the senators present. Treaties are normally sent to the Foreign Relations Committee for scrutiny before the Senate takes action. Foreign Relations has jurisdiction over all treaties, regardless of the subject matter. Treaties are read three times and debated on the floor in much the same manner as legislative proposals. After approval by the Senate, treaties are formally ratified by the president.

Trust Funds — Funds collected and used by the federal government for carrying out specific purposes and programs according to terms of a trust agreement or statute such as the Social Security and unemployment compensation trust funds. Such funds are administered by the government in a fiduciary capacity and are not available for the general purposes of the government.

Unanimous Consent — Proceedings of the House or Senate and action on legislation often take place upon the unanimous consent of the chamber, whether or not a rule of the chamber is being violated. Unanimous consent is used to expedite floor action and frequently is used in a routine fashion such as by a senator requesting the unanimous consent of the Senate to have specified members of his or her staff present on the floor during debate on a specific amendment.

Unanimous Consent Agreement — A device used in the Senate to expedite legislation. Much of the Senate's legislative business, dealing with both minor and controversial issues, is conducted through unanimous consent or unanimous consent agreements. On major legislation, such agreements usually are printed and transmitted to all senators in advance of floor debate. Once agreed to, they are binding on all members unless the Senate, by unanimous consent, agrees to modify them. An agreement may list the order in which various bills are to be considered, specify the length of time bills and contested amendments are to be debated and when they are to be voted upon, and, frequently, require that all amendments introduced be germane to the bill under consideration. In this regard, unanimous consent agreements are similar to the "rules" issued by the House Rules Committee for bills pending in the House.

Union Calendar — Bills that directly or indirectly appropriate money or raise revenue are placed on this House calendar according to the date they are reported from committee.

U.S. Code — A consolidation and codification of the general and permanent laws of the United States arranged by subject under 50 titles, the first six dealing with general or political subjects, and the other 44 alphabetically arranged from agriculture to war. The *U.S. Code* is updated annually, and a new set of bound volumes is published every six years. *(See also Law, Slip Laws, Statutes at Large.)*

Veto — Disapproval by the president of a bill or joint resolution (other than one proposing an amendment to the Constitution). When Congress is in session, the president must veto a bill within 10 days, excluding Sundays, after receiving it; otherwise, it becomes law without his signature. When the president vetoes a bill, he returns it to the house of origin along with a message stating his objections. *(See also Pocket Veto, Override a Veto.)*

Voice Vote — In either the House or Senate, members answer "aye" or "no" in chorus, and the presiding officer decides the result. The term also is used loosely to indicate action by unanimous consent or without objection.

Whip — *(See Majority and Minority Whip.)*

Without Objection — Used in lieu of a vote on noncontroversial motions, amendments, or bills that may be passed in either the House or Senate if no member voices an objection.

Yeas and Nays — The Constitution requires that yea-and-nay votes be taken and recorded when requested by one-fifth of the members present. In the House, the Speaker determines whether one-fifth of the members present requested a vote. In the Senate, practice requires only 11 members. The Constitution requires the yeas and nays on a veto override attempt. *(See Recorded Vote.)*

Yielding — When a member has been recognized to speak, no other member may speak unless he or she obtains permission from the member recognized. This permission is called yielding and usually is requested in the form, "Will the gentleman yield to me?" While this activity occasionally is seen in the Senate, the Senate has no rule or practice to parcel out time.

Constitution of the United States

We the People of the United States, in Order to form a more perfect Union, establish Justice, insure domestic Tranquility, provide for the common defence, promote the general Welfare, and secure the Blessings of Liberty to ourselves and our Posterity, do ordain and establish this Constitution for the United States of America.

ARTICLE I

Section 1. All legislative Powers herein granted shall be vested in a Congress of the United States, which shall consist of a Senate and House of Representatives.

Section 2. The House of Representatives shall be composed of Members chosen every second Year by the People of the several States, and the Electors in each State shall have the Qualifications requisite for Electors of the most numerous Branch of the State Legislature.

No Person shall be a Representative who shall not have attained to the age of twenty five Years, and been seven Years a Citizen of the United States, and who shall not, when elected, be an Inhabitant of that State in which he shall be chosen.

[Representatives and direct Taxes shall be apportioned among the several States which may be included within this Union, according to their respective Numbers, which shall be determined by adding to the whole Number of free Persons, including those bound to Service for a Term of Years, and excluding Indians not taxed, three fifths of all other Persons.][1] The actual Enumeration shall be made within three Years after the first Meeting of the Congress of the United States, and within every subsequent Term of ten Years, in such Manner as they shall by Law direct. The Number of Representatives shall not exceed one for every thirty Thousand, but each State shall have at Least one Representative; and until such enumeration shall be made, the State of New Hampshire shall be entitled to chuse three, Massachusetts eight, Rhode-Island and Providence Plantations one, Connecticut five, New-York six, New Jersey four, Pennsylvania eight, Delaware one, Maryland six, Virginia ten, North Carolina five, South Carolina five, and Georgia three.

When vacancies happen in the Representation from any State, the Executive Authority thereof shall issue Writs of Election to fill such Vacancies.

The House of Representatives shall chuse their Speaker and other Officers; and shall have the sole Power of Impeachment.

Section 3. The Senate of the United States shall be composed of two Senators from each State, [chosen by the Legislature thereof,][2] for six Years; and each Senator shall have one Vote.

Immediately after they shall be assembled in Consequence of the first Election, they shall be divided as equally as may be into three Classes. The Seats of the Senators of the first Class shall be vacated at the Expiration of the second Year, of the second Class at the Expiration of the fourth Year, and of the third Class at the Expiration of the sixth Year, so that one third may be chosen every second Year; [and if Vacancies happen by Resignation, or otherwise, during the Recess of the Legislature of any State, the Executive thereof may make temporary Appointments until the next Meeting of the Legislature, which shall then fill such Vacancies.][3]

No Person shall be a Senator who shall not have attained to the Age of thirty Years, and been nine Years a Citizen of the United States, and who shall not, when elected, be an Inhabitant of that State for which he shall be chosen.

The Vice President of the United States shall be President of the Senate, but shall have no Vote, unless they be equally divided.

The Senate shall chuse their other Officers, and also a President pro tempore, in the Absence of the Vice President, or when he shall exercise the Office of President of the United States.

The Senate shall have the sole Power to try all Impeachments. When sitting for that Purpose, they shall be on Oath or Affirmation. When the President of the United States is tried, the Chief Justice shall preside: And no Person shall be convicted without the Concurrence of two thirds of the Members present.

Judgment in Cases of Impeachment shall not extend further than to removal from Office, and disqualification to hold and enjoy any Office of honor, Trust or Profit under the United States: but the Party convicted shall nevertheless be liable and subject to Indictment, Trial, Judgment and Punishment, according to Law.

Section 4. The Times, Places and Manner of holding Elections for Senators and Representatives, shall be prescribed in each State by the Legislature thereof; but the Congress may at any time by Law make or alter such Regulations, except as to the Places of chusing Senators.

The Congress shall assemble at least once in every Year, and such Meeting shall [be on the first Monday in December],[4] unless they shall by Law appoint a different Day.

Section 5. Each House shall be the Judge of the Elections, Returns and Qualifications of its own Members, and a Majority of each shall constitute a Quorum to do Business; but a smaller Number may adjourn from day to day, and may be authorized to compel the Attendance of absent Members, in such Manner, and under such Penalties as each House may provide.

Each House may determine the Rules of its Proceedings, punish its Members for disorderly Behaviour, and, with the Concurrence of two thirds, expel a Member.

Each House shall keep a Journal of its Proceedings, and from time to time publish the same, excepting such Parts as may in their Judgment require Secrecy; and the Yeas and Nays of the Members of either House on any question shall, at the Desire of one fifth of those Present, be entered on the Journal.

Neither House, during the Session of Congress, shall, without the Consent of the other, adjourn for more than three days, nor to any other Place than that in which the two Houses shall be sitting.

Section 6. The Senators and Representatives shall receive a Compensation for their Services, to be ascertained by Law, and paid out of the Treasury of the United States. They shall in all Cases, except Treason, Felony and Breach of the Peace, be privileged from Arrest during their Attendance at the Session of their respective Houses, and in going to and returning from the same; and for any Speech or Debate in either House, they shall not be questioned in any other Place.

No Senator or Representative shall, during the Time for which he was elected, be appointed to any civil Office under the Authority of the United States, which shall have been created, or the Emoluments whereof shall have been encreased during such time; and no Person holding any Office under the United States, shall be a Member of either House during his Continuance in Office.

Section 7. All Bills for raising Revenue shall originate in the House of Representatives; but the Senate may propose or concur with Amendments as on other Bills.

Every Bill which shall have passed the House of Representatives and the Senate, shall, before it become a Law, be presented to the President of the United States; If he approve he shall sign it, but if not he shall return it, with his Objections to that House in which it shall have originated, who shall enter the Objections at large on their Journal, and proceed to reconsider it. If after such Reconsideration two thirds of that House shall agree to pass the Bill, it shall be sent, together with the Objections, to the other House, by which it shall likewise be reconsidered, and if approved by two thirds of that House, it shall become a Law. But in all such Cases the Votes of both Houses shall be determined by yeas and Nays, and the Names of the Persons voting for and against the Bill shall be entered on the Journal of each House respectively. If any Bill shall not be returned by the President within ten Days (Sundays excepted) after it shall have been presented to him, the Same shall be a Law, in like Manner as if he had signed it, unless the Congress by their Adjournment prevent its Return, in which Case it shall not be a Law.

Every Order, Resolution, or Vote to which the Concurrence of the Senate and House of Representatives may be necessary (except on a question of Adjournment) shall be presented to the President of the United States; and before the Same shall take Effect, shall be approved by him, or being disapproved by him, shall be repassed by two thirds of the Senate and House of Representatives, according to the Rules and Limitations prescribed in the Case of a Bill.

Section 8. The Congress shall have Power To lay and collect Taxes, Duties, Imposts and Excises, to pay the Debts and provide for the common Defence and general Welfare of the United States; but all Duties, Imposts and Excises shall be uniform throughout the United States;

To borrow Money on the credit of the United States;

To regulate Commerce with foreign Nations, and among the several States, and with the Indian Tribes;

To establish an uniform Rule of Naturalization, and uniform Laws on the subject of Bankruptcies throughout the United States;

To coin Money, regulate the Value thereof, and of foreign Coin, and fix the Standard of Weights and Measures;

To provide for the Punishment of counterfeiting the Securities and current Coin of the United States;

To establish Post Offices and post Roads;

To promote the Progress of Science and useful Arts, by securing for limited Times to Authors and Inventors the exclusive Right to their respective Writings and Discoveries;

To constitute Tribunals inferior to the supreme Court;

To define and punish Piracies and Felonies committed on the high Seas, and Offences against the Law of Nations;

To declare War, grant Letters of Marque and Reprisal, and make Rules concerning Captures on Land and Water;

To raise and support Armies, but no Appropriation of Money to that Use shall be for a longer Term than two Years;

To provide and maintain a Navy;

To make Rules for the Government and Regulation of the land and naval Forces;

To provide for calling forth the Militia to execute the Laws of the Union, suppress Insurrections and repel Invasions;

To provide for organizing, arming, and disciplining, the Militia, and for governing such Part of them as may be employed in the Service of the United States, reserving to the States respectively, the Appointment of the Officers, and the Authority of training the Militia according to the discipline prescribed by Congress;

To exercise exclusive Legislation in all Cases whatsoever, over such District (not exceeding ten Miles square) as may, by Cession of particular States, and the Acceptance of Congress, become the Seat of the Government of the United States, and to exercise like Authority over all Places purchased by the Consent of the Legislature of the State in which the Same shall be, for the Erection of Forts, Magazines, Arsenals, dock-Yards, and other needful Buildings; — And

To make all Laws which shall be necessary and proper for carrying into Execution the foregoing Powers, and all other Powers vested by this Constitution in the Government of the United States, or in any Department or Officer thereof.

Section 9. The Migration or Importation of such Persons as any of the States now existing shall think proper to admit, shall not be prohibited by the Congress prior to the Year one thousand eight hundred and eight, but a Tax or duty may be imposed on such Importation, not exceeding ten dollars for each Person.

The Privilege of the Writ of Habeas Corpus shall not be suspended, unless when in Cases of Rebellion or Invasion the public Safety may require it.

No Bill of Attainder or ex post facto Law shall be passed.

No Capitation, or other direct, Tax shall be laid, unless in Proportion to the Census or Enumeration herein before directed to be taken.[5]

No Tax or Duty shall be laid on Articles exported from any State.

No Preference shall be given by any Regulation of Commerce or Revenue to the Ports of one State over those of another; nor shall Vessels bound to, or from, one State, be obliged to enter, clear, or pay Duties in another.

No Money shall be drawn from the Treasury, but in Consequence of Appropriations made by Law; and a regular Statement and Account of the Receipts and Expenditures of all public Money shall be published from time to time.

No Title of Nobility shall be granted by the United States: And no Person holding any Office of Profit or Trust under them, shall, without the Consent of the Congress, accept of any present, Emolument, Office, or Title, of any kind whatever, from any King, Prince, or foreign State.

Section 10. No State shall enter into any Treaty, Alliance, or Confederation; grant Letters of Marque and Reprisal; coin Money; emit Bills of Credit; make any Thing but gold and silver Coin a Tender in Payment of Debts; pass any Bill of Attainder, ex post facto Law, or Law impairing the Obligation of Contracts, or grant any Title of Nobility.

No State shall, without the Consent of the Congress, **lay any Imposts or Duties on Imports or Exports, except what** may be absolutely necessary for executing it's inspection Laws: and the net Produce of all Duties and Imposts, laid by any State on Imports or Exports, shall be for the Use of the Treasury of the United States; and all such Laws shall be subject to the Revision and Controul of the Congress.

No State shall, without the Consent of Congress, lay any Duty of Tonnage, keep Troops, or Ships of War in time of Peace, enter into any Agreement or Compact with another State, or with a foreign Power, or engage in War, unless actually invaded, or in such imminent Danger as will not admit of delay.

ARTICLE II

Section 1. The executive Power shall be vested in a President of the United States of America. He shall hold his Office during the Term of four Years, and, together with the Vice President, chosen for the same Term, be elected, as follows

Each State shall appoint, in such Manner as the Legislature thereof may direct, a Number of Electors, equal to the whole Number of Senators and Representatives to which the State may be entitled in the Congress: but no Senator or Representative, or Person holding an Office of Trust or Profit under the United States, shall be appointed an Elector.

[The Electors shall meet in their respective States, and vote by Ballot for two Persons, of whom one at least shall not be an Inhabitant of the same State with themselves. And they shall make a List of all the Persons voted for, and of the Number of Votes for each; which List they shall sign and certify, and transmit sealed to the Seat of the Government of the United States, directed to the President of the Senate. The President of the Senate shall, in the Presence of the Senate and House of Representatives, open all the Certificates, and the Votes shall then be counted. The Person having the greatest Number of Votes shall be the President, if such Number be a Majority of the whole Number of Electors appointed; and if there be more than one who have such Majority, and have an equal Number of Votes, then the House of Representatives shall immediately chuse by Ballot one of them for President; and if no Person have a Majority, then from the five highest on the list the said House shall in like Manner chuse the President. But in chusing the President, the Votes shall be taken by States, the Representation from each State having one Vote; A quorum for this Purpose shall consist of a Member or Members from two thirds of the States, and a Majority of all the States shall be necessary to a Choice. In every Case, after the Choice of the President, the Person having the greatest Number of Votes of the Electors shall be the Vice President. But if there should remain two or more who have equal Votes, the Senate shall chuse from them by Ballot the Vice President.][6]

The Congress may determine the Time of chusing the Electors, and the Day on which they shall give their Votes; which Day shall be the same throughout the United States.

No Person except a natural born Citizen, or a Citizen of the United States, at the time of the Adoption of this Constitution, shall be eligible to the Office of President; neither shall any Person be eligible to that Office who shall not have attained to the Age of thirty five Years, and been fourteen Years a Resident within the United States.

In Case of the Removal of the President from Office, or of his Death, Resignation, or Inability to discharge the Powers and Duties of the said Office,[7] the Same shall devolve on the Vice President, and the Congress may by Law provide for the Case of Removal, Death, Resignation or Inability, both of the President and Vice President, declaring what Officer shall then act as President, and such Officer shall act accordingly, until the Disability be removed, or a President shall be elected.

The President shall, at stated Times, receive for his Services, a Compensation, which shall neither be encreased nor diminished during the Period for which he shall have been elected, and he shall not receive within that Period any other Emolument from the United States, or any of them.

Before he enter on the Execution of his Office, he shall take the following Oath or Affirmation: — "I do solemnly swear (or affirm) that I will faithfully execute the Office of President of the United States, and will to the best of my Ability, preserve, protect and defend the Constitution of the United States."

Section 2. The President shall be Commander in Chief of the Army and Navy of the United States, and of the Militia of the several States, when called into the actual Service of the United States; he may require the Opinion, in writing, of the principal Officer in each of the executive Departments, upon any Subject relating to the Duties of their respective Offices, and he shall have Power to grant Reprieves and Pardons for Offences against the United States, except in Cases of Impeachment.

He shall have Power, by and with the Advice and Consent of the Senate, to make Treaties, provided two thirds of the Senators present concur; and he shall nominate, and by and with the Advice and Consent of the Senate, shall appoint Ambassadors, other public Ministers and Consuls, Judges of the supreme Court, and all other Officers of the United States, whose Appointments are not herein otherwise provided for, and which shall be established by Law: but the Congress may by Law vest the Appointment of such inferior Officers, as they think proper, in the President alone, in the Courts of Law, or in the Heads of Departments.

The President shall have Power to fill up all Vacancies that may happen during the Recess of the Senate, by granting Commissions which shall expire at the End of their next Session.

Section 3. He shall from time to time give to the Congress Information of the State of the Union, and recommend to their Consideration such Measures as he shall judge necessary and expedient; he may, on extraordinary Occasions, convene both Houses, or either of them, and in Case of Disagreement between them, with Respect to the Time of Adjournment, he may adjourn them to such Time as he shall think proper; he shall receive Ambassadors and other public Ministers; he shall take Care that the Laws be faithfully executed, and shall Commission all the Officers of the United States.

Section 4. The President, Vice President and all civil Officers of the United States, shall be removed from Office on Impeachment for, and Conviction of, Treason, Bribery, or other high Crimes and Misdemeanors.

ARTICLE III

Section 1. The judicial Power of the United States, shall be vested in one supreme Court, and in such inferior Courts as the Congress may from time to time ordain and establish. The Judges, both of the supreme and inferior Courts, shall hold their Offices during good Behaviour, and shall, at stated Times, receive for their Services, a Compensation, which shall not be diminished during their Continuance in Office.

Section 2. The judicial Power shall extend to all Cases, in Law and Equity, arising under this Constitution, the Laws of the United States, and Treaties made, or which shall be made, under their Authority; — to all Cases affecting Ambassadors, other public Ministers and Consuls; — to all Cases of admiralty and maritime Jurisdiction; — to Controversies to which the United States shall be a Party; — to Controversies between two or more States; — between a State and Citizens of another State;[8] — between Citizens of different States; — between Citizens of the same State claiming Lands under Grants of different States, and between a State, or the Citizens thereof, and foreign States, Citizens or Subjects.

In all Cases affecting Ambassadors, other public Ministers and Consuls, and those in which a State shall be Party, the supreme Court shall have original Jurisdiction. In all the other Cases before mentioned, the supreme Court shall have appellate Jurisdiction, both as to Law and Fact, with such Exceptions, and under such Regulations as the Congress shall make.

The Trial of all Crimes, except in Cases of Impeachment, shall be by Jury; and such Trial shall be held in the State where the said Crimes shall have been committed; but when not committed within any State, the Trial shall be at such Place or Places as the Congress may by Law have directed.

Section 3. Treason against the United States, shall consist only in levying War against them, or in adhering to their Enemies, giving them Aid and Comfort. No Person shall be convicted of Treason unless on the Testimony of two Witnesses to the same overt Act, or on Confession in open Court.

The Congress shall have Power to declare the Punishment of Treason, but no Attainder of Treason shall work Corruption of Blood, or Forfeiture except during the Life of the Person attainted.

ARTICLE IV

Section 1. Full Faith and Credit shall be given in each State to the public Acts, Records, and judicial Proceedings of every other State. And the Congress may by general Laws prescribe the Manner in which such Acts, Records and Proceedings shall be proved, and the Effect thereof.

Section 2. The Citizens of each State shall be entitled to all Privileges and Immunities of Citizens in the several States.

A Person charged in any State with Treason, Felony, or other Crime, who shall flee from Justice, and be found in another State, shall on Demand of the executive Authority of the State from which he fled, be delivered up, to be removed to the State having Jurisdiction of the Crime.

[No Person held to Service or Labour in one State, under the Laws thereof, escaping into another, shall, in Consequence of any Law or Regulation therein, be discharged from such Service or Labour, but shall be delivered up on Claim of the Party to whom such Service or Labour may be due.][9]

Section 3. New States may be admitted by the Congress into this Union; but no new State shall be formed or erected within the Jurisdiction of any other State; nor any State be formed by the Junction of two or more States, or Parts of States, without the Consent of the Legislatures of the States concerned as well as of the Congress.

The Congress shall have Power to dispose of and make all needful Rules and Regulations respecting the Territory or other Property belonging to the United States; and nothing in this Constitution shall be so construed as to Prejudice any Claims of the United States, or of any particular State.

Section 4. The United States shall guarantee to every State in this Union a Republican Form of Government, and shall protect each of them against Invasion; and on Application of the Legislature, or of the Executive (when the Legislature cannot be convened) against domestic Violence.

ARTICLE V

The Congress, whenever two thirds of both Houses shall deem it necessary, shall propose Amendments to this Constitution, or, on the Application of the Legislatures of two thirds of the several States, shall call a Convention for proposing Amendments, which, in either Case, shall be valid to all Intents and Purposes, as Part of this Constitution, when ratified by the Legislatures of three fourths of the several States, or by Conventions in three fourths thereof, as the one or the other Mode of Ratification may be proposed by the Congress; Provided [that no Amendment which may be made prior to the Year One thousand eight hundred and eight shall in any Manner affect the first and fourth Clauses in the Ninth Section of the first Article; and][10] that no State, without its Consent, shall be deprived of its equal Suffrage in the Senate.

ARTICLE VI

All Debts contracted and Engagements entered into, before the Adoption of this Constitution, shall be as valid against the United States under this Constitution, as under the Confederation.

This Constitution, and the Laws of the United States which shall be made in Pursuance thereof; and all Treaties made, or which shall be made, under the Authority of the United States, shall be the supreme Law of the Land; and the Judges in every State shall be bound thereby, any Thing in the Constitution or Laws of any State to the Contrary notwithstanding.

The Senators and Representatives before mentioned, and the Members of the several State Legislatures, and all executive and judicial Officers, both of the United States and of the several States, shall be bound by Oath or Affirmation, to support this Constitution; but no religious Test shall ever be required as a Qualification to any Office or public Trust under the United States.

ARTICLE VII

The Ratification of the Conventions of nine States, shall be sufficient for the Establishment of this Constitution between the States so ratifying the Same.

Done in Convention by the Unanimous Consent of the States present the Seventeenth Day of September in the Year of our Lord one thousand seven hundred and Eighty seven and of the Independence of the United States of America the Twelfth. IN WITNESS whereof We have hereunto subscribed our Names,

George Washington,
President and
deputy from Virginia.

New Hampshire:	John Langdon
	Nicholas Gilman.
Massachusetts:	Nathaniel Gorham,
	Rufus King.
Connecticut:	William Samuel Johnson,
	Roger Sherman.
New York:	Alexander Hamilton.
New Jersey:	William Livingston,
	David Brearley,
	William Paterson,
	Jonathan Dayton.
Pennsylvania:	Benjamin Franklin,
	Thomas Mifflin,
	Robert Morris,

Delaware:

George Clymer,
Thomas FitzSimons,
Jared Ingersoll,
James Wilson,
Gouverneur Morris.
George Read,
Gunning Bedford Jr.,
John Dickinson,
Richard Bassett,
Jacob Broom.

Maryland:

James McHenry,
Daniel of St. Thomas Jenifer,
Daniel Carroll.

Virginia:

John Blair,
James Madison Jr.

North Carolina:

William Blount,
Richard Dobbs Spaight,
Hugh Williamson.

South Carolina:

John Rutledge,
Charles Cotesworth Pinckney,
Charles Pinckney,
Pierce Butler.

Georgia:

William Few,
Abraham Baldwin.

[The language of the original Constitution, not including the Amendments, was adopted by a convention of the states on September 17, 1787, and was subsequently ratified by the states on the following dates: Delaware, December 7, 1787; Pennsylvania, December 12, 1787; New Jersey, December 18, 1787; Georgia, January 2, 1788; Connecticut, January 9, 1788; Massachusetts, February 6, 1788; Maryland, April 28, 1788; South Carolina, May 23, 1788; New Hampshire, June 21, 1788.

Ratification was completed on June 21, 1788.

The Constitution subsequently was ratified by Virginia, June 25, 1788; New York, July 26, 1788; North Carolina, November 21, 1789; Rhode Island, May 29, 1790; and Vermont, January 10, 1791.]

Amendments

Amendment I

(First ten amendments ratified December 15, 1791.)

· Congress shall make no law respecting an establishment of religion, or prohibiting the free exercise thereof; or abridging the freedom of speech, or of the press; or the right of the people peaceably to assemble, and to petition the Government for a redress of grievances.

Amendment II

A well regulated Militia, being necessary to the security of a free State, the right of the people to keep and bear Arms, shall not be infringed.

Amendment III

No Soldier shall, in time of peace be quartered in any house, without the consent of the Owner, nor in time of war, but in a manner to be prescribed by law.

Amendment IV

The right of the people to be secure in their persons, houses, papers, and effects, against unreasonable searches and seizures, shall not be violated, and no Warrants shall issue, but upon probable cause, supported by Oath or affirmation, and particularly describing the place to be searched, and the persons or things to be seized.

Amendment V

No person shall be held to answer for a capital, or otherwise infamous crime, unless on a presentment or indictment of a Grand Jury, except in cases arising in the land or naval forces, or in the Militia, when in actual service in time of War or public danger; nor shall any person be subject for the same offence to be twice put in jeopardy of life or limb; nor shall be compelled in any criminal case to be a witness against himself, nor be deprived of life, liberty, or property, without due process of law; nor shall private property be taken for public use, without just compensation.

Amendment VI

In all criminal prosecutions, the accused shall enjoy the right to a speedy and public trial, by an impartial jury of the State and district wherein the crime shall have been committed, which district shall have been previously ascertained by law, and to be informed of the nature and cause of the accusation; to be confronted with the witnesses against him; to have compulsory process for obtaining witnesses in his favor, and to have the Assistance of Counsel for his defence.

Amendment VII

In Suits at common law, where the value in controversy shall exceed twenty dollars, the right of trial by jury shall be preserved, and no fact tried by a jury, shall be otherwise re-examined in any Court of the United States, than according to the rules of the common law.

Amendment VIII

Excessive bail shall not be required, nor excessive fines imposed, nor cruel and unusual punishments inflicted.

Amendment IX

The enumeration in the Constitution, of certain rights, shall not be construed to deny or disparage others retained by the people.

Amendment X

The powers not delegated to the United States by the Constitution, nor prohibited by it to the States, are reserved to the States respectively, or to the people.

Amendment XI (Ratified February 7, 1795)

The Judicial power of the United States shall not be construed to extend to any suit in law or equity, commenced or prosecuted against one of the United States by Citizens of another State, or by Citizens or Subjects of any Foreign State.

Amendment XII (Ratified June 15, 1804)

The Electors shall meet in their respective states and vote by ballot for President and Vice-President, one of whom, at least, shall not be an inhabitant of the same state with themselves; they shall name in their ballots the person voted for as President, and in distinct ballots the person voted for as Vice-President, and they shall make distinct lists of all persons voted for as President, and of all persons voted for as Vice-President, and of the number of votes for each, which lists they shall sign and certify, and transmit sealed to the seat of the government of the United States, directed to the President of the Senate; — The President of the Senate shall, in the presence of the Senate and House of Representatives, open all the certificates and the votes shall then be counted; — The person having the greatest number of votes for President, shall be the President, if such number be a majority of the whole number of Electors appointed; and if no person have such majority, then from the persons having the highest numbers not exceeding three on the list of those voted for as President, the House of Representatives shall choose immediately, by ballot, the President. But in choosing the President, the votes shall be taken by states, the representation from each state having one vote; a quorum for this purpose shall consist of a member or members from two-thirds of the states, and a majority of all the states shall be necessary to a choice. [And if the House of Representatives shall not choose a President whenever the right of choice shall devolve upon them, before the fourth day of March next following, then the Vice-President shall act as President, as in the case of the death or other constitutional disability of the President. —][11] The person having the greatest number of votes as Vice-President, shall be the Vice-President, if such number be a majority of the whole number of Electors appointed, and if no person have a majority, then from the two highest numbers on the list, the Senate shall choose the Vice-President; a quorum for the purpose shall consist of two-thirds of the whole number of Senators, and a majority of the whole number shall be necessary to a choice. But no person constitutionally ineligible to the office of President shall be eligible to that of Vice-President of the United States.

Amendment XIII (Ratified December 6, 1865)

Section 1. Neither slavery nor involuntary servitude, except as a punishment for crime whereof the party shall have been duly convicted, shall exist within the United States, or any place subject to their jurisdiction.

Section 2. Congress shall have power to enforce this article by appropriate legislation.

Amendment XIV (Ratified July 9, 1868)

Section 1. All persons born or naturalized in the United States, and subject to the jurisdiction thereof, are citizens of the United States and of the State wherein they reside. No State shall make or enforce any law which shall abridge the privileges or immunities of citizens of the United States; nor shall any State deprive any person of life, liberty, or property, without due process of law; nor deny to any person within its jurisdiction the equal protection of the laws.

Section 2. Representatives shall be apportioned among the several States according to their respective numbers, counting the whole number of persons in each State, excluding Indians not taxed. But when the right to vote at any election for the choice of electors for President and Vice President of the United States, Representatives in Congress, the Executive and Judicial officers of a State, or the members of the Legislature thereof, is denied to any of the male inhabitants of such State, being twenty-one years of age,[12] and citizens of the United States, or in any way abridged, except for participation in rebellion, or other crime, the basis of representation therein shall be reduced in the proportion which the number of such male citizens shall bear to the whole number of male citizens twenty-one years of age in such State.

Section 3. No person shall be a Senator or Representative in Congress, or elector of President and Vice President, or hold any office, civil or military, under the United States, or under any State, who, having previously taken an oath, as a member of Congress, or as an officer of the United States, or as a member of any State legislature, or as an executive or judicial officer of any State, to support the Constitution of the United States, shall have engaged in insurrection or rebellion against the same, or given aid or comfort to the enemies thereof. But Congress may by a vote of two-thirds of each House, remove such disability.

Section 4. The validity of the public debt of the United States, authorized by law, including debts incurred for payment of pensions and bounties for services in suppressing insurrection or rebellion, shall not be questioned. But neither the United States nor any State shall assume or pay any debt or obligation incurred in aid of insurrection or rebellion against the United States, or any claim for the loss or emancipation of any slave; but all such debts, obligations and claims shall be held illegal and void.

Section 5. The Congress shall have power to enforce, by appropriate legislation, the provisions of this article.

Amendment XV (Ratified February 3, 1870)

Section 1. The right of citizens of the United States to vote shall not be denied or abridged by the United States or by any State on account of race, color, or previous condition of servitude.

Section 2. The Congress shall have power to enforce this article by appropriate legislation.

Amendment XVI (Ratified February 3, 1913)

The Congress shall have power to lay and collect taxes on incomes, from whatever source derived, without apportionment among the several States, and without regard to any census or enumeration.

Amendment XVII (Ratified April 8, 1913)

The Senate of the United States shall be composed of two Senators from each State, elected by the people thereof, for six years; and each Senator shall have one vote. The electors in each State shall have the qualifications requisite for electors of the most numerous branch of the State legislatures.

When vacancies happen in the representation of any State in the Senate, the executive authority of such State shall issue writs of election to fill such vacancies: *Provided*, That the legislature of any State may empower the executive thereof to make temporary appointments until the people fill the vacancies by election as the legislature may direct.

This amendment shall not be so construed as to affect the election or term of any Senator chosen before it becomes valid as part of the Constitution.

Amendment XVIII (Ratified January 16, 1919)[13]

Section 1. After one year from the ratification of this article the manufacture, sale, or transportation of intoxicating liquors within, the importation thereof into, or the exportation thereof from the United States and all territory subject to the jurisdiction thereof for beverage purposes is hereby prohibited.

Section 2. The Congress and the several States shall have concurrent power to enforce this article by appropriate legislation.

Section 3. This article shall be inoperative unless it shall have been ratified as an amendment to the Constitution by the legislatures of the several States, as provided in the Constitution, within seven years from the date of the submission hereof to the States by the Congress.

Amendment XIX (Ratified August 18, 1920)

The right of citizens of the United States to vote shall not be denied or abridged by the United States or by any State on account of sex.

Congress shall have power to enforce this article by appropriate legislation.

Amendment XX (Ratified January 23, 1933)

Section 1. The terms of the President and Vice President shall end at noon on the 20th day of January, and the terms of Senators and Representatives at noon on the 3d day of January, of the years in which such terms would have ended if this article had not been ratified; and the terms of their successors shall then begin.

Section 2. The Congress shall assemble at least once in every year, and such meeting shall begin at noon on the 3d day of January, unless they shall by law appoint a different day.

Section 3.[14] If, at the time fixed for the beginning of the term of the President, the President elect shall have died, the Vice President elect shall become President. If a President shall not have been chosen before the time fixed for the beginning of his term, or if the President elect shall have failed to qualify, then the Vice President elect shall act as President until a President shall have qualified; and the Congress may by law provide for the case wherein neither a President elect nor a Vice President elect shall have qualified, declaring who shall then act as President, or the manner in which one who is to act shall be selected, and such person shall act accordingly until a President or Vice President shall have qualified.

Section 4. The Congress may by law provide for the case of the death of any of the persons from whom the House of Representatives may choose a President whenever the right of choice shall have devolved upon them, and for the case of the death of any of the persons from whom the Senate may choose a Vice President whenever the right of choice shall have devolved upon them.

Section 5. Sections 1 and 2 shall take effect on the 15th day of October following the ratification of this article.

Section 6. This article shall be inoperative unless it shall have been ratified as an amendment to the Constitution by the legislatures of three-fourths of the several States within seven years from the date of its submission.

Amendment XXI (Ratified December 5, 1933)

Section 1. The eighteenth article of amendment to the Constitution of the United States is hereby repealed.

Section 2. The transportation or importation into any State, Territory, or possession of the United States for delivery or use therein of intoxicating liquors, in violation of the laws thereof, is hereby prohibited.

Section 3. This article shall be inoperative unless it shall have been ratified as an amendment to the Constitution by conventions in the several States, as provided in the Constitution, within seven years from the date of the submission hereof to the States by the Congress.

Amendment XXII (Ratified February 27, 1951)

Section 1. No person shall be elected to the office of the President more than twice, and no person who has held the office of President, or acted as President, for more than two years of a term to which some other person was elected President shall be elected to the office of the President more than once. But this Article shall not apply to any person holding the office of President when this Article was proposed by the Congress, and shall not prevent any person who may be holding the office of President, or acting as President, during the term within which this Article become operative from holding the office of President or acting as President during the remainder of such term.

Section 2. This article shall be inoperative unless it shall have been ratified as an amendment to the Constitution by the legislatures of three-fourths of the several States within seven years from the date of its submission to the States by the Congress.

Amendment XXIII (Ratified March 29, 1961)

Section 1. The District constituting the seat of Government of the United States shall appoint in such manner as the Congress may direct:

A number of electors of President and Vice President equal to the whole number of Senators and Representatives in Congress to which the District would be entitled if it were a State, but in no event more than the least populous State; they shall be in addition to those appointed by the States, but they shall be considered, for the purposes of the election of President and Vice President, to be electors appointed by a State; and they shall meet in the District and perform such duties as provided by the twelfth article of amendment.

Section 2. The Congress shall have power to enforce this article by appropriate legislation.

Amendment XXIV (Ratified January 23, 1964)

Section 1. The right of citizens of the United States to vote in any primary or other election for President or Vice President, for electors for President or Vice President, or for Senator or Representative in Congress, shall not be denied or abridged by the United States or any State by reason of failure to pay any poll tax or other tax.

Section 2. The Congress shall have power to enforce this article by appropriate legislation.

Amendment XXV (Ratified February 10, 1967)

Section 1. In case of the removal of the President from office or of his death or resignation, the Vice President shall become President.

Section 2. Whenever there is a vacancy in the office of the Vice President, the President shall nominate a Vice President who shall take office upon confirmation by a majority vote of both Houses of Congress.

Section 3. Whenever the President transmits to the President pro tempore of the Senate and the Speaker of the House of Representatives his written declaration that he is unable to discharge the powers and duties of his office, and until he transmits to them a written declaration to the contrary, such powers and duties shall be discharged by the Vice President as Acting President.

Section 4. Whenever the Vice President and a majority of either the principal officers of the executive departments or of such other body as Congress may by law provide, transmit to the President pro tempore of the Senate and the Speaker of the House of Representatives their written declaration that the President is unable to discharge the powers and duties of his office, the Vice President shall immediately assume the powers and duties of the office as Acting President.

Thereafter, when the President transmits to the President pro tempore of the Senate and the Speaker of the House of Representatives his written declaration that no inability exists, he shall resume the powers and duties of his office unless the Vice President and a majority of either the principal officers of the executive department or of such other body as Congress may by law provide, transmit within four days to the President pro tempore of the Senate and the Speaker of the House of Representatives their written declaration that the President is unable to discharge the powers and duties of his office. Thereupon Congress shall decide the issue, assembling within forty-eight hours for that purpose if not in session. If the Congress, within twenty-one days after receipt of the latter written declaration, or, if Congress is not in session, within twenty-one days after Congress is required to assemble, determines by two-thirds vote of both Houses that the President is unable to discharge the powers and duties of his office, the Vice President shall continue to discharge the same as Acting President; otherwise, the President shall resume the powers and duties of his office.

Amendment XXVI (Ratified July 1, 1971)

Section 1. The right of citizens of the United States, who are eighteen years of age or older, to vote shall not be denied or abridged by the United States or by any State on account of age.

Section 2. The Congress shall have power to enforce this article by appropriate legislation.

Amendment XXVII (Ratified May 7, 1992)

No law varying the compensation for the services of the Senators and Representatives shall take effect, until an election of Representatives shall have intervened.

Notes

1. The part in brackets was changed by section 2 of the Fourteenth Amendment.

2. The part in brackets was changed by the first paragraph of the Seventeenth Amendment.

3. The part in brackets was changed by the second paragraph of the Seventeenth Amendment.

4. The part in brackets was changed by section 2 of the Twentieth Amendment.

5. The Sixteenth Amendment gave Congress the power to tax incomes.

6. The material in brackets has been superseded by the Twelfth Amendment.

7. This provision has been affected by the Twenty-fifth Amendment.

8. These clauses were affected by the Eleventh Amendment.

9. This paragraph has been superseded by the Thirteenth Amendment.

10. Obsolete.

11. The part in brackets has been superseded by section 3 of the Twentieth Amendment.

12. See the Nineteenth and Twenty-sixth Amendments.

13. This Amendment was repealed by section 1 of the Twenty-first Amendment.

14. See the Twenty-fifth Amendment.

SOURCE: U.S. Congress, House, Committee on the Judiciary, *The Constitution of the United States of America, as Amended*, 100th Cong., 1st sess., 1987, H Doc 100–94.

Index